The

TO ELI & HAZEL,
THANK YOU FOR ALL OF
YOUR ASSISTANCE, SUPPORT
AND ADICE THAT MADE
THIS JOURNEY POSSIBLE!!

Steve Urquhart

Enyeart, Steve

The Legacy Road: SHADOWING THE MARCH OF PRIVATE HENRY IRA BANKS AND THE ILLINOIS VOLUNTEERS' 102$^{ND}$ REGIMENT

ISBN 9778-1-312-70044-4

Cover, Layout & Text Design by The Author

This book is set in Times, Archive Roundhand and Bradley Hand Bold

PRINTED AND BOUND IN THE UNITED STATES OF AMERICA

# The Legacy Road

## SHADOWING THE MARCH OF PRIVATE HENRY IRA BANKS AND THE ILLINOIS VOLUNTEERS' 102ND REGIMENT

steve enyeart

LEGACY ROAD PRESS

**Dedicated to my father, Walter Ray Enyeart**

Who loved history.

# Chapter Guide

# An Introduction

SOME INSIGHT IN PREPARATION FOR OUR JOURNEY
UPON THE LEGACY ROAD

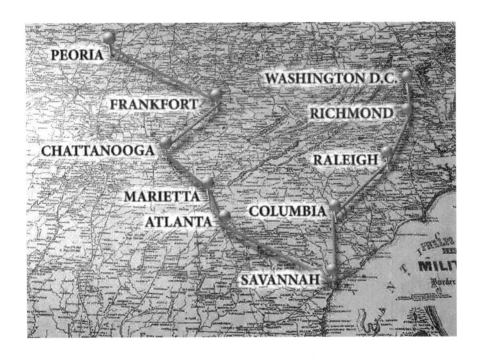

> *To better know the human being that you have become,*
> *identify the many parts of which you are the sum.*
>
> —*Anonymous*

I have a confession to make. I composed that rhyme at about the time I decided to embark on this journey that I call The Legacy Road. "Anonymous"? Well, for someone with such a narrow comprehension of his own identity, the shoe fit at the time. I had recently experienced the loss of my father, which nearly collapsed the only straining supports that held together what was left of our little nuclear family of five. With both parents now gone, I was overcome by an uncomfortable emptiness, which ignited an internal struggle between faith and doubt that began to agitate within. So conflicted, I could not, in good conscience assume title to that incisive verse that I wrote one Saturday afternoon nearly twelve years ago, yet I would choose to adopt it as my personal credo. In doing so, I found direction, clarity and restoration through the example, and unintentional expression of a mysterious ancestor who trudged through more turmoil and confusion than I would ever confront. Even while facing the chaos and horror of our nation's most devastating conflict, he would abide by his family and his faith with limited resources in reserve. As I pieced together the details, I was touched by his story, though it had never been brought to light until the fragments all systematically fell into alignment beneath my pen. Bearing witness to the gradual revelation of these events, I became compelled with a strong desire to follow in my great, great grand uncle's footsteps, so that is quite literally what I did.

An unexpected personal and spiritual journey seemed to materialize as I explored the meandering streams of cyberspace, by way of benevolent guides like Wikipedia, Google Earth, and Ancestry.com. These tools, and the genius mob of minds behind them are leading us at net speed into an equivocal future, while empowering us to connect remarkably with our personal past. Once mastered, they often dazzle us with their inexorable ability to connect all of our missing pieces, and provide answers to questions that span generations.

It was however, not the digital experience, but the physical pilgrimage that proved to be the life-altering antidote to my inevitable descent into a depressing identity crisis, or worse: mediocrity. Were it not for this adventure, I would have missed out on introductions to some new friends, distant relations and acquaintances who generously imparted support and encouragement that enabled me to endure along the path of restoration and discovery. To visit the places I had only read about, to hold fistfuls of the very earth upon which heroes fought for my freedom, and to experience the same sights and sounds seen and heard by an incredible family from which I descended, was a remarkably gracious gift for which I am forever grateful. I offer my heartfelt thanks and infinite love to my wife, Andi for her sacrifice, support, understanding, and patience during my absence, both physically and emotionally throughout the duration of this project.

A word of caution: I am not usually this obliging to extend invitation to the corridors of my personal and emotional interior. Upon entering, I would first advise you to duck! Ideas fly recklessly to and fro, colliding with each other at various speeds, as they constantly intertwine, and build momentum. Snapshots, music and soundbites by the score follow closely in tow. Some notions fall flat before they even begin to accelerate, and some just speed by uninterrupted, passing into oblivion, never to be seen again. Bring a towel…a stray "bad idea" may strike you, and they can be messy! They don't come along very often, but despite their foulness, and random eccentric origins, they too deserve to be entertained and investigated prior to their inevitable disposal. I suppose I have over two decades of "brainstorming" for advertising campaigns, logos, jingles and TV commercials to thank for the mental conditioning that developed this unusual pattern. There's always something in there being worked on, worked out, or worked over. Being raised in a creative household —influenced by a musical mother, and an artistic father who constantly fueled my young imagination— most likely customized this chaotic environment to accommodate such a hyperactive torrent of thoughts, images, and melody. I describe these frenetic surroundings to illustrate how powerful the impact of loss must have been, to make it all come to a grinding halt. In an instant, the static was reduced to an empty and silent void. This is the moment in my life when I was most vulnerable to internal collapse. This was the point in my timeline where the future ahead held no appeal, so when I was suddenly and inscrutably prompted, exploring the past seemed to be the only natural response.

For the most part, as members of the human race, we share an incurable obsession with the future. We seem to cling to an absolute that we've always known: there is an *unknown*. Unfortunately, the future's mysterious, opaque shroud offers us little choice but to wait for whatever lies beyond our blind horizons. Behind its great barriers the future could hold riches or poverty, success or failure, and finally, death in eternal darkness, or perhaps an afterlife in light...but only when the future sees fit to present it. When the uncertainty of the future becomes difficult to endure, I highly recommend a temporary "about-face."

Have you looked at yourself closely in the mirror lately? Your history is written all over your face. Where did you get those eyes? That cleft in your chin? That contagious laugh? Your hot temper, or calm disposition? Your DNA is like a bundle of gifts from your ancestors. Some you may cherish, others you might rather *regift*, if you could. Getting to know those anonymous benefactors in those old black and white photographs may help you distinguish who *you* really are, above and beneath the surface. Backtrack into your past for a while, and chances are great that you may find the clarity, identity, and confidence that will enable you to dismantle certain barriers, and carry you through this epic journey that we call "life."

It is my sincere wish that the experience I gained through many miles of travel and hours of research, as well as the many mistakes that I made along the way might somehow influence some who might choose a similar path. Open your mind and your heart to the vast array of possibilities that are out there, waiting to be explored. It has never been easier to unravel your DNA, and as you do, you may discover details about your true identity through those who cleared the paths for you, with their sweat, successes, trials, failures and sacrifices. Study their example, and you may find guidance, and even purpose for your own journey. If you're not too careful, your past may furtively sneak up on you like mine did, and offer you a generous gift from the most unlikely source you can imagine, just when you needed it the most.

—Steve Enyeart, Austin, Texas July 4, 2014

*Henry Ira Banks, taken shortly after his years of service as a Private in Company E, 102nd Regiment, Illinois Volunteers.*

# A President's Plea

*HARPER'S WEEKLY.*

*SATURDAY, APRIL 27, 1861.*

*By the President of the United States:*

*A PROCLAMATION.*

*Whereas, the laws of the United States have been for some time past and now are opposed, and the execution thereof obstructed, in the States of South Carolina, Georgia, Alabama, Florida, Mississippi, Louisiana, and Texas, by combinations too powerful to be suppressed by the ordinary course of judicial proceedings, or by the powers vested in the Marshals by law :*

*Now, therefore, I, ABRAHAM LINCOLN, President of the United States, in virtue of the power in me vested by the Constitution and the laws, have thought fit to call forth, and hereby do call forth, the Militia of the several States of the Union, to the aggregate number of 75,000, in order to suppress said combinations, and to cause the laws to be duly executed. The details for this object will be immediately communicated to the State authorities through the War Department.*

*I appeal to all loyal citizens to favor, facilitate, and aid this effort to maintain the honor, the integrity, and the existence of our National Union and the perpetuity of popular government, and to redress wrongs already long enough endured.*

Imagine the caloused fists of a 24-year-old Illinois farmer clenching that periodical tightly, as conviction —like a flame— ignites in his midsection. From inside the farmhouse, gazing out through the distorted windowpanes, which neatly frame the postcard panorama of freshly furrowed fields in which he and his brothers had tilled and toiled, he can scarcely tear his attention away. Knowing thoroughly in his heart that he may not live to observe this familiar vista again, he is in no apparent rush to begin provisioning for his forthcoming odyssey.

Yet, in September of 1862, Henry Ira Banks would not be one to deny his President's plea. He would follow his heart, and leave behind his 55-year-old widowed mother, and four younger brothers, in order to answer the call to arms against southern aggression. It was nearly a 21-mile trip from the farm in North Henderson, Illinois (present-day Alexis) to Knoxville, and about one-and-a-half hours by your average horse-drawn wagon. Upon their arrival on September 1, 1862, Henry and 31 other local farmers, laborers and merchants would swear their loyalty oath to God and country. Together, they embarked upon a journey through the dense murk of blue gun smoke, along a dimly lit trail paved by the confusion of contrasting politics, death, disease and mayhem. Their anchored camaraderie, and the hope and encouragement presented by corresponding friends and family would shore up their stamina during troubled times. Yet amidst the incessant tumult of the great war of the 1860's, I marvel at how one could maintain an unwavering faith and trust in a guiding creator. My great, great grand uncle Henry Banks found a simple way to preserve his faith, which, in turn, preserved him through many miles spent marching into strange and dangerous territory. One hundred and fifteen years later, and two thousand miles away from the Banks family homestead, I also gazed through a window at a panorama that was quite different than that of Illinois farmland, but I was no less inspired.

# History in the Making

I remember the distinct aroma of rain on warm concrete, which permeated the air on those pallid summer afternoons in western Washington State. School had let out two months prior, a non-eventful Little League season had recently ended, and I was spending a good portion of my free time alone at home, wearing grooves in my favorite stack of records, gradually blowing out the speakers in my parents' hi-fi. With very few neighborhood playmates, I spent many of my summer vacation days in isolation, and this day was no different. I was perched on our couch, peering out the front window at a sopping wet, steaming street, and the slick, black branches of the opposing Akebono, and Mt. Fuji cherry trees in our front yard, exploding with vibrant blossoms.

I was the quintessential "latchkey kid" with both parents absent, yet hard at work, hunched over their desks somewhere in the tightly packed grids of skyscrapers that towered over the bustling avenues of downtown Seattle. My two sisters had already graduated high school, and had vacated our family home in a Snohomish County suburb, near Lake Ballinger, which was named after a Civil War Veteran. The city of Mountlake Terrace was a maze of modest cinderblock ramblers and split-level, cedar-sided domiciles erected in the 1950's, purposefully poised to offer affordable housing to post-war baby-boomers.

My parents had purchased their little corner lot in 1954 —the same year that the city incorporated— and were never inclined to relocate. Early maps show mink farms, and great mill-owned parcels which once occupied the crowded subdivisions. Logs that were transported to Lake Ballinger were floated down McAleer Creek into Lake Washington, where they would be routed to a number of mills throughout the Puget Sound area. The leftover groves laden with Evergreens and Magnolias –whose branches were perfectly outfitted for climbing– guarded an abundant crisscrossed matrix of trails within a few blocks of my front door. On the rare occasion that fair weather prevailed, my imagination thrived in a wonderful outdoor environment where I spent my pleasurable youth.

As I sat on this day, observing our front yard, the rain showed no sign of relenting, but I was nonetheless adrenalized by the notion that it was Friday, and my parents and I would be packing that evening for a weekend east of the Cascade mountain range. There, the climate was arid and warm, as a general August rule. Our destination, somewhere along Highway 124 was a dot on the map called Lamar. Surrounding this diminutive whistle-stop was a 9000-acre wheat farm where my grandfather had once labored in the fields throughout numerous harvests, and had permanently stayed on as a sort of property caretaker in his retirement. He was invited by the local community to settle there, making his home in a converted 19th century two-story hotel. The front room window afforded a postcard view of the long gravel driveway, the horse corral, the great red barn, and a well-preserved log cabin, which had been constructed from hand-hewn cottonwoods in 1853.

A pioneer family from Missouri had originally settled in the little valley, completing their passage over the Oregon Trail, whose remnants of wagon wheel ruts were still visible throughout the region. Lamar had been a thriving little settlement in the mid-1800's, when the Hunt Railway had begun servicing the area. In its heyday, Lamar was complete with a Post Office, Restaurant, Hotel, Blacksmith Shop, Schoolhouse, Livery and Stables. The Touchet River meandered through the property, and its sandy shores had served as fishing and hunting sites for the local Nez Perce, Walla Walla and Cayuse indigenous tribes. Lewis and Clark had also camped here on their return trip to St. Louis in 1806, just a few miles down stream. Long abandoned, Lamar proper was now privately owned, serving as a staging area for combine and tractor maintenance, among other wheat harvesting operations. Local equestrians boarded horses in the corral attached to the giant barn, which also served as a parking garage for an ancient Studebaker whose blanket of dust obscured its original paint color, and seemed to get heavier each year. Now, imagine an unsupervised, tenacious and overtly curious 10-year-old, running loose in such a place for an entire weekend.

As my parents spent their Saturday visiting with my grandfather in the cool comfort of his living room, I investigated the historic outbuildings and other structures that dotted the property's perimeter. The log cabin which stood in plain view through the front window from my grandfather's Barcalounger, proved most noteworthy. I don't remember what compelled me to do so, but I decided to embark on an organized archaeological dig behind the old log cabin. I had heard somewhere that Pioneers once made a habit of burying their refuse, so after some patient surveying, I targeted a swath of earth, which bulged with a slight contour. I was ecstatic to bring to light a rusty, lucky horseshoe with the first pitch of my shovel.

The process of unearthing nails, tools, chards of fancy blue and white porcelain pottery, clear glass bottles of every shape and size, and various pieces of crockery and silverware took hours to complete in the blazing sun. I selected the bare bed of a conveniently parked pickup truck as my viewing area, and I strolled over to my Grandfather's house to announce to him, and my parents that my exhibit was officially open to the public. I don't remember if the audience was confused, or impressed, but I do recall that my treasures wound up in a cardboard box, which returned home with us, and eventually became a casualty of waning interest. Ironically, the contents most likely found their way to a subterranean resting place, forgotten once again. These days marked the beginning of my enthusiastic fascination with all things historic, and my memories of our numerous trips to Lamar are still so very vivid.

On Sunday morning, I rose early from my Grandfather's naugahyde sofa, where I would normally sleep, and headed out for a hike to a nearby hilltop in order to observe the sunrise. When I reached the summit, I scanned the horizon from end-to-end, and listened to the sounds of the prairie. It was so strangely quiet, that I could clearly hear conversations of waking neighbors, who were hundreds of yards away. The placid waters of the Touchet River were also within earshot, and I could see the reflection of the rising sun's amber rays glinting against its surface in the distance.

It was at this moment that I experienced a sensation that I have always found difficult to describe, but its acknowledgement is essential, nonetheless. My momentary sampling of tranquility was abruptly interrupted by an overwhelming perception of unseen, uninvited company. I became keenly aware of deliberate activity occurring all around me. There was, however no physical evidence of anything transpiring in my vicinity. No planting. No harvesting. No one had accompanied me on my hike, yet I felt surrounded by a human presence of many souls, though I could not see, hear, or touch them. In retrospect, I can compare my own perspective to that of a ghost, walking among the living, unnoticed. This experience lasted for about five minutes, until it evolved into an unsettling impression that I had worn out my welcome, and it was time for me to move on. I shuddered,

as the hairs on the back of my neck began to rise, and I ran back to the
safety of Lamar without looking back.

Perhaps it was the fear of ridicule that kept me from sharing the
details of this incident with anyone until about six years later, when my
father returned from a solo fishing trip near Ellensburg, Washington.

After punching the clock at Boeing's enormous facility in
Everett, Washington, my dad would often go fishing on his way home
from work. This was his personal escape. He would occasionally take
me along on his Saturday fishing trips too, but he often went alone. He
would rarely divulge any details about his day, aside from showing off
the occasional stringer of Cutthroats, or Rainbow trout. This particular
trip had been different than others, however and I could sense
excitement in his voice, as he shared the details of an incident that was
all too familiar. As the story goes, he had wandered off the trail, and
stumbled onto a location, hidden behind a great stand of Ponderosa,
that I later identified as Umtanum Creek Falls. With not a soul in sight,
he decided to strip down and take an impromptu swim in the deep basin
beneath the cascading water. When he returned to the creek's edge, he
evidently experienced a very similar encounter that I had wandered in
to, on that lonesome mound near Lamar. I remember him telling my
mother and I that what he had experienced was difficult to describe.
Never one to overanalyze things, he summed it up simply for us. All
around him he said, "I just felt Indians."

It wasn't until 1994, that I experienced another similar paradox.
I accompanied Andi —who was then my fiancé— on a long weekend
in Georgia to visit her best friend. We stayed a few nights in Susan's
modest apartment in the Buckhead suburb of Atlanta. My affinity for
the outdoors and exploration, and Andi's necessity for daily physical
exercise would not be denied, for within close proximity to the
apartment complex, there was a web of trails winding through miles of
forest. We woke early one morning, and quietly passed through the
front door, beyond the parking lot, and into the trees. We walked and
conversed for a few moments, and after we had trekked for about a half
a mile, the topography began to slope downward. The forest gradually
thinned out as we approached a wide river. Simultaneously, we stopped
to admire the pastoral scenery, which took us by surprise. A gentle
current of deep green and silver flowed before us, and made its way
through a series of broad curves, corkscrewing through a phalanx of
evergreens, which stood tall against the wind, forming an oscillating

horizon. It was here where I once again experienced that same energy, which stiffened the hairs on my neck. This time, however the intensity was much stronger, but I wasn't overcome by an uncomfortable sense of intrusion. Instead, I felt as if we were welcome, almost as if we were being hailed from across the river by a throng of souls. Andi was quick to notice that I was distracted, and I was careful to describe the phenomenon without raising any concern regarding my mental faculties. "Feels like we're being watched." I said. We continued traversing our trail, but I couldn't stop thinking about the event, which, to this day I conclude was a brush with the paranormal.

I later learned that the river we had stumbled upon was the Chattahoochee, whose confluence forked into the adjacent Peachtree Creek. I wasn't aware of this region's historic significance until a decade later, as I began to familiarize myself with the activity and conflicts that plagued the territory in the 1860's.

# *Good Spirits.*

That's how I summed up my father's demeanor as he spoke to me on the phone from his hospital bed, 3,000 miles away from my home in Colorado. He went on and on with amazement in his voice, about how polite his nurses had been, and how far technology had come, allowing him to watch his angioplasty procedure "LIVE on TV"!

One of my two sisters had alerted me by phone, earlier that day in 2003 that my Dad had driven himself from clinic-to-clinic in search of medical attention, in response to some pain in his chest. Healthcare bureaucracy denied him of his privileges, leaving him little choice but to shuttle himself to the nearest hospital emergency room. After some tests, he was diagnosed with having a mild cardiovascular "episode", and was swiftly scheduled for the operation to clear a blocked artery. For a 73 year-old man, most would conclude that this occurrence was anything but rare. My father, however was fairly active, an avid and capable outdoorsman, spending many mornings swimming at the community pool. His diet had recently declined in quality —consisting of mostly fast food— since my mother had passed on three years earlier, leaving only my sister to cook and clean for him periodically. Nevertheless, my father seemed healthier than most men at his age, and judging from his superficial condition, there was little cause for concern.

As our phone conversation came to a close, I told my Dad that I was happy he was in the clear, and I assured him that I would be on the first Seattle-bound flight to tend to his convalescence. He responded with his trademark sign-off: "Okay then, you carry on." His voice cracked slightly. I sensed some fear in his tone, and I was left with an uneasy feeling as I hung up the phone. At about half-past eleven that same evening, I was awakened by another phone call. I remember my reluctance to lift the receiver, but as I did, I heard my sister's voice, trembling this time, with the announcement that my father had unexpectedly passed on. The days that followed are a blur of sketchy details for me. Air travel, scheduling doctor and attorney meetings, errands and phone calls, and finally, the funeral.

Memories are faint, but plentiful of well-wishing relatives, friends, and friendly strangers who "knew me when I was this tall."

Ken, my best friend of twenty-plus years, and his wife Karen had interrupted their sailing trip in the San Juan Islands, and chartered a floatplane with no other reason but to attend the service —a gesture I will never forget.

The sun shone bright on the day that we buried my father, which is what he undoubtedly would have preferred, and as I watched the director close his casket, I quietly assured my sisters, "it's just us now...we're all that we have left." I wasn't really certain where that statement came from. I just felt the compulsion to say something that might mask over an uncharacteristic sensation of discomfort stirring within that was difficult to identify. This gathering had suddenly, and agonizingly become very anti-climactic, in my opinion. Both my father and mother were now gone, and though I was surrounded by siblings, cousins, aunts, uncles and lifelong friends, I felt completely isolated and alone. One-by-one, I scrutinized a linear array of snapshots from my strict religious upbringing and force-fed faith, which projected at fast-forward in my mind. For the first time that I could remember, my otherwise indelible beliefs were overshadowed by a shroud of doubt. My faith was on trial, or at least, under great suspicion.

Later that day, I found myself standing in the backyard of my Dad's house in Mountlake Terrace, which was the same home in which I was raised. I was surrounded by an assortment of his numerous half-finished projects. A broken fence, a sinking redwood deck permeated with dry rot, a weed-infested lawn and garden, and a jumbled heap of firewood, some cut and stacked, and some in need of cutting and stacking. I surrendered to a knee-jerk decision to finish something that my father didn't, and now couldn't. I wheeled away, axe in hand, at the scattered cluster of alder and cedar logs, until my hands blistered and bled. Inquisitive neighbors stopped by to converse, and though I did my best to be polite, I continued to manipulate axe, hammer and awl in conquest of completion.

Still dressed up for the funeral, panting and sweating beneath the summer sun, I stood back, leaning against the dull, rusty axe and admired the full cord of split logs that now rested, neatly stacked against the leaning fence. As I reflect, I don't believe either of my sisters could relate to my behavior. They never questioned my motives, though I'm sure my unorthodox method of dealing with our loss was confusing to them. One notion was irrefutable, however. With this endeavor behind me, I could now indeed "carry on".

# A Gift Unrecognized

The weekend was looming like an approaching squall, and neither my sisters nor I looked forward to poring through decades of my father's notes, hobbies and projects that littered his small den in a corner of the single-story rambler that we once called home. Still, the tasks at hand were necessary, and we busied ourselves with assertive determination to divide and conquer, with closure as our mutual incentive. Somehow, I found myself alone, surrounded by knee-deep mounds of good intentions: manuscripts, books, model planes, and trains. Many of the photos, sketches, paintings and books that I sifted through triggered indelible childhood flashbacks. I tried my best to soldier through the mountains of memories, organizing items for the "sell it" pile, the "keep it" pile, and the "ditch it" pile.

As my sisters dealt with similar duties in adjacent rooms, I stumbled upon an object that offered a welcome interruption to my progress. As I removed hangers full of clothes from my father's wardrobe, I discovered a small gray jewelry box tucked neatly away in an elusive cubby. As I opened the box, a pair of antique cufflinks emerged, made of copper and mother-of-pearl. Their styling was simple, and obviously antiquated, but their condition was pristine.

A palm-sized block of reddish-brown wood also occupied the jewelry box, and a quick glance revealed the name, "H.I. BANks" which was crudely carved upon its face. It appeared to be a rudimentary carving, perhaps created by a child, and I immediately recognized the "Banks" surname as my father's mother's maiden name. It was getting late, and I could not afford any more time hypothesizing. I stowed the mysterious treasures back into their box, set it aside, and continued clearing, cleaning, and organizing.

The estate sale was a burdensome affair for my sisters and I, although during the preparation, each of us had rediscovered many cherished mementos that sparked personal connections to our childhood. Simultaneously, chapters of our past, now proceeded to come to a close all at once, as we faced the finality of the event. We escorted strangers through our family home, as they perused boxes of books, my mother's enormous collection of Avon decanters, ancient record albums and knickknacks by the dozens. One insensitive "picker"

shouted to another in the next room, "nothing but junk in here!" I held
my tongue, and my temper, but shadowed him closely, and silently
throughout the house with my hands locked behind my back, until he
became obviously nervous, and quickly departed, empty-handed with
his partner in tow.

The sale was beginning to wear on my siblings. I have a clear
memory of my sister standing in the carport, staring off into space. Her
demoralized expression was too much to bear, given the circumstances.
I emotionally detached my concentration from all the personal items
spread out throughout the house, and the memories that they
represented. From some unknown depths I channeled a sort of snake oil
peddler persona, shadowing each prospect who darkened the doorstep,
acting as gregarious guide and salesman. This entire process needed to
end, so I did my best to capitalize on every opportunity to make the day
pass faster. We were exhausted by the time the sale was complete, and
a kind neighbor offered to take everything that was left over, in order to
sell it herself. We happily obliged, and hauled every remaining spec to
her garage with enthusiastic gratitude. The empty house was now ready
to list, and sell.

It wasn't long before I was on a 767 en route to my home in
Denver. Rising above Seattle's ever-present layers of gray, I chuckled
suddenly at the irony that I was flying home from my father's funeral in
a jet full of "wire bundles" that he and his department at Boeing's
Everett plant most likely installed. My wife, Andi would be waiting in
baggage claim. She had displayed incredible patience throughout the
entire ordeal, and held it all together with autonomous fortitude in my
absence. With a deep breath, I succumbed to my exhaustion, and after a
brief in-flight nap, I peered out the window through patchy clouds,
catching glimpses of the deep, sun-drenched canyons that twisted their
way through Utah and Arizona.

My mind embarked on its own twisted flight, as I wrestled once
again with my internal inquisition. A barrage of debate and dispute
subdued my faith in a Creator, my hope in an afterlife, and my
instinctive trust in a benevolent entity. A confidence and contentment
that had always been present was suddenly replaced by an unfamiliar
uneasiness, and anxiety.

For the first time, I was gripped with an uninvited panic, as the
767 passed over a thermal-rich mountainous area that some pilots call

"Red Table". The plane began to shake violently as it descended eastward over the Front Range, on a beeline vector to DIA. The turbulence made my heart race, and I felt as if the deeply anchored supports of faith that once held my soul in safe suspension were now reduced to threadbare tendrils. I quickly drained my styro cup full of coffee, burning my throat to avoid stains in my lap, and gripped the armrests with white-knuckled trepidation. I cursed the pilot under my breath, for his calm demeanor as he reassured every passenger via intercom that the turbulence was "common to the region". The plane's fitful bouncing subsided as abruptly as it began. We leveled out, passing quietly over downtown Denver, and onto the tarmac for a textbook landing. I took a deep breath, and exhaled with relief.

As she had promised, Andi was faithfully waiting for me at the baggage carousel, and that first glimpse of her covergirl smile was all it took for me to put my midair episode behind me. The drive home from the airport seemed like an eternity, but our home in Highlands Ranch was a welcome sight. It was a Sunday evening, and I was anxious to jump back into my routine. I was eager to mow my lawn, get under the hood of the Alfa Romeo I was restoring, to have a beer with some friends, and plan our next vacation –anything to divert my concentration away from the difficult days that were now behind me. By Monday, most everything was back to normal. My coworkers were inquisitive about my absence, and my family's well being. To their credit, the familiar sophomoric ad agency banter and playful exchange of insults and cacophony were sensitively, and noticeably held in check, at least for the time being.

*The small wooden block that emerged from my father's closet.*

*Walt Enyeart, my father at Ruby Creek in the Cascade Mountains, 1960's.*

# Cabin Fever

Winter arrived in Colorado with a vengeance. Andi and I spent four days sequestered in our home, with severe cabin fever, thanks to a relentless snowstorm. I had broken my right hand weeks before, and by virtue of necessity, I had discovered creative ways to manipulate the mouse attached to my iMac and surf the Internet, just for sanity's sake. Never one to favor the indoors, I pushed myself away from my terminal, bundled up, and forced open the front door. After several failed attempts to shovel the 5-foot snowdrifts that blanketed our driveway, I was desperate for a project.

I opened the filing cabinet in my study, and began to browse through some of my Father's notes that I had gathered and transferred into a manila folder. It was apparent that a decade or two before, my Dad had taken the initial steps of assembling our family tree, using what few resources were available at the time. Within the folder, I found some correspondence from distant cousins, some Xerox copies of overexposed black and white photos, and a fragmented flowchart, rendered in fading pencil. In addition, I came across a bound booklet of pages that were yellow, and worn from frequent examination. The title on the cover page said: "ENYEART FAMILY HISTORY". As I read page 1, the opening paragraph peaked my interest. The author pronounced the following:

> *ENYEARTS- The latter part of the Sixteenth Century, two brothers, younger sons of the Prince of Holland, of noble birth and great wealth, immigrated to America. The elder went to Pennsylvania and settled, the younger to New Jersey. About the year 1816, a descendant of the elder came west to Ohio and settled in Butler County. A few years later several families of Enyearts settled in Ohio, Warren, Butler, Montgomery and Miami Counties and some going to Indiana and Illinois. The Enyearts are lineal descendants of the Black Prince, famous in English History, and of Louis XIV of France, who, although perhaps very wicked and proud, well deserved the title of "Louis Le Grand" as he was called by the French people. With two such ancestors the Enyearts have every reason to keep a family record.*

Descended from Dutch, English, and French royalty? Really? This document was the obvious fabrication of some turn-of-the-century "genealogist" more interested in lining his pockets, rather than discovering the genuine truth. I have come to understand that there were cases of numerous families being "hoodwinked" by some of these unscrupulous operators in the early 1900's.

Even as a young boy, I often expressed interest in our family's origin, but all of my questions were typically met with answers loaded with conjecture, and sketchy second hand rumors. When I began to receive conflicting reports from different family members, my interest receded. I suppose that it would require nothing less than the interruptive assault of a 4-day blizzard, some twenty-five years later to awaken my curiosity once again. My father had done a fair job of organizing the little information that he had, and had even taken the time to depict his findings graphically in a branching grid, which represented the beginning of our family tree. With no Internet access, he had pieced together about four generations. I was impressed.

In the next year that followed, my position as Art Director for a Denver-based ad agency offered a few opportunities to travel back to the West Coast for meetings, conventions and photo sessions. When I could finagle a spare plane ticket, I brought Andi with me on a few occasions. I had always looked forward to flying, especially on the company tab, but since that tumultuous flight from Seattle, impending trips often prompted a degree of anxiety. Just being on the West Coast again —with our signature beach walks creatively woven into my schedule— was adequate compensation for my reluctance. After numerous heart-to-heart conversations, Andi and I made the collective decision to return to our Southern California roots. I had attended college in San Diego during the early nineties, and met my wife in our workplace shortly after graduation. We both missed the weather, the ocean, and the lifestyle that we had become accustomed to, before moving to Colorado.

We finally relocated to the Inland Empire in Southern California in November of 2004, and before we knew it, we were both working full-time in our chosen professions. We purchased a new home in the hills with a picturesque view of the Temescal Valley, and our "ocean-fix" was only 45 minutes away. I buried my brain into a new routine, and directed my complete focus on career, and the infinite joys of homeownership.

Three years passed, and after commuting 90 miles a day in gridlock, on the 91 Freeway, I began experiencing random panic attacks, occasionally waking abruptly with a racing heart. I made an appointment with my doctor, and after an intense cardio exam revealed nothing out of the ordinary, I was given a clean bill of health. While I was on the treadmill, shirtless, and tethered to an EKG by electrodes, I couldn't help but revert back to that flight to Denver from Seattle. It seemed silly to suggest any connection between traffic stress, and vertigo, so I decided to concentrate on the absolutes. I made certain that my doctor was aware of my family medical history, and that my father was recently deceased, due to a heart condition. He assured me that I some changes in order to reduce the stress in my life. This was about the time that I decided to take to the water for professional sailing instruction.

# Decatur Islanders

Summer had arrived, and my 40th birthday was approaching. Andi and I were invited to Seattle for a 10-day cruise with our friends, Ken and Karen aboard their sailboat in the San Juan Islands. I hadn't been home since my father's funeral, but we were both ready for a break and a chance to relax, so without hesitation we happily accepted the invitation. I didn't announce to any family members, or friends that I would be in the area, and there were two principal reasons behind this decision. The process of selling my father's house, and all of the probate issues that emerged during this time had driven my sisters apart more than ever. I was caught in the middle as usual, and there was just too much potential drama to dread, had I publicized our vacation plans. In addition, we had a full itinerary, and were at the mercy of the inlet's fluctuating tides. Landlubbers often have trouble comprehending the sea's stubbornness and unpredictability, so I chose to avoid hurt feelings by keeping our visit confidential.

Though I was raised in the Puget Sound area, I had rarely ventured out beyond land's end during my childhood, aside from the periodic ferry crossing. I had only been sailing about a half dozen times during my college days in San Diego, but this excursion would influence me beyond my expectation, and I would eventually surrender to the beckoning of the contagious pursuit of sailing that I still enjoy to this day.

The trip was everything I had hoped it would be, and more. The Western Washington summer weather was uncharacteristically fair, and I was spending my 40th birthday on the open water for 10 days with my best friend, and our best girls. What could be better?

Charles William Barkley, captain of the Imperial Eagle, a merchant vessel, had named the San Juan Islands, and the Strait of Juan de Fuca and active during the regional fur trade in the 1780's. Juan de Fuca, or Ioánnis Fokás happened to be a Greek with a transcribed Spanish name who was a ship's pilot under the orders of the Viceroy of New Spain. While searching for the fabled Northwest Passage, he had reported back to his homeport of Acapulco with news of a vast inlet positioned at approximately 47° latitude; its mouth guarded by a large island. It was hence referred to as the Strait of Anián. I thought it was unfortunate that Juan didn't receive the proper credit for his discovery for another two hundred years...so much for seventeenth-century public relations.

We navigated through the islands aboard the 48' ketch, docking in some of the most beautiful ports in the Pacific Northwest. Blake Island, Friday Harbor, Port Townsend, Roche Harbor, each destination offered a select variety of views, wildlife, history, and entertainment. We dined like royalty, hiked scenic trails, swam in the ice-cold water, and stayed up late into the night, scanning the clear skies for shooting stars and satellites. We spent one calm, quiet evening anchored in Brigantine Bay, on the western side of Decatur Island. This stop was a prerequisite in our float plan, since my father and his family had spent some years raising sheep on Decatur back in the 1930's.

My father had often regaled me with colorful accounts of his childhood on the island. He described how he and my uncle George would hunt for game, and fish the local waters in order to feed the family, after my Grandfather had set out for the mainland one morning, never to return. There were enduring rumors of my dad's occasional rowboat reconnaissance. Under cover of darkness, crossing Thatcher Pass to the local lumber mill, my father and his older brother, George would retrieve single giant logs, which would produce enough firewood to warm the house, and sell to neighboring islanders. My dad was convinced that the family might not have survived, were it not for a valiant rescue by his uncle Wendel, who served as the inter-island mail courier. I found photos from that period in my dad's files that confirm a hardscrabble existence for a single mother raising three boys, and two girls on a remote island during a remorseless depression.

My dad was a student of literature in college, and the files that I inherited contained reams of evidence, asserting that he was a shade tree historian as well. He described Decatur's origin to me on numerous occasions. Decatur Island was the namesake of Commodore Stephen Decatur, an American naval officer, noted for his heroic actions during the Barbary Wars, and his rapid rise to the rank of Captain while still in his twenties. His exploits read as an action-packed Hollywood blockbuster, and Lord Nelson himself is said to have honored his tactics with lavish praise.

We were stirred awake one morning to the faint cries of sheep, and once we were topside with our coffee, we spotted a dozen of them, unshorn, and roaming wild, poking around the rocks on the shore. I pondered at the notion that they must be descended from "The Original Enyeart Family Flock." Later in the day, we secured the boat, outfitted the tender, revved up the outboard, and the four of us were off to explore the lagoon on the opposite side of the island. I was excited to visit the original site of my father's house.

When I was about ten years old, I had accompanied my dad and Uncle Wendel on a passage to Decatur Island. Some blurry photos, and a 3' length of 8mm film are the only shreds of evidence left over from a trip that I scarcely remember. One memorable detail however is indelible. The trip had been cursed by motor failure, and there was more emphasis on repairs and rescue, rather than exploration and recollection. Unfortunately, that curse apparently still lingered in the present, for we had motored in the dinghy as far as Sylvan Cove, on Decatur's northwestern point, when we began to experience problems with the outboard. The motor was lugging, and blowing a lot of exhaust. Concerned, we decided to lighten the load, in order to increase the probability of safe navigation back to the sailboat. I volunteered to hike back to Brigantine Bay, and Ken would motor the girls back to safety, then row to shore and pick me up. I watched the inflatable disappear safely around the point, and I walked up a steep hill from the dock, through the Sylvan Cove Resort property, and back down a slope toward the bay.

As I hiked along the shoreline trail, I closed my eyes briefly and listened to the deafening quiet. I inhaled to take in the full bouquet of the towering sun splashed pines that formed a canopy above my route leading me to the shore. I stopped in my tracks, overwhelmed by the thought that I was negotiating the same trail that my father once followed when he was a barefoot kid in overalls. At that moment, I was struck by the realization that I had not taken any time to grieve for the sudden loss of my father. Knowing that it would take a while for my shipmates to return to the boat, I found a comfortable rock to sit upon, to take in the view of Thatcher Pass, and reflect on the life, and many wise words of a great, kind-hearted man.

I systematically rendered a timeline in my mind that I intentionally populated with memories of my dad, from my earliest recollection as a two-year-old, balancing with both feet planted in one of his outstretched hands, to our frequent fishing trips as a pre-teen in the Cascade mountain range. I acknowledged his often-futile attempts to connect with me during my awkward adolescence, then on through my late teens and twenties when we rarely spoke. Finally, I thought about the fishing trip we had taken just a year before he died.

I was grateful for his visit to Colorado that summer, shortly after my mother had passed away. We had driven from Denver to the wilderness just outside of Basalt, Colorado, where he would finally try his luck in some legendary fly-fishing waters that surrounded our campsite. We followed the advice of the local outfitters, and purchased the appropriate tackle, but despite our best efforts, neither of us managed to catch anything all weekend. Nevertheless, it was a richly rewarding getaway, filled with fireside conversations into the night, and relaxing recreation throughout the day. I was convinced that our once harmonious relationship had come full circle that weekend.

The sun was now sinking over the snowcapped Olympic range, which expanded in Technicolor beyond Trump Island's abiding silhouette. I rose from my perch, and jogged the remaining length of the trail down to the beach. Through the trees, I could see the ketch, still anchored in the bay, and judging from the muted laughter just offshore, it was clear that Captain and crew were now safely aboard. As I approached the clearing that led to the shoreline, it occurred to me that though I had heard many stories about our family's history on Decatur Island, I was now cohabitating with that history. This trail made it real. This trail made it relevant, and explicit. I was witnessing the very same scenery, the same sights, scents and sounds that my relatives had, nearly seventy years before. Every Decatur story that my father shared with me when I was young now took on a new light, and incredible clarity.

My imagination had been so far out of context, only mustering a pale, indistinct perception of my family's island heritage in the 1930's, before this day. It had been nearly thirty years since I last set foot on Decatur, and though little had changed on the island since then, a major transformation had just transpired within me. Unbeknown to skipper and crew, the man who was cast ashore at Sylvan Cove was not the same man who climbed back aboard the sailboat. I enjoyed the feeling of tracking historic, familial footprints, and I wanted more. Before, I could imagine the history. Now, I could revel in it.

All in all, my 40th birthday sailing cruise was an unforgettable experience. There were many moments of shared laughter, many adventures, and many gifts. However, this random diversion, which enabled me to spend a few solitary moments ashore was perhaps the best birthday gift of all.

# Don't Give Me That Look.

Shortly after returning home to California, Andi and I sold our home in the Inland Empire, and began renting a townhome in Newport Coast. Andi's commute was longer, but against traffic, and I was now only ten minutes from my office. First, and foremost, the Pacific was just as close, and we could take our beach walks at Crystal Cove whenever the ocean beckoned. While preparing for our move, I stumbled upon two boxes that my sister had delivered, just a few months prior to our relocation from Denver to California. They contained the collection of personal mementos that I had set aside before the estate sale commenced. Honestly, in my attempt to distance myself from the consequential stress, which resulted from the ordeal of finalizing my father's affairs, I had all but forgotten about the boxes, and their contents.

Packing up the house was a tedious process, but the two "mystery boxes" emerging from our attic offered an opportunity to take a break from lifting, and moving furniture. These were the boxes that I had filled with items set aside at my father's house after his passing. I opened the first box, which was filled with items that my mother had saved in her hope chest —some of my baby clothes, toys, and my first pair of shoes, carefully preserved over time. The second box had been packed with a bit more carelessness. It contained an unorganized heap of odds and ends, which included all of my school year books, a few books by Hemingway, and some written about Hemingway. Finally the bottom of the box revealed a familiar item, which was insignificant in appearance, but what it contained was poised to endow some life-altering effects.

I opened the small grey jewelry box, and removed the ruddy little wooden block, which I studied closer than I had previously, when I first encountered it prior to my dad's estate sale. I now recognized it as a meticulously hand-carved, palm-sized wooden bible. Andi walked into the room, where I sat at my desk, studying the details on the book. I held it up to allow the ambient light to spill over its face, so she could study it as well. The faint initials, "H. I. BANks" were crudely carved into the back cover, and on the spine, were two stacked words in all caps which read: HOLY BIBLE. Toward the bottom of the spine a more faint etching revealed the date: "1862, Dc 6." The front cover featured some cryptic abbreviations that were indecipherable at first glance. They read: "CoE 102 RE ILL Vo".

I studied the gibberish for a few moments, and it suddenly just rolled off my tongue: "Company E, One-hundred-and-second Regiment, Illinois Volunteers." I looked for an expression of approval from my wife, but she obviously wasn't as excited as I was. I raised the wooden block closer to her face, exposing the date on the spine. "Eighteen-sixty-two", I said. "This guy was in the Civil War!" Andi gave me "that look". "Don't give me that look" I said with a smile. It was the identical expression that my mother would give me when the occasional 4-letter word would slip out if I dropped something fragile, or slammed my finger in the door as a kid. For Andi, "that look" was usually in response to one of my spontaneous brainstorm ideas that might require some rethinking. Sensing that I was already committed to learning more, she rolled her eyes, returning to her packing chores, mumbling something about my infatuation with the History Channel.

# Me, Myself
# and a Macintosh

In the days that followed, I spent my evenings at our townhome in Newport Coast, in order to supervise painting and other preparations, while Andi stayed at the house in Corona, continuing to pack. I had since stuffed my SUV with a week's worth of clothes, an air mattress, and my trusty iMac computer. On my first night alone at the townhome, I plugged in the iMac, and activated the power switch, bringing the system alive with the familiar Apple orchestral tone. I hadn't yet ordered cable or Internet activation, so I scanned for Wi-Fi, and pumped my fist as I discovered a careless neighbor's non-encrypted Linksys router, and proceeded to establish a full-bar connection. I launched Safari, and my default Yahoo portal now opened up an entire virtual universe, just waiting to be explored. Where to begin? It seemed sensible to initiate my search by looking up the 102nd Regiment online.

At the top of the page of my search results, Wikipedia listed the 102nd Regiment, Illinois Volunteers, a regiment in the Union Army during the American Civil War. Their service record was explained as follows:

> The 102nd Illinois Infantry was organized at Knoxville, Illinois and mustered in for three years service on September 1, 1862.

> The regiment was attached to Ward's Brigade, Dumont's 12th Division, Army of the Ohio, to November 1862. Ward's Brigade, Post of Gallatin, Tennessee, Department of the Cumberland, to June 1863. 2nd Brigade, 3rd Division, Reserve Corps, Army of the Cumberland, to August 1863. Ward's Brigade, Post of Nashville, Tennessee, Department of the Cumberland, to January 1864. 1st Brigade, 1st Division, XI Corps, Army of the Cumberland, to April, 1864. 1st Brigade, 3rd Division, XX Corps, Army of the Cumberland, and Army of Georgia, to June, 1865.

*The 102nd Illinois Infantry mustered out of service on June 6, 1865 and discharged at Chicago, Illinois on June 14, 1865.*

The description of the miles covered by the 102nd left little doubt that this regiment saw some serious action. I was impressed to find a list of the regiment's noteworthy engagements which was posted in a separate column:

*-Atlanta Campaign*

*-Battle of Resaca*

*-Battle of Kennesaw Mountain*

*-Battle of Peachtree Creek*

*-Siege of Atlanta*

*-Battle of Jonesboro*

*-Sherman's March to the Sea*

*-Carolinas Campaign*

*-Battle of Bentonville*

I continued to navigate via Google, and arrived at a site labeled: civilwar.ilgenweb.net. It featured a comprehensive search function, which allowed me to separate the regiment by company. I selected Co. E, which was linked to Mercer County, Illinois. My smile broadened as an alphabetical roster appeared. I thought to myself, "It can't be this easy." Listed fifth from the top was none other than Private Banks, Henry of Suez, Illinois! The page didn't reveal any additional information, other than the date that Henry was mustered in: September 2nd, 1862. I calculated that this date was exactly 104 years before my date of birth. I was relieved to read that Henry was mustered out on June 6th, 1865, whereas many others who served in his company were not as fortunate. The list featured other Volunteers from Suez.

*- Killed at Resaca, Ga., May 15th, 1865.*

*- Died at Chattanooga, Jun 4, 1864. Wounds.*

*- Died at Gallatin, Tenn. Dec 8, 1862*

This last poor fellow's epitaph caused me to stop reading, only because the date coincided with that which was inscribed on Henry's wooden bible. Dc. 6, 1862. I presumed that Henry was most likely at this place called Gallatin when his comrade had expired. I had never heard of Gallatin before, and my overall familiarity with American history as it pertained to the Civil War was probably just a step or two beyond that which I retained from my school days. I remembered a high school test question clearly, which required us to list the Great War's alternative titles. The War of Secession. The War of Northern Aggression. The War of Southern Independence. The War Against the States. The Freedom War. I had always found it fascinating that though the war left the universal impact of the high cost of over 600,000 souls, its purpose, origin and outcome also affected many Americans on a personal level, which ultimately produced this diverse variety of labels. On that note, I always deemed the term "Civil War" as one of the greatest examples of an oxymoron.

Further research revealed a brief history of Company E's origination, which I discovered at: www.illinoiscivilwar.org.

*"**Company E.** --- On August 7 a meeting was held at Brown's school house in North Henderson township, at which Dan. M. Sedwick enlisted eighteen men. Thomas Likely, of the same township (now of Norwood), was present and stated that he had enrolled eight men, and proposed to unite with Sedwick, which was done. By the 14th they had eighty-four. On that day the men met at the same place and organized by electing Likely captain, Sedwick, first lieutenant, and T. G. Brown, second lieutenant. The following were the non-commissioned officers appointed: Sample B. Moore, first or orderly sergeant; John Allison, William J. Abdill, Jonathan E. Lafferty, and Albert Bridger, sergeants; Thomas Simpson, Henry M. Carmichael, John Tidball, Lyman Bryant, Allen Dunn, Henry W. Mauck, Robert Godfrey, and John T. Morford, corporals. Sometime in the last week of August, Lieutenant Sedwick started from Bridger's Corners (now Suez) with thirty-two men, and going through Scott's grove, met Captain Likely one mile south of that place with about the same number, from whence they proceeded in*

*wagons through Galesburg to Knoxville, arriving there in the*
*evening, where the rest of the company joined them."*

I was impressed to find so many details recorded in this text, which was identified only as "A Mercer County History." I decided that my first task would be to learn more about Henry, the man, before I wandered too far off track, which is so easy to do when researching online. I selected a link to the Database of Illinois Civil War Veterans, which is a branch of the Illinois State Archives. I entered the company, and Regiment number, and in response to my query, a list of officers and enlisted men, all according to their rank spilled out onto the screen before me. Again, fifth from the top of the list was *Banks, Henry, a Private from Suez, Mercer County, Illinois.* When I selected his name, a digital version of his ILLINOIS CIVIL WAR DETAIL REPORT appeared. "Joined: August 9, 1862. Age: 24. Height: 5' 9". Eyes: Gray. Complexion: Light. Marital Status: Single. Occupation: Farmer. Nativity: Putnam Co, NY."

I was overcome by the sudden realization that I was presently reading the physical description of a Civil War Union Private, proudly representing Lincoln's home state, who survived three years of heavy engagement and was undeniably an ancestor of mine. Of this, I was certain, for I recalled the mention of Putnam County, NY somewhere before…perhaps in my father's genealogical scribblings, or elsewhere. Returning to my search, I scrolled down through a few pertinent links, which proved that there was a healthy share of information on the worldwide web relating to the Illinois Volunteers. The link I selected, however, would prove to be the most valuable discovery of all. I was led to a page at a site that I had perused many times before, in search of eBooks: www.books.google.com, which featured the title: "OUR REGIMENT: A History of the 102nd Illinois Infantry Volunteers, with Sketches of the Atlanta Campaign, the Georgia Raid, and the Campaign of the Carolinas."

*Sergeant Major Stephen F. Fleharty, whose journal, fresh from the battlefields was a splendid gift and guide that revealed many details about Henry, and the 102nd Regiment's movements during the Civil War.*

# Fleharty's Journal

I was excited to find a free 200-page pdf, derived from a publication, which documented the history of Henry's regiment, during the Great War. I wondered, what the chances were that I would locate a book, which documented, and was dedicated to this single infantry regiment? On the first page, it was noted that the initial publishing of this volume was recorded as 1865. A heartfelt dedication followed:

> *"OFFICERS, NON-COM. OFFICERS & PRIVATES of the 102d ILLINOIS INFANTRY VOLUNTEERS, To you, one and all, as a testimonial of enduring regard for the Generous and the Brave, this volume is respectfully dedicated."*

A quick scan of the first chapter revealed that the book was indeed written from a first-person autobiographical format. Knowing that the 102nd was mustered out earlier in the same year of publication, I was thankful, and deeply inspired that the author, Sergeant Major Stephen F. Fleharty had kept a daily journal —whenever his duty allowed him the convenience— and that he completed his project while the details were still so fresh in his mind. I had never before read such a copious collection of dates, places, and events, meticulously recorded with palpable detail. Aside from Fleharty's journal, he had also regaled the general public, especially family and friends of his Illinois brethren with a newspaper column that appeared in two publications in Rock Island, Illinois. The Argus, and The Union published his column entitled, "Jottings From Dixie" which offered accurate depiction of the 102nd Regiment's exploits.

Engrossed, the advance of each page filled with Fleharty's eloquent prose drew me closer into the regiment's movements, until I felt as if I was moving right along with the 102nd. I couldn't march alongside the volunteers in the mid-nineteenth century, but a 21st-century means of virtual tracking emerged, which turned out to be the next best thing. I skipped through Fleharty's book while tracing the regiments' steps by way of "Google Earth" satellite imagery. It was very much like following the troops' movements in a digital hot air balloon...only 145 years forward in time. I launched with the 102nd from Knoxville, Illinois, and followed the railroad tracks, which lead to Peoria, and on to their camp at "Lost River" near Bowling Green,

Kentucky, where the regiment prepared to cross over into Tennessee to join Ward's Brigade in November of 1862.

My eyes were watery, and sore from fatigue. I gave them a rub, and leaned back in my chair, as my spine popped in a few places, for I had been frozen in a sort of contortion, in order to scan to-and-fro from computer screen to notepad, and back again. Glancing at the clock on my desk, I became suspicious that the batteries were drained of power, so I squinted at my watch, and rose from my chair, with a groan of disbelief. My research session had begun at about 5:30 pm. It was now approaching 4 a.m. It was a task to tear myself away from my terminal, and attempt to catch some shuteye, but I managed to get an hour of sack time before rising at 6am to get ready for another workday. After a 15-minute commute, I would sit at another computer for eight more hours. The entire day would drag, more so than usual.

Once my responsibilities were completed at my place of employment, I rushed home to tend to some chores to prepare our new place of residence. Before sundown, I took a jog around our new neighborhood, and reflected on all that I had discovered during the previous evening. I pondered at the possibility that Henry might possibly have been my great-great grandfather. On a few occasions, I witnessed older family members referring to "Grandpa Banks", and my first inclination was to assume that he and Henry were one-in-the-same, but I had to be certain. I walked up the drive toward our townhome. I passed the parallel rows of giant date palms, which flanked our complex as the setting sun cast long shadows across the blacktop. I arrived at my doorstep, and ascended the stairs to take my place, yet again before my iMac, and I resumed my research from where I had left off the night before.

In the church where I was raised, I had once heard a guest speaker mention that the Mormons were especially adept at compiling and recording genealogical records. His comment was confirmed when I searched online for Mormon Genealogy, which resulted in a link titled: FamilySearch.org, which turned out to be a very helpful find. I consulted Henry's CIVIL WAR DETAIL REPORT to obtain his approximate birth date, and birthplace, which gave me enough information to narrow my search with pinpoint accuracy. Listed with his nine siblings, the 4$^{th}$ eldest son of Nathan O. Banks Jr., and Cynthia Irish of Putnam County, New York was born, February 17$^{th}$, 1838, and later died at the young age of 51 in 1889. No additional information was available, but I knew I had just scratched the surface of the abundant sources I had yet to explore, in order to find those elusive answers.

My next objective, while flipping through Fleharty's book, was to learn where Henry was stationed on that particular date, inscribed on the spine of the wooden bible. According to the journal's detailed account, Henry's regiment was camped out at a little burg called Gallatin, Tennessee. Though the events of the exact day of Dc. 6 are not mentioned in Fleharty's pages, Henry and his company would be stationed here for the long haul.

Fleharty wrote:

> *We reached Gallatin in the evening — Nov. 26th — little thinking then that we would remain there six long months. But such was to be our destiny.*

I concluded that during this six-month period, Henry had some time on his hands to do a little whittling, but a bible? Why not? I didn't suspect that Henry decided to mimic some customary whittling exercise that may have prevailed in his day, for I had yet to find record of another hand-carved bible created during the Civil War. What I did know was that Henry descended from a family of hard-working farmers, whose homestead was built among a community of Quakers in upstate New York. Family records indicated that his mother was herself, a minister. Religion was undoubtedly a very influential component of Henry's early life, and his probable intention was to keep his faith in check. Though manifested in the crude form of this small talisman, I like to think that this block of wood — personally fashioned, and engraved by Private Henry Ira Banks of Company E— served its purpose through many marches and skirmishes, across acres of horrific carnage, and dreadful experiences not suited for the eyes and ears of a 24-year old farmer from rural Illinois.

Fleharty described the appalling conditions at the Winter Camp at Gallatin as follows:

> *During the dark days of our sojourn in Gallatin, the mortality on account of disease in the different regiments was absolutely frightful. Daily, almost hourly, the sound of muffled drum and the plaintive dirge fell upon our ears. In addition to*

*all this, weather was for a long time very inclement. Cold rains were frequent, and occasionally snow fell.*

As I continued my tour with the 102$^{nd}$ via Google Earth, I was quick to order a hardcopy of Fleharty's book, and in doing so, I selected priority delivery, which brought it to my doorstep 2 days later. "OUR REGIMENT" held a favorable surprise within its final pages. A complete list of the enlisted was included, each according to their company. Under the heading of "ROLL OF COMPANY "E" among the listing of PRIVATES is where I found a report which summoned a certain empathy within.

> *Henry Banks, North Henderson, Ill—wounded at New Hope Church.*

It was now clear that Henry didn't make it through the war completely unscathed. Scanning through the pages again, my second objective was to learn about this location where Henry was wounded, and what part he played in the action.

In Chapter VII, Fleharty witnessed Company E on May 26th, 1863 being deployed to protect a work party charged with building the regiment's Winter quarters which was later to be called Fort Thomas. An over-zealous Captain D.M. Sedwick led the company too close to the enemy in a morning fog, and seven men were wounded in a skirmish with the rebels. Not before Henry's company *"let fly with their Spencer rifles in such an effective manner, that the rebels were compelled to retire, temporarily abandoning two field pieces which they had placed in an advanced position."*

As I read the blow-by-blow description of the skirmish, I shifted my focus to Henry's bible, which stood beneath my desk lamp. For the first time, I looked outside of Henry's inscriptions, and studied the material. It exhibited some signs of expected wear, scratches, and shine from over 100 years of handling, storage and transport. However, a reddish, gummy substance, scattered in small droplets was present, and I was not quick to rule out the possibility that it may have been evidence of a wound, or simply residue left over by a careless handler. This was yet another mystery that begged to be solved, but it would have to wait, as I had yet to establish Henry's identity as it pertained to my connection as his descendant.

My great-great-great grandfather David Irish Banks with his grandchildren.
My grandmother, Mary Banks-Enyeart-Felch is far left.

My mother and sisters and "Harmony" in front of the old log home at Lamar Station,
near Walla Walla, WA. That's me riding point in my first pair of cowboy boots!

# Roots That Bind

It was January 26th, 2009. Andi was on a business trip, and I had some time to kill on a crisp, sunny Saturday. I had decided to contact one of the eldest, and closest of known Banks relatives of mine. My father's first cousin, Hazel lived with her husband, Eli and their family, just a few miles away in Chula Vista. The Rico family had been wonderful hosts when I arrived in San Diego back in 1990 to attend college. They made it a priority to include me in their weekend and holiday gatherings, and accepted me as part of their throng, despite the fact that we had never previously met. Having some family nearby took some of the sting out of the difficulties that came with adjusting to a new city, and routine. This trip to their home was no exception. Of course, I was invited with open arms to visit the Ricos at their cozy home, just South of San Diego, and when I arrived, I was treated to a delicious lunch, and reflective conversation. Hazel was the daughter of my grandmother Mary's brother, John "Henry" Banks. I presented Henry's bible to Hazel and Eli, and described to them how it came into my care, and that I was curious if Henry was my great-great grandfather. Hazel wasn't sure, but she smiled with a twinkle in her eye, and excused herself from the living room where we had gathered after lunch. She returned in a minute or two, holding a large dark green book. I recognized it immediately.

Back in 1977, a 12-hour mini-series aired on ABC that was the most-watched telecast of all time, according to the Neilsen ratings. Alex Haley's "ROOTS" sent many viewers rummaging through old photo albums, and dusty trunks to piece together the details of their own family histories. Hazel's sister, Pat was one of them. The book Hazel held was the Banks Family History, an abundant collection of photographs, correspondence and old family stories, methodically arranged within a hardbound cover, which bore the title in a gold foil stamp: "Roots That Bind". I had a faint memory of cousin Pat staying at our home in the summer of 1978 for a few days. Our home was just one of many stops on her tour to gather information for her collection. She had passed away some years later, but she had left quite a legacy within the yellowing pages of her anthology. My parents had ordered a copy of Pat's book when it was completed, and it graced our coffee table for years. I had leafed through it many times as a kid, and at the time, I found some of the older sepia photos of scowling faces a little haunting. It wound up in the possession of one of my sisters during the estate sale drama. Had I known it would later serve as such an instrumental tool, I would have set it aside for myself.

Hazel and I flipped through some of the first pages in the book, which listed the same Banks family that I had discovered on FamilySearch.org, and Henry was included as I expected. One of the sepia photographs featured an elderly gentleman surrounded by eleven young children in their Sunday best outfits. Henry's date of death predated the photograph by about 21 years, so I knew that I was looking at one of his many siblings. The children were listed by name, along with "great grandfather, "David I. Banks". The first child in the photo was my grandmother, Mary, which made it clear that Henry Banks was not my great-great grandfather, but rather, my great-great grand uncle. I perused the pages that followed, which featured descriptions of each sibling's family history that cousin Pat recounted with a consistent, flattering flourish. Pat had obviously approached her project as a labor of love, for her attention to detail, and organization of the forward-extending branches of each sibling's line, often including the most trivial of tidbits were exemplary. Henry's account however, was mysteriously absent. Hazel graciously loaned Pat's book to me, and wished me luck with my search for answers. I promised her that I would stay in touch, and share my discoveries with her as they occurred. What I didn't know at the time was that the details would be more elusive than I expected.

I turned the key to start up my SUV, and headed north on Interstate 5, eventually passing the familiar stand of San Diego's high rise buildings glinting from the sun which was presently setting over Point Loma, not far from the spot, in 1542 where the West Coast hosted its first European visitor, Juan Rodríguez Cabrillo, the renowned Portuguese explorer. My mind flooded with the blur of my first five years as a college student, and resident of San Diego. The city had taken permanent residence in the recesses of my heart and soul, for it represented infinite memories, and rights of passage for a twenty-something wide-eyed Seattle transplant. It was the city that offered my first divine taste of independence. It's where I met lifelong friends, and ultimately, the love of my life. Whenever opportunity was kind enough to offer an encounter with my favorite city, I would inevitably depart with great reluctance, but always whisper to her: "I'll be back, and maybe next time, to stay."

Through the corner of my eye, cousin Pat's green hardcover rested in the passenger seat, beckoning me to explore its pages, though I had done so dozens of times before, as a teenager. With hands gripped to the wheel, I gave much consideration to the many deliberate routes that Henry's wooden bible must have taken in order to wind up in my possession. Had it somehow been passed on to my great-great-grandfather, David Irish Banks? He was close to Henry in age —only a year and a few months older— but there were nine other siblings who could have ultimately become the guardian of Henry's token. Had David passed the palm-sized wooden block along to his son, who was my great-grandfather, Willis Banks? Why him, and not one of Willis' seven siblings? Had Great Grandfather Willis entrusted it to my grandmother, Mary Almira Banks, who was a sister to my father's four uncles, and aunt who could have acquired the little book just as easily? My father had two brothers, and two sisters, yet Henry's memento found its way into Dad's den, 140 years after its completion in 1862. Finally, why was it that I was the one who had discovered Henry's bible on a shelf in Dad's study, instead of one of my two sisters? I shook my head to clear the impossible math from my brain as the twisting ribbons of bright headlights, and crimson taillights tugged my attention away to the miles of highway that fanned out before me. I smiled as I drew the only conclusion that made any sense to me: Who else would better qualify as its caretaker? It was at that moment that I made a solemn oath to get to know everything about Uncle Henry and his mysterious heirloom that history would reveal, and to undertake this pursuit, but only until the trail ran cold.

In the months that followed, I capitalized on sporadic periods of leisure time to pursue and refine my new pastime of Banks family genealogy. I enlisted with hundreds of other subscribers at Ancestry.com, in gleeful concurrence with their modest monthly fee. A multitude of powerful research instruments were suddenly at my command, and I took full advantage of their attributes.

I consulted the 1850 U.S. Federal Census, which corroborated many of the details concerning the Banks family, with which I was already acquainted. Henry's father, Nathan O. Banks Jr. however, was mysteriously absent from the listing. This would lead me down another tributary path of exploration.

The 1860 Census listed Cynthia Banks, Farmer (56), and five of her sons: Henry (22), Egbert (20), William (19), George Fox (17), and

John J. (13). They were all now residing in Mercer County, IL, just as Henry's Civil War Detail Report had mentioned. Though my great-great grandfather, David Irish Banks was not listed with his brothers, I found him a few pages, and 20 miles away, living in Monmouth, IL with his wife, Mary, and their 6 year old daughter. Their son, who would be my great grandfather Willus David Banks wouldn't appear on the scene until 13 years later.

The 1870 census had been recorded five years after the Civil War came to a close. Yet, it featured Henry, who had apparently remained single, and was now a 30 year old farmer, living with younger brother, John J. (23) and mother, Cynthia, now 65 years old, in the Elm Creek township of Saline County, Kansas. Curious as usual, I entered this new location in the search field at EPodunk.com, which is a search engine that lists just about every community known to man, from the most obscure dot on the map, to the most heavily populated metropolis. EPodunk.com listed Elm Creek as a community in the Salina metro area. Subsequent research for historic photos impressed upon me Salina's similarity to Hill Valley, California, which was the fictitious location for the film, "Back to the Future". The Classic Revival style courthouse even sported a nearly identical clock upon its façade, beneath the steeply pitched peak of its roofline in the early days. Shortly after the Civil War, the Kansas Pacific Railroad opened up a direct route to the Salina area, bringing in settlers from all directions. Salina had survived a brief stint as a cattle-trading post, which the city's website described as follows:

> The businessmen had expended a good deal of money to secure the trade that would be derived from the town being made a trading point for cattle, but having secured it, the people soon discovered that it was not such a desirable thing to have after all. The trade in itself was good enough, and the business of the merchants in town was greatly increased thereby, but the town became infested with such a crowd of disreputable character, both male and female, that whatever advantage was gained in trade was more than counterbalanced by loss in morals. When the cattle trade moved westward two years afterwards, the citizens of Salina were more than rejoiced at its departure than they were at its coming. Salina was a mill town and a trading center, and that's the way they liked it.

It was difficult for me to conjure the image of Henry rubbing elbows with the rustlers, cowboys and outlaws of the Old West, but I could easily imagine him and brother John loading up the wagon, and "goin' to town" for supplies, or to "dicker" with brokers over the best price for a bushel of their wheat and alfalfa.

Fishing for more information, in the 1880 Federal Census I found Henry Ira Banks, 42 tending a farm in Pleasant Valley, Kansas. I was amused by the coincidence that I was presently the same age. Listed in the same household was Henry's wife, Tilla, 48 and a live-in German-born laborer, Theadore Siffens, 23. Henry's younger brother, William was living just a few doors down. The story was beginning to unfold, page-by-page before my eyes, and I was happy for Henry that he had finally married, though no children were listed. I assumed that since he and his wife were in advanced years, a family was not part of their equation. Tending a farm in the 19th century was thirsty work, and a brood of strapping sons was the hope of most hard-working agrarians in those early days. I hoped that by some enigmatic swing of providence, that the 1890 Census would disclose evidence that might provide a path to a descendant to whom I might pass Henry's bible.

I had already established that Henry hadn't survived the 1880's, and that he would not be mentioned in the 1890 census, but I was hopeful that his widow's movements in the next decade might possibly offer some clues as to where he died, where he was buried, and if he left an heir. To my displeasure, an article I located on Ancestry.com delivered the following blow:

> *Some said it was a cigarette. Some said it was a conspiracy. But no one really knows for sure what started the fire on January 10, 1921, that destroyed a large portion of the 1890 U.S. federal census. What everyone agrees on is this: it was a tragedy of immense proportion. The census, with critical historical information on more than 6 million people in the U.S., was being stored in the basement of the United States Commerce Department. The other census records were inside a fire- and water-proof vault when the flames started, but the 1890 census was sitting just outside its protective walls. Firemen rushed to the scene to put the fire out, but what wasn't already destroyed by fire and smoke was drowned in water: 25% was said to have been destroyed by the flames; 50% by the smoke and water that followed it. And what happened to*

*the remaining 25%? Most of it was shuffled around from place
to place until it was finally destroyed in the 1930s.*

I decided to go back to my cousin Pat's book to determine,
whether or not there was any mention of Henry throughout the
enormous body of her research. Flipping through the photos, which
corresponded with Henry's parents and siblings, I happened to spot a
pair of photos that featured an older bearded gentleman, sporting a
shiny medal on the lapel of his dapper vintage suit. I held my breath as
I scanned the preceding pages for an index. It identified the elderly man
as Egbert Banks, Civil War Veteran. Ancestry.com listed Henry's
younger brother as an enlisted Private attached to Company E, of
Iowa's 11th Infantry Regiment. While his older brother went off to fight
the rebellion, Egbert left Illinois for Iowa only to be recruited in 1864
to serve the Union cause, even if it was for just a few months. In
retrospect, I realized that the date of the photo was from the teens, so
my suspicion that the man in the photo might be Henry was a figment
of wishful thinking, and nothing more. I continued, however to search
for facts about Uncle Egbert, and I began with a random Internet
search. To my surprise, I found the following excerpt online from the
book "The History of Clinton County Iowa" by L. P. Allen (1879):

> *EGBERT BANKS, farmer, Sec. 5; P. O. Welton; born
> in Putnam Co., N. Y., in 1839; his father was drowned at
> Albany, N.Y., about 1849; after the death of his father, he lived
> in the family of his uncle, in Dutchess Co., N. Y., for four years;
> he also lived in Connecticut one year; lived for some time in
> Fairfax Co., Va., went to Illinois in 1854; he came to Clinton
> Co. in the fall of 1864. Fall of 1864, went as a recruit in the
> 11th I. V. I.; was on detached duty at Ringgold, Ga., until
> February, 1865; was afterward engaged in the battle of
> Kingston, N. C.; was mustered out of service with his regiment
> in July, 1865. He married, 1867, Elizabeth Dannatt, a native of
> Lincolnshire, England; has two children-Caroline and Benjamin
> D. Mr. Dannatt has a well-improved farm of 120 acres.*

The dates did, in fact jibe with those in the Banks family book,
and subsequently, I discovered that my great-great-great grandfather's
death was attributed to drowning in Albany, NY in 1849. I later
identified the medal pictured on Egbert's chest as a Grand Army of the
Republic Membership Medal. The GAR, according to Wikipedia was a
fraternal organization composed of veterans of the Union Army who

had served in the Civil War. They were among the first organized advocacy groups in American politics. The organization was eventually succeeded by the Sons of Union Veterans of the Civil War (SUVCW).

I continued to meticulously scour through the pages of my cousin's book, studying every detail in photographs, postcards and letters between family members, including those of my great, great grandfather David Banks, who was quite the prolific correspondent. After hours of reading by lamplight in my study, I was coming up empty in my search for the slightest shred of evidence that might lead me to Henry's whereabouts. I was approaching the book's final pages, upon which my cousin had featured numerous Xerox copies of letters collected from various descendants of the original Banks family of Putnam County, NY. The Banks' infinite progeny had since canvassed the nation. Some had settled in Los Angeles, Santa Barbara, and San Bernardino, California. Others had meandered south to Missouri, Iowa and along the Oregon trail northwest to Oregon and Washington State, where my direct lineage had proliferated. One letter in particular engaged me, with its neatly practiced, feminine cursive. It was from one of Henry's nieces, Annie L. Banks of Long Island, NY. She was the daughter of Daniel Banks, Henry's older brother. In Annie's heartfelt exchange with a close cousin, she expressed some concerns about her uncles and their farms, regarding the devastating effect from a phenomenon of biblical proportions that made national headlines in 1874:

> "...what fearfully horrible things those grasshoppers must be to destroy so much. I feel very sorry for Grandmother, Uncle John, George, and **Henry**, but we must expect to meet with disappointments in this world."

A recent episode on the History Channel came to mind, and a cross-reference with answers.com confirmed my supposition that Henry and his brothers had been victimized by the locust plague of 1874.

> *July 20–30, 1874. The Rocky Mountain locust, long a pest in the American Midwest, became an even bigger threat in the summer of 1874. Beginning in late July, the largest recorded swarm of this insect descended on the Great Plains. It is estimated that 124 billion insects formed a swarm 1,800 miles long and 110 miles wide that ranged from Canada and the*

*Dakotas down to Texas. Contemporary accounts said that the locusts blocked out the sun and devastated farms in mere minutes. The swarms continued in smaller size for the next several years and caused an estimated $200 million in crop destruction.*

After exploring the entire volume, I set my cousin's book aside, grateful that I found some trivial details regarding Henry's life, yet disappointed that I had little to show for my investment of time spent researching every page, but such is the way of inquisitive scrutineers. At the very least, I was now quite well-versed in Banks family history.

Like most early settlers, most of the men, and even some of the women were classified as farmers in the U.S. Census records. I pondered over the many generations of shared agricultural knowledge that must have been exchanged between fathers, sons, and grandsons, since Henry's early childhood in Putnam County, NY. The thought aroused a childhood memory of mine. I recalled the strong scent of Golden Delicious apples that hung in clusters on an impressive tree standing guard before a garden path in the backyard of my mother's parents' residence in picturesque Skagit Valley, WA. I remembered listening intently to lessons about soil and seasons, as I rode on the shoulders of my grandfather, who was a retired dairy farmer. Reaching out to grasp the tops of six-foot tall corn stocks, ripe for harvest, I couldn't have been much older than five or six, but the memory was vivid enough, that I could recollect how warm the sun was on that day. My own father, who was an accomplished gardener in his own backyard for as long as I could remember, also passed along grains of horticultural advice to me. Even so, I calculated the hundreds of dollars that I had spent during my tenure as a suburban homeowner on tree, shrub and sod replacement. Despite my impressive farming heritage, it was painfully apparent that the Banks family green thumb gene had either skipped a generation, or recessed altogether.

# Picking Up Stakes

The holidays were approaching, and in typical fashion, my workload at the ad agency began to increase, as my spare time that I usually devoted to research began to taper off. After examining two intimidating historic books cover-to-cover, and poring over all existing census records, and antiquated documents, Henry's trail began to run cold. I considered this period an unintentional hiatus, though some evidence had unexpectedly managed to trickle in. I obtained a copy of Henry's Civil War Pension Application through the National Archives, to see if an heir had submitted the application. However, a lackluster clerk had left imperative fields blank on the document, depriving me of the evidence I was hoping for. Concurrently, I had contacted the Kansas State Historical Society, in attempt to locate Henry's gravesite. Their helpful staff rifled through their records, and referenced neighboring cemeteries, but came up empty, as did their counterparts at the State of Illinois. I was looking at an empty nine-year timeline, which spanned from the 1880 Federal Census where I found the final record of Henry's life, to the 24th of July, 1889, which was the solitary record of Henry's death, according to familysearch.org, and the details in my cousin Pat's book. I took stock in all that I had learned about my own family tree, and the deep, emerging admiration for hard-working people who were so devoted to their families, their country, and their way of life, for which they would eagerly sacrifice so much. I placed Henry's bible back in the box where I had found it, and though I tucked it away out of sight, Henry's story was not out of mind. It occupied my thoughts, constantly.

In April, 2009 I flew home to Seattle to attend my grandmother's 100th birthday party. She was living in a nursing home, suffering from dementia. I use the term "suffering" very loosely, as her physical health was tip-top, though her memory was on a constant, and consistent decline. I arrived early, and assisted my sisters and the rest home staff with the preparations. Relatives from my mother's side soon began to parade into the chapel. I hadn't seen many of them since my father's funeral, four years before. My cousin, Ken Vanden Hoorn had since retired, and had become a very skilled genealogist. He had brought with him albums filled with photographs of my grandmother's parents, who were immigrants from Friesland, a province which lies in the northernmost portion of the Netherlands. He had composed her family tree, which spanned back through numerous generations to Holland. I leafed forward to where the Banks family connected, thanks to my parents' fortunate introduction. I didn't get very far before my attention was diverted by grandson duties, but I did make a point to spend some time conversing with Ken, in order to learn more about his efforts. I was intrigued by the immense compilation of data that I assumed must have kept him occupied for hours. I shared with him my testimony, as it involved Henry's bible, and my investigation that I had thought had come to a close. I was encouraged by his painstaking approach to gathering information, and analytically piecing together the details that would have otherwise been forever lost. I promised that I would correspond with him when I returned to California, and that I would compose a summary of my own discoveries and send him a copy. It had been months since I had put any effort toward my research, but I anticipated that this little assignment could potentially be the boost I needed to get the wheels spinning once again.

I began scribbling some notes on the plane, en route to Orange County the following day, and before the week was out, I had recorded every detail that I could gather at the time. I read through the first draft, and was happy with the result, and amazed at what I had learned in such a brief period; but it was missing an ending. Nevertheless, I emailed a draft off to Ken in response to a set of DVD's that he had sent to me as he had previously promised. They were loaded with the research he had shared with me at my grandmother's party. I included the following note:

> Ken,
>
> Thank you for all of the research...I am looking through the DVD's now. I have attached some pages from a project that is on-going. I'm trying to obtain closure, and find out if my great-great grand uncle had any children, and where he is buried. I've hit the wall so far. Read on, and let me know if you have any suggestions. I've scoured the cemetery websites, etc. with no luck.
>
> I hope you enjoy the attached...it's been a fun ride so far. I am such a nerd...following Henry's march with Google Earth, stopping at the same places he stopped, viewing photos of the same things he saw, only 150 years later.

*Thanks again.*

*Steve*

At the very least, it was the beginning of something. The project would have ended here, had I not persisted.

Andi and I were starting to feel the sting of the declining economy in 2009, which was intensifying like a relentless tsunami across the states, and California was no exception. By November, we were both jobless, and struggling to survive financially, through some very tempestuous trials, that tested and stretched our relationship to its very limits. After months of job-hunting between infrequent freelance assignments, and with no prospects on the horizon, my self-esteem was taking a severe beating. It didn't seem to matter how often I had reminded myself that I had been through layoffs, and transitional periods of unemployment before. I was in a dark place, and was finding it more difficult, with each passing day to recover. We made the mutual decision to take a break, as we both were in desperate need of a temporary scenery change. As Andi accompanied her stepmother, and some friends on a visit to Sweden, I decided to take a few days, and reclaim some perspective for myself. I didn't waste any time. On the same morning I drove Andi to the John Wayne airport to wish her bon voyage, I left the west coast in my rear view, and followed Highway 40 East through the Mojave desert.

I have always enjoyed the road. I find peace in a moving landscape, or seascape for some reason. Being idle for too long has always made me restless and fidgety, but if I can find an excuse to be on the move, I will capitalize upon it. One such trip occurred while I was attending college in San Diego. I had hitched a ride with a co-worker to Seattle, to surprise my family for the holidays. Sitting in my hotel room, early in the morning on Christmas Eve, I had the phone receiver in my grasp, ready to announce to my mother that I was in town. A sudden kneejerk decision caused me to retract. I dialed the front desk instead. Later, a Mitsubishi Montero with keys, and a full tank of gas was waiting in the driveway, just as the concierge had promised. I jumped in behind the wheel, strapped myself in and headed East. My destination? Lamar, WA —the forever home of my Grandfather, and my childhood summer playground near Walla Walla, where my love of history was born.

I wasn't proud that I hadn't been east of the Cascades to visit my Grandpa Dan in nearly a decade. However, since I had the time and the transportation, I decided to resolve that matter. The impromptu road trip had restored some peace of mind, eradicated some guilt, and instilled a warm satisfaction that my gesture had made my grandfather's Christmas, which he would have otherwise spent alone. That visit would be our first real man-to-man exchange, but our last meeting before his passing.

Suffice it to say that as I now drove through the California desert, all the burdensome issues that occupied my thoughts instantly diminished in size. Once I arrived at the end of my journey, I was gazing across the impossible expanse at the Southern rim of the Grand Canyon. Observing its striking panoramas for the first time, I finally understood why those who visit the canyon are so verbally challenged. Though the scenery is spectacular from all angles, the experience defies description.

While in Arizona, I took a big bite of life, almost as if it were my last. My approach to this break was open-ended —casting all cares to the wind— it was time to enjoy some warm weather in God's country, and some laughter and mayhem with my nephew, Ande who lived in Phoenix, and Ken, my best friend since childhood who had flown out from Seattle for our annual "Lost Weekend". We hiked through the canyons in Sedona, spent three days boating on Lake Powell, walked in the shadows of lawmen and outlaws in Tombstone, and strolled the sidewalk with throngs of Japanese tourists in the towns that still thrived along Route 66. The last thing I wanted was to return to the coast with a case of tourist's remorse. It was my intention to see it all, and do it all, near to the point of exhaustion. We succeeded.

The sun was high in the desert sky, as I descended through the familiar bend in the Barstow Freeway spanning parallel to the Cajon Wash, which emptied into the Santa Ana River. As the sparse inland terrain gave way to neatly aligned date palms, and cloned red-roofed dwellings, I finally passed through the Orange Curtain, devoid of the hopelessness, which had driven me away. With improved mental stability and heightened stamina, I was ready to face reality, and resign to the gravity of our current condition. Andi and I reunited, and after examining the books, and discussing our options, we arrived at the mutual decision to pickup stakes, and relocate to a market that hadn't yet been affected by the national jobless trend. Coincidentally, I would be embarking on yet another road trip through the same Arizona desert passage I had traversed only nine days prior, only this time my route would extend dramatically, to Austin, Texas.

Andi had many ties in Austin, and her father still resided in a Houston suburb, where she was born and raised. A graduate of the University of Texas, Andi was familiar with the area, though Austin had experienced some very rapid growth since her sorority days, rendering its skyline and suburbs somewhat unrecognizable. She would be tying up all the loose ends in Newport, while I focused on locating temporary housing, and securing full-time employment. The 1400-mile drive from Newport to Austin passed by with a blur. No detours to witness roadside attractions, or historic markers this time. My only diversions were for reasons of sleep, refueling, or dining with "The Colonel". Once I arrived at my destination, I opened the drivers-side door, which let in a rush of blistering air that stole my breath. Austin was experiencing a record heat wave, which was in high contrast to the mellow summer sea breeze that I had just left behind. I scanned the area, with its infinite rolling hills, sprawling with great oaks, and mesquite trees, each heavily populated with deafening cicadas. "Where the hell am I?" I murmured to myself.

Years before, when we had returned to California after living for nearly ten years in Denver, I had labeled myself an incurable "Suburban Coastal Dweller". Yet here I was, working against my grain once again, making preparations to relocate far inland, by virtue of necessity. By and by, this outrageous decision would prove to be advantageous for both Andi and I on many levels —both personal, and professional— but I never dreamed that Texas would disclose the elusive answers that I assumed were forever cloaked in obscurity.

# Correspondence and Clues

After spending a month in the Austin area, emailing draft-after-draft of my professional resume to innumerable sources, I came up empty, without a single interview on my calendar. I began networking with local professionals, and attended numerous social functions in effort to establish some contacts. It was immediately apparent that the subject on every tongue was the current depressed state of financial affairs —both on a national, and local scale. Mingling with a cocktail in one hand, and a growing stack of business cards in another, I had to continuously remind myself to be patient and hopeful, but cautiously realistic. This was a different kind of recession, leaving devastating damage in its wake —with no end in sight— and it was affecting everyone, one way or another.

In the morning, I would fly back to Orange County, and segue from the role of Hunter to Scout, primed and ready for yet another cross-country drive. Andi and I were joined by a throng of kind-hearted friends who offered their assistance as we proceeded to jam a 3-bedroom townhome full of belongings into a moving truck that was nearly bursting at the seam. Our last evening in Newport Coast, California was spent on the same air mattress that I slept on, during those nights when I began my pursuit after Uncle Henry. It had been nearly two years since I sat down at my iMac to open this new chapter in my life that was as mysterious and engaging as it was stimulating. Recently, however, my focus had shifted to the matters at hand, and all of my research, books, and Henry's wooden bible were packed away somewhere in a box in the back of a U-Haul truck, just outside my front door. God only knew when it would surface again.

Salty mist. Crashing waves. Crying gulls. My eyes were intentionally closed, in order to give way to my other senses, as I devoured every sensation that my last visit to Corona del Mar beach would offer. The sun had just rose, and the fire pits —still smoldering from the evening before— peppered the salty air with a pungent, but beautifully mixed aroma that is second only to my favorite scent —sun drenched pines. My eyes stretched open wide, as my bare feet suddenly stung with the frigid intrusion of a teasing Pacific wave. I wasn't certain when I would see, or feel the coast again, and I knew I would regret missing this opportunity to bid the ocean farewell in my own way. I spent about 30 minutes strolling the beach from the long jetty to the north, which flanked Pirate's Cove, and the mouth of Newport Harbor, all the way South to the tide pools at Little Corona. I returned to the car, both refreshed, and tortured all at once. I joined Andi at the townhome, loaded her sports car on a trailer attached to our rented, diesel-guzzling beast of burden, and we lit out for Texas to open a new chapter. I described our journey in an email that I sent to Sandi, my sister who was a flight attendant stationed in Portland, Oregon shortly after our arrival in the Lone Star State.

*Sandi,*

*Well...here we are, Austin, Texas...our new home.*
*We packed up a 24' moving truck on July 1st with no room to spare. As a matter of fact, we had to leave some things behind with some friends in Newport Beach who graciously agreed to donate them for us. Andi and I drove cross-country with her Saturn Sky on a flat bed trailer attached to our truck, and a trio of cats in their carriers riding with us in the cab, howling non-stop through three states. We felt like the Clampets. We meant to leave at 6am, but circumstances didn't allow us to pull out until 2pm! We arrived at our hotel in Las Cruces, New Mexico at about 3:30 am on the 2nd. Collapsed. We crossed the border into Texas at about 3pm (we lost 2 hours due to the time zones) and arrived at our townhome in Austin at about 230 am on the 3rd. By that time, the cats had grown accustomed to the movement and noise of the truck, and were lying in our laps watching the passing scenery and lights. We were so impressed. Since then we've been unpacking, hanging pictures and moving furniture...jamming a 3 bedroom townhome full of stuff into a 2 bedroom townhome...it hasn't been easy, but it's all looking good. We are in a great location, and can see sunsets over Lake Travis every night from our patio. There are great restaurants everywhere, and a sailing club that I can join just a few miles away in Lakeway, TX. I look forward to getting back into that, and taking friends out for a sail on the lake. Monday we resume our efforts to find jobs. California is in such poor shape right now, and though it was painful to leave, we won't miss the financial strain. I have been networking a lot here, with no promises yet...but at least people call back, and follow-up, which is more than I can say for CA. It sounds like we're having our first houseguests tonight (some of Andi's Austin friends) so I*

*had better snap to it and attack the HONEYDOO list. Our new info is down below. Drop us a line, or come visit if you can take 106° in the shade. FYI: It looks like Alaska begins nonstop flights from Seattle to Austin in August.*

*Well, take care of yourself, and stay in touch.*

*Love,*

*Steve & Andi*

Andi and I celebrated our nation's 233rd birthday watching a spectacular display of fireworks over Lake Travis from our balcony, which offered a favorable vantage point. We spent a good portion of our first Sunday arranging furniture, and making numerous trips back-and-forth to our storage unit. Monday brought with it a very busy regimen of scouring the classifieds, crafting resumes, and firing off emails. Fortunately, the statistics concerning the Austin employment outlook eventually proved to be true. Before too long, I was employed full-time as an in-house Creative Director at a locally headquartered company. A prominent homebuilder eventually recruited Andi, and though our new environment was unfamiliar, we were at least better off financially for the time-being, and in full-throttle recovery mode.

Once my home office was fully functional, I began to catch up with my emails and communication, which had lapsed somewhat, due to my job-hunting priorities. I retrieved some correspondence from my cousin, Ken who had located a very random, but valuable posting on the Internet, since our live discussion in April. He wrote:

*Steve,*

*This is what I can tell you regarding Henry:*

*Henry Banks*
*Born: Feb 17, 1838 in Oblong, Duchess County, NY*
*Died: 10:15 pm Wed, Jul 24, 1889 in Baird, TX*
*Buried: Ross Cemetery, Baird, Texas*
*Married: Apr 22, 1888*
*To   Bowlus*

*Born: Apr 25, 1860 in Sandusky County, Ohio*
*Died: in Oakland, Calif*
*Dtr of William Henry Bowlus & Barbara Ann Beck*

Inclined to investigate the origin of this random posting, I requested the actual link from my cousin, Ken who had discovered it on rootsweb.com. Once I received it, I learned that the individual who had posted the information had fortunately left her email address for reference.

She wrote: *"I am a descendant of the Bowlus family through William Henry. I have a book written on this family from 1940 by a descendant of this family now deceased."*

She continued: *"William Henry Bowlus, born in 1821 married Barbara Ann Beck, and apparently had 11 children. Emma Bowlus, their 8<sup>th</sup> child married one Henry I. Banks, April 22<sup>nd</sup>, 1888. He died July 24, 1889, Baird, TX at 10:15 p.m. Wednesday night, and is buried at Ross Cemetery, Baird, TX."*

I had to read this posting twice, in order for the irony to finally sink in. A quick glance at Google Earth confirmed that if the cryptic, and random entry that my cousin had just sent me was accurate, then Henry's final resting place was just a 3-hour drive from my new home address in Texas! I have come to learn that when coincidences of this nature avail themselves —the ones that tend to bowl you over— it pays to follow up with obedience, and pay close attention to what comes next. With great anticipation, I typed up a brief query and sent it off to the mysterious source, hopeful for a response:

*Hello.*
*I just found your entry on Rootsweb about your family book, which you transcribed. Without knowing it, you've probably just provided a very important clue to the final resting place of an ancestor that I have been researching for a long time. Apparently, Emma Bowlus was married to my great-great uncle Henry I Banks for only a year before he died, and was buried in Baird, TX at Ross Cemetery. I live in Austin now, so I am looking forward to a drive up to Baird to hopefully find what I have been looking for. Attached, you will find documentation from my search, and Henry's connection to the Civil War. I will continue to try to track down a photo of him,*

*if one even exists.*
*I would love to get copies of the pages in the book you described.*
*Feel free to contact me if you wish.*
*Thank you!*

*—Steve Enyeart*

A response came almost instantly, and the email I received from Junior Ramsey was cordial, inquisitive, and rich with information.

*Hi Steve, well I do not remember what I posted or where but I do have the pgs in the book and I certainly can make copies and mail them to you at yr address below. Emma being the daughter of Wm Henry Grant and Barbary Ann.*
*Emma was md 3x....lst to a Gain, then to Banks, then to Crawford*
*In 1940 when this book was written she was still living. Since Gain is buried at Ross cem in Baird I would imagine she is too. Most of the Bowlus that lived in Baird are buried there. Emma had 3 kids w/Gain but they all died within 2 yrs of birth then they got div Apr 3 1888.*
*thats when she md yr Henry Banks 19 days later!! [Apr 22 1888] and it says he died in the next yr 1889.*

*Do you know why he died so sudden? I have no kids listed for them.*
*Also says his bible does not show dob so author must had his bible too.*
*[I have not read yr attachment yet] then she md Crawford, had twins [boy, girl] then a girl born/died 1900 and a boy who lived to 1936 in CA. In 1940 both twins were still alive both living CA.*
*If you'd like me to send the above info in email*
*I do not mind doing that.*
*My relation to Wm Henry Bowlus is this way.*
*his son Wm Grant Bowlus was 11th child md Bertha Belle Rice. I knew her she was my gr grandma and she was living at Baird and I use to visit there with her with my granny who was her dau also name Bertha [md a Ramsey] So Emma Bowlus was [8th child of Wm Henry]and Wm Grant were sis/bro*
*I guess that makes them my gr grand aunt/gr grandpa ?*
*Let me know what you'd like.*

*So you are related to the Banks and not Bowlus then?*
*I will read the attachment and get back to you*
*thanks for writing.*
*I live in NE Wa, my bro and I came up here from TX after our*
*Dad died in 1970. We had lived here bef as our Dad was a col*
*and bomber pilot and we all loved it here.*
*I've lived on a ranch here 30 yrs.*
*...Junior*

I was elated to receive Junior's correspondence, and confirmation. Checking the mailbox one day, on my way home from work, I discovered an envelope from Newport, WA. It contained a hard copy of the pages that listed the genealogy of Emma Bowlus-Gain-Banks-Crawford, which included her brief history as Uncle Henry's wife.

Junior, who was also a genealogy enthusiast, had later located more information about Henry that a researcher had posted while looking for unrelated information through microfiche at a local university. Her reason for posting her findings was unknown. Something compelled her to broadcast the article, perhaps by the slim chance that someone might find it useful.

Indeed, it was useful, and indeed the chance was slim, but I was grateful for this stranger's benevolent response to the article she found, and the time she spent transcribing it for my benefit. It was Henry's official "Notice of Probate" published in the Baird Star Newspaper, just months after his death. Though scant in its details, it revealed just enough to render a more vivid depiction of Henry's brief term as a Texan.

*Baird Weekly Star - Thursday October 10, 1889*
*NOTICE OF PROBATE:*

*To the Sheriff or any constable of Callahan County Greetings:*
*You are herby commanded to cause to be published in some*
*newspaper published in said county once a week for four*
*consecutive weeks, previous to the return day hereof the*
*following citation:*

*The State of Texas:*
*To all persons interested in the estate of H I Banks, deceased,*

*Emma Banks has filed in the County Court of Callahan County, an aplication to probate the nuncupative will of said H I Banks, deceased; said application alleging in substance, that said H I Banks died in Baird on the 24th day of July AD 1889, leaving real and personal property of the estimated value of eight hundred dollars, and a nuncupative will duly executed; that the testamentary words of said will were in substance as follows: I bequeath al my real and personal property to my wife, Emma Bank that the witnesses to said testamentary words were Emma Banks, \* W H [William Henry] Bowles [Bowlus] and Mrs. W H Bowles; that all of said witnesses to said will reside in the county of Callahan and State of Texas; that said H I Banks at the time of his death resided in Baird, Callahan County, Texas; that Emma Banks, the applicant is the surviving wife of said H I Banks and resides in Callahan County, Texas; that no executor was named in said will; that the names and residences of the heirs at law of the said H I Banks were unknown to the applicant Which said application will be heard at the November term 1889 of this said court, to be holden on the first Monday in November, 1889 at the Court House thereof, In the town of Baird, at which time all persons interested in said estate may appear and contest said application, if they are proper. Herein fail not, under penalty of the law and of this writ make due return.*

*Issued the first day of October 1889*
*Witness L N Jackson clerk of said court and the seal therof at office in the town of baird the first day of Octboer 1889*
*J N Jackson clerk County Court Callahan County the foregoing is a true copy of original citation,*
*I certify. J W Jones? Sheriff Callahan Co. TX Oct 2, 1889*

*A note from the poster:*
*Note: I am not related to this family, **I just found this in newspaper***

I found it interesting that Henry's surviving heirs and their places of residence were unknown to his widow, and I wondered if his siblings ever learned what became of him, due in part to Emma's lack of information, available technology, or concern, perhaps. The many samples of collected correspondence between his siblings that I had observed up to this point bore no mention of Henry's name.

Still, thanks to the kindness of a few individuals who were just as passionate about genealogy as I was now becoming, I was drawing closer to a conclusion. The events of Henry's life were gradually coming into sharper focus, and these new revelations energized me to once again reinstate my pursuit, from where it had since stalled out.

I made a call to the Callahan County courthouse early on a Monday morning, and did my best to summarize the story, which wound up droning on and on with the brevity of a bar exam. A very cordial young lady patiently listened to my testimony, and replied in her Hill Country drawl, "Y'all need to be speaking to our Veteran's Affairs man...he's fixin' to come in to the office anytime now." She transferred me to the voicemail of Tom Ivey, who also had a heavy Texas twang, and judging by the tone of his voicemail greeting, and the prescriptive detail with which he described how I was to leave my message, I knew I had the right guy. I left a brief message outlining the reason for my call.

Later that same week, my cell phone rang, and the voice on the other end of the line was unmistakable. It was Tom Ivey, Veteran's Officer of Callahan County, Texas. He was hesitant to believe that there was a Union Private buried in Baird, Texas! I spelled out the details of my search as briefly, and poignantly as possible. He seemed intrigued. We established a wonderful rapport, and arrived at the mutual decision that we needed to meet in person. Tom invited me to meet him for lunch on the following Saturday in downtown Baird. In the days that preceded my drive from Austin toward Abilene, Tom and his staff scoured the microfilm collection that was housed in the courthouse. A few items surfaced that were helpful, and Tom was quick to forward hard copies to me by mail.

One item was a copy of Uncle Henry's Notice of Probate — previously mentioned— as it appeared in the Baird Star Newspaper. Also included was a document originating from the Baird courthouse showing Henry's widow, Emma failing to appear in court on November 1, 1889, which was the date when her application to assume Henry's real and personal property was supposed to be read before the court. It is unknown if she ever returned for her claim at a later date.

# Bound for Baird, Texas

In the 1870's Texas was the center of the nation's cattle business, and it became obvious to some, that the expansion of the westward branching railroad would serve as an effective conduit for which to move cattle to demanding northern markets. Construction camps began to spout up virtually overnight, and one camp in particular became the town of Baird. Named after a director of the Texas and Pacific Railway, Matthew Baird, the little town really began to flourish once rail service was established to Ft. Worth on December 14th, 1880. The railroad put forth a national advertising campaign, announcing cheap land to be settled around the community, and soon a sizeable population began to multiply. It is quite possible that shortly after Henry sold off his acreage in Kansas, his new bride Emma, whose family's homestead was in Baird may have convinced him to leave his farm for new employment opportunities. Baird had much to offer Henry professionally, with the new railroad, numerous cattle ranchers, or perhaps the local lumber mill, owned and operated by the Bowlus family.

From a manila envelope sent to me by Tom Ivey, I removed an amusing black and white photo of a "Mr. Bowlus", (William Grant Bowlus) taken at about 1917, during World War I. He was posing proudly in front of his hardware store's façade, which was festooned with bunting and banners featuring hand-scrawled "anti-Kaiser", and "pro-American" messages. I pondered over the fact that for a brief period, this man was Uncle Henry's brother-in-law. Judging from William's obvious soft-spot for veterans, I hoped that he and the Bowlus family treated Henry with the same deserving respect which was evident in the photo.

It was early Saturday morning, September 6th, 2009, and since Andi had flown back to California to visit some friends the day before, I was on my own for the weekend. Before dawn, I was on the road, bound for Baird. The drive was long, but scenic, over hill and dale through some of the most picturesque landscapes that the Texas Hill Country could offer. Since the hour was early, I had hardly any company on the highway, so I wasn't modest about negotiating some of the curves beyond the posted limits.

With some of my best friends in California and Colorado being professional photographers, I had become familiar with a phenomenon they referred to as "magic hour." This is a window of opportunity that only presents itself shortly after dawn, and just before dusk, offering pristine conditions for photographing landscapes and other subjects dependent on ambient light. Somewhere North of Cedar Park, magic hour arrived in its prime, and made it difficult for me to keep my eyes on the road. I passed grand old oaks by the score, with their corkscrewing branches twisting in random chaos, and forming perfectly symmetrical canopies of shimmering green. Endless groves of mesquite, prickly pear cacti and sage carpeted the panorama from horizon to horizon. I encountered an innumerable population of deer along this stretch of highway, some standing, some running, and some that unfortunately didn't make it back safely from the creek. My route led me through a small town that appeared frozen in time, on my way to Baird, Texas called "Cross Plains." It's name rang a familiar bell with me for some reason, and as I followed a detour that led me through a quaint residential area, where I spotted a modest, white single-story home with a large sign in the front yard which read: *"Historic Home of Robert E. Howard."* I grinned ear-to-ear, and muttered to myself, *"no-way."*

As an eighth and ninth grader, I had found Howard's stories of fantasy swordplay fiction so beguiling, and the characters who emerged from them —larger than life, and formidable— were my heroes, despite their perennial moral complexity. In the 1930's and 1940's Howard created an alternate world similar to those of Tolkien, and C.S. Lewis. Howard's Cimmerian realm however, was much more tawdry and promiscuous, with danger and dread lying in wait around every corner —the perfect combination for an introverted and rebellious teen, hopelessly plagued with creative aspirations. Paired with my admiration for the equally transporting qualities I discovered in the art of Boris Vallejo, and Frank Frazetta, the stories of King Kull, and Conan the Barbarian perpetuated my imagination through my artistic efforts, and my short-lived phase of all-night reading and drawing marathons. As fate would have it, the Howard home was closed, as it was early on a Saturday morning, so I continued North toward Baird, disgruntled, but hopeful.

After leaving the town of Cross Plains in my rear view, it seemed like I had traveled a hundred miles north via Highway 283 without seeing any sign of life, when gradual hints of civilization began to emerge. Random turnoffs to endless gravel roads increased in frequency. A pair of garishly painted pintos stood like bookends, staring out at me from their barbed-wire barriers, their pasture littered with dozens of classic autos, now rusty deteriorating hulks, sunken partially into the earth. Finally, a road sign announced that Baird was only a few miles ahead. Along with my Canon G9 digital still camera, I had also packed a small Panasonic video camera, and kept it within reach in the passenger seat, just in case I spotted something worth documenting during my drive. I decided that the trip itself was reason enough, so I passed the time recording a brief narrative on-camera as I drove, chronicling the events, which had led up to the trip. This exercise proved to be an effective method to help me avoid road-coma, and to record details that I might eventually forget, though at the time, I wasn't sure what I was to do with it all.

Eventually, I lost interest in listening to my own voice, and pulled off the highway. I drove down a long thoroughfare that led me to an old, 2-story brick building, which I later identified as the Callahan County courthouse. I turned left down Market Street and struggled to locate the "Whistle Stop" café, where I was to meet up with Tom Ivey. I had perused the town's official website before leaving Austin, and now, as I drove past the nearly abandoned sidewalks it became clear why Baird was known as "The Antique Capitol of Central Texas." Antique stores lined each side of the street all the way down to its abrupt end where another ominous historic brick building stood. Here stood the Baird Railroad Depot, Visitor's Center and Transportation Museum. Just like the home of Robert E. Howard, it too was closed. Denied! Again!

I turned around, and drove up Market Street in the opposite direction, and spotted the tiny sign above "The Whistle Stop Café." I entered the restaurant, and suffice it to say, it was exactly how I had pictured it. An elderly gentleman sat alone at a four-top table near the kitchen, and I approached him slowly. He peered over his newspaper, and addressed me in his unmistakable drawl. "You must be Steve." I shook his hand firmly, and took my place across from him at his table. We ordered lunch, and had a good conversation, in person this time. I was impressed that he respectfully referred to my great-great uncle as "Mister Banks." We reaffirmed many details throughout our conversation, and when the dishes were cleared, he insisted on treating me to lunch. I obliged, and we made our way out to our vehicles. I followed Tom and his two large canines who rode in the cab of his pickup truck beyond the Baird city limits, and out to Highway 283, which became Cherry Street, after crossing North over Highway 20. Eventually, we turned down a narrow gravel road, which led to Ross Cemetery where Henry was reportedly interred in 1889. I was surprised and a bit intimidated at how large the graveyard was. Tom assured me that the dates on the headstones followed a chronological pattern, for the most part, and he would lead me to where the dates coincided with Henry's date of death. We strolled along parallel paths that oddly had street names like "Live Oak", "Red Bud", and "Pear", all along inspecting each headstone for names and dates.

Finally, we reached a large plot with a handful of older markers, which shared the familiar surname: "Bowlus." We had discovered Henry's in-laws, who were buried together with other members of the Bowlus family who had lived before them, and after. "Well," Tom said, "like I told you on the phone, there's a good number of unmarked plots in this general area." "I wouldn't be surprised if Mr. Banks wound up in one of them." I wasn't giving up that easily, and though I nodded in agreement to Tom's comment, I continued to inspect each grave in the vicinity, until I wandered far into the twentieth century stones. It was a typical September afternoon in Central Texas, and the temperature was well into the 90's. I walked carefully between plots, both marked, and unmarked, and eventually arrived next to Tom, who was resting on his truck's tailgate, in the shade with his two panting companions. He was studying a large paper scroll. He slid it over to me, and I recognized it as an old plot plan for Ross Cemetery. "Here's something interesting." He said, pointing to a small rectangle on the fading schematic. I couldn't believe my eyes. Just as each plot was identified with a surname, this small speck belonged to "Banks". Its proximity to the "Bowlus" family plot, and the similarity in age shared by other graves nearby, made it unmistakable. This had to be where they laid Uncle Henry to rest! I turned to Mr. Ivey and said, "My God Tom, I think we've found him." He agreed.

I carried the scroll over to the Banks plot. It was a bare, non-descript stretch of sod, and I stood before it with thoughts racing through my mind faster than I could measure. I took an inventory of the multitude of events, which led me to this place, and the years of discovery that culminated to this very moment. I marveled at the coincidental parallel of Henry's impromptu relocation to Texas —of all places— and my own migration to the lone star state. I was overwhelmed by the chance discovery of Henry's bible in my father's study, and the coincidental encounters with perfect strangers who unknowingly guided me, thus far with their helpful assistance and advice. I shook Tom's hand, and thanked him for his time and efforts, wishing I could repeat the gesture with every one of my contributors.

I surveyed the area once again, and documented every detail with photographs, in order to keep my facts together for future reference. According to Tom's schematic, it was unclear whether or not there was once a marker, or headstone present during the survey in the 1940's. I presented an idea to Tom, who was in absolute agreement. "I think Henry deserves a stone," I said. "A Civil War veteran, wounded in action should have a bona-fide Union Infantry marker."

I only had a photograph of Henry's small wooden bible to share with Tom while I was in Baird. The relic itself was somewhere safe in our storage unit, back in Austin, or so I assumed. After spending the afternoon at Uncle Henry's graveside, it became a new priority to locate it. Since Andi and her friends had been in charge of packing up my office in California while I was job-hunting three states away, I assumed it had been stowed safely, but with the slight risk of it being misplaced, or lost while out from under my supervision, I was almost afraid to begin looking for it. Nevertheless, I shared the photographs of Henry's memento with Mr. Ivey, and we discussed details of what it would take to procure the proper Civil War era headstone from the Veteran's Administration. Since Tom was in charge of organizing Veteran's services and the like for Callahan County, he had been through this exercise before. He would draft up the necessary forms for me. We agreed that I had reached the end of my search, and had already collected all the proof that was necessary to appease those in charge at the V.A., but I wasn't yet satisfied. I wasn't ready to close the book of Henry's biography quite yet. I had found the place, which marked his death, yet there was so much more to learn about his life.

Tom and I said our goodbyes, with a promise to stay in touch, and to continue to keep our "eyes peeled" for anything of interest relating to the case of Henry Ira Banks, and his short-lived term as a Texan. I watched in my rear view as Tom waved in my direction. He stood with a garden hose in his hand, watering a tree, which shaded some of the plots that surrounded Henry's. I noticed one of Tom's loyal dogs, which had crept up next to him, and sat against his leg, earning the reward of a pat on the head. Dust arose from the dirt and gravel driveway, which suddenly obscured the scene, and I shifted my attention to another long stretch of highway opening up ahead of me. However, something inside prompted me to choose a detour, and for one final glance, I drove slowly through Baird, past the ancient courthouse, and down Market Street once again. I parked at the end of the empty avenue where the Train Depot stood, stepped out of my SUV with camera in hand, and scanned the scene for photo-ops. As I snapped a few frames, I studied the townscape, mentally peeling away the antique signs, and gaudy, modern facades in order to visualize, and contemplate the scenery through Uncle Henry's eyes, at the moment of his arrival in 1889. I walked up the sidewalk in the opposite direction of the train depot, the most likely "jumping-off" point for a transplanted Kansas farmer and his new bride, ready to start a new life together in an established, and growing Texas town. I imagined a bustling anthill of activity that once filled, and flanked the street. I imagined a street abuzz with horses, coaches, wagons and folks crowned with bowlers and bonnets, going about their daily exercises fueled by nineteenth-century supply and demand. I strolled for a while, in Henry's footsteps.

Instead of making a beeline for Austin, I decided to stick around the general area for a while, and reflect on the day. As a force of habit, I sought out a venue where I could participate in a personal custom of "celebrating the small victories," that I had adapted during my recent period of unemployment in California. I wandered about twenty miles up Highway 20 through Clyde, and finally arrived in Abilene. After driving through the city, which seemed almost as abandoned as Baird had been, I pulled up to a stoplight, and spotted a humble establishment called "The Lucky Mule." "Perfect," I whispered. With ample parking, I pulled into the closest stall, and locked up the Hummer. As I passed through the heavy front doors, the aroma of stale beer and cigarette smoke nearly bowled me over. I wandered into the dark bar, walking to the rhythm of Molly Hatchet who provided a suitable soundtrack. I sidled up to the bar, and ordered a premium scotch. The bartendress clued into my mood, and asked, "What are we celebrating?" I smiled and answered, "Just met up with a long-lost relative." I didn't know where to begin describing my adventure, so before she could ask for details, I just ordered a second round, and drank a toast to Uncle Henry. Savoring the last few sips, I entered a few notes into my smart phone, though I didn't know at that time how valuable all of the documented details would soon become. The drive back to Austin would undoubtedly be long, but I would have much to process in my head and heart, along the way.

As was often my ritual on sunny Sunday mornings, I shared my trusty patio chair with Popeye, one of our three feline companions, while Andi went to the gym for an early morning workout. Our modest balcony overlooked the basin at the east end of Lake Travis, the peninsula of Hudson Bend, and an indecisive little landmass which local sailors referred to as "Sometimes Island", which appeared and disappeared with the constant rising and falling of the lake's water levels. I was busy organizing and uploading video and stills to my laptop from my trip to Baird, and making notes while the details were still fresh in my mind. I made a point to post a few photos on my Facebook page, creating a new photo album to share with friends and family members. I briefly studied the title I had given the album: "Looking For Uncle Henry." Looking? I had indeed found Henry, at least I had found his remains, but I hadn't yet really come to know that much about him. The details I had since gathered were spotty at best. "Well, he's been buried for 120 years, what do you expect?" I thought to myself. I reflected on the fascination that I had experienced while walking down Baird's Market Street promenade, and how those few steps had been so satisfying in my efforts to become better acquainted with my mysterious ancestor.

Suddenly, a familiar notion crept out of my subconscious, that I had dismissed the evening before, assuming it was the product of road fatigue during my drive home from Baird. I pondered over it more carefully this time. "Would it be crazy to do it?" "Is this some mid-life crisis effect?" "If it's such a far-fetched idea, then why can I not stop thinking about it?" I ran up to our master bedroom, and pulled open the top drawer to my nightstand. I grasped the small, green hardcover that I had not yet completed, and had nonchalantly neglected since the beginning of the new year. "Our Regiment" held within its pages a veritable road map that its author, Stephen Fleharty had drafted with vigilance and great detail through his epic documentation of the war. I could quite easily follow Henry's movements, from end-to-end, beginning with that trip from the family farm in Illinois to the schoolhouse where he swore his oath with his fellow Volunteers. I could travel through eight states, stopping to march through the same battlefields where Henry and his brothers in blue engaged the Confederate juggernaut. I could learn a great deal about Henry with each step, and maybe a little more about myself, not to mention the important cause that my ancestors chose to fight for, by visiting these sites in person. After all, I had at my disposal, the most prolific tour guide I could ever hope to follow: Sergeant Major Fleharty, himself.

I sipped my coffee, and gazed out into the distance at a spectrum of colorful genoas and spinnakers from a fleet of J-22 sailboats whose crews were in the midst of one of their beer can regattas. I was missing out on a good wind day, and I envied the sailors out enjoying the elements, but I was more than satisfied with my current post.

*Mary Almyra Banks, my grandmother in the 1920's*

*Top left: Egbert Banks, about the time of his enlistment. Top right: Cynthia Banks, the family matriarch in her period Quaker garb. Bottom, l-r: Egbert Banks, Eliza Banks, George Fox Banks, Mary Banks, and David Irish Banks, taken in 1895.*

# A New Branch for the Family Tree

Thankfully, after contorting my every limb to bushwhack through heaps of furniture, while digging through layer upon layer of banker boxes, I ferreted out the wooden bible, which was carefully wrapped in tissue. I found it lodged safely in the bottom of a large crate, at the very back of our storage unit, of course. After returning all the furnishings and boxes to their original place in the unit, I returned home, wrapped Henry's bible in a chamois cloth and placed it in a safe cavity, just beneath my iMac's monitor as a reminder to keep better track of it. Here, it was always within reach, should I need inspiration, as I continued to document my search for answers.

Over the next few months I managed to compile a good quantity of notes, photos, and video that I had collected since the initial discovery of Henry's wooden souvenir. Sitting down one night at my laptop, I expanded on an abbreviated summary that I had written while I was still living in California. I scanned images from my cousin Pat's book, and gathered more from bookmarked websites, placing them as inset visuals nested within the text. It didn't take long before I had completed the second draft.

While searching online for additional photographic reference, I located a pair of needles in a haystack. The first was a photograph of Henry's Commanding Officer, Captain Dan M. Sedwick, now bald and silver, sporting a Santa-esque beard. The image had been scanned from a booklet that commemorated a gathering of Veterans on the 50th Anniversary of the war's first shot, which occurred at Fort Sumter. Henry, of course hadn't survived long enough to attend, otherwise, I would have perused every page to discover any shred of evidence leading to his image or written reference. The second image that the Internet surrendered to my collection triggered a double-take. A scanned tintype photograph of Private Andrew Boger provoked me to laugh out loud. Here was a young Union soldier, listed in Henry's very unit. Sporting the stylish goatee, and long brown hair, posing proudly with a stern glare, in full-dress uniform, minus his hat. He was frozen in an odd, yet deliberate position. He intentionally rested both of his

hands on his chest, articulating them both into the tightly cropped
frame of the waist-up photograph, as if to show that he had managed to
escape the war with all appendages intact. I found Private Boger listed
in Fleharty's book as being discharged in early 1862 somewhere near
Louisville, Kentucky, hands and all. No reason for his discharge was
given, but I did find record of his plea for Civil War pension on a
public family genealogy page at ancestry.com. Boger's brief appeal
paints a dour picture of the period's infant mortality rate, which had
been reported to average nearly 35%, nationwide.

> *"Civil War Pension Affidavits of Andrew Boger, Pension No.
> 1048368, Co. E, 102 Ill. Vol. Infantry. "Mr. Andrew Boger
> Crainville, Republic Co, Kansas. I am married Abigail Boger
> maiden Abigail Brown. Married April 8, 1860 at Cameron,
> Warren Co, Illinois by Maximalin Haley. Certificate of marriage
> and recorded in Monmouth, Illinois. Were you previously
> married? No. Have you any children living? I have four Franklin
> P. Boger Birth August 29, 1864; Edward Boger Birth October 5,
> 1866; Wyatt Boger Birth Febuary 23, 1872; James E. Boger
> Birth Febuay 15, 1874; Date of Reply, November 22, 1897.
> [Signed] Andrew Boger."*

> *Another affidavit in his pension file, "born: 1836 November 26
> Penn near Warriors Mark; post office at enlistment: Lucy, IL
> [not currently on map]; wife: Abigail Brown; marriage: April 8,
> 1860 at Coldbrook, Warren County Illinois by Maximalin Haley;
> any official or church record of marriage: no; Were you
> previously married: I never had but one woman; present wife
> married before: my wife was never married before; has there
> been a separation; no sepration; all children living or dead: Ella
> Boger Feb 23 1861 dead, Henry Boger Nov 10, 1862 dead;
> Frank Boger August 29, 1864, Edward Boger October 5, 1866
> dead, Wyatt Boger Feb 23, 1872, James Boger Feb 15, 1874.
> March 24, 1915 signed Andrew Boger."*

As I navigated from one link to another, I had to stop myself,
and reestablish my primary objective. The Internet has a curious way of
enticing navigators down unknown corridors, with succulent
breadcrumbs, and if you lose track of your intended research target, all
you ultimately consume is valuable time. I decided that if I was to get a
proper introduction to my ancestor, it was necessary to start at the very
beginning. That beginning —according to sources previously

discovered— would commence somewhere in Putnam County, New York, on February 17th, 1838. Henry's birthday.

Since the first appropriation of public money for weather services was not granted to The Franklin Institute of Philadelphia until the same year of Henry's birth, one could only speculate what the weather was like on that Saturday in February. Based on present weather trends in the general vicinity, I presumed that Henry's first breaths were taken in a frigid, wintery wonderland. To tag Henry's first day with more relevance, I cross-referenced The History Channel's listing of events, which also occurred in 1838:

08JAN1838: The first telegraph message is sent using Samuel Morse's code of dots and dashes.

26JAN1838: Tennessee becomes the first state to prohibit alcohol

16FEB1838: Kentucky passes a law allowing women to attend school, under "certain conditions."

18FEB1838: British Physicist, Ernst Mach is born, after whom "mach speed" measurements are named.

21APR1838: American naturalist, John Muir is born.

27APR1838: A fire destroys nearly half of Charleston, NC.

28JUN1838: Queen Victoria is crowned in Westminster Abbey.

According to my cousin's book, "Roots that Bind," Uncle Henry and his siblings came from a Quaker family. Being raised in a rather strict religious home myself, I wondered what Henry's experience was like as a sheltered teenager, particularly with the exciting city and world capitol of Manhattan only 70 miles away. It was a difficult picture for me to conjure, so I accessed my dictionary to get a simple definition:

**Quaker** |kwākər|
**noun** *a member of the Religious Society of Friends, a Christian movement founded by George Fox c. 1650 and devoted to peaceful principles. Central to the Quakers' belief is the*

*doctrine of the "Inner Light," or sense of Christ's direct
working in the soul. This has led them to reject both formal
ministry and all set forms of worship.*

I once studied many of the different religious persuasions of the
world in high school, and until then, when Quakers came to mind I
couldn't get that image of the guy on the oatmeal box out of my head.
Quakers are most often thought of as uber-conservative, separatist,
holier-than-thou types, much like the Mennonites or Amish. Their very
name however, is widely rumored to reference a curious custom that
they share with many charismatic churches of today. My dictionary
offered the following description:

> **ORIGIN** from **quake** + er, *perhaps alluding to George Fox's
> direction to his followers to "tremble at the name of the Lord,"
> or from fits supposedly experienced by worshipers when moved
> by the Spirit.*

Once I had moved out of my parents' house at 17, I was living
in a basement apartment with three other members of a fledgling heavy
metal band, whose minions were ultimately diverted to follow the
grungy stylings of Nirvana, Pearl Jam and Alice In Chains. It was
during this period that I "strayed from the flock" of our family church;
a Conservative Baptist congregation where my mother had been a
permanent fixture at the organ bench since I was in preschool. I took up
with a couple of other local church youth groups, just to test the waters,
and (let's be honest here) to meet girls. This was my initial exposure to
"charismatic" worship, and the common practice of the raising, and
"laying on" of hands, spoken prophecy urged from the pulpit, and
speaking in tongues, which never did sit very well with *my* spirit. But,
the music was cool with guitars and drums and no organ, directed by
worship leaders with long hair like mine. I always left with a thought-
provoking message to take with me every week, which kept me
grounded, and helped me keep my head screwed on straight, for the
time being. I had never attended a Quaker church, however, and
probably wouldn't, even if it was conveniently next door.

My cousin Pat's book briefly mentioned that Henry's mother,
Cynthia Irish-Banks had been a minister, and at the time of her
research, Pat mentioned that a distant cousin still had Cynthia's pulpit
in her home. From what I have read in historic documents, the idea of a
woman leading a congregation was quite radical in the 19th century. I

have come to understand that since the institution of the early church, the ordination of women was traditionally frowned upon, undoubtedly contributed to the Apostle Paul's opinion, as it is poignantly expressed in his letter to Timothy in the New Testament: *"But I suffer not a woman to teach, nor to usurp authority over the man, but to be in silence."* To the best of my knowledge, Paul remained a single man through his adult life until his death at the hands of the Romans in the first century, and I will leave it at that.

Examining my expanding quiver of research documents, the town of Patterson, and Putnam County, New York were mentioned in recurrent reference to Henry's place of origin. Accessing Google Earth, I climbed aboard my digital hot air balloon once again, and drifted from Texas into a region of deep green topography, just shy of the Connecticut border. The area undulated with rolling hills, and thick wooded forests, flanked by numerous ponds and silver creeks, which seemed to unravel in all directions. Property boundaries seemed uniquely expansive, with farms and large estates spread out from one another at a substantial distance. I conducted a quick word search on Google, and typed the following phrase: *"Patterson New York History."* The link that I selected first, was a page at rootsweb.com that offered a profile of Putnam County, which was published in 1841 by John Barber, author of the Connecticut and Massachusetts Historical Collections. It read:

> *Putnam county was taken from Dutchess (County) in 1812; greatest length 21, greatest breadth 12 miles. The Highlands extend across the western part. The highest point is about 1,580 feet above the Hudson. The remainder of the county, though generally uneven, has some handsome plains, with a soil various, and some of it fertile. The mountains abound with iron ore of good quality. Butter, beef, wool, calves, lambs, sheep, fowls, and the many other species of "marketing" are produced here in great quantities for the New York market, and their returns are rapidly enriching the producer. The evidences of prosperity are everywhere visible. Within a few years the lands have doubled in value and price. The county is watered easterly and centrally by the main branches of the Croton. It is divided into six towns. Pop. 12,825.*

Another search led me to the Town of Patterson's Historic website at historicpatterson.org. I perused the smartly-organized and maintained site, and boned up on the region's historic roots, and some of the families who settled in the area. I was immediately drawn to the top of their homepage, crowned by a neatly organized row of thumbnail photos, which featured historic homes. I felt my body temperature rise a few degrees, when the notion hit me that I could possibly be looking at a photo of the Banks family home. I shook off the ridiculous idea, and embraced the reality that in a region whose population boasted over 12,000 souls in 1841, the likelihood of finding, and even identifying such a photo was extremely remote.

Still, I was hopeful to find something of interest that would give me an improved impression of how the Banks family thrived in early 19th century New York. Fortunately, Patterson's historic website had a direct contact email for general information, so I fired off a quick inquiry asking for assistance.

On the following cool winter evening, I took a seat at my iMac after a long, hard workout at our neighborhood health club, with the intention of spending about an hour or so researching Henry's history before a much-needed shower. I checked my email, and was excited to find a response to the email I had sent on the previous evening:

*"Steve, your email to the Town of Patterson was passed on to me as president of the Historical Society. On March 15, 1830 Nathan O. Banks purchased a farm which is at the east end of Haviland Hollow Rd and appears on the 1854 map of Putnam County as belonging to S.[tephan] Whitehead (recorded in Liber G, page 217). The Patterson portion of that map can be viewed on our website at www.pattersonhistoricalsociety.org or for the whole county at www.HRVH.org --search 1854 map. Haviland Hollow Road is about the center of the map, running west to east to the Connecticut border. The house on the property still stands, but whether it dates from the 1830's is not known at this time. Depending on when the family moved in and when the census was conducted that year they may appear in the 1830 Census, and certainly should be in the 1840 Census. -- That assumes that the property purchased in 1830 was where the family lived.*

*—Ron Taylor"*

*Before: The former Nathan O. Banks family home in Putnam County, New York, in the 1880's
(Photographer unknown; from the collections of the Patterson NY Historical Society,
image copyright by them)*

*After: The former Banks family home in Haviland Hollow, as it appears today.
(Photographer Ron Taylor; from the collections of the Patterson NY Historical Society,
image copyright by them)*

Naturally, I was thrilled to find a helpful source that was obviously well-equipped to assist me with my search for Henry's birthplace. I logged onto Yahoo, and entered the link to the Hudson River Valley Heritage website that Mr. Taylor had furnished. Keying in my query for the 1854 map, I conjured up the image of an antiquated document, printed in great detail, yet fading in color. The web designer had the forethought to program a comprehensive zoom feature, which allowed the end user to zoom into concentrated areas. I targeted the Connecticut border at midpage, as Mr. Taylor had instructed, and in doing so, I located Haviland Hollow. It appeared as a vast valley flanked by highlands, which were divided by a meandering stream called "Quaker Brook."

A road ran alongside the water, and was dotted with marks that represented structures, barns and homes -most of which were identified with corresponding names. I traced the map East toward the Connecticut border, and found a property belonging to S. Whitehead, which was the last farm in the hollow, before crossing the state line. As Ron had mentioned in his email, this was supposedly the home where Henry was raised. I needed to be certain, so just out of curiosity, I jumped onto Ancestry.com, to inspect the census from 1850, which was just 4 years prior to the year of the Putnam County map's print date. I searched for Nathan O. Banks in New York. My search came up empty, however, I did get a "hit" when I entered Henry's mother's name, which ushered me to the 1850 Census. I located a list of the entire family at dwelling number 213 on page 39, written on the 22$^{nd}$ of August, 1850. Cynthia and Henry —then just 15 years old— and all nine of his living siblings were present, but his father, Nathan was not mentioned. I made note of the names of neighbors, who were recorded as living in adjacent properties to the Banks family residence. Orange B. Thomas and wife occupied dwelling number 212, and 214 belonged to John Bouton and family. When I clicked over to the 1854 map, once again, my presumption was confirmed that the Whitehead family property was indeed flanked by the O. B. Thomas, and J. Bouton residences, and therefore, had to be the Banks family farm.

I leaned back in my chair, and stretched my arms to the ceiling, in celebration, and as they remained suspended, I was suddenly, although subtly reminded that I hadn't yet showered as I had intended. It had taken approximately three hours of research, but I was quite certain that I had located the spot where Henry was born and raised. I rose to step away from my iMac, but quickly slumped into my office chair again, as I heard my email chime. Apparently, I wasn't the only one burning the midnight oil, hopelessly stationed at my terminal that evening. Ron Taylor had sent a follow-up to his original email, which came with two jpegs attached. He wrote:

> *"I have attached the two abstracts, the full deeds might have more information as would any will on file, but that would take going to the County Records Office which would have to be a paid research trip. If you note, the debt sale is short 32 acres of the original purchase, so some more deed searching is needed to get the whole story of the land."*

I inspected the attachments, and found neatly typed transcriptions from the original deeds for both the initial purchase of the Banks farm, and the sale of the same. The land was deeded to Nathan O. Banks by Nicholas Wanzer dated March 13th, 1830 for the substantial sale price of $1790.00. I was intrigued by the description of the property, presented through an antiquated method of measurement that was customary for that early period:

> *"Beginning at a River or brook adjoining the land of David Haviland late of Patterson deceased; thence running North eleven deg. West five chains; thence North two deg. West one chain and ninety links; thence North one deg. West two chains and seventy links; thence North thirteen deg. West four chains and twenty-five links; thence North fifty deg. West four chains and twenty-five links; thence North fifty deg. etc. etc.*
> *Containing one hundred thirty two acres of land more or less."*

According to the 1910 *Manual of the Principal Instruments used in American Engineering and Surveying*, the garden variety Surveyor's chain was described as follows:

> *"The ordinary Gunter's or surveyor's chain is sixty-six feet or four poles long, and is composed of one hundred links, connected each to each by two rings, and furnished with a tally mark at the end of every ten links. A link in measurement includes a ring at each end, and is seven and ninety two one hundredths inches long. In all the chains which we make the rings are oval and are sawed and well closed, the ends of the wore forming the hook being also filed and bent close to the link, to avoid kinking. The oval rings are about one third*

*stronger than round ones."*

Mr. Taylor closed his letter with the following statement:

*"…most of the information we have is because of the efforts of
Minnie Barnum Durga who was born in that house in 1861 and
who later in life documented the Hollow and surrounding area
with more than 600 photos, collections of reminiscences, and
some genealogical research; all of which we are preparing for
publication."*

For some reason, Minnie Barnum Durga's name sounded
familiar to me, and I recalled the Barnum name associated with one of
the images of those old historic homes that I had seen on the Patterson
historic website. I accessed my bookmarks within my Safari browser,
and scrolled through the content on a page dedicated to Haviland
Hollow, *"one of the oldest areas in the town of Patterson."* Exploring
among the thumbnail photos taken by Mrs. Barnum Durga about 1913
of historic homes of the Hollow, my attention was diverted to one two-
story home in particular which was posted with this description:

*"The George Barnum home, located on Haviland Hollow Road.
The house still stands. George and Susan Barnum moved here in
1856 and lived here until they died. George died in 1882, Susan
in 1917."*

The description of the Barnum home's location coincided with
that of the residence purchased by Stephen Whitehead from Nathan O.
Banks. A quick glance at the 1860 census showed George and Susan
Barnum, with daughter, Minnie, and her siblings. Shifting to the 1850
census, I found the Banks family in Patterson, New York on page 39,
living between the Orange B. Thomas family, and that of John Bouton.
It was irrefutable. I was looking at a photo of the home where Henry
was born and raised. Fortunately, there were two clear grayscale photos
that I was able to download from the thumbnail's link. I printed half a
dozen copies, and trimmed them out to share with family, or anyone
who would express interest in our genealogy.

It was only through the unsolicited assistance of a like-minded
historian, and some simple deductive reasoning that I was able to
identify the Banks home. I enjoyed the entire process, and the
satisfaction of the final payoff. The pursuit of it all struck a familiar

chord within. It reminded me of my brief tenure as a skip-tracer for the Credit Card department at Seattle First National Bank. I developed some creative detective skills during that time while in my early twenties, just prior to my relocation to San Diego to attend college. Once transplanted, I was dependent on those skills for survival during the first few months I spent living in a new city with no money, few friends, and bills piling up for tuition and books. At an early age, I had been trained by some prolific loss-prevention specialists, and fraud investigators, and somehow I had managed to retain some of those instincts, which were once again coming in quite handy twenty-some years later.

While I had previously explored some of the Census reports, I made note that Henry's father, Nathan O. Banks was absent from the 1850 records. His eldest son, Willis, then 21, was listed as head of the household. It was a grim reminder that the family had suffered a great loss, due to Nathan O. Banks' drowning in Albany, New York in 1849. The official report was described in a brief article, which appeared in *The Albany Argus*, dated 10 October, 1849:

> *"Melancholy Occurrence.—Last evening a most melancholy accident occurred at the steam-boat landing. MR. NATHAN O. BANKS, Jr. of Patterson, Putnam County, who arrived in the train from the west and while attempting to pass on board the Isaac Newton, with his wife, owing to the darkness of night, walked off the dock, his wife being on the plank, and before assistance could be rendered was drowned. His body was recovered at about 10 last night, an inquest held Coroner OSBORNE, and a verdict returned of accidental drowning. Mr Banks was a respectable member of the Society of Friends, 53 years of age."*

The Hudson River Maritime Museum website described The Isaac Newton in a passage written by Fred Erving Dayton as follows:

> *"William Brown built Isaac Newton in 1846, larger than any previous river steamer, 1,332 tons, 338 feet length, 40 feet beam, 10.6 feet depth of hold and about 5 feet draught, with engine by the Allaire Works having cylinder 81½ inches diameter by 12 feet stroke. Steam was generated in two iron boilers, 38 feet length, 12.6 feet wide and 10.6 feet high with 4,540 square feet of heating surface and 161 square feet of*

*grate. Isaac Newton consumed four tons of anthracite coal per hour, then considered a prodigal amount. The wheels were 39 feet diameter with double buckets."*

By the 1860 census, Cynthia, now widowed was no longer living in Patterson, New York, but in the West Mercer Township of the state of Illinois. She settled there along with her youngest sons, Henry (22), Egbert (20), William (19), George (17), and John James (13). Two years later, Henry would enlist with the Illinois Volunteers. I would have liked to have been a fly on the wall in their home when the discussions occurred concerning Henry's enlistment.

A kind volunteer at a local museum had helped shed some light on this period for me, with a fortuitous find.

*"Hello Steve,*

*We were lucky, we had the land record book we needed at the museum.*

*On Sept. 28, 1859, Cynthia Banks bought the East 1/2 of the NW Qtr of Section 28 in Suez township from B. Harrington and sold the same parcel on Mar. 1, 1865 to John Lafferty.*

*That parcel lies a little north and east of the town of Norwood. If you have a plat book of Mercer County you should be able to find it very easily. I hope this is what you needed for your history."*

Though my eyes were becoming heavy, I located a map of the Suez Township on the Internet that was rendered in 1874, nearly 15 years after Cynthia had sold her parcel to Mr. Lafferty. I found it curious that the transaction had occurred only a few weeks before Henry was mustered out at Washington. The top half of the 640 acre Section #28 was presently owned by John Lafferty, except for the 80-acre parcel in the Northeastern corner, which belonged to Thomas Likely. This landowner had been Henry's Captain during the first few months of the 102nd Illinois' operations. A posting on rootsweb.com mentioned the Lafferty home as a rendezvous point for the annual reunion and basket dinner of Company C, 102nd Regiment which was held each July.

This brief exercise in surveying illustrated for me, how common it was for many of those who fought in the Civil War to find themselves marching along side of their neighbors from home. It was now approaching 1:00 am, and I had a busy Monday to prepare for at my new job, so I shut down my iMac, and reluctantly slinked away to take my shower, and retire for the night.

*The Isaac Newton Steamship, upon which Nathan O. Banks Jr. was boarding when he drowned in the Hudson River. He left behind 10 children and a widow. (Illustrated by Nathaniel Currier, 1885)*

*A portrait of Cynthia Irish-Banks rendered most likely in the 1840's. (From the collection of Marie Prestmo)*

# A Welcome Diversion

After braving a record summer in Austin, with the temperatures blazing into the triple-digits for more than forty consecutive days, it hardly seemed likely that snow would fall one afternoon in the following month of February. Yet, as I moused away at packaging die lines, and web pages at my employer's North Austin headquarters, through a West-facing window I noticed flakes falling. After living for nearly a decade in Denver, Andi and I had had our share of the white stuff. Still, I followed my astonished native Texan co-workers out into the parking lot to enjoy the attraction. The flurries only lasted about twenty minutes, but I enjoyed standing back and observing, as some of my associates momentarily transformed into giggling adolescents.

Andi and I had been living in Austin for about seven months, and we were both relieved to be gainfully employed in each of our chosen industries, but we were both primed and ready for our "Ocean Fix." For our 15th anniversary, I planned a surprise trip in March, though I didn't reveal our destination to my wife until we arrived at the gate at George Bush Intercontinental Airport in Houston. Our plane would land in Guanacaste, Costa Rica. In between rainforest hikes, jungle zipline adventures, monkey spotting, sailing and river-rafting, I capitalized on some leisure time by the pool and beach, to read through Fleharty's "Our Regiment" once again. My mindset, and approach this time was different, in that I was plotting a course to physically follow the regiment's route, with stops at key locations that were concurrent with their rebel encounters during their three years of service in the 1860's. I would have to be economical with the stops along the way, which would include mandatory visits to Gallatin, Resaca, Kennesaw Mountain, The New Hope Church site, Peachtree Creek, and Savannah. The South Carolina capitol of Columbia could not be missed. Finally, all would culminate in Washington D.C., where Henry's unit was mustered out 13 days after the Grand Review that paraded down Pennsylvania Avenue on May 23rd and 24th, 1865.

When we returned home to Austin, I began outlining my plans, and sharing my intentions with a few friends to gauge their impressions pertaining to my forthcoming pilgrimage. I received support from the entire panel, but one response resonated profoundly. "Sounds like a great trip, but what do you plan to do with what you learn, when it's all

behind you?" Jeff had agreed to ride along with me on a long drive to
Dallas, to inspect a sailboat I was interested in buying. I do remember
warning him that it was a long drive, and I had suggested that he bring
along a good book. "You *are* a good book", he said. It had been a long
time since I was so deeply affected by as fine a compliment as this.
After inspecting the boat (I decided to pass) I shared a pint or two with
Jeff on our way home to Austin. Once he had planted that question in
my head, it would not stop repeating in my thoughts. *"What do you
plan to do with it?"* I dropped Jeff off at his house, and before pulling
into my garage, I had the entire outline completed, at least in my head. I
couldn't wait to begin writing. If I'd known then what I was in for, I
may have scrapped the whole idea.

Once you make the decision to approach the process of seeking
out your heritage, it is advisable to be prepared for anything. On-ramps
to answers often masquerade as barricades and dead ends in disguise.
Persistence, and tenacity pay off in ways that will defy explanation, so
long as they are paired with patience...lots of patience. In the months
that followed my sudden decision to write my first manuscript, I
realized that there was a very important component missing from the
entire project. I had scoured through source after source ad nauseum,
even to the point of locating and contacting "Banks" and "Bowlus"
family members who were receptive to what I had since discovered, but
had little more to contribute. Historians and genealogists headquartered
in New York, Illinois, Kansas and Texas had all been very cordial,
cooperative, and eager to assist, but I had reached a point where I felt
as if I was chasing a ghost. Henry had been deceased since 1889 after
all, and I was resigned to the fact that without a face to match his name,
Henry was just that, and only that...a name. Acquiring a photo of
Uncle Henry was next to impossible. A drought of some kind had
swooped in without warning, and took the steam out of the momentum
that had driven me to complete my first few pages.

As a young Art Director in Denver, I spent many evening hours
under the gun, fighting impossible deadlines that demanded original
concepts, sometimes by the dozen. I was no stranger to writer's block.
As was often the case, I would routinely walk away from the project at
hand, to focus on a completely unrelated subject, or engage in an
irrelevant activity that would often generate fresh, original ideas. My
best concepts often came to me while behind the wheel in a bumper-to-
bumper commute. Why, I wondered, would that technique be
ineffective now, struggling with the first pages in my manuscript?

A distraction could be just the ticket.

Only a few days had passed before an opportunity presented itself. While conversing on the phone with my friend Ken, he offered up a challenge. I recall describing to him how my manuscript pages had been spilling out, one-by-one in rapid succession, and then, I had suddenly hit the wall. Without a beat he said, "I have a project for you, if you're interested."

As a boy, Ken had spent a few years living in Cocoa Beach, Florida, with his parents who managed a beachside motel in the early 1970's. Cocoa Beach was then a popular draw for surfers and snowbirds from all over, and the constant transient traffic passing through the property often contributed some odd leftovers that wound up in the lost-and-found box behind the front desk. Somehow, a class ring from Georgia Tech had unfortunately separated from its owner, and wound up in the possession of Ken's father. Despite his numerous efforts to engage the university to locate its rightful owner, all attempts failed, and the ring remained unclaimed. The ring had since survived a major relocation to Seattle, and many more moves from home-to-home, spending years in desk drawers, shoeboxes, and closets until Ken found it, and began to examine it closely. It showed signs of some wear, but despite its age, the ring was still in good condition.     Inside the ring, he discovered the faint initials "T. J. Irwin" which were etched in flourishy script. Embellished upon the gold ring were the tell-tale numerals, indicating that it had been awarded to a member of the graduating class of 1928. Ken emailed some macro-set photos along with a link that he had discovered online at the Georgia Tech archives. I wasn't surprised that he had located a photo of "Thomas Jared Irwin" listed alphabetically in the Engineering section of "BLUEPRINT", Georgia Tech's yearbook, printed in 1928. "You've done most of the work already" I said, "but I'll be glad to take over, from here." Ken obliged, and sent the ring on its way to me via FedEx.

In the following weeks, I set aside my manuscript, and began to work on the Irwin case. First, as Ken's father had done nearly forty years before, I contacted the Alumni Association at Georgia Tech by phone. Their records revealed only what I already knew: Thomas Jared Irwin earned a degree in General Engineering in 1928. I learned through researching the current online Alumni newsletter that the President and CEO of Georgia Tech's Alumni Association had held his present post since 1999. His last name was Irwin. The irony.

I called the main number at the Alumni office for the second time, and asked to be connected to Mr. Irwin directly. I left a voicemail message at his extension, explaining the reason for my attempt to contact him. Mr. Irwin promptly returned my call, and we conversed for a few moments about the discovery of the class ring, and my intention to locate any of Thomas J. Irwin's direct descendants. "You wouldn't happen to be related, would you?" I asked. Mr. Irwin laughed, and said "no." "I figured that it couldn't be that easy," I said, "but it never hurts to ask." Mr. Irwin wished me luck, and asked me to keep him posted with my progress.

Once again, I was taking full advantage of my monthly membership dues to Ancestry.com, and tapped into their treasure trove of resources, beginning with the U.S. Census records. I found a T. Jared Irwin, age: 27, living with wife, Mildred, and daughter, Anne in the 1930 Federal Census. The corresponding address listed was in Fulton, Georgia, just a few miles from Georgia Tech. With no son listed, I knew that establishing a link with Mr. Irwin through his daughter would be time-consuming, so on a hunch, I accessed the online White Pages, and in so doing, I found a Thomas J. Irwin Jr. living in Jasper, Georgia. Excited, I picked up my Blackberry, and dialed directory assistance. The operator announced that the corresponding phone number was unlisted. Hastily, I typed and printed a quick letter, and dropped it in a mailbox along the route to my office the following morning. It simply said:

> I am attempting to locate Thomas Jared Irwin Jr. of Georgia. I have recently found a personal item that I believe belonged to Thomas Irwin Sr. who was a graduate of the Georgia Tech's class of 1927. Please respond, if I have the correct party.
>
> Sincerely,
>
> Steve Enyeart

I was careful not to give away any details about he ring, since I wasn't certain if the resident I was reaching out to was indeed related, due to the common nature of the Irwin name.

In a roundabout way, I received a response a few days later, on my Facebook page! It abruptly said: "My father was Thomas Jared Irwin Sr. What do you want?"

Apparently, my postings and photographs that littered my social network site were being carefully scanned and scrutinized by Mr. Irwin, but proved satisfactory enough to spur a succinct response. I presumed that I had made the correct connection, and under the circumstances, didn't blame him for being wary of my intentions. Still, I had to be 100% certain of his identity, so I put together a montage of portraits clipped from the 1927 yearbook, which included a likeness of Thomas Jared Irwin Sr. Since my previous inquiry —neatly typed and professionally formatted— had raised some suspicion, I enclosed a hand-written letter this time, requesting a positive identification.

The holidays were quickly approaching, and the ensuing chaos that predictably accompanies the season was in full tilt, as I scrambled daily, racing the clock to meet deadlines, and to attack my endless to-do list. Checking the mail one day, a letter surfaced which I immediately recognized as the self-addressed, stamped envelope that I had included with the portrait lineup that I had sent to Mr. Irwin in Georgia. I swiftly tore open the letter, and was pleased to find the correct image of T.J. Irwin circled in ballpoint pen. Scrawled next to the circled photograph was a cryptic message: *"By the way, he graduated in 1928."* "Well," I thought, "then you're in for a pair of surprises." I found it difficult to sleep that evening, and postponed my sporadic morning sessions with the elliptical machine the following morning. I couldn't wait to pull into the driveway at my office. Before our daily morning meeting, I mounted the class ring in a framed shadowbox, with the help of my coworker, Raul. I enlarged the portrait of T.J. Irwin, and matted it within the frame next to the ring. I wrapped it up, and brought it to the post office during my lunch hour, and enclosed the following letter:

*Dear Mr. Irwin,*

*I am happy to present you with what I have come to know as your father's class ring, from Georgia Institute of Technology. It has indeed been on a long journey, and I am honored to have played a part in its full circle back to its proper place.*

*This is how I understand the ring's history:*

*My friend's parents used to manage a motel in Cocoa Beach, Florida in the 1960's and 1970's. From time-to-time, they would find personal items left behind in the motel rooms, on the property, or even in the sand at the beach nearby. According to my friend's father, Mr. Irwin's ring wound up in the lost and found at The Silver Sands Motel in Cocoa Beach, Florida back in 1972, or thereabouts. He remembers attempts to locate the owner by name, but had no luck. He took additional steps, and contacted officials at Georgia Tech, who were not able to assist him with his search for the rightful owner. Finally, the ring disappeared, and moved from box-to-drawer-to-box again, through the family's relocation from Florida to Washington State, then to various locations within the Seattle area.*

*Only within the last year, did the ring resurface again, and as my friend took note of my growing interest in tracing my own genealogy, he offered me the challenge of locating the ring's owner's family. It only took a glance at some Census records, the yearbook pages from the Georgia Tech's archives, and the local White Pages to finally locate your address, and complete the process. My friend and his father will be elated when they learn that the ring has finally been returned after all these years. I hope that you will forgive the intrusion on your privacy, though I'm certain that now you will understand the reason for my persistence.*

*I would only ask for one favor from you. I realize that it has been nearly 40 years since the ring was found in Cocoa Beach, but if there are any details you can share with me, pertaining to how and when the ring was lost, I would be very grateful.*

*This has been a fun and fulfilling experience for me, and it is my sincere hope that the ring remains in your family for many generations to come.*

*Happy Holidays!*

The Irwin case was indeed a challenge, but Ken had already done a good amount of the fieldwork necessary to locate the ring's owner. Together, we attained closure, and returned the ring to T.J. Irwin's family. It was a brief, but satisfying distraction, providing the motivational ramp-up that I needed to pick up where I left off in my adventures with Uncle Henry. As I filed the Irwin case away, and shifted my focus once again to my own family mysteries, I was clueless to the significance of the ring's return, and the weight of the irony that it brought with it upon its arrival at the Irwin family's doorstep.

I was browsing through the local bookstore during my lunch hour, engrossed in my Civil War research as my BlackBerry chimed. The email response I received from Mr. Irwin caused me to locate the closest chair I could find. I was floored.

> *"My Father and Mom did spend time at The Silver Sands Motel. I think most of the dates were in the late 60's and early 70's. I was serving in the U S Army much of that time but do remember at least one trip there with them. Seems to me the Motel was on the beach. In the late 60's, early 70's they moved from Atlanta to Woodstock, Ga. to a home he had built on Lake Allatoona, sold the house in Atlanta. Your friends moving the Ring around probably made it harder to locate him and Tech was not user friendly at that time. When I was first contacted by you I thought that this was some sort of scam so I was not very cooperative and I was not aware that the ring had been lost. I was never told about it. My Dad had a Tech ring and only yesterday did I find out that it was given to him by a classmate named Herb Reed, they were best friends, Dad helped Herb build his house on the lake. I guess Herb gave it to him in appreciation. So I always saw him with a ring. Only one of my three sisters knew about all of this and I found out about it last night. My father died in 1987 and was buried with Herb's replacement ring, how odd to now have the original ring that was lost.*
>
> *Thank you for your work tracing this mystery.*
> *Best Regards,*
>
> *Thomas Jared Irwin, Jr."*

I couldn't help but wonder if there were spiritual influences at work behind this entire episode, from the very get-go. While others might be quick to write off the experience as mere coincidence, I classified it as a serendipitous joint venture between two pairs of lifelong friends, which culminated into the presentation of an unexpected gift (message?) to a family from their departed father. Was it just coincidence? Did that class ring surface at just the right time, and fall into the possession of just the right person, after being hidden from view for decades? I knew the ring would be an important find to the Irwin family, but I was not aware of the powerful bond that it represented. One question remained unanswered, however. Did Thomas Jared Irwin, Sr., deceased, have a hand in completing this "coincidental" connection?

Given my history with the unexplained, it was a fair question.

Coincidentally, while hiking in the canyons near his home outside of Scottsdale, Arizona, Ken's German Shepherd sniffed out a beaded necklace buried in the earth. Upon closer inspection, Ken discovered yet another mysterious ring attached to the necklace. This time, it appeared to be a platinum wedding band with initials and a date inscribed inside. To date, the case is still unsolved, but we continue to investigate.

# Postcards from the Hereafter

Months before, I had embarked on a business trip to Pocahontas, Arkansas, of all places. It was a small dot on the map, not far from the city of Jonesboro, but an important hub for the manufacturing functions of my employer. Though many locals have their theory of how Pocahontas got its name, a friendly and knowledgeable employee at the local history museum satisfied my curiosity with a simple explanation. When Randolph County broke off from Lawrence County in 1835, someone thought it might be cute to name the new county seat after the famous daughter of Chief Powhatan, which was the name of Lawrence County's seat. Despite the many rumors, and an impressive statue that stands in the local city park, Pocahontas, herself never set foot in Arkansas, to my knowledge.

I was to fly from Austin on American Airlines to Little Rock, and drive the remaining 140 miles via rental car. I typically flew on United, Continental, or Alaska, when traveling on vacation, to the coast, or to Seattle, which was most often the case. This trip was an exception. My ticket had been purchased by the secretary who reported to my C.F.O. and C.E.O., both of whom would be traveling with me. Needless to say, I was on my best behavior. I had my laptop at the ready. I ordered a coffee instead of a cocktail, and was extremely polite to the flight attendant. Though it was completely out of character for me, I went as far as to follow along as she blathered on, over the intercom about the important steps in the "unlikely event of a water landing." As I flipped the laminated pages in the instruction pamphlet that I had pulled from the seat pocket in front of me, I suddenly froze. I looked closer to study a series of photographs that featured a group of passengers demonstrating the consecutive stages of evacuation. I felt a warm sensation rush through my body in a split second, and my palms began to sweat. There, in one of the photos, on the receiving end of the inflatable slide was my late father. His glasses and receding hairline, his backyard gardener tan, and signature rolled-up shirtsleeves of a career draftsman were unmistakable.

I must have studied that photograph for at least twenty minutes, talking myself in-and-out of the identity of the man in the photo. I quarreled within over the remoteness of my knee-jerk decision to opt for the emergency pamphlet in lieu of the in-flight magazine. I finally laughed out loud, and surrendered to the astonishment that had held my thoughts hostage as we taxied along the tarmac, lifted off, and finally leveled out at high altitude. I had over two hours, strapped in my chair between two snoring fifty-something business-types to think it through. Why did this photo wind up in a pamphlet that I was never inclined to read, on a flight that I would never reserve, on an airline that I rarely, if ever patronized? I would never know how my dad wound up posing in a photo shoot, presumably arranged at Boeing's plant number 3, where he worked as a draftsman while I was in high school. For all I knew, he may have come home from work one day in the 1980's, and told me all about it. As an extremely rebellious teen, I could have cared less. Now, as an empathetic adult, I would happily share in his enthusiasm. Kudos, Dad. Perhaps your indelible image will save a life or two one day. Maybe it already has.

Coincidence?

I would agree, were it not for a related experience that still defies explanation for me, to this day.

In 1999, my mother had passed away at 65, due to unfortunate complications from Melanoma. Thankfully, her suffering didn't last long beyond her initial diagnosis. However, the pain of her absence was felt by the entire family in a profound sense, since her bout with the disease was not prolonged. We weren't granted a satisfactory number of days to spend quality time with her, and to say our goodbyes. Then again, who is to say how much time is adequate in such a circumstance?

After Mom's funeral, Andi and I returned to our home, which was at the time, in the suburbs of Denver. We gradually phased back into the frenetic pace, and demanding schedules of our deadline-driven careers. At the advertising agency where I had been employed for five years, a project was assigned to me just days after I had returned from a few days of bereavement leave. The job seemed custom-tailored for me, since it involved drafting a conceptual print campaign for the local music scene in Seattle. The creative brief featured a directive to explore "Familiar Seattle Icons." I often welcomed jobs that were simple, and lacked challenge, especially after immersion in a high-stress, complicated assignment, or, as in the case of my recent loss, an emotionally taxing event. *"Give me a stack of layouts to trim for a presentation, or some whitepaper decks to collate and staple! Something brainless to work on for a while, and I'll be primed for when the next bomb drops!"* That was the general tone of my occasional rant.

I began my assignment as always, making a list of terms for a wordplay exercise. Combining terms would sometimes relegate the amount of labor needed to arrive at that perfect headline, visual, or a combination of both. The most effective ads, in my opinion were those that didn't require much time and effort on the reader's part to perceive. As far as I was concerned, the "seven-second rule" of outdoor advertising applied to magazine and newspaper page-flippers as much as it did to commuting motorists. So, often to my copywriter partners' chagrin, I always strove to present ads that featured simple, but hard-working visuals, that needed only to be paired with a simple headline of one or two words, or no headline at all. Naturally, as I approached the regional focus of this assignment, I began listing terms that were unmistakably relative to Seattle's culture and geography. I began with the obvious:

*Birthplace of Grunge. The Space Needle. Puget Sound.*
*Elliott Bay. Pioneer Square. Pike Place Market. Microsoft.*
*The Olympic Mountain Range. Mount Rainier. Ferries.*

If there was one thing I knew about the younger urban demographic of the Seattle area, it was their cynical disdain for preachy advertising at a local level from a non-local influence. *"Don't tell me what to do." "Don't tell me what I already know." "Don't EVEN THINK of pretending you know more than I do about my own turf."*

A more effective strategy was needed. I began exploring some of the more obscure, and ambiguous icons that only a Seattle native would be familiar with.

The first visual that came to mind was the streamlined passenger ferry, the "Kalakala." Resembling a hybrid of an airstream trailer and an electric razor, it ruled the waters of Puget Sound in silvery glory from 1935 to 1967, and in its heyday, was the 2$^{nd}$ most-photographed man-made structure in the world, next to the Eiffel Tower. It had since been mothballed, and relocated to Alaska where it sat for years, with an uncertain fate. The Kalakala had earned a resurgence of attention in the local headlines at the time, and a public outcry to resurrect the old rusty hulk to its original shining art deco condition, which is why it became a subject of my interest, worthy of exploration.

Reaching way back to early weekday mornings as a preschooler, I wondered if Seattle icon, and campy local celebrity, J.P. Patches (aka: Chris Wedes) would still resonate, somehow with our target consumer. Since the 1950's, the eccentric "Mayor of the City Dump" entertained children, and their supervising parents with a mix of improvisational comedy, cartoons and slapstick during his morning program. In that era, it seemed that every major market, for the most part had their local clown, hobo, train engineer, zookeeper, or drag-queen, as morning television host. My roll model came to life on the small screen in clown-white makeup, a red rubber nose, and a quilted ragged jacket, festooned with about a thousand colorful metal buttons. He talked to a rubber chicken and a stuffed dog, and shared his unrehearsed adventures with an eclectic swarm of twisted sidekicks, all portrayed by his brilliant co-star, Bob Newman. Occasionally, when I was just a toddler, my mother would covertly contact the television station early in the morning, and I would wake to a personal "Happy Birthday to Stephen" from J.P., himself through his magical "I.C.U.2." TV set. I have always attributed my sarcasm, moderately warped sense of humor, and my chosen profession in creative arts and broadcast to those early influences and boisterous shenanigans.

Just a few clicks into my online research for J.P. Patches imagery led me to a black and white candid photo taken in his studio sometime in the late 1950's. I would have moved on to another image quickly, but my attention was captured by a familiar detail in the background. I studied the photo for a few minutes, and rose from my desk, and stepped away from my office, cupping my open mouth with one hand. I walked between the buzzing cubicles, alive with activity as always, but all sound was somehow obscured as I wandered out into the long hallway of the second floor of our building. I strolled from one end to the other at a slower pace than normal. I took my time, trying to piece together the impossible happenstance that I had just experienced. It was only days after my family and I had buried my mother, yet, there in that random photo, she sat in a folding chair against the wall of a Seattle television studio, in her mid-twenties, looking toward me, smiling, with a birthday cake in her lap. As I made my way back to my desk, I vaguely recalled an incident that Mom had proudly shared with me, when I was a child, sitting on the floor while she adjusted the rabbit ears on our black and white Zenith television. As I studied the photo in detail, it all came back to me in a rush.

My youngest of two older sisters had been born on the same day that the J. P. Patches television show had premiered. On the Show's first anniversary, an invitation was broadcast statewide to all 1-year-olds, and their parents to appear on the show to join in the celebration. This explained the crowd of toddlers crawling around on the floor, surrounding the grinning clown in the foreground of the photo, and the dozen or so women, seated in the background, who flanked my mother. She seemed to be the only woman —front-and-center— who was aware of the camera, which captured the moment. Typical Mom.

I stared at the photograph for a while, unable to persuade myself to write it off as a fluke. That evening, I called my father, and shared my remarkable discovery with him. He paused, uncharacteristically silent, and responded with a testimony of his own. As he slept, he had a dream a few nights before my call. He was returning home from a day at his office, and walked through the front door of our home. Seated at the table was my mother. She was in her twenties, and dressed up, similar to how she appeared in the photo I had just found. In his dream, my father asked her what heaven was like. She smiled, and said, "Wonderful." Brief, but enduring; that was the extent of his dream. Dad marveled at the similarities that his dream, and my photograph shared in common.

Months passed, and February brought an opportunity to travel to Seattle for a meeting at our regional office in the Northwest. I spent the evening with my father, and shared the photograph with him. I had since had the picture mounted, matted and framed. My sister joined us both for dinner that evening, and I handed her the wrapped photo as a birthday gift. As she unwrapped it, I didn't say a word. Instead, I studied her face as she examined the photo. When she made the connection at last, I knew I had made her day. She wept. My sister called me later that year, and reported that Mr. Wedes (J.P. Patches, himself) had dropped by the radio station where she worked, to conduct some business. She introduced herself, and invited him into her office where the photo hung on the wall. As Mr. Wedes examined the photograph, she told him the entire story. He was touched.

What were the chances that a photograph of this nature would unexpectedly present itself with such perfect timing? What were the odds of it happening twice? Both of my parents were very artistically expressive, talented and creative people, not to mention exceedingly spiritual. There couldn't be a more suitable method for them to express the notion that "all is well," than through a photograph.

Postcards from the afterlife? Maybe.

# *Reaching Out*

Refreshed, energized, and inspired, I continued the pursuit of my elusive ancestor, intently poring over page after page of documents that I had collected since the initial discovery of Henry's bible. However, my newfound resoluteness would only spark a fleeting flame. My file folder was bulging at the seams with notes, photocopies, scribblings, and photographs of places, and family members, fellow soldiers and acquaintances that Henry had most likely encountered during his short life. Still, I could not place a face with his name. The description in his ILLINOIS CIVIL WAR DETAIL REPORT: "Age: 24, Height: 5' 9", Eyes: Gray, Complexion: Light" was all I had to imagine, but it wasn't enough to justify my continuation. I would have happily settled for a group photo of the 102nd Illinois Volunteers, which I could study, with the satisfaction that his face was perhaps one of many, posing proudly in uniform alongside his comrades, but despite my many efforts to obtain it, I was denied that wish as well.

Weeks passed, and I had exhausted all obvious avenues of exploration, going as far as to correspond with some of my older relatives, and those who descended from Henry's second wife, Emma Bowlus through her subsequent marriage. At one time, I had people in four states, simultaneously sifting through dusty photo albums, old family letters, and shoeboxes full of nameless faces, hunting for Henry Banks, but despite their empathetic cooperation and shared excitement, all had come up empty. It was getting more difficult for me to continue my quest without a photograph, and my enthusiasm began to wane. I could conjure only a blurred image of Henry's face, based on the growing collection of photographs of his mother and siblings, which I had indirectly acquired. It was suddenly, and decidedly evident that the idea of tracing Henry's steps any further was seemingly imprudent. Though I purported to be an expert in the Banks family heritage at the very least, my venture to graduate to the rank of genealogist was now under great scrutiny by my worst critic. Myself.

One winter evening, I opened my laptop, and began looking through my expanding family tree on Ancestry.com. It was apparent that had it not been for the discovery of Henry's bible, I would not have found so many family connections that were now interwoven through branch after branch of the Banks family lineage. With a previous familiarity that was obscured by rumor and conjecture, the details were all falling into place, and I knew exactly how I fit into the big picture. With the help of Ancestry.com, and other sources, I had made direct ancestral connections with two colonial patriots who were documented as serving in the Revolutionary War, a Mayflower passenger, and a Mohawk princess. One of my most thought-provoking discoveries, however, was the evolution of the Banks surname over time. Though there were familial echoes of its English roots, and even a rumor of a connection to Sir Joseph Banks, who sailed the Pacific with the infamous Captain James Cook, I learned that the name originated in Germany, of all places. According to my cousin Ken's GEDCOM, a 4-year-old Palatine boy named Johan Jacob Heisterbach joined his parents as a passenger on a ship that sailed from London to New York in 1710.

The Clermont State Historic Site published a wonderful summary on their website which explained the German Palatine migration that occurred in the early 18th century.

> In 1709, a rumor began to spread through southwestern Germany, spread [sic] by a "golden book." Few people at the time could read, but many heard the promises that the book seemed to make. By the time that rumor had done its work, almost 15,000 people had left their homes to travel to a far off land.

> The "golden book" was titled (when translated) "A Complete and Detailed Report of the Renowned District of Carolina Located in English America" and was written by a German minister by the name of Joshua Kocherthal.

> Kocherthal's work was a promotional tract written to encourage immigration to Carolina. It was probably created by consulting a number of other promotional tracts, since Kocherthal had not visited Carolina by that point. It was short, straightforward and easy to read aloud to semi-literate audiences. Kocherthal praised Carolina for its fertile soil, its low taxes and its religious freedoms.

> All of this must have appealed to his audience in Germany, but the first edition printed in 1706 didn't immediately get people moving. But in 1708, Kocherthal

*managed to convince the British Crown to settle him and a group of forty colonists in Carolina by claiming to be refugees from French Catholic oppression. With this experience, Kocherthal was able to add an appendix to later editions of his book.*

*England's monarch, Queen Anne, had agreed to support Kocherthal's group, not only by funding their travels but also by supporting the colonists until they could get established. Kocherthal's report of this in the third and fourth editions of his book struck a chord with his audience: Queen Anne was colonizing Carolina and was willing to pay the way of refugees looking for a new start.*

*Perhaps Queen Anne might be willing to support another group from along the Rhine? While Kocherthal made no promises in his book, the possibility was there. In the alchemy of rumor, "possibly" became "definitely," and word began to spread of this new opportunity for all those willing to head to England.*

*This rumor found fertile ground in southwestern Germany. The region was as war-torn as any in history, having suffered through the Thirty Years War, the War of the Palatine Succession and the War of the Spanish Succession in the course of a single century. The Thirty Years War alone had cost the region more than 50% of its population. Plague and famine followed war, followed by another war, and so on.*

*The powers that be had dealt with the problem by settling immigrants from other regions into the battle scarred area. Southwestern Germany became a mix of ethnicities, religions and languages. They were settled on abandoned land and allowed some religious freedom in order that they might settle and start paying taxes.*

*When residents of the Rhine Valley began to appear in England looking for their free trip across the Atlantic, they were labeled "poor Palatine refugees." In order to understand what happened after that, it's important to see that this was inaccurate. They were not refugees, since they were not just running from but also running to: they were headed off to find*

*easy prosperity in Carolina. They were not – at least not all –*
*Palatines, since they came from all over southwestern*
*Germany, and may have been an entirely different nationality*
*just a generation before.*

*And if they were poor, they didn't necessarily start out*
*that way. Most sold what they couldn't carry in order to*
*finance their trip to England. There they would be taken care*
*of by Queen Anne, just as they were promised. Only, this was a*
*promise that England was not aware it had made.*

Wikipedia succinctly described the means in which the
Heisterbach family arrived in the new world.

*The Germans transported to New York in the summer*
*of 1710 totaled about 2800 people in ten ships, the largest*
*group of immigrants to enter the colony before the American*
*Revolution. Because of their refugee status and weakened*
*condition, as well as shipboard diseases, they had a high rate of*
*fatality.*

Despite the prevailing reports of attrition, Nichlaus (53),
Christina Catherine (10), and Jacob (4) Heisterbach were all included in
the list of Palatines remaining in New York, according to the Colonial
Census of 1710. Nichlaus' wife, Gertraudt apparently died in 1709,
perhaps during, or as a result of the long voyage aboard one of the
British ships, whose passenger lists reported their presence aboard. The
reports bear witness to the place where this particular group of
Palatines disembarked. Nutten Island, which is known today as
Governor's Island was designated as one of the Palatine emigrants'
new settlements, as proven by surviving documents from the Court of
Kensington. Apparently, this was a preplanned site of permanence for
the Palatines, since a clear and direct motion was passed by the court:
*"Huts are to be made for them."*

And thus began the illustrious American history of the Banks
family, formerly known as the O'Banks family, formerly known as the
Oysterbanks family, formerly known as the Heisterbachs, from
Bacharach, on the Rhine. It is clear that many Palatines were put to
work immediately, most likely making tar for the waterproofing of
British Navy ships, in order to repay their debt to the crown, in
exchange for their safe passage. Certain "Subsistence Lists" have

surfaced, listing a staggering number of Palatine adults, and their children and orphans who were, in many cases assigned to apprenticeships, as in Henry's great-grandfather, Jacob's case. Though I searched the sources at my immediate disposal, I had no luck locating a record of the Heisterbach family members on such a list. Yet, I assumed that they arrived in the new world as "denizens of the kingdom," indebted to her majesty, Queen Anne for a period of time. One thing is for certain, however. The Heisterbach family eventually settled in the colony of Connecticut, and thrived in the local Quaker farming community for three generations.

It was satisfying to have stitched together a somewhat complete fabric of my ancestors' history, which mapped all the way back to 16$^{th}$ century Germany. Incidentally, just a brief paddle up the Rhine, near Konigswinter, the discovery of an ancient structure called "Heisterbach Abbey" peaked my interest, but it would have to be bookmarked in GoogleEarth for future exploration, since it was late in the evening. I remember resigning to the conclusion that even if I had fallen short in my efforts to gather a full documentation of Henry's life, at least I had filled in some blanks regarding our family's legitimate heritage, and debunked some false conclusions in the process.

As I began shutting down my laptop, with the intention of setting my project aside —perhaps indefinitely— I responded to a fleeting idea that popped into my head with an impulsive action. Remembering that Henry's mother, Cynthia Banks had been a Quaker minister, I wondered if anything had been published about her online. I typed her name into my browser, just out of curiosity. In response to my query, a brief quotation from an obscure blog stood out from among the other listed results:

> "As I've researched my background, I've found fascinating people who lived quiet, yet courageous lives. My great, great grandmother Cynthia Irish Banks inspires me with her ability to keep going after her husband died, leaving her with 10 children, five of whom were dependent on her."
>
> —Posted by Mary Emma Allen at 9:35 AM

I quickly identified Mrs. Allen as a published author living in New Hampshire, who also happened to be my cousin by way of Henry's older brother, Willis. I explored her many blog entries posted online before I finally located her email address. It was attached to a posting of Mary's that dated back a few years, so it was doubtful that her email address was current. Mine had also changed innumerous times throughout our moves between different states. Just the same, I fired off an introduction to her, with hopeful anticipation, and staggered off to bed.

> *Hello Mary.*
>
> *Before I write too much, I wanted to see if this is still a good email for you. I found your email address in a very old post on the Internet.*
>
> *I too am a descendant of Cynthia Irish Banks, and am in the middle of writing my first book about one of her sons, Henry.*
>
> *Please contact me, and let me know if you are receiving email here.*
>
> *Thank you!*
>
> *Steve Enyeart*

I arrived home from work the following day at about 6pm, and raced to my iMac to check my email. I had been preoccupied at work throughout the day, thinking about the cryptic introduction I had sent to Mary Allen the night before. How fascinating it would be to make contact with another writer in the family, who not only had an obvious interest in her "Banks" roots, but attributed her tenacity to the widowed matriarch, her great-great grandmother, Cynthia.

As all other "coincidental connections," this attempt to reach out to yet another complete stranger was met with prompt and enthusiastic response. I had no idea at the time how valuable this contact would become, in piecing together the details of Henry's life, both during and after the Civil War.

> *"Hello Steve,*
>
> *Yes, this is still a good e-mail for me. I'm delighted to connect with another cousin descended from Cynthia. I didn't*

*realize Henry Ira Banks had any children. I'd only heard of the wife he was married to when he died. Recently, I found some more info about him and it appeared he had a first wife when he lived in Iowa.*

*What do you have of his early life, Cynthia's ancestry, and Henry Ira's Civil War service? I grew up in NYS, near where Cynthia was born and lived before she moved to Iowa, after her husband's death. She was an amazing woman, and I'm researching her with the idea of writing about her...at least for family background. Whenever I encounter difficulties, I think of Grandma Cynthia and how she kept going midst obstacles.*

*I've made contact with descendants of Henry's brothers William and Daniel. I'm descended from Willis who was my paternal grandmother's father. The information I have is that Henry Ira is buried in Baird.*

*Mary Emma"*

After reading Mary Emma's cordial response, I smiled, took a deep breath, and stretched out my arms, crossed my fingers, and cracked my knuckles, preparing to type my way into the beginning of a wonderful exchange with my distant cousin. Though I had to correct her misconception that I was Henry's direct descendant, all the other information contained in the body of her email was dead-on accurate.

*Mary Emma...*

*Thanks for getting back to me so soon.*

*First, I'm not a direct descendant of Henry's. His brother David Irish Banks was my grgr Grandfather. David's son, Willus was my gr Grandfather.*

*An item that Henry made while he was in the Civil War fell into my possession, and I could type up the whole story for you, but I would rather just attach a pdf that I prepared a while back when I began gathering facts. (file is attached, along with an excerpt from my first draft of a book I'm writing)*

*At the beckoning of friends and family members, I am writing a book about my search for answers about our heritage. This is my first attempt at writing, and it has really become incredible therapy for me. After looking at some of your work, I'm certain that you understand where I'm coming from.*

*During my research, I have found photos of Cynthia, a photo of a Sampler she stitched as a teenager, and a photo of the home that I believe was the Banks family residence in Putnam County. I will send these files to you if you wish.*

*I am VERY interested in the facts that you have regarding the Banks family history in New York, and their exploits as farmers in Kansas, where they settled in the 1870's.*

*I'm rambling.*

*Please see the pdf, and give it a read when you have a few minutes.*

*So nice to make your acquaintance!*

*Sincerely,*

*Steve Enyeart*

I exchanged a few more notes with Mary, and finally, we decided to speak on the phone. I called her at her home one evening, and we exchanged notes about our Banks family roots for approximately 30 minutes. I was bubbling over with information, and I was so excited to share it with someone who could relate to, and benefit from it, that I could scarcely get the words out of my mouth fast enough. As I attempted to articulate the numerous connections and discoveries that I had made since Henry's bible dropped into my life, I was unaware that as I rhapsodized, Mary had been thumbing through a photo album that had belonged to her grandmother. She politely interrupted me, and uttered a phrase that left me dumbstruck.

*"I'm looking at a photograph of Henry Ira Banks. It is signed by him, and is dated 1872."*

I went silent for a few seconds, overwhelmed by the impossible fortuity that once again seemed to grace this quixotic mission of mine.

*"And here is another,"* Mary pronounced, before I could conjugate a single word. *"He is younger in this photo, leaning against a tall table."*

Bonus! *"Mary,"* I said quietly, and stern, *"if I can get copies of those photos, you will be my new best friend."*

Mary laughed. I sensed a familiar tone in her laughter that I tried hard to dismiss, but I could not ignore the unmistakable lilt in her voice, which echoed with a calm and comforting temperament. I believe it was a reminiscent trace of my Grandmother, Mary Banks-Enyeart. We spoke for a few more minutes, promising to stay in touch.

During that same evening when I had considered resigning my position as Henry Banks' chronicler, I was given a marvelous gift, which was the final missing piece that would prompt me to continue. I didn't need a building to fall on me, or the sky to open up to a chorus of angels and harps. It was incontestable. I was encouraged to finish what I had started. To decide otherwise would be disobedient. I decided to follow through with the original objective of retracing Henry's path. My motivation wasn't entirely altruistic, for I hoped that I would somehow obtain some personal benefit from the experience, whether emotional or spiritual. I also thought of my many cousins and their children. Of course, my own nephews and niece also came to mind as I envisioned future generations who somewhere, sometime, might find this information helpful in their own search for answers. At the very least, I could provide some entertaining hijinks, fumbling with my obsolete 21st century technology.

# Face to Face
## with Uncle Henry

Checking the mail one afternoon, I found a manila envelope nesting the typical stack of bills, catalogs and direct mail ads. Despite the uncharacteristic 90° conditions of a January afternoon in central Texas, I tore open the envelope on the hood of my SUV, because the anticipation was just too much to bear. The envelope was from Mary Allen, and its contents included scanned copies of two vintage photographs featuring Henry Ira Banks. A broad smile spanned across my face, as I was finally introduced —face-to-face— to my great-great uncle Henry.

I studied the first photograph, which was a full-length likeness, featuring a lean, late-teen, or 20-something, fair-haired, well-dressed young man in a long coat, satiny vest complimented by a neatly-fastened bow tie. Wearing square-toed dark leather boots with a high sheen, both his expression and posture exuded a certain degree of pride, standing tall, resting his right hand on a small table, which was festooned with a garish brocade tablecloth. A simple wooden chair with a shiny varnish was placed halfway into the frame, I supposed this prop was included to achieve visual balance. It was difficult for me to discern whether the photo had been taken before, or after Henry's service in the Civil War. I later discovered that this photo had been mislabeled, and was actually a likeness of Henry's younger brother, Egbert. This taught me a valuable lesson, and I would be careful to substantiate all sources, if possible as my journey progressed.

The second photograph was a headshot, and offered more detail of Henry's features, the most prominent of which, were his steel gray eyes. He seemed noticeably tired in the photograph. His eyelids drooped slightly, and his gaze seemingly was fixed on a distant subject. He appeared in full, bushy beard, with dark hair. He was dressed in a suit and vest with a bowtie. Henry's signature was featured at the bottom of the card that the photo was affixed to, and he had dated the image in 1872, making him about 34 years old when the photograph had been taken. I applauded Henry for placing his signature on the picture, as well as the year. Otherwise, anyone who could qualify to identify his likeness would now be long-deceased. A good lesson: the forethought of a sharp and responsible ancestor.

I thought about some of the old photographs that I had previously acquired from my parents' photo albums after they had passed away. I recall one Saturday afternoon, spent in my garage in California, sifting through literally hundreds of their pictures, which were all very interesting, but had no value whatsoever, due to their lack of identification. I wondered if there were to be more lessons that my encounter with Henry would teach me.

I noticed that Mary's envelope had a certain heft that begged investigation. Upon inspection, I found a set of stapled pages, which featured neat, formatted text from an inkjet printer. I read the first paragraph, and before I knew it, the sun had set, and I had read all 12 pages in their entirety. It was a vast collection of correspondence between Henry, his mother Cynthia, and his brother Egbert. All letters were sent to or from various posts during Henry's years of service as a Union Infantry Volunteer. Unbelievable!

I placed the photographs of Henry back in the envelope, gathered the rest of the mail that I had strewn across the hood of my SUV, and aimed for home. I parked in the driveway, grabbed my belongings, and stepped up to the porch. I stopped in my tracks, and peeked around the corner to the dense forest of oaks and mesquite, which flanked the property behind our townhome. A bright red cardinal sat atop an exposed branch, calling out to his neighbors across the wooded ravine. His vibrant feathers were amplified by what I refer to as *"one of those crazy Texas skies"* that sends rosy sunbeams piercing through cotton clouds that roll across the hill country at sundown.

As a random response, I took a seat on the lawn, beholding the Technicolor scenery passing before my eyes. Just as I had stood at the end of Market Street in downtown Baird, Texas, imagining the same perspective that Henry would have, when he arrived in 1889, I wondered if a descendant of mine would ever sit in my current spot, and in the same manner, observe this panorama 120 years from now. I wondered if Uncle Henry —as he whittled away on his wooden bible in 1862— ever imagined how far his souvenir would travel, through both distance and time, or the impact it would have on a great-great-grand-nephew. Now that I had finally become somewhat formally introduced to the man, seen his face, identified his birthplace, and his final resting place, it was time to begin filling in some of the gaps. I was ecstatic to hold in my grasp, a fresh volume of information ready to be examined. As I ascended the stairs to the second story of our townhome, I moved slowly as I read one of the letters aloud, savoring every word, like a fine cigar.

The Xerox copies of the 5" x 8" pages were splashed with faint, delicate cursive from the deliberate hand of Egbert Banks, Uncle Henry's younger brother. The letter was dated November 28th, 1895, addressed to one of Egbert's nephews, though he is never mentioned by name.

Egbert, then 56 years old, would only live 2 years and 5 months after he sealed and sent his letter, which chronicled a certain journey traveled by train with my great, great grandfather David, Egbert and Henry's older brother. Their apparent purpose was to visit relatives in neighboring states. Egbert wrote about generously assisting with money, labor and supplies, to get some of the family back on their feet. Along the way, Egbert would also celebrate his part in the war with others who served, as a proud, medal-wearing member of the G. A. R. (Great Army of the Republic). Studying copies of a collection of family photographs that I have seen in the homes of relatives, and in my cousin Pat's Banks family book, I discovered that they were all taken during Egbert and David's 1895 trip. I had no doubt that the photo sessions were most likely arranged by Egbert as well.

Egbert opened his greeting with a slight rant about friends and family still living in his native Putnam County, N.Y., who wouldn't respond to his letters. At the time, he was farming in Clinton, Iowa, and drafted a ten-page narrative, in which he shared news with his nephew about the condition of his hogs, the price tag for bushels of wheat and corn, the weather, pests and other items of note that were newsworthy to the farming population. By page six of the letter, I had settled into my chair on the balcony, and continued to read by the diminishing light of the setting sun, when I arrived at Egbert's reference to my great-great grandfather David.

*David and I went to Salina, Kansas we started from marchal town (Marshalltown, IA) sept 24 on a excursion ticket good till oct 17 we went to councial bluffs (Council Bluffs, IA) then down the mesura valley (Missouri Valley, IA) to Kansas City then to saline (Salina, KS) changing cars at councial*

*bluffs and Kansas city we left marscaltown the 24ᵗʰ 2 a.m. the
G.A.R. state encampment was in progresss we tuckit in (took it
in) and then went out to brother George which is 4 miles nearly
north of salina*

Finally, my investment of seven-plus years of reading,
research, correspondence, and the tireless distillation of facts and
figures from generations of family rumor and opinion all culminated at
the pinnacle of a single paragraph that I found myself reading over and
over again. Uncle Egbert continued:

*I rote to Uncel Henry I Banks' widow in Texas to find
where he was berade (buried) she is mared (married) a gain
and lives at Wetherford he was bered at baird Texas I made
araingments with a man in Salina who gets tomb stones of the
government for soldiers the government furnish them for free of
cost.*

Whether or not it was a convenient excuse for closure, or a
legitimate directive from an other-worldly source, I finally came to
realize my place in this mysterious exploit. Egbert and David's
honorable intention to award their brother a proper Union headstone
had never been accomplished. I had walked the graves at the cemetery
in Baird, myself, and found numerous headstones that predated 1895,
when Egbert and David had traveled to Kansas. Henry's plot was
marked clearly on old cemetery records, but no stone, evidence of an
eroded marker, or even a leftover divot in the lawn was present. Had
Egbert and David paid for a stone that was never delivered? Had a
stone been set, and then destroyed somehow? Doubtful, considering the
condition of other stones that were present, and much older. After
reading Egbert's passage regarding Henry, I decided instantly, with
certainty and conviction that Henry's little wooden bible fell into my
hands in order to complete some unfinished Banks family business. I
was happy to assume the torch, and see to the fulfillment of my
ancestors' mission. I wasted no time drafting the appropriate forms and
copying the many supporting documents I had since gathered for the
Veteran's Administration. As I collected all papers into a manilla
envelope, I made certain to follow all of the specific requirements
outlined on their website to a "T". There were still missing details that
the V.A. required, in order to generate a stone for Henry, so the open
envelope remained on my desk as a reminder, as I continued in
diligence to pursue additional intel the best that I could.

*My 3rd cousin, Mary Emma Allen, and husband, James Allen. Mary contributed the priceless collection of Henry's letters that were preserved in a family album.*

*3ʳᵈ Cousin Delilah Beougher and her husband, Max. Dee assisted me in locating Henry's farm, and the Banks family cemetery in Salina, Kansas.*

*Henry Ira Banks, Gentleman Farmer, Salina, KS*

# Salina, Kansas

Salina, Kansas had been mentioned in many of the resources that I had collected since the beginning of my research. I contacted the Smoky Hill History Museum, which seemed to have an immaculately comprehensive website, and a well-organized collection of resources available to the public. I acquired from the museum's staff, an early map of the Saline County area dating back to 1903, along with an early land title document naming Henry I. Banks as the grantee. I imported the museum's jpeg of the illustrated map into GoogleEarth, and placed it as a separate, semi-transparent layer, and after some minor adjustments, I aligned it perfectly with the base layer of current satellite imagery, using creeks, ponds and railroad tracks as reference points. On the historic map, the Salina area was checkered with connecting squares, which were arranged in numeric order, according to established townships. Recalling the heading on the 1880 census page that registered Henry and his first wife, Tilly, the township of Pleasant Valley would be my target area. Between the townships of Glendale and Elm Creek, in the upper left quadrant of the map is where I found the municipality I was looking for.

In his 1972 book, *"Picture Trails, Past to Present: Pleasant Valley Township, Saline County, Kansas,"* Harry Craig Hughes offered a historic summary of the area during the late 1800's.

> *Following the Civil War and passage of the U.S. Homestead Act by the Federal Government, many citizens from the eastern United States and immigrants from Europe, migrated to the unsettled areas of the western United States, beginning in the 1860's.*

> *Pleasant Valley township, in northwest Saline County, included 36 square miles bordered on the south by Mulberry Creek and on the north by the Saline River. Its landscape is made up of about 90% rolling prairie upland and 10% fertile creek and river valley land.*

> *Almost half of the area, including its uneven numbered sections, was originally U.S. land grants to railroads. The*

*revenue from sale of this real estate to settlers provided funds to finance railroad construction.*

*In 1785, Congress adopted a "Rectangular System" of land surveys, measured by baselines at right angles to each other. Twenty sets of baselines were established in the U.S. The ones from which Pleasant Valley was measured includes the baseline running east and west along the northern border of Kansas, and the 6th Principal Meridian running south from this baseline through central Kansas, along the east border of Saline county.*

*Township borders were surveyed at 6-mile intervals from these lines. Pleasant Valley became township #13 south from the baseline and within Range 4 west of the meridian. In 1858, the 36 sections, each 1-mile square, within its bounds were surveyed and designated.*

It was #34 of these 36 sections that I concluded to be Henry's farm which, according to local records he had purchased in 1876. I zoomed into the image of the antique map, and located the parcel that was identified numerically. I slowly adjusted the opacity slider tool in GoogleEarth's layer control palette to dissolve the 1903 map on the top layer. This revealed the bottom layer and what seemed to be a currently occupied residence on the GoogleEarth satellite image.

I felt the sweat begin to bead up on my forehead, as I zoomed in as close as the imagery's sharpest resolution would allow. As details of the property began to emerge, it appeared that Henry's farm was still in full operation. Grooves in the earth spiderwebbed out from cylindrical structures, which could only be evidence of cattle, and their hoof prints, which led between food and water sources. I deciphered certain objects as farm and irrigation equipment, and eventually began to perceive elongated shadows of cows grazing in their pasture, adjacent to a collection of buildings, which I supposed were a barn, and the current owner's residence.

Before I could talk myself out of my compulsion to contact the current owner, for fear that I was invading the peace of a private citizen, I had identified the house number and street of the current resident of parcel #34, and my phone's receiver was already against my ear. It was ringing.

*"Hello?"*

The voice on the other end of the line was obviously that of an elderly gentleman.

*"Hi, is this Mr. Claussen?"* I asked.

*"Yes it is."* He answered.

I didn't know where to begin. I didn't want to come across as a potentially fraudulent solicitor, or bamboozler, so I was very careful not to sound professional in the least bit.

*"Mister Claussen, I'm so glad I was able to find you. My name's Steve, I live in Austin, Texas, and I'm studying my family history. I believe you and I have a mutual connection."*

I waited for Mr. Claussen to break the silence, or to hang up, I wasn't sure which it would be. To my relief, he seemed genuinely intrigued, and invited me to divulge more intelligence. I explained how his farm had once belonged to Henry—once a Private in the Civil War— and how I had become acquainted with all the details that eventually led up to this phone call. Mr. Claussen immediately recognized Henry's name from somewhere. I was delighted to hear that Mr. Claussen had lived on the property since the 1950's, and that he had a collection of early photographs of the farm, some of which featured the original house, which he described as "fancy." Unfortunately, it had since been demolished as a result of termite infestation, but I was excited by the notion that I might eventually possess a photo of the home that Henry had built in the 1870's.

Our conversation swayed from the historical to the present. I described what I did for a living, and what it was like living in Austin, Texas. We expressed our mutual disdain for the intense heat that the summer of 2011 had wrought upon both Kansas and Texas, and the adverse affect it was having on local crops. Mr. Claussen changed the subject to his days as a tank driver in WWII, memories of raising his family on his farm, and his reminiscence of the once-thriving livestock business in Saline County. Though it wasn't currently the operation that it used to be, he still kept a few head of cattle on his farm, and "walked and talked with them every day."

We must have spoken for nearly 30 minutes, when he said,

> *"Well, I could just go on talking to you for hours, this sounds like such a wonderful story. You are welcome to come out and visit us here anytime, and see the place for yourself."*

> I answered, *"I just might take you up on that someday, Mr. Claussen, I'm planning a road trip next June."*
> *"Not till June? Why, I'm 86 years old."*

I knew what he was getting at, and I didn't want to disappoint him. I got the feeling that this little adventure could be a welcome stimulus for the aging Kansas farmer. Just as I always intended, Henry's story was already making an impact on the lives of others, and the book hadn't even been written yet. I assured Mr. Claussen that I would see what I could do to make it to Kansas before Winter.

September approached, as did my 45th birthday. True to her form, Andi pestered me about what I wanted as a gift. For some reason, it was always difficult for me to rattle off a list of things that could fill this void, or that, but this year was different. *"I want a round-trip plane ticket for my birthday. I think it's time for me to go back to Denver,"* I said. Andi's response surprised me. *"I think you're right,"* she said, *"It's been seven years."*

Since moving from Colorado to California in 2004, I hadn't returned to Denver except to transfer planes on business trips, or vacations. I spent nearly 10 years creating award-winning beer ads and promotions with many good friends and talented colleagues in Colorado, who I now recognized only as Facebook icons. Staying away was my own warped method of being assertive, and focusing on the path of personal progress. Picking up stakes, and moving to a new state with no job prospects on the horizon was indeed a difficult step, back in 2004, and I needed all of my faculties available to remain motivated. That future in California that I was so intent on establishing was now history, and as we were now finally settling into a new home in Texas, I was ready to visit with my some of my old pals.

It was the day after the tenth anniversary of Al Qaida's attack on the World Trade Center, and the Pentagon. Coincidentally, I was on an American Airlines 737 en route to New York City for a series of meetings. I had been reflecting often about those unfolding events, where I was, and the friends and colleagues with whom I had witnessed that horrific experience. On the morning of September 11th, 2001, I answered my ringing cell phone while en route to my office in Lakewood, Colorado. It was Andi, hysterically describing what she was watching on the morning news.

We had both been getting ready for work with the television on in the background. We must have passed it a dozen times, oblivious to the imagery of those two smoldering towers. Only after I had backed out of the driveway, had her attention been diverted to the screen. What she was describing seemed so surreal and improbable, that I could hardly believe my ears. By the time I arrived at work, the cubicles were deserted, but there was commotion emanating from my Creative Director's office. I entered to find the entire Creative staff seated on the floor, gathered around the television, watching intently as the news broke about the plane that struck the second tower.

The rest of the day was a blur, though I remember hearing the announcement of the early office closure over the P.A. System. Some of us gathered at a local bar to absorb the coverage, and a few cocktails. Though I have always been described as a calm, even-keeled personality, and an incurable optimist, always slow to anger, that day would aggressively test that degree of my character to the point of near collapse. I couldn't believe some of the phrases and expletives that were coming out of my mouth, as I broadcast my reaction to the emerging news details that grew increasingly dire. My anger flared, fueled by the frustration that whoever was to blame for the senseless, heartless and selfish attack on my country, had yet to be identified. I had my own theory, and it eventually proved to be true.

I arrived at home in the afternoon to find Andi perched with our cats in front of the TV. I joined her, wrapping my arm around her shoulder. We didn't exchange a word. Later that evening, we chose to turn off the television, our eyes tired and bloodshot from watching clip after clip of the chaos that ensued in lower Manhattan. We felt helpless, insulted, and violated, as I am sure many Americans did that night as they retired for the evening.

The next morning began like any other, with my exercise routine, shower, and breakfast on the run. I made a random stop at a local coffee shop to curtail the drowsy effects of a restless night. I stood in line behind a team of 5 construction workers in overalls, and hardhats who were next to be served. I suddenly pushed past them to the counter, and announced to the cashier that I would be paying for their coffee, and mine. She looked at me as if I had three heads. I turned to face the crew behind me. They also were dumbstruck. "I insist," I said. They all nodded, smiled, and a couple patted me on the back. It took them a minute, but they "got it." They knew what I was doing, and why I was doing it, possibly even before I realized it myself. It was truly an impulsive action. When I finally ordered my own coffee, the cashier smiled at me and said, "that was a really nice gesture." I responded, "I had to do *something*."

While I was making my travel plans to spend an October weekend in Denver, it occurred to me that Salina, Kansas was only a few hours East of downtown. Hell, I-70 ran straight through Henry's 160-acre property. It would be a straight shot! Flat, and straight. I hadn't even thought of what I would do with my free Saturday while I was in Denver, so I decided that the travel portion of my quest to follow Uncle Henry would begin that day, with a visit to his former farm. I contacted Mr. Claussen in the evening, and shared the news that I would be stopping by his property at around noon. He seemed thrilled, and motivated to begin hunting for his old photos and documents. I was energized, with a trip to look forward to in the coming weeks that would hopefully pay off.

I drafted a quick letter, and sent it to Mr. Claussen in order to give him some background, in case he needed to explain this stranger's visit to his wife and family, he would be aptly equipped with the details. Though my letter was rushed and ponderous, it was a rewarding exercise for me to summarize the particulars of my research in a succinct, single page.

*Dear Mr. Claussen,*

*As I promised, I am enclosing some of the material that I spoke to you about a few nights ago, regarding Mr. Henry Banks, who I believe was the original owner of your land in Salina, KS.*

*I have included a photographs of Henry that a distant cousin in New Hampshire found in an old photo album.*

*The photo was taken in 1871 at a photography studio in Salina that used to be located on the corner of Santa Fe and Iron Avenue. 1871 was the year that Henry settled in the Salina area, and I am happy that he signed the photo, or I would have never identified him.*

*Also attached is a copy of an old outline map of Saline County, and a map of the Pleasant Valley Township area, which clearly shows where Henry I. Banks settled.*

*Mr. Banks was my great-great grandfather David Irish Banks' younger brother. The Banks family's original home was in Putnam County, N.Y. They were Quakers, and descendants of Palatine Germans who came to America in the 1700's. After Henry's father drowned in an accident in Albany, N.Y., the family picked up stakes, and relocated to a farm in North Henderson, Illinois, which is in Mercer County, not far from the Iowa state border. Both my great-great Grandfather David I. Banks, and his brother Egbert Banks later settled in Clinton, and Center City, Iowa.*

*My uncles Henry and Egbert both enlisted to fight in the Civil War in 1862. My cousin has furnished some letters that were exchanged between them and other family members while they were skirmishing in the field.*

*It is quite an interesting path that I have been following for the last 8 years or so. My parents both passed away before I was 40, and I took the loss pretty hard. While going through some of my father's things, I found an old palm-sized wooden bible that had some strange carvings on it. I began investigating their meaning, and it turned out to be a piece of trench art that Uncle Henry had crafted while he was stationed at Gallatin, Tennessee during what he thought would be 9 months as a Volunteer in the Civil War. He would instead, serve for 3 years as he blended in with Sherman's forces, as they burned Atlanta, sacked Savannah, then marched through the Carolinas, until Lee's surrender at Appomattox in 1865.*

*I think this distraction has helped me deal with my loss, by resurrecting details of my Uncle's life. It's difficult to explain, but the coincidences through circumstances that I have experienced have been nothing short of miraculous, and I have made some very fine friends during my search for answers.*

*The way I see it, Henry's bible wound up in my hands for a reason, and I have recently discovered why. Through a letter written by Henry's brother, Egbert, it seems that he and my great-great grandfather took a trip on an open-ended train ticket in the late 1800's. As they traveled to Salina, Kansas, they met with a man who was supposedly going to order and erect a Union Army headstone for their brother, Henry, who had died in 1889. His widow had been married to him for just over a year, and buried him near her family's plot in Baird, TX without a headstone, then remarried soon after. In Henry's probate letter, his widow states that she had no idea how to reach his next of kin.*

*When I learned where Henry was buried, I had just moved to Austin, TX. I drove to the cemetery, and found an old map from the 1940's that showed where Henry was laid to rest.*

*No headstone.*

*Henry's brothers wanted a proper stone placed for their younger brother, who fought for the Union, and was wounded at New Hope Church, GA during a brave skirmish with a heavily armed confederate garrison. I have decided to take on the responsibility of placing a proper stone for Uncle Henry in their honor.*

*I am ordering a stone to be placed next July 24th, One-hundred and twenty-three years after Henry's untimely passing. I still don't know how he died. All material that I have examined doesn't give a cause of death.*

*I have also attached an outline that documents all of the incidents that led up to my discovery of Henry's grave. I hope you enjoy reading it.*

*Next May and June, I hope to follow the actual path that Henry's unit traversed during the Civil War, and visit some of the actual places where he fought, marched and camped.*

*With this goal in mind, I also hope to include a visit to your place in Kansas, with your permission.*

*Please write back, and let me know you received this letter, and if you have discovered any information concerning my uncle, Henry Ira Banks. I appreciate you being so receptive, and eager to assist me.*

*I hope you are well, and that the heat wave subsides soon.*

*Sincerely,*

*Steve Enyeart*

*Austin, TX*

Recently, Andi and I had just moved into our first home in Austin, and I was staring at a "honeydo" list as long as my arm. As the husband of a professional Interior Designer, there was no shortage of chores and projects that required immediate attention. Mirrors, fixtures, photos, art, furnishings and hardware were distributed in piles throughout our new suburban domicile. The tedious process of transferring each item to their place on our blank walls caused me to adopt an appropriate nickname for myself: "The HangMan."

Admittedly, it wasn't the most favorable time to be leaving town with so many loose ends yet to be fastened. For instance, to my chagrin, my morning began with a cold shower at 4:30 a.m., due to a faulty hot water heater. My inspection and repair efforts caused me to nearly miss my flight, but with a fortuitous procession of green lights, and no bags to check, I breezed through the security line at Bergstrom International Airport, arriving at my gate with time to spare. The Airbus dropped me down into the mile-high city right on schedule, affording me an astounding view of The Rockies painted in hues of cyan and sienna, reflecting the rising sun. This time I wouldn't be hopping on another bird bound for Seattle or L.A. for business purposes. After 7 years, it was high time to pay Denver a visit on my own dime.

I selected a new Ford Focus, which had previously proved to offer the right amount of performance and payload for our periodic road trips to Houston, and ample headroom for my 6'4" frame. I was surprised by my auto-pilot memory, as I merged onto Southbound I-25, a route I had followed countless times as a resident commuter. I detoured through our former neighborhood in Highlands Ranch, and parked across the street from our former home, just off the scenic Wildcat Reserve Parkway. I was pleased that the present owner was still capitalizing on my sweat equity, and my "custom" water feature still bubbled in a flagstone pond before the front steps. I snapped a photo with my smartphone, attached it to a text, and sent it off to Andi, who was at her office. Only seconds later, I heard her ringtone, and answered my phone promptly. She was in tears. "What's wrong?" I asked. "That was a little abrupt, and unexpected," Andi choked. "It just bought back so many memories."  She was right. It was a wonderful home that we enjoyed very much, during a time in our lives that was abundant and full of fun and fellowship with great neighbors, and friends who were more like extended family. Our home was a semi-custom structure that we designed together. Andi approached the décor with her typical aptitude, as I installed all of our landscaping, fencing and sprawling backyard deck. Some of the parties we hosted in that house were legendary. Who could forget the sensational time we had with friends and colleagues at our Hawaiian Christmas party of 2002? What a riot!

As we continued our phone conversation, I laid out my plans and schedule to Andi, as I usually did when on the road. I took one last look at the old Enyeart digs, and drove away wearing a mischievous grin. I wondered as I rolled out of the neighborhood if anyone would ever unearth that time capsule that I placed inconspicuously somewhere within the walls. Time will tell.

After a brief hike along the rambling trails of South Valley Park in Morrison, I drove East to Lakewood, and parked at a restaurant near the ad agency where I once worked. I had previously arranged a meeting for lunch with my 3rd cousin Dee, who was the great grand daughter of Henry's brother, William. My cousin Mary Emma in New Hampshire had introduced us via email, since we both were in common pursuit of Banks family details. Since Dee and her husband Max coincidentally lived in Lakewood, CO, I couldn't pass up an introduction. Dee and her husband, Max joined me at the table, and I immediately recognized some of Dee's unmistakable "Banks" features that reminded me of my late grandmother. Dee had been raised on a farm near Grinnell, KS, and had many details to share, regarding the Banks family members who lived in the Salina area in the 1870's and '80s. She produced a copy of her family tree, and photographs of great, great, great grandmother Cynthia's headstone. She knew the exact whereabouts of the small cemetery where Cynthia was buried, and gave me written directions. Dee and Max seemed fascinated by Henry's small wooden bible, and I explained the details of its discovery as they closely examined it. We had a wonderful exchange of information, and said goodbye, with a promise to stay in touch.

I spent the rest of the day with friends, and former colleagues, many of whom I hadn't seen for seven years. I was caught up on all the agency scuttlebutt, and news that I had missed out on as a now former employee. Everyone, it seemed had been affected in their own way by the economic downturn of the previous years, and the agency that I left had taken on a new, but not-so-alluring character. It was clear that I had made the right decision to relocate when I did. There had been a scant, lingering microbe of regret floating around in my subconscious, which had been permanently eradicated, as a result of this visit. To some extent, it was liberating.

Saturday morning arrived with a cloudless violet sky, and rising before dawn, I poured myself a generous cup of java to-go. There was moisture in the autumn air, which had obscured my windshield with condensation. Idling for a few moments, I let the defroster do its thing, as I set my GPS to Salina, Kansas. It calculated an approximate ETA of 12:30 pm. My heart sank a little. Truthfully, this was my initial realization of just how far a drive I was in for. Had I driven from my home in Austin, it wouldn't have been much more than two additional hours on the road. "What am I doing?" I asked aloud. My destination was 6.5 hours away, and I hesitated as apprehension did its best to take root. Ultimately, stubborn foolhardiness triumphed, and I aimed my Ford eastward, down the I-70 corridor toward the Colorado/Kansas border. I watched the blinding sun rise over the endless plains of Western Kansas, as I set my Satellite Radio to the '40's channel. This selection was so beyond the norm for me, but for some reason Glen Miller, Tommy Dorsey, Les Paul and Mary Ford offered an appropriate soundtrack to a scenic, but monotonous landscape, which diminished toward the horizon in my rearview mirror.

I was no stranger to long road trips. As a family of 5, with my father as our diligent sole provider, we rarely traveled by air or rail when I was a youngster. Dad preferred to experience new horizons from ground level, so as not to miss the details. It was up to each one of us to find ways to pass the time in our own unique ways. One such trip came to mind while I was en route to Uncle Henry's Kansas homestead. In the summer of 1981 my parents and I traveled in our 1972 Volkswagen Squareback Wagon from Seattle to Burns Lake, British Columbia to visit some extended family. They allowed me to invite a friend along for the 700 mile drive. Of course, my best friend Ken would unflinchingly accept my invitation.

Responding to boredom and monotony, it's quite remarkable how creative a couple of ninth graders can get with an implement as rudimentary as a whoopee cushion. Stopping at a small truck stop cafe near Kamloops, B.C., we rushed through our breakfast, and excused ourselves to set up an elaborate stunt in the Men's room. The restaurant was cozy, but obviously popular, as every seat was occupied. The restroom doors were frivolously poised just a few feet away from a row of tables where locals, and travelers alike were innocently enjoying their omelets and oatmeal. With my buddy stationed at the sink, and I in a locked stall, we laid in wait for our first victim. It didn't take long before the restroom door hinges squealed to life, and in walked contestant number one. When he was finished at the sink, I heard my signal, which was Ken's subtle cough. It was perfect timing that we were after, and we nailed it on the first try. From the shadowy safety of the locked stall, I squeezed with all my might as the cushion roared with flatulent harmonies, echoing against the tile walls, and out through the open doorway, where our victim stood red-faced before an appalled assembly of diners. After three or four sessions, my parents became wise to our little gag, confiscated our instrument, and dragged us out to the car, as we snickered uncontrollably.

About twenty miles outside of Denver, my head jerked with a double-take as I spotted a large pirate ship in an open field on the south side of I-70. A mirage? On the contrary. Festooned with hand-carved skulls, and shredded fabric sails that were eerily flowing with the sweeping winds from the plains, it was an unexpected, but welcome sight against an unvarying backdrop of grassland cattle and barbed wire. According to a local news station's online post, the landowner who is "as elusive as Captain Jack" built this enormous pirate ship from styrofoam, frayed rope, and rusty nails for no other reason but to perplex commuters and truckers who happened to pass by.

The signs along the interstate to "Kanorado" were clear indicators that the border between states was not far ahead. Since it was a Saturday, traffic was moderate, and weather was superb. I was anxious to finally visit Henry's post-war spread, and to explore the property for any leftover trace of his former occupancy. As I had so often done before, (but not very much lately) I said a brief prayer to God that I would come away with something in exchange for my far-fetched efforts. He would not disappoint.

Near Colby, the highway took a sharp right turn Southeast for about 30 miles, leading me into a sort of "crop circle" encounter. Obviously, center-pivot irrigation was the method of choice in this region to nourish crops. Enormous green circular fields flanked the highway for miles. As I approached Oakley, I was enticed time-and-again by tempting signage, beckoning for me to behold "Live Rattlesnakes," "The World's Largest Prairie Dog," "Roscoe the Miniature Donkey", and "The LIVE 6-legged Steer!" Unfortunately, I had not prepared adequately for this one-day junket. Had I known about the colorful network of roadside attractions that I would encounter en route to Salina, I would have allowed myself more time to follow the exit ramps, and enrich my famished intellect. Still, just pondering over the progressive "Burmashave-style" campaign of homespun billboards provided some welcome amusement and tested my willpower, but I resisted and stayed the course toward Salina.

The remaining miles of my road trip featured much more than just bovines and hay bails. Among the many diversions en route to Henry's farm were the strangely incongruous Cathedral Rocks near Grinnell, the beautiful twin spires of St. Fidelis Church, aka "Cathedral of the Plains" in Victoria, not to mention the Museum of Natural History in Hays, and their wonderful collection of prehistoric dinosaur bones and fossils.

Somewhere near the junction where the arterial of highway 156 leads southwest to Great Bend, the landscape began to assume an entirely different appearance. The garrisons of modern windmills atop quilts of crop circles gave way to lush rolling mounds of green, divided by deeply pitched valleys crowded with groves of stately Cottonwoods and American Elms in various stages of prismatic transition. This was certainly a bucolic postcard view that I didn't expect. This road was a metaphor to my continuing quest for answers, which began with just a meager desire for truth. Every blind corner that I approached —at times with trepidation— seemed to hold an unexpected reward in nearly every case. After all of this time, I still hadn't shaken the habit of placing my trust in presupposition. So far, the boring, nondescript, lonely drive that I had momentarily dreaded earlier that morning had me rubbernecking in amazement, all the way from Denver to Pleasant Valley.

I was getting close to the turnoff to Hedville, which was just a stone's throw from Uncle Henry's homestead. Before long, I was turning onto the dirt road that led to the farm that I had located on GoogleEarth. I turned into an unpaved driveway that led me deep into the property. I grinned ear-to-ear as I coasted through a small village of antique buildings, crippled vehicles and rustic farm equipment. I remember thinking to myself that this was a "Picker's Paradise." A dog barked loud and aggressive. I couldn't locate the source, but from the sound of it, I didn't feel threatened. An old red barn stood at the end of the driveway, and looked like it was conjured directly from a Steinbeck novel. In hand-hewn woodblock letters, the word: COW was spelled out in a vertical orientation. I chuckled, then mumbled to myself: "This must be the place."

It was approximately 12:45 pm as I stepped out of the car to look around for the owner's house. I stretched my back, which was aching from the 6-hour haul, and took in a deep breath of warm air, sweet with fresh hay and old dust. For a moment, I was back at my grandfather's roost in Lamar, WA, where I had first inhaled that medley of pungent scents with which I was so familiar. I had driven into the wrong driveway somehow, and wound up behind the farmhouse, which I could see through thick brush and trees. I got back into my rental car, and carefully backed out of the narrow driveway.

The dirt road led to another driveway. This one was neatly paved with loose gray gravel, and some trees had been cut away to make room for a large satellite dish. I followed the driveway up to the modest, split-level farmhouse, where I was hailed by a tall, slender figure in well-worn blue overalls and a baseball cap. As he approached, I rolled down my window and called out "Mister Claussen?" I kept the motor running, I suppose in case I needed to make a quick getaway. After all, I was a long way from home. "That's a nice car. Is that a Ford?" he asked. I shut off the motor and stepped out of the car into the "crunch" of the gravel driveway. "Sorry I'm a little late," I said. We shook hands, and walked in tandem up the drive where I was introduced to "Zip," the dog whose barking had since subsided to a low gravelly growl. I got the feeling from his cautious and standoffish behavior that visitors to the Claussen farm were few and far between.

Virgil led me to the back of his home, across a cement patio, and up a step through the back door into the kitchen. It was a sparse, yet comfortable space that reminded me a great deal of my own childhood home. I smelled home-baked goods and coffee that transported me to occasional weekends at my Dutch grandparents home in rural Mount Vernon, Washington, where my Grandmother all-to-often spoiled my family with her instinctive culinary talents. Appliances and furnishings were dated, but utilitarian, and a no-frills décor richly complimented a simple, salt-of-the-earth lifestyle. Virgil stepped into a room adjacent to the kitchen, where I remained standing, reviewing prerequisite questions in my head that I was otherwise likely to forget to ask. Soon, he returned to the kitchen with "Thea" in tow.

Virgil's wife had a familiar accent that I remembered from our recent exchange on the telephone. She was petite, sandy-haired and dressed nicely for a Saturday on the farm. The three of us sat down at the kitchen table, where I reminded the Claussens of the reason for my visit. I cleared up some confusion for them, which I am certain was a product of my own excitement as I had previously droned on over the phone, and in my letter with all the details that I had unearthed since Henry's bible fell into my hands. I produced the little block of wood that I was carrying in my camera bag, wrapped in a small piece of chamois. Both Virgil and Thea examined the bible, and both seemed intrigued as I reminded them that it had almost certainly spent some time here on their farm, perhaps in a drawer or chest when Henry was the landowner. Here it was, once again occupying the same space that it had, some 130 years before.

I described the circumstances that most likely led to Henry's decision to carve the small souvenir from his six-month station in Gallatin, Tennessee in 1862. I told Virgil and Thea that I had recently been researching Civil War era "trench art", to learn if there were any additional records of bibles being carved by soldiers, either Union or Confederate. Virgil's eyes lit up, and I could tell I struck a nerve. "I have something to show you" he said. Virgil lunged up from the table, and disappeared into his living room. Seconds later he came marching back into the kitchen, wearing glasses this time, which transformed him into the spitting image of my grandfather. His large hands dwarfed a small green jeep that was cupped in his palms. It was approximately 10 inches long, and rich with detail, from the white star emblazoned on the hood, to the articulating glass windscreen, red reflectors on the front and back corner panels, and whitewall tires all around. It looked like a Revell model kit that I would have built as a tween in the 1970's.

Virgil carefully placed it on the kitchen table before me. "Do you know who made this jeep for me?" he asked. I examined it closely, determining promptly that it was not fashioned from a plastic cheap store-bought model kit. On the contrary, it was fashioned by hand, out of chunks of wood. Even the round tires were hand-carved with precise detail right down to the tread pattern, and the delicate spokes of the steering wheel seemed to be evocative of the real deal. "Someone *made* this?" I asked. "Yep. German soldiers held prisoner at Dachau, gave it to me as a Christmas present." I was speechless. "Go ahead" Virgil said, as he clued into my eagerness to hold the jeep for a closer look. "What were you doing at Dachau?" I asked, as I carefully examined the keepsake. Virgil spelled out the details of his post-war assignment in 1945, watching over Nazi captives as a prison guard at the notorious concentration camp. I knew some of its history, and the grim newsreel images captured shortly after the camp was liberated flashed through my mind, as Virgil narrated in tandem. "I guess those fellas liked me for some reason." "Anyway, they made this jeep for me out of scraps from around the camp." Virgil continued. "They did a real nice job with the paint too." "I kept it just like they made it, all these years." As I listened intently to Mr. Claussen's account, I pieced together the rest of the story. "Did you bring Thea back to the states from Germany?" I asked. "Sure did." He said with a smile, and a wink, aimed across the table at his bride. I leaned forward toward both Virgil and Thea, resting my folded hands on top of the table, and looked them both in the eye. "Now *that* is a fascinating story." I said.

We chatted for a little longer about the family they had raised, who were now scattered about, and their history with the farm, which they bought in 1956, not long after Virgil brought Thea to the states from Germany. Apparently, there were just a few buildings on the property at that time, including an old farmhouse that they lived in until termites forced its demolition in 1963, once the construction of their current home was completed. Virgil handed me a black and white photo of the house, as it stood in the 1950's. "You can have that if you want." He said kindly. Instead, I promised him I would scan a copy for myself, and return it by mail. "The old house is still here, it's just in piles." Virgil said. "Can I see it? I asked eagerly." "Sure!"

I followed Virgil out the back door, making sure to grab my Canon G9 digital camera. I snapped photos of everything I could that appeared as if it was from Henry's era. Virgil pointed out an old barn, and some stone foundations where original structures no loner stood. We passed by the original water pump, manufactured in Fairbury, Nebraska that hadn't drawn from its well in decades. Finally, we arrived at the edge of a giant chasm in the earth, next to a large pile of neatly arranged stone blocks, decaying wooden planks, and composition shingles. It appeared as if the entire house was still here, just deconstructed. Virgil pointed into the hole, and stated, "They say there was a big well here, that opened up next to the old house." "I believe someone fell in once or twice." I snapped a few photographs, from different angles, and suddenly lost my footing. Instinctively, I reached out to break my fall, and braced my arm against a large stone object that jutted out from the earth about 30 inches. It was a stone obelisk-like object, about 9 inches wide, and crowned with what appeared to be a 4-inch wide iron ring. I rose to my feet, and examined the platform where I stood. I had seen this familiar hardscape treatment somewhere before. I was standing on top of a waist-high wall of stacked, hand-hewn stone blocks that spanned about 20 feet across. A 6-foot wide staircase escalated up through the center of the wall. The staircase was flanked by the stone post that broke my fall, and its twin stood just a few feet away. "Do you know what those are?" asked Virgil? I thought for a moment, and offered up my best guess. "Horse hitches?" "That's right!" he said. This sent my imagination spiraling into hyperspeed rewind. I suddenly, and clearly remembered where I had seen this identical design before. The photograph that I had found on the Town of Patterson Historical Society's website of the Banks family home in Haviland Hollow featured a similar wall surrounding the foundation, built with dry-stacked stones, and flanked with two opposing hitching posts!

Who might have hitched their horses up to these posts when they came calling on Henry and Tilla Banks in Salina, back in the day? I could imagine ascending the stone steps at dusk, and approaching the quaint little cottage with its brick chimney billowing aromatic smoke from a warm, welcoming fire. Since Henry's first wife, Tilla was mentioned in the 1880 Federal Census as "keeping house," I would expect her to be the first to greet me at the door. I couldn't picture her.

Who was she?

Tilla seemed to fall off the map shortly after Henry was remarried to Emma Bowlus-Gain, who abruptly brought Henry to her family home in Texas, only days after her divorce from her first husband was finalized. I wasn't the only one who assumed that Henry and Tilla had also divorced. My volunteer contacts at The Smoky Hill Genealogical Society in Salina thought this may have been the case, since Henry and Emma made such a hasty exit to the Lone Star State. However, no records ever surfaced except for both of Henry's marriage certificates. There was no sign of Tilla, Tillie, or Matilda Banks in the 1890 Census that matched her date of birth, though if she had remarried, it would be very difficult to locate her under her new married name. It was yet another mystery to solve in this exciting, yet perplexing journey.

Alas, nothing now remained of the old farmhouse but a tidy cluster of piled rubble and a short stone foundation marking the structure's former perimeter. I at least had photographic proof of its former self, while in its bygone heyday as my great, great Uncle's Kansas residence. For that, I was grateful.

Virgil and I continued to peruse the property and old structures that were likely to have been in use during Henry's era. We passed through a barbed wire gate, and into a stand of tall trees that were arranged in a perfect line, like a hedgerow. I recalled the Google Earth image of Henry's property, which was divided into fourths by these dark green living boundaries. I don't remember Virgil's exact words, but he mentioned something about leaving the trees where they were, instead of clearing the property for pasture, out of respect for whomever went through the trouble of planting them in the first place. Henry was the first ploughman that came to mind. Perhaps a certain German-born immigrant named Theodore Siffens, also listed in the 1880 Census as a household resident was there at Henry's side to share the sweat.

Virgil and I reached a clearing beyond the trees, when I heard him say, "Well, you're sure an interesting fella...why, we figured you for an older guy than you are." I wasn't sure how to respond, but I knew Virgil's observation came from a good place. "I guess so," I said. "Most guys like me would typically be on the couch watching football on a Saturday like this, but I came out to tour your farm instead!" Virgil laughed a little, then suddenly bellowed loudly, deep from his diaphragm, through a raised, cupped hand. It startled me a little, but when I turned toward the direction of his call, I saw a herd of Angus and Hereford cows, up to their hocks in a still pond. They began walking toward Virgil, as he continued to call them. "Oh, wow...they're awesome." I said. Virgil continued to call the herd with his trademark "whoop, whoop" as they drew closer. I was amazed by the command he seemed to have over these animals, and how they responded to him with trust, at least until they spotted the "stranger" at Virgil's side, which made them all freeze in unison. Livestock was Virgil's livelihood, but I was also witnessing a man, confident, content and at peace with his passion. I couldn't shake it, that gnawing envy.

We walked back to the house together, returning to the kitchen where Thea was waiting. We sat at the table again, and I continued to drill the Claussens about their history with the farm. Virgil mentioned to me that his farm was widely known as "The Old Hoops Place", figuring that "Hoops" was the original titleholder to the farm. Though he had heard my uncle's name somewhere before, he wasn't certain of the context. Virgil reached into a cabinet in the kitchen, and produced an antique leather binder that held together a stack of scrolled legal-sized documents. I knew instantly what he was about to share. Virgil handed me the original Abstract of Title to the farm, and I dove into it like an 8-year-old on Christmas morning. I leafed through the many layers of pages, back to the first, and earliest document.

*"Dated March 1ˢᵗ, 1876. Recorded April 13, 1878, at 2pm Book "M" of Deeds, page 437-8. Consideration: Granted.*

*The United States of America to Henry I. Banks Homestead Certificate No. 1689 Application 12017. To all whom these Presents shall come, Greetings:*

*Whereas, There has been deposited in the General Land Office of the United States a Certificate of the Register of the Land Office at Salina, Kansas, whereby it appears that pursuant to the Act of Congress approved 20ᵗʰ May, 1862, to secure homesteads to actual settlers on the Public Domain, and the acts supplemental thereto, the claim of Henry I. Banks, has been established and duly consummated, in conformity to law for the South East Quarter of Section Thirty-four, in Township Thirteen South of Range Four West, in the District of Lands subject to sale, at Salina, Kansas, containing, one-hundred and sixty acres according to the Official Plat of the Survey of the said land returned to the General Land Office by the Surveyor General.*

*Now Know ye, That there is therefore, granted by the United States unto the said Henry I. Banks, the tract of land above described. To have and to hold the said tract of land with the appurtenances thereof, unto the said Henry I. Banks, and to his heirs and assigns forever.*

*In Testimony whereof, I,* **Ulysees S. Grant, President of the United States of America,** *have caused these letters to be made Patent, and the seal of the General Land Office to be hereunto affixed. Given under my hand at the city of Washington, the first day of March, in the year of our Lord one thousand eight hundred and seventy six, and the Independence of the United States, the one hundredth. (SEAL). By the President. U.S. Grant, By D. D. Cone, Secretary*

I looked up at Virgil and Thea from the binder and said, "Do you know how incredible this is?" "I've got goosebumps right now, this was signed by Ulysses S. Grant!" I wondered aloud how Henry must have felt, when he received his final approval from the former Commander of Union Forces that he once served under. I beamed with pride. Not only was my dear Uncle Henry a Civil War Veteran, but he was also a *true* pioneer of the "westward movement."

I expressed my thanks and enthusiasm to Vigil and Thea, "This is an incredible find that shows Henry Banks as the original landowner." I politely asked if I could capture a few photos of the documents. Virgil obliged. There were 19 pages in all, that mentioned Henry's name, and it became obvious that Henry and Tilla Banks were both just as busy selling off parcels of their land, as they were at farming. The final transaction on page 19 was dated March 15th, 1888, recorded on the 17th at 5:20 pm. An 80-acre parcel, more or less was sold to Alice E. Edie for the consideration of $2,000.00. Signed, Henry I. Banks, a widower. "Did I read that correctly?" I thought.

"This is very interesting," I mumbled, as Virgil and Thea looked on. I was still under the impression that Uncle Henry and his wife, Tilla had divorced before he remarried and moved to Texas. Clearly, I had assumed incorrectly, but I was excited to have a new mystery to unravel. By this time, I had become hopelessly addicted to the chase.

It was time to say goodbye to the Claussens, for it was getting late in the afternoon, and I had a very long drive ahead of me, from Salina back to Denver. I thanked Virgil for his generosity, and freeing up an afternoon to let me poke around on his property. I asked my new friends if I could take a photo of them before hitting the road. They posed for me in their front yard, insisting on including their pets in the frame, which raised my level of admiration for Virgil and Thea at least a notch or two. Zip, the growling hound and I were now on speaking terms.

Virgil gave me driving directions to a small cemetery where Henry's mother, Cynthia was supposedly buried. I listened politely and recorded Virgil's details, even though my cousin Dee had previously furnished the same. Meanwhile, Thea had disappeared into the house, but returned promptly with a Tupperware tub filled with German Pound Cake. That earned Thea a generous, but gentle bearhug. Her homemade treats would sustain me all the way back to Colorado, and save me from the ill effects of off-ramp fast food. *Danke für die Imbisse, Frau Claussen!*

Virgil expressed once again how he enjoyed my visit, and I shook his hand firmly as I hopped back into my Ford. I promised that I would stay in touch, and keep him posted on my progress with my book. I drove down the gravel driveway, and exchanged a friendly wave with the Claussens, as I made my way South toward the old Ohio Township, to hunt for an obscure graveyard, and hopefully my great, great, great grandmother.

I enjoyed my brief visit with Virgil and Thea, and was leaving with much, much more than I had when I arrived. The drive from Denver was worth every flat, lonely mile, though I was overcome with an intuition that Virgil and Thea rarely had visitors. Just the same, I was honored to have been a welcome guest in the home of such an endearing couple with such a heartfelt history, even if it was just for one afternoon. Sadly, I learned later that Thea had passed away shortly after my visit to the Claussen farm.

I hadn't driven far before I spotted a sign on the side of the dirt road that stretched southward from Henry's farm. In whitewashed wrought iron, the sign read: "FAIRVIEW CEMETERY OHIO TOWNSHIP." I parked along the roadside, and approached the cemetery, which was clearly populated with about a dozen headstones. Someone had been taking care of this modest patch of earth, mowing the grass, and maintaining the grounds. I strolled between the stones, and spotted a taller one that seemed to stand out from among the rest. Cynthia's stone was not hard to find. I knelt down beside her monument to read the sincere inscription. It read:

> "How we miss the dear Mother. How she cared for my infant days. How she guided me over life's sands. How peaceful she went to the Heavenly home."

Hers was an impressive, lavishly designed 4-sided marble gravestone, adorned with floral embellishments, leaving little doubt that the family spared no expense for its creation. This marker was a grand testament to a sorely missed, and deeply admired lady. Cynthia had passed away on April 19, 1877, which aged her stone 134 years, and I was amazed at how well it had held up, season after season. I hoped that the stone I had on order for Uncle Henry would prove to be as robust.

I snapped a few photos of the family markers, including that of William Banks, who was Henry's brother. I had previously identified William's farm on my antique map of Pleasant Valley, which was just a mile or two Northeast of Henry's land. William had obviously remained in the Salina area, while Henry decided to pick up stakes after the death of his wife, Tilla. I looked carefully around the small cemetery for any sign of a headstone that may have been erected for Tilla Banks, but all present monuments were spoken for.

It was getting late in the day, and the sun was flirting with the horizon in the West, so I wedged myself in behind the wheel of my Ford Focus, and set my GPS for Denver. My flight home passed by quickly, since I spent the entire trip noodling some notes in my journal, while the details were still fresh in my mind. By the time I had arrived home in Austin, an envelope was waiting in the mailbox from my cousin Mary in New Hampshire. I tore it open anxiously, and flipped through the stack of pages, identifying them as Henry's widow's affidavits for Henry's Civil War Pension Benefits.

*left: Virgil Claussen with his jeep, a gift from the German prisoners over whom he stood guard during WWII. Right: Thea Claussen and friend on the farm in Salina, KS which was Uncle Henry's former homestead, granted to him by the U. S. Government*

*At Fairview Cemetery, just after locating my gr, gr, gr Grandmother Cynthia's grave*

# A Sad Revelation

Little did she know, but with the details about Henry's past that Emma Bowlus-Gain-Banks-Crawford outlined in her request for government assistance, the peculiar widow was equipping me with a significant list of facts that would otherwise require many hours of hit-and-miss investigation. The specifics of Uncle Henry's story had taken some years to piece together, but for the first time, I was confident that I was getting very near to closing the circle.

Based on the staggering volume of claims and affidavits in my lap, I gathered that Emma had pursued those pension benefits with an intense degree of passion. Her petitions spanned over a period of a decade or more, with her initial request earning the devastating and curt response: *"No record of Henry I. Banks found."* If only Emma had the extensive sources of the Internet at her disposal back then.

I scoured through her inquiries and submissions of evidence drafted by attorneys, including Henry's own brother, Daniel, who was a prominent attorney living in Long Island, New York at the time. In his general affidavit, he stated the following:

> *"In the matter of the claim for widow, said widow being Emma Crawford, formerly wife of Henry I. Banks, Private, U.S.A. Personally came before me, a Notary Public in and for the County of aforesaid Daniel G. Banks of Sea Cliff, Queens County, State of New York, a person of lawful age, who, duly sworn, declares in relation to the aforesaid claim as follows: that he was personally acquainted with Henry I. Banks and that of his own certain knowledge that Henry I. Banks did not serve in the Army of the United States prior to his enlistment on August 9th, 1862."*

I found it curious that Daniel Banks did not go out of his way to claim that he and Henry were siblings, but chose to state only the facts that pertained to Emma's plea for her Civil War Widow's Pension.

Another document dated May 2nd, 1889 from the Department of the Interior's Bureau of Pensions confirmed Henry's injury at the Battle of New Hope Church, Georgia on May 26th, 1864, but did not divulge the nature of the wounds. However, the same record mentioned that Henry had also suffered a "wounded finger," just days before the skirmish, on May 15th, 1864. This was during the Battle at Resaca, GA.

Some years later, Emma had contacted a Union Veteran who had served with Henry during their post at Lavergne, Tennessee in 1862. In an effort to stack the deck in her favor, I suppose, the testimony of Private William Artman of the 102nd Regiment's Company "E" revealed to me at last, in detail, the cause of Uncle Henry's death in 1889. It was not what I expected.

> "...while in the line of duty, and without fault or improper conduct on his part, on or near Lavergne, State of Tennessee, said soldier incurred Chronic Diarrhea. I know the fact by reason of my acquaintance with him from the time we enlisted in the said company when he was a sound, able-bodied man and continued in good health up to the time we arrived at LaVergne after a march from Louisville, KY. Soon after our arrival in LaVergne, he was complaining of the said disease, and was excused from duty by the Regimental surgeon by reason of said disease, and he continued to have chronic diarrhea as long as I knew him in the service."

Once again, I consulted Stephen Fleharty's excellent journal, "Our Regiment," to confirm Private Artman's ranking as a legitimate witness. Indeed, his name was listed first, preceding Henry's, which was second in alphabetical order of Privates in Company "E." The adjoining reference stated that William Artman was also wounded at the battle of Resaca.

I looked to a few sources online, regarding the condition that caused Henry's death, and found it common knowledge that this ailment claimed more lives than shells and bullets during the war. One source stated that throughout the war, the Union reported 1,739,135 cases of either diarrhea or dysentery, of which 57,265 were casualties. Generally, at any given time, 25% of the army was stricken with one of the conditions.

Uncle Henry was undeniably a casualty of war. His suffering, however was prolonged over a 27-year bout with a debilitating disease that finally claimed his life in 1889, after the sale of his Kansas farm, and his eventual relocation to Texas with his new bride, who was twenty-two years his junior.

In a general affidavit, signed by B.A. Bowlus dated April 8th, 1889, the facts were further verified:

> *"In the matter of claim for pension of Emma Crawford, widow of Henry I. Banks, Co. E, 102nd Ill. Vols. Personally came before me, a County Clerk in and for aforesaid County and State, B.A. Bowlus, age 65, Baird, Callahan County, Texas. A person of lawful age, who, being duly sworn declares in relation to the aforesaid case as follows: That affiant was acquainted with Henry I. Banks for about 10 years, preceding his death. As a nurse, she attended said Banks in his last sickness and his death was caused by diarrhea contracted during the time he was serving in the U. S. Army 1861-1865. That he said Henry I Banks suffered all the time from his discharge to date of his death from said disease, so contracted as aforesaid. I further declare that I have no interest in said case, and I am not concerned in its prosecution."*

It was unclear if Emma was a nurse by trade, or if the term "nurse" was used in the general sense in this case. I had yet to uncover any evidence that Emma Bowlus-Gain-Banks-Crawford was ever employed beyond the status of homemaker.

At last, in her original declaration for Pension of a Widow, she revealed details that resolved the mystery behind Henry's first wife, Tilla. In the section of the document that asks for details *"if either widow, or veteran have been previously married, so state and give date of death, or divorce of former spouse"* she claims the following:

> *"Both had been previously married. Former wife of Henry I. Banks died July 12, 1887 – Emma Gain divorced from her first husband, April 3rd, 1888."*

It was the details within these documents that enabled me to finally locate Tilla Robinson-Banks, who was laid to rest at Gypsum Hill Cemetery in Salina, Kansas. A volunteer from the local genealogical society took it upon herself to drive across town to locate the exact plot where Tilla was buried, though she found no gravestone. Of course, I added the action item of ordering a stone for Tilla to my to-do list.

Emma would marry Henry less than a year after Tilla had passed on. Curious.

These pension documents that my cousin had produced were just the evidence I needed to include with my petition for a Government-issued Civil War Union headstone for Henry, so I copied the documents, and included them in the same envelope with the completed official forms I had prepared for the V.A. I was closer than ever to finalizing this matter of family business: the procurement of a headstone for Uncle Henry, originally intended, but not realized by my great-great grandfather David Banks, and his brother, Egbert during their train trip west to Salina, Kansas in 1895.

I sealed the envelope, hustled up the hill to our mailbox, and sped my bulging envelope off to Washington. While walking back to our townhome, I was overcome by the irony that I had just recently completed a request for yet another headstone, but for a different Veteran. My father-in-law had just passed away from the unfortunate symptoms of Alzheimer's disease. Andi was devastated, since her mother had passed away years before, and with both my mother and father long gone, we were fresh out of parents. We had just spent a few days in Houston, where we said our goodbyes to a great man who also served in the United States Armed Forces in the 1950's. I couldn't help but reflect back to my own father's funeral, and I was floored by the realization that nearly a decade had passed since my sisters and I had buried him. When we returned to our home in Austin, Andi and I each dealt with our grief in our own unique ways. Andi spent her day organizing family photos, while I chose to cozy up to my laptop, and complete this chapter.

# *Invaluable References*

My father was in love with history, —not necessarily the facts, figures, and timelines— but the fascinating stories, and the enchanting men and women who lived through those significant adventures of their time. I looked back on the moment that I stood in the backyard of my childhood home, splitting the firewood stack that Dad had never completed. I could almost hear him say, *"Oh, so you want to complete a project, do you? Why don't you see what you can make of this little wooden bible that I've kept hidden in my study for umpteen years? That should keep you busy."*

As you might expect from a Literature Major, my father had an extensive library in his study at our home in Washington State. One of the earliest memories I can recall was leafing through his collection of publications from some of the National Parks that he visited over the years. Some of the books were published long before I was born, yet they were full of wonderful photographs, maps, and renderings that peaked my interest, even as an elementary school-aged kid. I was intrigued to the point of hypnosis by the photographic details revealing the otherworldly landscapes of Craters of the Moon National Monument, and the sprawling bastions of Fort Vancouver. The gory particulars of The Whitman Massacre at Waiilatpu sparked a lifelong sympathy for the plight of the Native American, despite the austere methods chosen by the Cayuse to confront the source of a devastating measles epidemic in this case. Imagine my delight when I found some of these treasures once again online at the National Parks Service website on their Historical Handbook Series page.

In its early days, the National Park Service recognized education as one of the primary objectives of park management. For this reason, the Field Division of Education of the National Park Service was established. Formed in 1929, its principal intent was to employ and educate park guides (then called Ranger-Naturalists). The department also published a number of reports, which were essential in the development of interpretive programs and museum exhibits. As it happened, many of the books were written by some of the most widely recognized authors and historians of the modern era.

This rediscovered trove of crucial literature gave me an idea. I began to reference some of the battlefields that were also featured in Sergeant Major Stephen Fleharty's journals —actual soil where Uncle Henry most certainly marched, fought, and bled for his country. Many of these sites were now National Parks, and with some of the books and brochures being written in the 1940's, and others in the 1960's, I could rely on the decisive accuracy in the detailed accounts, many of which may had otherwise been forgotten, disregarded or become lost in obscurity. I was adrenalized by the discovery of these sources, for they would be of great value to me in creating a more precise commentary, especially as I visited these sites in person.

April was approaching, giving way to Spring in the Central Texas Hill Country, and our brief winter had surrendered to blankets of colorful wildflowers and sunny days with 80° temps. This season had become a welcome respite for me that preceded the inevitable discomfort of unbearable humidity, month-long periods of triple-digits, and staggering utility bills, as a consequence.

Invitations began to fill up my voicemail from my fellow sailors, looking for able-bodied crew for weekend outings on Lake Travis. The morning was cooler, as a thick layer of fog had rushed in to occupy the winding canyons that encircled our community, so I decided to take my mountain bike out for a stretch, and explore some local trails. After covering a single-track trail near our home, I ventured off on an unfamiliar path that dropped me down into a heavy patch of forest. The trail twisted around through the shaded canopy of trees, and led me to the edge of "Bear Creek," where it ran parallel with the water that was rushing with fresh rainfall. Finally, after about 30 minutes of smooth, level topography, the trail ended at the edge of the fast-moving currents that interrupted my steady ride. My route clearly continued on the opposite side, up a steep grade. A Good Samaritan had strategically placed a series of boulders across the currents, which made for an effortless and splash-free crossing.

Once across, I dug in, and cranked hard up the hill where the slick, muddy trail led to a plateau. As I reached the top, I found myself in the midst of a sprawling expanse of black, charred trees. It was the grim reminder of a devastating fire that had occurred just months before, on Labor Day weekend, 2011. I walked my bike at a leisurely pace beneath the beating sun, and clear blue sky among a horde of twisted black limbs rising from the earth, scorched bare. The air still wreaked of smoke and soot, as if the fire still smoldered.

I marveled at this surreal landscape, and couldn't help but compare the evidence of recent devastation to the many photos of Civil War battlefields that I had beheld, and how the forests appeared in the fresh aftermath. As I emerged from the treeline, and began to pedal home, my mind raced with the vast inventory of locations where Uncle Henry had made camp, or exchanged gunfire with the rebels during his experience in the field. Fort Thomas at Gallatin, TN, Lavergne, Lookout Mountain, Resaca, GA, Kennesaw Mountain, New Hope Church, Peachtree Creek; I knew I couldn't visit all of them, but I would do my damndest.

Yes, Spring was here. It wouldn't be long now, before I embarked upon the pilgrimage of a lifetime. I had just over a month to prepare, so I knew I had little time to waste. Of course, the first necessity an explorer needs before venturing out, is a map. I would tap a very reliable resource for imperative waypoints, in order to create the most effective itinerary. My delegated cartographer would be Frederick H. Dyer (2 Jul 1849 - 21 Sep 1917).

In July, 1863 —so the story goes— Dyer ran away from school with a friend at the age of 14, to join the army. At the last minute, his sidekick reluctantly changed his mind about enlisting. Since his friend's aunt had provided guardian consent, he assumed her surname, and enlisted as a minor into Company "C" of the 7th Connecticut Infantry Regiment as a drummer boy. His unit saw action in several conflicts during the war, until he was mustered out with his unit on July 20, 1865.

In 1867, Dyer joined the Grand Army of the Republic, and became very involved with the organization. It was during this time that he began collecting historic accounts of the Civil War, while interacting with other veterans, including General William Tecumseh Sherman, himself. Forty years later, Dyer published an accurate account of the Union Army's exploits in three complete volumes, widely known as *"The Dyer Compendium of the War of the Rebellion,"* first published in 1909.

Fortunately, Dyer did not overlook the exploits of the Illinois Volunteers' 102nd Regiment. His timeline proved to be an extremely beneficial resource, enabling me to draft a thorough itinerary, while paralleling many key locations where Uncle Henry had served. Dyer's reminiscence was not as fresh as Fleharty's journal, but his condensed summaries were easier to reference, contrasting the explicative content in *"Our Regiment."*

Another resource gave me great insight into the gradual establishment of the 102$^{nd}$, and offered more intimate details regarding the events of each Company's formation. At illinoiscivilwar.org, a thoughtful poem preceded the summary, written in 1862 by *Edward Howard Norton Patterson*, who was a close acquaintance of *Edgar Allan Poe*.

> *"Tis midnight in the camp,*
> *The tired soldiers sleep, and dream, perchance*
> *Of home, perchance of conflicts past, and others*
> *Coming on the morrow. Braves, sleep on !*
> *Let the cool night winds soothe your slumbers deep,*
> *That you may rise refreshed. Your country looks*
> *To you, and such as you, to guard her honor*
> *from traitors' foul contaminating touch.*
>
> *Yet, one is vigilant ;*
> *With measured tread he paces on his beat-*
> *The midnight sentinel. The moonbeams play*
> *Upon his burnished bayonet, and its rays*
> *Fall gently on a calm, sweet, upturned face,*
> *That smiles upon the soldier from its frame."*

*"From a Mercer County, Illinois History"*

***Company E.*** --- *On August 7 a meeting was held at Brown's schoolhouse in North Henderson township, at which Dan. M. Sedwick enlisted eighteen men. Thomas Likely, of the same township (now of Norwood), was present and stated that he had enrolled eight men, and proposed to unite with Sedwick, which was done. By the 14th they had eighty-four. On that day the men met at the same place and organized by electing Likely captain, Sedwick, first lieutenant, and T. G. Brown, second lieutenant. The following were the non-commissioned officers appointed: Sample B. Moore, first or orderly sergeant; John Allison, William J. Abdill, Jonathan E. Lafferty, and Albert Bridger, sergeants; Thomas Simpson, Henry M. Carmichael, John Tidball, Lyman Bryant, Allen Dunn, Henry W. Mauck,*

*Robert Godfrey, and John T. Morford, corporals. Some time in the last week of August Lieutenant Sedwick started from Bridger's Corners (now Suez) with thirty-two men, and going through Scott's grove, met Captain Likely one mile south of that place with about the same number, from whence they proceeded in wagons through Galesburg to Knoxville, arriving there in the evening, where the rest of the company joined them.*

With every document, account, journal entry, and reflection that I happened to discover and read, the more familiar I was becoming with the repeated names of those whose roles were key in the movements of the 102$^{nd}$. It reminded me of a little game that I developed years ago, when I was in High School. I wasn't always the most ardent reader of books, truth be told. Yet, in the rare instance that I was assigned a novel to peruse in order to pass a class, I approached it cinematically. I grazed through the first few pages, and developed each character in my mind's eye, before I began to navigate with them, through their experiences. I cast the film first, allowing me to picture each character, which, by assigning them a popular film celebrity's face, mannerisms and voice, made each story easier for me to follow. Without naming names, this made for some very interesting encounters and exchanges that Hollywood would NEVER pair together.

So now, before we begin the first leg of our journey to cast our shadows on some of the same soil where Uncle Henry Ira Banks and the 102$^{nd}$ marched, camped, drilled, foraged, and fought, let's roll the opening title credits, and give each character a proper introduction.

# A Star-studded Cast

### Daniel Butterfield

b:) 31Oct 1831
d:) 17Jul 1901

Daniel Butterfield's choice to enter a military career proved to be a wise one, as he found himself on the "fast track" early in his career. On April 16th, 1861 he joined the Army as a first sergeant in Washington, D.C. Within two weeks he rose to the rank of Colonel in the 12th New York Militia, which became the 12th New York Infantry. By July he commanded an entire brigade and by September he was promoted to Brigadier General!

Joining Major General George B. McClellan's Army of the Potomac for the Peninsula Campaign in the V Corps, he served under Major General Fitz John Porter. Despite wounds received in battle, his acts of valor in the Seven Days Battles, at Gaines' Mill on June 27, 1862 were recognized thirty years later in 1892 with the Medal of Honor. The citation read: *"Seized the colors of the 83rd Pennsylvania Volunteers at a critical moment and, under a galling fire of the enemy, encouraged the depleted ranks to renewed exertion."*

Butterfield is credited with the composition of "Taps", probably the most famous bugle call ever written. He wrote this composition to replace the customary firing of three rifle volleys at the end of burials during battle. "Taps" also replaced Tattoo, the French bugle call to signal "lights out". Butterfield's bugler, Oliver W. Norton of the 83rd Pennsylvania Volunteers was the first to sound the new call. It didn't take long before "Taps" was sounded by buglers throughout the Union regiments, and the Confederate armies adopted it as well.

Butterfield also commanded at the Second Battle of Bull Run and at Antietam, he became division commander, and then V Corps commander for the Battle of Fredericksburg. Once Major General Joseph Hooker replaced Ambrose Burnside as Army of the Potomac commander after his infamous "Mud March", Butterfield became Hooker's chief of staff in January 1863. He was finally promoted to major general in March 1863.

Butterfield is also credited with the introduction of distinctive hat and shoulder patches displayed to identify the unit each soldier belongs to. Most were designed by Butterfield, himself. This practice is still in use by today's Army, and other branches of the service.
Butterfield was wounded by a spent artillery shell fragment at Gettysburg on July 3, 1863, and was later removed as chief of staff on July 14, 1863.

After healing from his wounds at Gettysburg, Daniel Butterfield returned to duty as chief of staff once again for Hooker, who was now commanding two corps in the Army of the Cumberland at Chattanooga, Tennessee. Once these two corps (the XI and XII Corps) were combined to form the XX Corps, Butterfield was assigned to lead the 3rd Division through the first half of Sherman's Atlanta Campaign. Succumbing to illness, he did not complete his service through the war in the field, tending instead to administrative duties at Vicksburg, Mississippi.

Butterfield's father, John Warren Butterfield was co-founder of American Express, and a co-owner of the Overland Stage Company. The "Butterfield Stage" once ran through modern-day Corona, California, not far from where my wife and I once made our home in Temescal Canyon, near Interstate 15 in Riverside County. The station was within walking distance from our front door, and I visited that spot numerous times.

### William McMurtry
b:) 20Feb 1801
d:) 10April 1875

McMurtry was born in Mercer County, Kentucky to James and Elizabeth (Lucas) McMurtry. William married Ruth Champion (1795–1864, also of Mercer County, Kentucky), on November 23, 1826. In 1829, William and his young family moved to Knox County, Illinois along with his father and brother James and his wife. It was here that William McMurtry's home remained until his death. McMurtry was known as a close personal friend of fellow Illinois Democrat Stephen A. Douglas and remained a prominent voice in the state's Democratic party in the years preceding the Civil War.

During the Black Hawk War, McMurtry organized a group of between 70 and 90 men from Knox and Warren counties — which consisted of nearly all the able-bodied men from the area — to form a battalion of mounted rangers with him serving as captain and his brother James serving as sergeant. At the outset of the Civil War, he organized the 102nd Illinois Infantry, which was made up of men from Knox County, and others. William McMurtry's leadership would only last a couple of months, before receiving an honorable discharge due to poor health attributed to his advanced age, and quite possibly due to his "habit of intemperance". His resignation is said to have been forced by both officers and enlisted men of the 102nd. Just the same, while organizing at the Knox County Fairgrounds in Knoxville, IL in the Fall of 1862, the 102nd Regiment recognized their station as "Camp McMurtry".

At home, McMurtry was known as a bright man, despite his modest formal education, he was an avid reader and reportedly a good neighbor. William was a freemason and treasurer of the local Grand Lodge. He and his wife Ruth had five children. William McMurtry died in Henderson, Illinois; a town founded near his farm home after he and his family had settled there. McMurtry became the 11th Lieutenant Governor of Illinois after his service during the Civil War.

**Colonel Franklin C. Smith**
b:) 14Jul 1824
d:) 19Aug 1891

Civil War Union Brevet Brigadier General Smith was commissioned Lieutenant Colonel on September 8, 1862 and was shortly thereafter promoted to Colonel assuming command of the regiment on October 24, 1862. He led the 102nd for the entire duration of the Civil War though he was wounded at Big Shanty, June 15, 1864, during the Atlanta Campaign. For distinguished service and leadership, he was brevetted Brigadier General of the U.S. Volunteers on March 13, 1865. In April 1865, he marched the 102nd into Raleigh, North Carolina where the army remained until the Confederate surrender. A native of New York, he is listed in the 1870 Census at 46, as a lawyer, married to Sarah, with three children living at home.

### John Bell Hood (CSA)
b:) 01Jun 1824
d:) 30Aug 1879

Hood excelled as a brigade and division leader, though he was notoriously uncooperative as a corps commander, and was an unqualified disaster at the head of an army, which he all but destroyed. A Kentucky-born West Pointer (1853), he became associated with Texas while with the 2nd Cavalry.

Resigning his first lieutenant's commission on April 16, 1861, he joined the South. His impressive record includes the following assignments: First Lieutenant, Cavalry (Spring 1861); Colonel, 4th Texas (October 1, 1861); commanding Texas Brigade, Whiting's Division (known as Forces Near Dumfries and in the Potomac District until March and the Valley District in June), Department of Northern Virginia (February 20 - June 1862); Brigadier General, CSA (March 3, 1862); commanding Texas Brigade, Whiting's Division, 2nd Corps, Army of Northern Virginia (June 26 - July 1862); commanding the division, 1st Corps, same army (July-August 30, 1862; September 14, 1862 - February 25, 1863; and May - July 2, 1863); Major General, CSA (October 10, 1862); commanding division in the Department of Virginia and North Carolina (February 25 - April 1, 1863); in the Department of Southern Virginia (April 1 - May 1863); temporarily commanding the corps (September 20, 1863); Lieutenant General, CSA (February 1, 1864); commanding 2nd Corps, Army of Tennessee (February 28 - July 18, 1864); temporary rank of General, CSA, and commanding the army (July 18, 1864 - January 23, 1865); and also commanding Department of Tennessee and Georgia (August 15, 1864 - January 25, 1865).

Hood organized cavalry on the Peninsula and participated at the small action at West Point and saw later action at Seven Pines and Seven Days Battles. He delivered a powerful attack at 2nd Bull Run but was arrested by General Nathan G. Evans after a dispute over some captured ambulances. Allowed to accompany his division while under arrest, he was released by Robert E. Lee on the morning of South Mountain.

After distinguishing himself at Antietam he was promoted to major general and fought at Fredericksburg. Service followed in southeastern Virginia where he led his division at Gettysburg, suffering a crippling wound in his arm.

He resumed command as Longstreet was headed for Georgia and while commanding the corps at Chickamauga he was wounded again, this time in the leg. Recovering in Richmond from the amputation, he received a promotion and was permanently assigned to the Army of Tennessee.

It was at this time that Hood underwent a change. He had a great deal of difficulty coordinating with the other corps commanders during the Atlanta Campaign, especially General Hardee. With the army having fallen back to the outskirts of Atlanta, Hood was appointed a temporary general and replaced Joe Johnston.

In a series of disastrous attacks over the next several days he failed to drive Sherman from the city. After a siege he was forced to evacuate and resorted to attacking Union supply lines to force Sherman northward. Failing in these attempts, he launched a move into middle Tennessee, hoping that a threat to the Ohio Valley might dislodge the enemy from Georgia. After a missed opportunity at Spring Hill, he threw his infantry into a bloody frontal attack at Franklin that decimated them.

Besieging the Union forces in Nashville, he attacked in mid-December 1864 and his army was annihilated. Retreating into the deep South with the fragments of the army he relinquished his command and his temporary commission in January 1865. After the war he settled in New Orleans and became a prosperous merchant until an 1878 financial crisis. He died the next year in a yellow fever epidemic. His memoirs are entitled "Advance and Retreat". (McMurry, Richard M., John Bell Hood and the War for Southern Independence)

**Major General Joseph Hooker**
b:) Nov 13, 1814
d:) Oct 31, 1879

Joseph Hooker was a career United States Army officer, achieving the rank of Major General in the Union Army during the Civil War. Although he served throughout the war, usually with distinction, Hooker is perhaps best remembered for his stunning defeat by Confederate General Robert E. Lee at the Battle of Chancellorsville in 1863.

After graduating from the United States Military Academy in 1837, Hooker served in the Seminole Wars and the Mexican-American War, receiving three brevet promotions. Resigning from the Army in 1853, he pursued farming, land development, and (unsuccessfully) politics in California. After the start of the Civil War he returned to the Army as a brigadier general. He distinguished himself as an aggressive combat commander, leading a division in the Battle of Williamsburg, May 5, 1862, resulting in his promotion to major general.

As a corps commander, he led the initial Union attacks at the Battle of Antietam, in which he was wounded. At the Battle of Fredericksburg, he commanded a "Grand Division" of two corps, and was ordered to conduct numerous futile frontal assaults that resulted in numerous casualties. Throughout this period, he conspired against and openly criticized his army commanders. Following the defeat at Fredericksburg, he was given command of the Army of the Potomac.

Hooker planned an audacious campaign against Robert E. Lee, but he was defeated by the Confederate Army at the Battle of Chancellorsville. Hooker suddenly lacked the nerve to marshal the strength of his larger army against Lee, who boldly divided his army and routed a Union corps with a flank attack by Stonewall Jackson. Hooker began to pursue Lee at the start of the Gettysburg Campaign, but his poor performance at Chancellorsville prompted Abraham Lincoln to relieve him from command just prior to the Battle of Gettysburg.

He returned to combat eventually, leading two corps from the Army of the Potomac to help relieve the besieged Union Army at Chattanooga, Tennessee, achieving an important victory at the Battle of Lookout Mountain during the Chattanooga Campaign. Hooker continued in the Western Theater under the command of William T. Sherman, but left before the end of the Atlanta Campaign when he was bypassed for a promotion to command the Army of the Tennessee.

Hooker became known as "Fighting Joe" following a journalist's clerical error reporting from the Battle of Williamsburg; however, the nickname stuck. His personal reputation was as a hard-drinking ladies' man, and his headquarters was legendary for parties and gambling, although historical evidence discounts any heavy drinking by the general himself.

**George H. "Pap" Thomas**
b:) Jul 13, 1816
d:) Mar 28, 1870

At the outbreak of the Civil War, 19 of the 36 officers in the 2nd U.S. Cavalry resigned, including three of Thomas's superiors—Albert Sidney Johnston, Robert E. Lee, and William J. Hardee. Many Southern-born officers were torn between loyalty to their states and loyalty to their country. Thomas struggled with the decision but opted to remain with the United States. His Northern-born wife probably helped influence his decision. In response, his family turned his picture against the wall, destroyed his letters, and never spoke to him again.

Thomas was promoted in rapid succession to be lieutenant colonel (on April 25, 1861, replacing Robert E. Lee, Confederate) and colonel (May 3, replacing Albert Sidney Johnston, Confederate) in the regular army, and brigadier general of volunteers (August 17).

Commanding the "Center" wing of the newly renamed Army of the Cumberland, Thomas gave an impressive performance at the Battle of Stones River, holding the center of the retreating Union line and once again preventing a victory by Confederate Corps Commander, Braxton Bragg. Thomas was in charge of the most important part of the maneuvering from Decherd to Chattanooga during the Tullahoma Campaign (June 22 – July 3, 1863) and the crossing of the Tennessee River.

At the Battle of Chickamauga on September 19, 1863, now commanding the XIV Corps, he once again held a desperate position against Braxton Bragg's onslaught while the Union line on his right collapsed. Thomas rallied broken and scattered units together on Horseshoe Ridge to prevent a significant Union defeat from becoming a hopeless rout. Future President James Garfield, a field officer for the Army of the Cumberland, visited Thomas during the battle, carrying orders from General William Rosecrans to retreat; when Thomas said he would have to stay behind to ensure the Army's safety, Garfield told Rosecrans that Thomas was "standing like a rock." After the battle he became widely known by the nickname *"The Rock of Chickamauga"*, representing his determination to hold a vital position against strong odds.

In command of the Army of the Cumberland shortly before the Battles for Chattanooga (November 23 – November 25, 1863), Thomas led a stunning Union victory that was highlighted by his troops storming the Confederate line on Missionary Ridge. As the Army of the Cumberland advanced further than ordered, General Grant, on Orchard Knob asked Thomas, "Who ordered the advance?" Thomas replied, "I don't know. I did not."

During Major General William Tecumseh Sherman's advance through Georgia in the spring of 1864, the Army of the Cumberland numbered over 60,000 men, and Thomas's staff did the logistics and engineering for Sherman's entire army group, including developing a novel series of Cumberland pontoons. At the Battle of Peachtree Creek (July 20, 1864), Thomas's defense severely damaged Lt. General John B. Hood's army in its first attempt to break the siege of Atlanta.

When Hood broke away from Atlanta in the autumn of 1864, menaced Sherman's long line of communications, and endeavored to force Sherman to follow him, Sherman abandoned his communications and embarked on the March to the Sea. Thomas stayed behind to fight Hood in the Franklin-Nashville Campaign. Thomas, with a smaller force, raced with Hood to reach Nashville, where he was to receive reinforcements.

At the Battle of Franklin on November 30, 1864, a large part of Thomas's force, under command of Major General John M. Schofield, dealt Hood a strong defeat and held him in check long enough to cover the concentration of Union forces in Nashville. At Nashville, Thomas had to organize his forces, which had been drawn from all parts of the West and which included many young troops and even quartermaster employees. He declined to attack until his army was ready and the ice covering the ground had melted enough for his men to move. The North, including General Grant himself (now general-in-chief of all Union armies), grew impatient at the delay. Major General John A. Logan was sent with an order to replace Thomas, and soon afterwards Grant started a journey west from City Point, Virginia to take command in person.

Thomas attacked on December 15, 1864, in the Battle of Nashville and effectively destroyed Hood's command in two days of fighting. Thomas sent his wife, Frances Lucretia Kellogg Thomas, the following telegram, the only communication surviving of the Thomases' correspondence: *"We have whipped the enemy, taken many prisoners and considerable artillery."*

Thomas was appointed a major general in the regular army, with date of rank of his Nashville victory, and received the Thanks of Congress:

*...to Major-General George H. Thomas and the officers and soldiers under his command for their skill and dauntless courage, by which the rebel army under General Hood was signally defeated and driven from the state of Tennessee.*

### Joseph Eggleston Johnston (CSA)

b:) Feb 3, 1807
d:) Mar 21, 1891

Johnston was a career U.S. Army Officer, serving with distinction in the Mexican-American War and Seminole Wars, and was also one of the most senior General officers in the Confederate States Army during the American Civil War.

He was trained as a Civil Engineer at the U.S. Military Academy. He served in Florida, Texas, and Kansas, and fought with distinction in the Mexican-American War and by 1860 achieved the rank of brigadier general as Quartermaster General of the U.S. Army. When his native state of Virginia seceded from the Union, Johnston resigned his commission, the highest-ranking officer to join the Confederacy. To his dismay, however, he was appointed only the fourth ranking full general in the Confederate Army.

Johnston's effectiveness in the Civil War was undercut by tensions with Confederate President Jefferson Davis, who often criticized him for a lack of aggressiveness, and victory eluded him in most campaigns he personally commanded. However, he was the senior Confederate Commander at the First Battle of Bull Run in 1861. He defended the Confederate capital of Richmond, Virginia, during the 1862 Peninsula Campaign, withdrawing under the pressure of a superior force under Union Major General George B. McClellan. In his only offensive action during the campaign, he suffered a severe wound at the Battle of Seven Pines, after which he was replaced in command by his classmate at West Point, Robert E. Lee. In 1863, in command of the Department of the West, he was criticized for his actions and failures in the Vicksburg Campaign. In 1864, he fought against Union Major General William T. Sherman in the Atlanta Campaign, but was relieved of command after withdrawing from northwest Georgia to the outskirts of the city. In the final days of the war, he was returned to command of the small remaining forces in the Carolinas Campaign and surrendered his armies to Sherman on April 26, 1865. Two of his major opponents, Grant and Sherman, made comments highly respectful of his actions in the war, and they became close friends with Johnston in subsequent years.

Following the end of the war, Johnston was an executive in the railroad and insurance businesses. He served a term in Congress and was Commissioner of Railroads under Grover Cleveland. He died of pneumonia after serving in inclement weather as a pallbearer at the funeral of one who he had befriended later in life; his former adversary, William T. Sherman.

## Captain Thomas Likely

b:) Jan 29, 1823
d:) Jun 1, 1896

Captain Thomas Likely and his wife, Miss Diana Doyle were married in 1844, and both hailed from Huntingdon County, Pennsylvania, where my Enyeart family ancestors flourished at the time. According to an 1860 map of the Suez Township in Mercer County, Illinois, Cynthia Banks and family were close neighbors to Likely's 160 acre farm on Duck Creek. After the war, he was appointed the position of Mercer County Judge, where he served for four years. Captain Likely had resigned early-on, during the period that the regiment was encamped at Gallatin, Tennessee. According to a published document that records the history of Mercer and Henderson County, Likely resigned by reason of "disabilities". Some officers, however could not easily bear the burden that accompanied the duty of sending men into combat, which often resulted in staggering losses. Yet, Likely's decision may as well have been based on a disagreement with leadership, since there was a great deal of personnel shuffling during the encampment at Gallatin. I can only offer speculation, but the fact remains that during this reorganization, the rank of Captain would be passed along to Dan M. Sedwick. During my research, I did manage to locate and purchase an original Provision Return (No. 13) "for 1 day, commencing Sept. 11th 1862" while the regiment was stationed at Camp McMurtry, aka: Knox County Fairgrounds, Knoxville, Illinois. The document was signed by Captain Likely, approving sustenance and rations for the hungry troopers of Company E as follows:

Number of Men: 95
Number of Women: left blank
Number of Rations: 95
Fresh Beef: 95
Pork: left blank
Flour: 95
Corn Meal: left blank
Beans: 95
Rice: 95
Coffee: 95
Sugar: 95
Vinegar: 95
Candles" 95

Soap: 95
Salt: 95
(hand-written) Potatoes: 95

This rare and significant document is now mounted and framed behind museum glass, where it hangs with honor in my study.

### Major Dan M. Sedwick

b:) Jul 31, 1834
d:) Jan 7, 1924

Sedwick came to Mercer County in 1855 and made his home at Bridger's Corners. Aug. 7, 1862, he enlisted in Company E, One Hundred and Second Illinois Volunteer Infantry, and upon the organization of the company he was elected Lieutenant, afterwards Captain, and later brevetted Major by President Lincoln.

Sedwick took part in the battles of Resaca, New Hope Church, Kennesaw, Peach Tree Creek, Atlanta and joined Sherman on his memorable "March to the Sea," and at Hilton Head, S.C., was given command of a regiment on detached duty. He resumed his position with the 102nd at Goldsboro, N.C. marching on to Raleigh, then on to Washington, where he took part in the "Grand Review," and was mustered out June 6, 1865.

After the close of the war he returned to Bridger's Corners where he was in the mercantile business from 1865 to 1870. In 1869 he purchased a local farm, and devoted himself to general farming and stock raising. On Sept. 3, 1857, he was married to Frances A. Bridger, daughter of Henry and Elizabeth Bridger, and they raised six children.

Politically, Sedwick was a Republican, and had been Supervisor of Suez Township for fifteen years; was Chairman of the Board of Supervisors and of the Building Committee during the building of the Mercer County Court House; represented Mercer and Henderson Counties in the House of Representatives in 1865-6, and was Justice of the Peace for several terms. Member of Viola Post, No. 44, G.A.R."

## Sergeant Major Stephen F. Fleharty

b:) 06Sep 1836
d:) 09May 1899

S.F. Fleharty was the designated regimental scribe and spokesman, keeping a copious journal of daily events experienced by the 102nd Illinois Volunteers. His book, "Our Regiment" was published in the same year the Civil War ended, and therefore remains one of the most accurate collections of its kind. Fleharty concluded his book with a comprehensive list of all officers and enlisted men that served in the 102nd Regiment according to their company. Their fates, injuries and other details offer some invaluable insight for historians and genealogists alike.

While serving in Company C, he sent a number of dispatches back to *The Rock Island Daily Argus* newspaper, and later to *The Rock Island Weekly Union*. He called his column *Jottings from Dixie,* and there were fifty-five letters in all. Many of his letters were sent home accompanied by casualty lists.

Aside from the details of battlefield movements, and colorful descriptions of life in camp, Fleharty was often motivated to record more intimate situations that he witnessed while he was enlisted. Fleharty aptly documented the struggles of "the Negro", and their peculiar culture, in order to educate his audience in the north about the very race they were fighting to set free.

Fleharty's writing style was very fluid, sophisticated, but not stuffy. A politically aware dry wit and sense of humor engages the reader throughout his manuscripts. After the war, Fleharty held positions as a newspaper publisher, mail courier, and land speculator. He also sold copies of his book, even receiving praise from William T. Sherman, and the compliment that it had found a place in his personal "War Library". Fleharty never married, and unfortunately contracted Tuberculosis later in life, when he relocated to Tampa, Florida for the warm climate. He later moved to North Carolina where he passed away from the disease in 1899.

### William Thomas Ward

b:)Aug 9, 1808
d:) Oct 12, 1878

William T. Ward was born in Amelia County, Virginia. He attended common schools and then St. Mary's College near Lebanon, Kentucky. Ward studied law and was admitted to the bar, beginning practice in Greensburg, Kentucky.

Ward served in the Mexican-American War as Major of the 4th Kentucky Volunteers from 1847 to 1848. In 1850, Ward served as a member of the Kentucky House of Representatives. He was elected to represent the Kentucky 4th Congressional District to U.S. Congress as a member of the Whig Party, serving in the House of Representatives 32nd Congress (March 4, 1851 to March 3, 1853). He did not stand for renomination in 1852.

With the outbreak of the Civil War, Ward was commissioned as a Brigadier General in the Union Army, serving in that capacity throughout the war. Ward led a brigade in the XX Corps during the early stages of the Atlanta Campaign. After Major General Daniel Butterfield went on leave, Ward commanded the 3rd division, XX Corps for the remainder of the campaign, displaying valiant leadership at the battle of Peachtree Creek. He also led the division through Sherman's March to the Sea and the Carolinas Campaign.

After the war was over, he returned to the private practice of law in Louisville, Kentucky.

Ward died in 1878 and was buried in the Cave Hill Cemetery in Louisville, Kentucky.

## Benjamin Harrison

b:) Aug 20, 1833
d:) Mar 13, 1901

Harrison, a grandson of President William Henry Harrison, was born in North Bend, Ohio, and moved to Indianapolis, Indiana, at age 21, eventually becoming a prominent politician there. During the American Civil War, he served the Union as a brigadier general in the XX Corps of the Army of the Cumberland. After the war, he unsuccessfully ran for the governorship of Indiana but was later elected to the U.S. Senate by the Indiana legislature.

A Republican, he was elected to the presidency in 1888, defeating the Democratic incumbent Grover Cleveland. His administration is remembered most for economic legislation, including the McKinley Tariff and the Sherman Antitrust Act, and for annual federal spending that reached one billion dollars for the first time.

Democrats attacked the "Billion Dollar Congress." They used the issue, along with the growing unpopularity of the high tariff, to defeat the Republicans, in both the 1890 mid-term elections and in Harrison's bid for re-election in 1892. Harrison advocated, although unsuccessfully, federal education funding and legislation to protect voting rights for African Americans. He saw the admittance of six states into the Union.

Defeated by Cleveland in his bid for re-election in 1892, Harrison returned to private life in Indianapolis. He later represented the Republic of Venezuela in an international case against the United Kingdom. In 1900, he traveled to Europe as part of the case and, after a brief stay, returned to Indianapolis. He died the following year from complications from influenza. He is to date the only U.S. President from Indiana and the only one to be the grandson of another President.

Harrison wanted to enlist to participate in the Civil War, but worried about how to support his young family. In 1862, President Abraham Lincoln issued a call for more recruits. While visiting Governor Oliver Morton, Harrison found him distressing over the shortage of men who had responded to the latest call. Harrison told the governor, "If I can be of any service, I will go".

Morton asked Harrison if he could help recruit a regiment, though he would not ask him to serve. Harrison recruited throughout northern Indiana to raise a regiment. Morton offered him the command, but Harrison declined, as he had no military experience. He was commissioned as a Second Lieutenant. In August 1862, when the regiment left Indiana to join the Union Army at Louisville, Kentucky, Harrison was promoted by Morton to the rank of Colonel, and his regiment was commissioned as the 70th Indiana Infantry.

For much of its first two years, the 70th Indiana performed reconnaissance duty and guarded railroads in Kentucky and Tennessee. In 1864, Harrison and his regiment joined William T. Sherman's Atlanta Campaign and moved to the front lines. On January 2, 1864, Harrison was promoted to command the 1st Brigade of the 1st Division of the XX Corps. He commanded the brigade at the Battles of Resaca, Cassville, New Hope Church, Lost Mountain, Kennesaw Mountain, Marietta, Peachtree Creek and Atlanta.

When Sherman's main force began its March to the Sea, Harrison's brigade was transferred to the District of Etowah and participated in the Battle of Nashville. On March 22, 1865, Harrison earned his final promotion, to the rank of Brigadier General. He rode in the Grand Review in Washington, D.C. before mustering out on June 8, 1865.

# Henry's Place in the War

According to William R. Scaife's 1992 publication, "Order of Battle" a comprehensive document listing the order of Federal and Confederate forces engaged in The Campaign For Atlanta, William Tecumseh Sherman commanded 112,819 men as of May 31, 1864. Sherman's forces were divided into three columns. The Army of The Tennessee, commanded by Major General James B. MacPherson, then by John E. "Black Jack" Logan, and later by Major General Oliver O. Howard.

The Army of The Ohio formed the second column, commanded by Major General John M. Scofield, and later by Major General Jacob E. Cox. Finally, The Army of The Cumberland rounded out Sherman's grand Army, commanded by Major General George H. "Pap" Thomas. The Army of The Cumberland was divided by three units: the IV Army Corps, the XIV Army Corps, and the XX Army Corps. The XX Corps was commanded by Major General Joseph Hooker, and later by Brigadier General Alphaeus S. Williams, who was later replaced by Major General Henry W. Slocum.

The XX Army Corps was divided into three divisions, which were subsequently divided into three brigades, each, along with their respective artillery detachments. The third division of the XX Army Corps was commanded by Major General Daniel Butterfield, and later was commanded by Brigadier General William T. Ward. Consequently, Ward would command the First Brigade before his promotion, and replacement as Brigade Leader by Colonel Benjamin Harrison, who would become our 23rd President of the United States. The First Brigade was composed of five regiments, the 79th Ohio, the 70th Indiana, the 129th Illinois, the 105th Illinois, and finally, the 102nd Illinois Volunteers, commanded by Colonel Franklin C. Smith.

In preparation for the Georgia Campaign, the XX Army Corps was divided into three divisions, which were subsequently divided into three brigades, each, along with their respective artillery detachments. The third division of the XX Army Corps was commanded by Major General Daniel Butterfield, and later by Brigadier General William T. Ward. Consequently, Ward would command the First Brigade before his promotion, and eventual replacement by brigade leader, Colonel

Benjamin Harrison. The First Brigade was composed of five regiments, the 79th Ohio, 70th Indiana, 129th Illinois, 105th Illinois, and finally, the 102nd Illinois Volunteers, commanded by Colonel Franklin C. Smith.

The 102nd Regiment was composed of 921 men, who were divided into ten companies, "A" through "K". There is no mention however, of a Company "J". I imagine that the difficulty in discerning the characters "I" and "J" was to be avoided. This stands to reason. Case in point: Henry is listed in certain census and military records as both Henry I. Banks, and Henry J. Banks.

Company E had an estimated roster of 95 men, once they organized and mustered in at Knoxville, Illinois on September 2nd, 1862. Their ranks would be whittled down to about 50 by the morning of May 24th, 1865 as the surviving throng marched down Pennsylvania Avenue before the Grand Review in Washington, following Lee's surrender.

And so, to sum up Henry's place in the war, he was a Private in Company E, 102nd Illinois Volunteer Infantry, First Brigade, Third Division, XX (20th) Corp, Army of the Cumberland, Military Division of the Mississippi, United States Army. Whew! For those of us who respond more favorably to visual aids, an illustrated diagram representing Henry's chain of command is hereby presented.

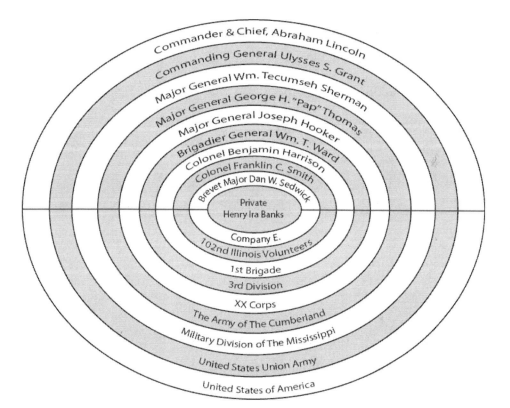

Year 64

July the 27
Before Atlanta
Georgia

Dear Brother with plesure I seat myself here behind bregtworkes to scratch you a few lines to let you know that I am still in the land of the liveing in the midsts of the turers of ware & the battlesfields of our common enemy I have bin in severl battells sence I wrote to you I beleve I had bin in the battell of wadacheo before then I have bin in ... since then I have bin looking very ... diently for a letere from you for a long time but it had bin in vain so far but still I have hope left that there must be one on the road but for all this I felt it my duty to write to you I have had good helth all of the time & stand it as

# Marching in Lock-Step

It was difficult for me to decide in what order to present the movements of Private Henry Ira Banks, Sergeant Major Stephen F. Fleharty, and my own as I began the exercise of following the path that was so generously marked for navigation by both soldiers. As he opened many of his letters, Henry was thoughtful enough to divulge his whereabouts, even calculating the distance between his campsites and towns, rivers, etc. In similar fashion, Fleharty would take the journey a step further and describe the topography, terrain, landmarks and hazards. These navigational aids would tempt me to no end, often keeping me awake at night, imagining how the landscape appeared, and how their adventure affected the two troopers, physically, mentally, emotionally.

For an Illinois farm boy, and a small town printer, their enlistment was an enormous gamble, and somehow, —though we were separated by generations— I wanted to be dealt in. After many hours of exposure to the letters and journal entries describing the march that covered 11 states, and several hundred miles, I concluded that a chronological order of observation would be easiest for the observer to follow. Henry's letters are written posthaste, with events described in fresh recollection, but with a shortage of paper, ink and leisure time, the details are sparsely presented in most cases, yet his inquiries give some insight into family affairs in Illinois, Iowa and New York. Fleharty's journal entries were obviously pored over, and thoughtfully edited prior to the publishing of his book, "Our Regiment" in 1865.

Once I perused both collections and compared the authors' perspectives, I could hardly wait to pack my own gear in preparation to follow their path. To document the journey, I decided to transcribe my notes from the field last, which would follow Henry's letters, allowing Fleharty's colorful and detailed commentary to lead and properly establish the locations, scenes and mood of each day.

And so, the journey begins.

## The Schoolhouse Gathering

On August 7, 1862 a meeting was held at Brown's schoolhouse in North Henderson township, (present day Norwood, IL) at which Dan M. Sedwick enlisted eighteen men. Thomas Likely, of the same township, was present and stated that he had enrolled eight men, and proposed to unite with Sedwick, which was done. By the 14th they had eighty-four. On that day the men met at the same place and organized by electing Likely captain, Sedwick, first lieutenant, and T. G. Brown, second lieutenant. Some time in the last week of August, Lieutenant Sedwick started from Bridger's Corners (now Suez) with thirty-two men, and going through Scott's Grove, met Captain Likely one mile south of that place with about the same number, from whence they proceeded in wagons through Galesburg to Knoxville, arriving there in the evening, where the rest of the company joined them.

## Camp McMurtry, aka: The Knox County Fairgrounds

Established in 1851, the 52-acre fairgrounds proved to be the perfect place to organize a Union Army regiment. Here, young farmers, laborers and school chums would don their blue uniforms, and for the first time, recognize their new identity, duty and cause which they were to defend. This activity reminded me of the excitement I felt as a twelve-year-old, stepping through the front door of the gear shack next to our neighborhood ballpark to suit up for the first time in my Little League uniform. The team had previously drilled and practiced a few times, the coaches had assigned us our respectful positions, and a couple of would-be teammates had even bowed out. Jersey number 17 seemed to fit me the best, and remains my lucky number to this day. I earned my place on the team, proud to wear the mighty orange and white of the Mountlake Terrace Cougars. I was initiated. I belonged to an elite force, and I couldn't wait to step onto the mound and begin launching fastballs.

The atmosphere must have been electric on the fairgrounds as the drills commenced, with lines and columns forming, and moving in tighter, and tighter choreography, orchestrated in sync with each sharply barked command. The men of the 102nd must have drilled and

trained hard during those crisp October days spent at the Knox County
Fairgrounds, for it is widely rumored that the presence of the troops
caused such damage to the huge facility, that the fair was cancelled for
the year of 1862. Though none of Henry's discovered letters were
written during his time at his first encampment with the 102nd, I deemed
it important enough to establish it as a launching point into Henry's
long march.

Sergeant Major Stephen F. Fleharty described the general mood
that prevailed at Knoxville.

*And those were days of turmoil. All were patriotic, of
course; but the patriotism of many was of such a character that
it led them to believe they could best serve their country in some
exalted position. Hence there was much wire-pulling, and many
who had expected to wear what the boys called "pumpkin rind,"
or compelled to march by the side of those who were lured into
the service by pure patriotism, and $13 a month, with
allowances.*

*The wonder with us was, that amid such contention, so
many good and faithful men received commissions. There were
some who afterwards proved failures. I need not mention their
names here. They are fixed in the minds of the men of the
Regiment, indelibly.*

*I will not, by any personal allusions, resurrect the
bitter feelings of jealousy that existed for a time at Knoxville;
doubtless the experience of the 102nd was the experience of all
regiments, in this respect. Suffice it to say that the extreme
desire for official preferment had a very demoralizing tendency.
Men of battle or no capacity aspired to the highest positions in
the regiment. An incident illustrating this recklessly ambitious
spirit was subsequently related to me as having occurred when
the regiment was at Knoxville.*

*One of the newly promoted captains was but half
satisfied with his responsible position, and learning that the
adjutancy was vacant, a bright idea struck him. Forthwith he
went to wire-pulling, and approaching a lieutenant, explained to
him that he desired to be promoted to adjutant of the regiment,*

*and asked for his support! The regiment was mustered into
service on September 2, 1862 –921 strong. So at least says the
morning report of that date.*

*The soldiers were soon all clothed in the army blue,
and were fast becoming initiated into the mysteries of their
profession. With surprising dignity they paced to and fro when
on duty with the old mud-filled, broken locked muskets in their
hands! All were anxious to leave Knoxville; willing to go
anywhere; willing to do anything rather than remain imprisoned
there. At length the order came, and on 22 September, a bright
and beautiful day, the right wing was marched on board a train
of cars, and there receiving the loving adieus of dear friends,
they glided away from their homes and hearthstones – away to a
new encampment at Peoria. The left wing was transferred to the
new rendezvous on the following day.*

## Encampment at Frankfort

After enlisting, gearing up, and fitting out for the fight of their
lives, Henry and the 102nd began their adventure with some quickly-
paced marches during the day, and a brief pause each night as they
would set up camp in different locations, only to strike them again each
morning.

From Louisville, Kentucky the XX Corps marched fifteen
miles on October 3rd, 1862, camped at Shelbyville, and moved again at
a rapid trot to Frankfort, Kentucky. They would camp and drill here in
extreme exposure until the 17th of October, 1862, when they finally
received their tents. Once they were pitched, they would strike camp
the following day, and so it went for Henry and Company throughout
those early days of service.

Sergeant Major Stephen F. Fleharty enlightens us from pages
in his journal, leading with his impression of the fair belles of
Shelbyville, Kentucky.

*Monday evening, October 6th, the forward trot was
resumed. We were ordered to proceed two miles east of
Shelbyville and encamp for the night,—and went almost "on*

*the double quick." There were many pretty and patriotic young*
*ladies in the beautiful village of Shelbyville, but we could not*
*halt to talk with the fair creatures. There is in our minds at*
*this time a dim recollection of a panoramic scene like this: A*
*lovely collection of houses, crowded awnings; waving flags;*
*wavy tresses, blue eyes, pearly teeth and rosy cheeks, and that*
*was all they would let us see of Shelbyville.*

*Wednesday morning, the 8th, we continued on towards*
*Frankfort. Soon there were rumors of fighting in advance, and*
*presently an order came to give way to the right and left, and*
*permit a body of cavalry to pass.*

*There was a dense cloud of dust in the rear, which*
*increased and enveloped everything as the horsemen passed*
*by. Late in the evening we entered a narrow defile where the*
*dust in the road was deep, and light as flour. At that moment a*
*battery was ordered up from the rear, and it came thundering*
*by—the horses in a sweeping trot, raising a cloud of dust that*
*filled the atmosphere from hill-top to hill-top and veiled the*
*face of the rising moon. The terrible machinery of war seemed*
*about to be let loose. At length the column filed off into a*
*plowed field; we slept a couple of hours, were aroused by the*
*unwelcome notes of the bugle sounding "forward" and were*
*quickly on the road again. Continuing down the narrow pass*
*we debouched at length near the city of Frankfort. The rebels*
*had attempted to burn the bridge, but our cavalry was too*
*quick for them.*

*As we marched over the bridge and into the city, the*
*moon shone brightly and all things were hushed in deep*
*repose. There was little, save the marching columns, to*
*indicate the existence of war. The faithful cavalry boys were*
*resting at the roadside near the bridge. Some sleeping on their*
*horses—some on the ground. We filed through the quiet*
*streets, then up, up, up a hill that seemed as if it would reach*
*the sky—found a comparatively level surface, formed in the*
*line of battle, stacked arms and slept, the sweet sleep that is*
*seldom enjoyed, save by weary soldiers.*

*At daylight the right wing of the regiment was ordered*
*to a new position in support of a masked battery. It will be*

*recollected that here, on the slope of a hill that made an angle of at least forty-five degrees with the plane of the horizon, Acting Adjutant Ogden endeavored to have battalion drill. Among other lessons he attempted "firing by file" and "by platoon." The men were quite awkward, as they had never been taught these things. Ogden became impatient, declared we ought to have understood these exercises, thought we "never would learn anything," and marched us in a short time to camp. We changed camp twice while at Frankfort.*

*During the last week of our stay there the regiment was encamped two miles east of the city. The men were supplied with bell tents-which were but a slight improvement upon the cedar houses they had learned to construct. In the bell tents we were crowded so closely, that comfortable sleeping was out of the question-to escape being "overlaid" was as much as could be hoped for under such circumstances. The practice of "standing at arms" was observed, for a time, at Frankfort. This ceremony consisted in forming a line of battle an hour or two before daylight, and remaining in line until sunrise,-or so at least it was ordered, but the letter of the law was not obeyed and the troops were usually dismissed at dawn of day. The design was a good one-namely, to guard against surprise. But the men were aroused at an earlier hour than was necessary; - the mornings were very cold, and coming out of their warm beds they stood shivering as with an ague. Many became sick in consequence of the exposure, and the obnoxious practice was abandoned.*

It was here at Frankfort that Henry wrote his first letter home to his Mother, Cynthia Irish-Banks. Throughout the letter, he addressed her in an Olde English manner, apparently to pay respect to their Quaker heritage. ("I received thy letter" and "hope the (thee) will succeed in finding help" etc.)

*Camp near Frankford ken  Oct 18th 1862*

*Dear Mother (Cynthia Banks)*
*I received thy letter yesterday I was regoist (rejoiced) to get a letter from home for the first time I offand (often) allmost giveup getting one I am sory Wm is sick (Wm. N. Banks,*

*Henry's younger brother) he is so grate hand to work it will go hard with him  still I am in hopes he will get well  I exspect the boys (Henry's other brothers) are bisy making molass and gathering corn I would like to be their to help rather than be here exsposed to the nite air and but a littell to eat  I am in hopes we will now do better  we received our tents yesterday before that we have lade out in the open air uprate (upright) meny are sick  still we have bin blest by not having eny rain  there has not bin but too rains and them small wones (ones)  they say that there has not bin but a littell rain sens July  I exspect the has received my last letter that I rote th 14 I beleav it was  we are encamped in the same plase yet how long we are goin to stay I can ot tell  we may stay a month and maby not  to days camp life is a shifting life I like it very well iff I could eat entirely well  I have had the diare (diarrhea) more or less ever sens I have bin in this camp  this morning when I awoke my hed felt very bad it felt as iff it had bin used for a mall (maul)  I was sory to hear of the deth of Henry B Wanzers wife. (former neighbors in Fairfield, CT)  he will shurely be fonely glad to hear that gran mother is still smart  the spoke about working hard  the must be carful and not over do  I hope the will succeed in getting some help (on the Illinois family farm) we have a battery to support here of to guns onell (only) I hav  sean nor hird aney thing of the rebels nether  do I beleav we ever will  we take priseners ocasionely  they say that brags (General Braxton Bragg, C.S.A.) armey torge (toward) to cumber land gap I think when he gets their he will meat something  we haf to get up every morning at the fireing of the canon whitch is at fore (4am) and stand in line of battle with our guns until ? ? unless sick. I told them I was sick and got red (rid) of the job I had  rather be reported on the sick list than stand there  it is a tiresome job spesely for one that is a little sick and weak  tell the some of the boys to write and lett me know how there hogs look and how doing  I hear that they are still ?? with the ?? yet and there corn turns out and all sutsh things  I am glad to heare of eny thing from home  I will now close be causus (cautious?) and of good shear  give my best respects to all I remain as ever thy Sone (son) H I Banks*

*write sone (soon)*

*Directions*
*Con E 102 reg*
*Ills vol*
*Care of Cap Likely*
*By the way of Louis vill*


☆ ☆ ☆


My visit to Frankfort, Kentucky was deliberately included in my itinerary, however, it would be necessary to pass through on my way home to Texas from my travels on the East Coast. In keeping the entries of my journal in chronological order, details of my visit to Frankfort will unfold toward the end of this chapter. Meanwhile...

## *Gallatin, Tennessee & Fort Thomas*

Henry had arrived at Gallatin with his unit on November 26th, 1862, according to Stephen Fleharty's book, "Our Regiment." This was about a month after his letter to Cynthia was written. Henry and his unit would remain until May, in an environment described by Fleharty as having a "frightful mortality rate," due to disease, and severe weather. Among the suffering, Henry was apparently no exception.

> *On the morning of the 25th of Nov. we resumed the march southward in the direction of Gallatin. After marching a few hours, and while passing through a deep valley, loud cheers were borne to our ears from the head of the column. We had found the "Tennessee Line."*

> *At a late hour that evening, when expecting every moment to be halted for the night, the column commenced descending a narrow valley —down, down, down; deeper and darker, and only room enough at the bottom for the road! Where would an encampment be found? The question was soon answered. A halt was ordered. The men stacked arms. The wagon trail halted in the road. A fence on a hillside near by, afforded fuel. Owing to the lateness of the hour and the inequalities of the ground we were unable to pitch our tents,*

*and slept in Indian style by the brightly blazing camp fires.*

*We continued on at an early hour the next morning and passed through what appeared to be the nucleus of a town. The only thing we saw there worth commenting upon, was a satirical representation of Bragg and Buell crudely charcoaled on the door of a blacksmith shop,— one smoking a pipe, the other a cigar, and apparently chatting in a jovial, hail-fellow-well-met style. It was thought that the soldiers of both armies could appreciate the caricatures. The town or neighborhood was called Rock House Valley.*

*We reached Gallatin in the evening—Nov. 26th—little thinking then that we would remain there six long months. But such was to be our destiny.*

*Gallatin is a pleasant village of about two thousand inhabitants; has some neat residences, and the people had exhibited taste and refinement in decorating their grounds and ornamenting their buildings. The pretty groves of evergreens in which the neatly painted white cottages were cozily nestled, presented a pleasant picture during those cold December days.*

*The weather became excessively cold a few days after our arrival. Considerable snow fell. Rude chimneys were hastily constructed in our tents, but with all his labor, the soldier was only comfortable when snugly stowed away in his bed. When the weather became more moderate, the brigade commenced work on Fort Thomas. Finally the 102d was ordered to finish the fort and garrison it until further orders.*

*While in our first camp at Gallatin an installment of luxuries from home was received by several companies of the regiment. Cans of preserves, piles of cakes, green apples, dried apples, cheese and choice butter! What a princely bill of fare for soldiers! Many were the delighted recipients of warm mittens, gloves, stockings, and a host of minor articles, such as pins, needles, thread, ink, pens, writing paper and postage stamps. The lucky ones liberally shared their luxuries with those who unfortunately received none. For many days there was a heavy discount on "fat pork and hard crackers." After a bountiful meal of the good things that had been dispatched it was common for the men to gather about their camp-fires and smoke their fragrant cigars with all the gravity becoming gentlemen of leisure.*

*The articles were contributed by friends at home. The soldiers were much indebted to Captain J. A. Jordan for his zeal and perseverance in taking charge of the goods, shipping them to their destination and delivering them in person to the men.*

Note: This is most likely the period when Henry was in the process of carving his little wooden bible. The date carved on the spine was recorded as "Dc 6 1862".

*About the first of December the command of the Post at Gallatin was given to Brigadier General E. A. Paine. General Dumont, our division commander, had resigned, and all the troops at the Post were ordered to report to General Paine. The General had made a speech to us shortly after our arrival. He referred to the anomalous position of the amateur soldier;—characterized the strict discipline necessary to the proper discharge of the soldier's duties as repulsive to the feelings of Americans, yet urged its absolute necessity, and asked us to preserve untarnished the brilliant name Illinois had already won in the annals of the war. He was followed by General Ward, who is a very fluent speaker. He paid a glowing tribute to Illinois soldiers, and his speech of course was well-received.*

*Our brigade was ordered into winter quarters about the 10th of December. The 70th Indiana Regiment camped near the race-course, northeast of the town—a detachment from that regiment was stationed at Sandersville.*

*The 105th Illinois Regiment went into camp about a half mile east of town, and the 79th Ohio Regiment camped about the same distance north.*

*The 102nd went into winter quarters at Fort Thomas on the 12th of December. Companies I, K, and G were detailed the following day as Provost Guards, and were assigned comfortable quarters in houses around the Public Square. Co.*

*C was sent to Station Creek—three miles south of town—to guard a railroad bridge, and was there soon established in good quarters. The company had a splendid position,—the men led a free and easy life; foraging extensively and consequently living like princes. The companies that remained at Fort Thomas constructed underground chimneys, or fire-places in their tents, and thus all were prepared for inclement weather. Thus divided, the regiment passed the gloomiest period of its term of service.*

*During the dark days of our sojourn in Gallatin, the mortality on account of disease was absolutely frightful. Daily, almost hourly, the sound of the muffled drum and the plaintive dirge fell upon our ears.*

*In addition to all this, the weather was for a long time very inclement. Cold rains were frequent, and occasionally snow fell.*

*The only class of people that seemed contented amid so much misery was the colored community. They enjoyed their usual festivities, cotillion parties, etc. My mind reverts to one or two sable lasses who were accustomed to dance on the pavement with every manifestation of ecstatic delight when the martial bands would play, on their return from the burial of a soldier. A funeral was evidently a treat to these miserable creatures.*

*At the opening of Spring the regiment had dwindled away from nine-hundred and twenty-one to a small fraction over seven-hundred men. But a brighter day was at hand. The regiment had passed through the ordeal of purification. Much of the useless material, rank and file, had been thrown off as an effete encumbrance.*

*Lieutenant Colonel Smith commenced the work of introducing some ideas of discipline into the minds of the men. He conducted battalion drill every day and ordered company and squad drill. Harmony was in a measure secured by the officers. A strong prejudice existed against the Colonel, but the soldiers were treated by him as friends and as fellow citizens—temporarily subservient to the military powers. He thus won their confidence and in a measure overcame their prejudice. Under his command the highest possible degree of personal liberty, consistent with the good of service, was enjoyed by the men.*

*The brigade was transferred from Gallatin to LaVergne by railroad on the first day of June, 1863. From that place the 102nd marched on the 2d to Stewart's Creek. The regiment was there divided. Co.'s E, K and G camped near the railroad bridge across Stewart's Creek, and were under the immediate command of Lieutenant Colonel Mannon. The intermediate time was occupied in drilling, visiting our friends at the front—visiting the Murfreesboro battle-ground, and picking blackberries—varying the routine of exercises by an occasional scout.*

Henry's brother, Egbert Banks was at home in North Henderson, IL apparently tending the farm with his younger brothers, William, George, and John James. Egbert would not remain for long, for like his older brother, Henry, he too would answer the call to arms, and fall in with the 17th Corps, 11th Iowa Regiment, Company A, despite Henry's expressed misgivings about soldiering. The two brothers exchanged correspondence often during the war, and set out upon occasion to find each other during their service. They were eventually united in the field on one occasion when both of their companies gathered at Richmond, Virginia.

*Gallatan Tennessee  Dec 22th, 1862*

*Dear Brother (Egbert Banks)*

*I resived your letter last weak with pesure  glad to hear that you wer all well  I am getting better slowly  I had a letter from  mother last weak they wer well  She wrote that she was no going east on the account of it costing more than she expected  she sed she was going back home and take another start  I rote to her and directed it home  she sed she wold be home by the time my letter got there so I directed it home  write and let me know the particulars about it  I suppose you have got dun picking corn by this time  we are going to make our winter Quarters here  we do pickitt duty and garding  that is all we are worth we are in camp close to the brest works that commands the town I think of no particular nuse at present we have not had no fiting yet to do & another thing I don't belive we ever will there is more than half of our men sick hardly enoff to stand guard Will Torbart is beter but stil keps weak has the rumitis(m?) Will Stuard has bin complaining but getting better James Lee has bin sick but is getting better he looks bad Harve Lafferty keeps strong and ruged as a bare the wether is fine here & dry we are gont to have bred befor long There is an oven making I am tired of the darned crackers and sowbelly we now draw flower but have nothing to coock it in we get nofe to eat if we had something to coock it in that is the gratest difficulty here, camp life is a hard life take it all in all but I am goin to try to stick it threw long or short I hope it will be the latter I send my best respect to you all I remain as ever your Brother*

*H I Banks*

*Tennessee*

*To E Banks*

In his letter to Egbert, Henry had mentioned Harve Lafferty, whom I eventually identified as James Harvey Lafferty, also hailing from the Suez township in Mercer County, Illinois. His obituary from *The Alexis Argus*, dated June 23, 1921 states that members of the 102nd had attended his funeral as honorary pallbearers. The paper also mentioned that at that time, there were only nine known survivors of the regiment.

Even this early in the war, obvious traces of melancholia are evident throughout the body of Henry's letter to his mother, Cynthia Irish Banks, written just three months after the date that he carved onto his wooden bible, "Dc 6 1862". Henry apparently tended to a pick and shovel, once Winter eased into Spring, and quite possibly participated in structural improvements on Fort Thomas.

Gallatin, Tennessee
Mar the 27 1863

Dear Mother

I received thy very welcome lettuer to day I was very glad to hear from thee & the wrest of my friends & brothers Sory to hear that Willis (brother) was not well I my self have the hardest cold that I ever had in my life & a sore throat with it I was so hoars at first that I could not hardly speak above a whisper but I feal very smart otherwise. I have had a little cold all winter this is a hard plase to gett wred of a cold one is exposed so much in being up nites on guard wrain or shine heat or cold and then make his bed on the hard ground or in the open are (air) every fellow it seams has to look out for him self hear in the army I got a letur from Lyda Jane (sister in Iowa) last weak they wer then all well I have not hird from the boys (brothers in Iowa) in some time they were then all well when they saw uncle Jonathan Dorland & family I wod to God that I could have bin their to enjoy time with them and the wrest of my dear friends that I soften (so often) think of down hear in Tennessee in the land of blood shed and vengence I would to God that this war woud soon come to a finell close so that this nation could live once more in peas & enjoy the cumforts of life but the  prospects that is now before us looks dull in my eyes Still I live in hopes If I dident I woud dy in dispair I must now quit writing for I am cauld out in fatigue duty to dig out treas and stumps in our camp there is a detale of a bout 100 men made every day we haf to dig them up one thousand yards from the fort I think we have a summers job of it well I must go write away This evening I set down to finish scribeling theas treas are dug up so the wrebels cant have a chance to dog behind them We are under a different Curnell a Jenneral than we have bin our curnells name is Smith and Jenneral Sweat (Sweet) he has ordered the fort to be made stronger & all theas treas to be dugg out the prospect is we will stay hear all sumer to hold this town and fourt drill and stand guard this town is on the Louisvill & Nashvill RR & I have come to the conclusion to be wresind (resigned) to my lot to stay until the ware comes to a close for I see no way in getting out afit (of it) unless you are nearly ded I theank of no *more nuse (news) this time  write afften give my love to all inquiring friends  I wremain as ever thy Son*

*Henry I. Banks*

I was instantly amused by Henry's misspelling pattern, and his creative method of word-smithing by way of phonetic pronunciation, e.g. "theas treas" = "these trees." All amusement aside, I found his soulful and introspective opinions inspiring, especially those concerning the futility of war.

This letter and many more, were found by Mary Emma Allen in a collection of papers which belonged to her grandmother, Ella Banks-Place. Mrs. Place was the daughter of Henry's older brother, Willis H. Banks. (b: 16Aug 1829 – d: 07Mar 1881). Cynthia Banks had forwarded this letter from Henry to his older brother, Willis with much concern, which is clearly apparent in her introduction. With her sentences still seasoned with purposeful Quaker pronouns, she wrote:

*I have got another letter from Henry Ira. I feel much discouraged about him Somehow I all the time thought he had gone only for 9 mo. And now he says he had made up his mind to try to stand it till the war was over  oh dear when will that be  goodness alone knows  I will send this letter with this and will give thee directions so thee can write to him  I suppose a letter does him a great deal of good*

*Henry I. Banks*
*Company E 102 Regiment Ill. Volunteers*
*By the way of Louisville, Tennessee*
*Care of Captain Likely*

Though Captain Thomas Likely saw to the diligent delivery of Henry's mail, I learned that he would resign his position indefinitely within the next month. He was not alone. Many other officers resigned while posted at Gallatin. I was encouraged, and honored that Henry had survived the ordeals at Gallatin, and continued on with the remaining throng that was the 102nd, to stand against the Confederate threat. Henry and Company E would need that hardened bark, as they would be called upon, over and over again to defend work parties, to recon blind across fog-laden fields, and to put their lives at risk for the benefit of their regiment. There must have been something special about the team that composed Company E in particular, for the examples of their gallantry are numerous throughout Fleharty's journal.

Tapping into the published 128 volumes of the "Official Records of the Union and Confederate Armies" there are a few noteworthy references to Fort Thomas and events that occurred there during the war. For instance, the following represents a site survey that was composed in 1865. The corresponding report offers a comprehensive description of Fort Thomas, its design and proximity to the railroad depot.

> *Union Correspondence, Orders, And Returns Relating To Operations In Kentucky, Southwestern Virginia, Tennessee, Northern And Central Georgia, Mississippi, Alabama, And West Florida, From March 16 To June 30, 1865.*

> *GALLATIN is twenty-eight miles from Nashville, on the Louisville road. Near the depot stands Fort Thomas, a star redoubt, with six salients built upon a slight elevation. But a short distance beyond is a higher crest, from which the fort is not defiladed. An interior bomb-proof block-house would have made this work quite strong. It is now capable of good defense. Its parapet, however, between five and six feet thick, is rather too slight as against artillery. The ditch is deep and a good obstacle; the scarp and counterscarp are revetted with sods, and the parapet is preserved in the same manner; logs and rails form the breast-height revetment. In each salient is a platform and three embrasures to allow the guns to fire in three directions. These embrasures are not deep, made of logs, and are entirely too open at the throat. The command of the fort is high and the terre-plein is from eight to nine feet below the interior crest. The enclosed space is about equivalent to a square of 200 feet sides. Within the fort is a magazine in fair condition and covered with earth from three to four feet thick. There are also two water-tanks. At the entranceway is a draw bridge which is covered by a redan-shaped traverse. The fort is*

*kept in very good order by the First Ohio Battery, who garrison it. Their barracks are near, between the work and the railroad. Fort Thomas will doubtless be held and there will be no expenditures of any amount connected with its preservation.*

An official report from Colonel Benjamin Sweet describes a rare encounter with the Confederate Army during the 102nd's occupation of Fort Thomas. Sweet's glowing report describing the actions of a heroic locomotive engineer illustrates the significant role that the railroad played in war efforts, whether for troop transport, or the logistics of moving supplies and provisions.

*APRIL 27, 1863.--Skirmish at Negro Head Cut, near Woodburn, Ky.*

*No. 3.--Report of Colonel Benjamin J. Sweet, Twenty-first Wisconsin Infantry.*

*FORT THOMAS, Gallatin, Tenn., April 28, 1863.*

*CAPTAIN: In obedience to orders from your headquarters, yesterday morning, April 27, 1863, I took from my command 150 men, of the One hundred and second Illinois Volunteers, Colonel Smith, and placed them on the 9.30 a.m. up-passenger train, engine No. 4, Frank Bassett engineer, on the Louisville and Nashville Railroad, with instructions from you to repel any attack which might be made on the train, save its passengers, and prevent damage to the railroad. On the tram was also a guard of 25 men from Company H, One hundred and eleventh Ohio Volunteers, under First Lieutenant Dowling, of same company, stationed at Bowling Green, Ky. The train left the depot at Gallatin about 10 a.m.*

*Arriving at Franklin, Ky., information gathered there indicating the belief that an attempt might be made near that place to tear up the track before the evening down-train should arrive, Lieutenant Conger, Company C, One hundred and second Illinois Volunteers, an intelligent officer, was left there with 50 men, with instructions to save the track, and, if attacked, to make his fight in the town, using the houses near the depot as a shelter, if necessary. Leaving Franklin at about 11.30, when running through Negro Head Cut, between Franklin and Woodburn, distant from Franklin 3, from Woodburn 2 miles, where a train was attacked and burned some weeks ago, the cool, watchful engineer, Frank Bassett, saw ahead on the track that one end of a rail on the east side had been turned out some 4 inches, to run the train off, and though running at ordinary speed, and fired at again and again from behind trees not more than 4 rods distant, stood firmly at his post, keeping the train under control, and bringing it to a halt when the fore wheels of the engine were 10 feet from the end of the broken track.*

    *On the right of the railroad, up and down, nearly, perhaps more than a mile, is a thick wood, crowding close on to the road, the trees of which, at a distance of about 4 or 5 rods along the train, made a cover for the enemy, from which, while the train was yet in motion, he fired indiscriminately, upon the ladies' car in the rear as well as upon all the other passenger cars of the train. Though much crowded in the cars, our men at once, while the train was moving, returned the fire through the car windows with coolness and deadly aim. Then, as the train halted, fell out rapidly on the side opposite the enemy, and, from under cover of the railroad grade, loaded and fired over the track and under the cars. This being what the enemy did not bargain for, he broke and fled.*

    *Finding that the train guard, under Lieutenant Dowling, Company II, One hundred and eleventh Ohio Volunteers, had most experience and drill as skirmishers, I deployed it, under his command, and, supporting him with Company C, One hundred and second Illinois Volunteers, Lieutenant Shaw, pursued the flying train-robbers rapidly through the dense wood, which extends some 100 rods from the railroad, hunting them from cover. They mounted their horses, which had been left well in their rear, under the protection of a crest, and escaped, except those killed or badly wounded. Followed some 2 miles with skirmishers, and scoured the wood and country with ready-made scouts mounted upon 6 captured horses. I recalled skirmishers and scouts and their supports, having meanwhile broken the wire.*

*Telegraphed Lieutenant Conger, at Franklin, General Judah, at Bowling Green, and you at Gallatin.*

*The track being repaired, our own wounded and those of the enemy then found being placed in the cars, took the train again until meeting the down-passenger train from Louisville, 3 miles south of Bowling Green; changed cars, and returned to this post, taking on the command of Lieutenant Conger at Franklin, the object of the expedition having been accomplished. Officers and men all showed good fighting qualities; and my thanks are due to Colonel Smith and his command, Lieutenant Dowling, Company H, One hundred and eleventh Ohio Volunteers, and his command, from Bowling Green, as well as to Lieutenant [A. H.] Trego, One hundred and second Illinois Volunteers, acting adjutant to me, and Lieutenant Hall, Thirteenth Indiana Battery, for their courage and resolution.*

*The passengers on the train behaved well, keeping quiet till the fight was over.*

*This attack was made by 52 men, detailed from the brigade of the rebel General Wharton, or Horton, to avenge the capture of the rebel trains at McMinnville, and was led by Captain Gordon, accompanied by Captain Jones, of Morgan's command, who selected the place of attack. The party crossed Cumberland River, near Hartsville, on the night of April 25. Arrived near the place of attack about daylight, April 27.*

*Our loss is 5 men of the One hundred and second Illinois wounded, 2 mortally, whose names will be found below.(\*) The rebel loss is known to be 4 killed, who have been found and buried, and 4 wounded; 6 horses and their equipments captured, which were sent under charge of Lieutenant Dowling to Bowling Green.*

*All of which is respectfully submitted.*

*I have the honor to be, yours, to command,*
*B. J. SWEET, Colonel Twenty-first Regt. Wisconsin Vols., Comdg. Fort Thomas.*

One other letter from Henry had been bundled in with others, and had somehow become partially shredded, most likely by rodents. It is however presented here in the best interpretation that I can offer. I won't attempt to decipher the missing portions of dialogue. Instead, I will leave this assignment to you, the reader. The letter's origin and date was decipherable, at least. It has considerable significance, for it records the collective celebration of the regiment as they crossed over into the land of Dixie, which I found to be very inspiring.

*Galiton, in camp Nov 2 (1862) Tennessee*

*Dear Brother I received your lett the 25 last Munday with grate plesure____when we wer in line for ____martch*

*We left scots vill the 25 for Gallitin we are now in the land dixsy as we cawl it we left scots vill at 10 martch 20 miles the first day martch till in the nite then lade down on __ground__side of the ____a valley with out____the martch & a ____er put on the martch____martch 15 miles got to____galliton at 4 in the eve___t in camp west of the town on nise ground the___0 days martch we crossed the line between Kentucky & Tennessee at 2 oclock the solgers cheared as they passt the line the first days martch we ___threw some ruff cuntrey rockey all timber and good to the last day the cuntry began to gett better more farm___this is very nise cuntry h____ ___ars pass threw this ____I cant tell I stood___martch very well I am____ning strength we are ____from corinth 26 from ___Will torbet is not better he__t very poor and looks bad___dont think he can s_____it we have very nice wether here __ow there has not bin eny rain of eny acount yet I exspecand to gett some posteg stamps ___your last Letter but I ___they did not come don't forget to send a dollar worth & 5 dollars green back for I am now out of paper & posteg stamps _____thing when we wer ___martch & I was a c_____to se the timber af___ the fenses when we__would make the rails f_____a site to se it Lan____is unwell I supose you be bisy now in your corn ___ tell george to write & william to for I like to heare from home I would like to be there to help you pick corn an ___ceap batch I think I would enjoy my self eny how I think so pleas write often I you hafto write y___nite I think of no m___ present give my love to___as ever___*

Now, with a full quiver of insight, it was finally time to initiate my expedition into Tennessee and Georgia, with Fleharty's journal and Uncle Henry's letters as my roadmap. My objective was to locate, or get as close as I could to the exact spots where Henry sat down to write his letters to relatives back home. Throughout my pilgrimage, I was resolute to jot down my notes at the end of each day, in order to capture as many details, thoughts and moods that I could retain. As I reflect upon the experience, I recollect my enthusiasm reaching a fever pitch as I stepped off the plane in Nashville. The anticipation leading up to that moment drove me to the point of near exhaustion, due to lack of sleep, a pattern which would continue long into the week, for various reasons. My journaling begins in the wee-hours of Independence Day, 2013, amidst a swarm of fireflies, beneath thunderous skies and rain-soaked pines, recollecting on my arrival in Tennessee.

### Wednesday, July 3, 2013 – Flight to Nashville, TN

I must have dozed off for about two hours, or so. Otherwise, I didn't sleep a wink on the night of July 2nd, 2013. I couldn't wait to get on the road, and the only obstacles in my path were the 40-minute drive to the airport and the 3.5-hour flight from Austin. I hadn't packed more than I would need to make it from Nashville to Atlanta and back. Still, my enormous sea bag was bursting at the seams, with clothes, a daypack, a 2-man tent, a lantern and sleeping bag, for I wouldn't be checking in at The Hilton. If I were to move forward with this escapade and find the exact locations where Uncle Henry stopped to write his Civil War letters that I had recently acquired, then I would do my damnedest to rough it "soldier-style". What better way to spend Independence Day than camping under the stars in the Deep South?

Based on past experience, I made a concerted effort to reserve a direct flight to Nashville from Austin, while bypassing DFW at all costs. I have a more intimate history with that airport than I care to think about, due to canceled flights, weather related delays, and poorly-timed layovers. Once airborne, I buried my face into my iPad, poring over details of my forthcoming adventure.

We landed in Nashville, incident-free, and I made a beeline to baggage claim to pick up my sea bag. I stepped up to the carousel before a loitering throng of grumpy passengers squinting for their luggage, tapping their feet, and glancing at their watches. I made an announcement to lighten the mood. *"Everyone, please let me know if you spot a big black bag."* It took a few seconds for some to react, since there was a veritable sea of black ballistic nylon floating past us. A well-dressed woman turned to me and said, *"Really dude?"* I counted about half a dozen conversions from grimace to grin, and my work was done here. Finally, my giant duffle was riding on my shoulder, and I was hoofing it to the stall where my rental car waited. I knew I would be covering some distance, so I opted for a compact model for efficient fuel economy. Comfort was a feature that I would just have to sacrifice, but to what degree? This would be a continuing theme throughout my route, as I followed the march of Federal Troops into enemy territory, but the ghosts of Southern Sons would soon have their vengeance.

Finally, I was moving northbound on the 65 Freeway, en route to Gallatin, Tennessee, the Sumner County seat, named for the former U. S. Secretary of State, Albert Gallatin, established in 1802, population: 30,678.

As I drew closer to Gallatin, the weather grew more and more inclement, and my windshield wipers were gradually becoming ineffectual. Still, I drove onward with my trusty GPS app guiding the way. I had previously spoken on the phone to a very gregarious elderly woman who I assumed was the curator at the Sumner County Museum, who was assured that despite the national holiday, the facility would be open for business on the Fourth of July. As I often did while I drove en route to landmarks and historic sites, I reviewed my mental notes, remembering that my octogenarian contact at the museum had knowledge of a Civil War fort that once stood at the intersection of Blythe and West Eastland Avenue. I viewed an image online of a historic map of Gallatin while we spoke, and confirmed the location of "Fort Thomas" exactly where she stated that it once stood. She didn't seem to possess any further intel regarding this site in particular, but she wasn't shy about voicing opinions on other unrelated matters that resulted from the defeat of the South during the War of the Rebellion. In her case, it seemed, the resentment was still fresh. I was truly looking forward to spending some time in conversation with this lady, for she seemed very sharp, inquisitive, and most likely had a better handle on the local history than most.

The rain continued to pour as I parked the car on Main Street beneath a cluster of beautifully preserved historic brick facades that flanked the Sumner County Courthouse, where, according to a nearby historic marker, the first African-American volunteers took their oath to join the Union cause as "The Thirteenth United States Coloured Infantry". As I read the plaque, I was impressed by the enormous gravity of this event, considering the time and place where, and when it occurred. I couldn't imagine what it would take to make such a bold stand. Though the weather had not improved, I spent some time walking around the square that surrounded the courthouse, imagining what the general climate was like for the local townfolk of an "occupied" city, which Gallatin most certainly was, from 1862-1870. I found my way back to the car, and continued driving along Main Street until I slid into the gravel driveway of the Museum which was clearly marked, and positioned at the rear of a preserved historic residence called Trousdale Place. This impressive Flemish-style brick structure was the former home of William Trousdale (1790-1872), governor of Tennessee (1849-1851) and U.S. minister to Brazil (1853-1857). He was considered the "Elder Statesman" of Gallatin during the occupation, and opened his grand home for various uses for the occupying Union forces, despite his staunch confederate loyalty.

The rain had increased in its intensity and volume, so I donned my wide-brimmed hiker hat, and abandoned my vehicle. As I approached the front door to the museum, it dawned on me that mine was the only vehicle in the parking lot. The sign hanging in the window of the museum's front door confirmed my surmounting fear. "CLOSED FOR THE HOLIDAY". I was inclined to call down curses on the old woman who balked on her invitation, but I recoiled, took a deep breath, and directed my concentration to locating the Fort Thomas site, where Uncle Henry had spent six long months in camp, carved his wooden bible, and wrote one of his first letters home. It wasn't far to the intersection where Water Street doglegged, transformed into West Eastland Street and crossed Town Creek, and the railroad tracks. Referring to my bookmarked historic map, I was parking at the very spot where the train depot once stood. Fort Thomas had been built in 1862 on a high point nearby, to afford a broad view of the city and its citizens, and to serve as a visual deterrent discouraging Confederate troublemakers from disrupting the railroad operations. I hiked up the hill to the intersection of West Eastland and Blythe. A small convenience store now occupied a corner, along with a church, and some odd unmarked, windowless buildings behind barbed wire fencing that I perceived to be a government installation of some sort. There was no marker or sign that identified the spot where the fort once stood. I was satisfied, however that I had located the spot where Henry had spent his first months in the war. I returned to my vehicle, and drove in concentric circles around the location, just to make certain I wasn't missing any details.

By this time, I was ready for some lunch, so I kept an eye out for a place to grab a bite. I drove down West Eastland Street, back across Town Creek, and up Water Street again when I spotted a couple of local gentleman in faded baseball caps, conversing on a bench in front of some sort of luncheonette. One was a cross between Santa Claus and a member of ZZ Topp. His beard was yellowed, and stained around the mouth, most likely from tobacco, bourbon, or both. As I drove by at a snail's pace, I watched the twosome rock back and forth on the wooden bench beneath a rusting red metal awning, both of them roaring with laughter, despite the torrent pounding the street before them which was beginning to flood. The scene was rich with "patina" and though the establishment seemed a bit suspect, I nudged my rental car into an empty spot in the alley behind the building excited and simultaneously skittish.

I locked the car, and rushed to round the corner leading to the cafe, with the intention of striking up a conversation with the two gents, but I was denied the privilege, as an old Chevy pickup sped off with the pair seated in the cab, sheltered from the rain. I stood in front of the diner, and gulped hard as I mustered the courage to step inside. I sidled up to the counter, where a matronly, apron-clad young lady worked the grill and register with a prowess. She owned the Water Street Lunch Rush! That rush consisted of myself, and a 60-something local man, who had his nose buried in the paper, in spite of the national news that blared out of the tinny speaker of the small television hoisted above the smoking grill, sizzling and popping with grease, oozing with rust, and bits of charcoal. Still my appetite dominated my common sense, and I proceeded to order a hamburger and a diet coke.

Out of respect for the establishment, and the help, I will not pronounce on the sad state of my meal upon its arrival. Suffice it to say that I managed to choke down every last crumb, and got right down to business. *"So...(cough)...are either of you familiar with the history of this part of Gallatin?"* I could tell by the blank stares from both the hostess and patron that I would need to be more specific. *"As it pertains to the Civil War"* I said. Still nothing. I continued, *"There was a fort over by the train depot, up on the ridge where the church is...did you know?"* Finally the gentleman spoke up. *"I don't know much about the history here."* The waitress snapped her towel over her shoulder, and returned to her grill. *"Hey thanks. Y'all have a great day"* I said, as I pushed through the squeaky screen door, and out into the deluge that now flooded the storm drains flanking the aptly-named "Water Street".

My attempt to drum up some local scuttlebutt was a dismal fail, and I needed a drink. I sprinted to my car, but managed to soak myself through to the skin, anyway. The windshield steamed up with the humidity and moisture that I introduced to the interior. I crept out of the parking lot with the defroster blowing at full blast, and made my way up Water Street at a careful crawl, at least until the fog cleared, and I could see clearly.

I found a bar that once was the town pharmacy near the courthouse. The original bold signage from the 1950's was still intact inside the establishment, which stated: "PRESCRIPTIONS" above the bar. It was stacked floor-to-ceiling with an impressive selection of hard liquor. I prescribed myself a cold local microbrew, as I plotted out the next leg of my trip, which would be LaVergne, Tennessee.

## LaVergne, Tennessee

As I flipped through my photo collection and video clips from that first day of tracking Henry's march, a trace of that euphoric energy is profoundly evident in my demeanor. Unfortunately that verve can't easily be summoned on cue, but the excitement and anticipation of the unknown that waits around the next corner presents an intoxicating combination of anticipation and dread. I suppose this was the same

combination that fueled the bravado shared by Sergeant Fleharty and
the men of the 102$^{nd}$, as they finally struck camp at Gallatin, Tennessee.

*The brigade was transferred from Gallatin to
LaVergne by railroad, on the first day of June, 1863. From
that place the 102d marched on the 2d to Stewart's Creek. The
regiment was there divided. Co's E, K and G camped near the
railroad bridge across Stewart's Creek, and were under the
immediate command of Lieutenant Colonel Mannon. Co. H,
Captain Hiram Elliott commanding, was stationed at Overall's
Creek, in close proximity to the battle-ground of Murfreesboro.
Co. B at Smyrna. The remaining companies were stationed
about three-fourths of a mile from the railroad bridge, at
Stewart's Creek near a small fort. There, Colonel Smith
established regimental headquarters. Thus located we
remained until the 19$^{th}$ day of August.*

*The intermediate time was spent drilling, visiting our
friends at the front—visiting the Murfreesboro battle-ground,
and picking blackberries—varying the routine of exercises by
an occasional scout.*

*Those battalion drills—somewhat obnoxious to us then,
on account of the excessive heat—did much to prepare us for
subsequent active campaigns.*

*Those were pleasant days in our regimental history.
The citizens were generally hospitable. The young ladies of the
neighborhood were pretty, and many of them accomplished.
They loved to sing the "Bonny Blue Flag" and the "Home
Spun Dress" to our men. (Both contain lyrics that celebrate
Southern Rights) In return, the singers of the regiment
sometimes favored them with the "Star Spangled Banner," and
the "Song of a Thousand Years" or "Rally Round the Flag,
Boys."*

*Blackberries!—how natural the transition from pretty
girls to luscious blackberries! This tempting fruit grew in
unparalleled abundance in that vicinity. There were immense
quantities within the picket lines, and a few miles from camp
there were large fields of briars burdened with berries.
Morning, noon and evening they were placed on our table, and
we had stewed blackberries, blackberry pies, dumplings and*

blackberries, and blackberries with milk—the latter a substitute for cream.

While encamped at LaVergne, tents were entirely ignored. A large number of elegant log huts had been vacated by the regiments, which returned to Nashville. These were removed to our encampment and placed in regular order—forming a village of about fifty houses, with three streets.

In these commodious huts, which were furnished with fireplace, bunks, tables, etc., we were well prepared for the approaching winter.

Guerillas were quite bold and troublesome during the time we were at Stewart's Creek. A detachment of the 10$^{th}$ Ohio Cavalry, which was encamped near us, and was under the command of Colonel Smith, was often sent out after the miscreants, and was occasionally reinforced by a squad of mounted men from the 102d. Often, these parties would have a jolly time before returning.

On one occasion about sunset, word ran through camp that a scouting party was going out-he object being to intercept a number of rebels, who, report said were to meet at a house south of Stone River, preparatory to going south. All available horses and mules were quickly saddled, and we were soon en route for the barrens beyond the river. A number of the 10$^{th}$ Ohio cavalry accompanied us. A repentant rebel who had made known the intentions of the rebels to the Colonel, was to act as guide. We rode to his house, but the guide could not be found—his lady stating that he had gone to the house of a neighbor. To the house of the neighbor we galloped. "Not there—had been there that afternoon." Thence we hurried away to Stone River, forming a long line in single file as we crossed the historic little stream. At a farm house beyond, a colored guide was procured, to pilot us to a house about two hours distant where it was thought that the migratory guide could be found. "Cuffey" led off quite briskly and for miles we dashed along through the brush at a break-neck speed. At length the senseless haste of the guide was moderated, and we—six men of the 102d—discovered that we were far in advance of the main party. Reaching the house we learned that our "guide" had not been there.

*Knowing that we were so far away from the main body of the detachment that they could not find us, and confident that we could not find them, we were left to our own resources.*

*"Take us to Jefferson" said Mike—a mule mounted Lieutenant, addressing the guide—and for Jefferson, a small town two miles up the river, we started. Mike was full of mischief and yelled out to the guide, "Forward! Faster!" and away we went through the brush over logs and into dense bodies of cedars. "Faster!" yelled the Lieutenant, and over the rocks, leaping, slipping and stumbling—the horses' shoes striking fire—onward we rode. At length the mad cap was induced to rein in his steed. Refording Stone River we rode into Jefferson—an antiquated little village, picturesquely located. All the inhabitants were wrapt in slumber. The moon had fairly risen and its silvery light rendered the scene really romantic.*

*Dispensing with our guide who did not seem to appreciate the romance or necessity of our night ride, we continued on towards camp. But another idiosyncrasy seized upon "Mike." He would have a swim in Stone River. Lieutenant W. dashed off with him. The remainder of the party rode leisurely into camp, which was reached at two o'clock in the morning. The swimmers came in shortly afterwards and the entire detachment an hour or two later.—having failed to accomplish the purpose for which it was sent.*

*Shortly after our arrival at LaVergne, Col Smith received an order to have four companies at that place mounted, and by a bit of skillful diplomacy he secured for the use of these companies, two-hundred and twenty-five of the celebrated Spencer Rifles—also each man was supplied with one of Colt's or Remington's revolvers. Horses were foraged from the country. Several expeditions were made to the vicinity of Duck River for this purpose. In a brief period the four companies were mounted.*

*From that time until the regiment was ordered to the front, the duties devolving upon the men, were more severe than are usually experienced by troops in garrison.*

*At one time the four companies at LaVergne were compelled to assist in patrolling the railroad, besides furnishing details for fatigue duty, picket duty, scouting, and being engaged in the work of getting out railroad ties.*

*The companies at the stockades were similarly employed, save that they had no scouting to do.*

No letters were ever recovered from Henry during his 7-month station at LaVergne, TN, which is not to say that he did not write home during that period. He would refer to his experience there in a letter written to brother, Willis, however while he was camped at Lookout Mountain, later along his march into Georgia. Still, I managed to spend some time in the area, and in particular, at the Stones River battlefield, or "Murfreesboro", as it is otherwise known.

Highway 24 would carry me through Nashville once again, and another 30 minutes or so would pass until I reached LaVergne. LaVergne was a significant spot, since it was mentioned in the Civil War Widow's Pension demands of Emma Bowlus-Gain-Banks as the location where Henry had first contracted his lethal intestinal disorder. Also, though it was short-lived, the "Battle of LaVergne" that occurred on October 6th, 1862 was featured in many major newspapers at the time, including The New York Times.

As I drove South, I spotted a few directional signs to "Lebanon" which would potentially take me about 1.5 hours off course. Since I was on a schedule to get to my campground before sundown, I had to bypass the exits, while I surmised that the town's unique name just had to have a story behind it, so I made a mental note to research its origin. As suspected, it turns out that the founders of Lebanon bestowed upon it this title because of the area's abundance of cedar trees, referring to the "Cedars of Lebanon" mentioned numerous times in the Old Testament. When I learned of this detail, the first thought I had was of the reddish hue in the wood Henry chose to craft his palm-sized bible. I had seen my share of cedar when I lived in Washington State, especially while working three summers as a roofer, sometimes hauling bundles of cedar shakes by hand, up ladders to dizzying heights. Henry's bible appeared to be a softer material like cedar tends to be, and received the knife easily, as evidenced in Henry's etchings. It mattered little whether or not the wood block was from the nearby Lebanon cedar forest, but the ironic biblical parallel offered something for me to scratch my head over.

In camp, here in the LaVergne area, Henry had shared some of his exploits in a letter to his brother Willis, and more details leading to his actual whereabouts were divulged once again in Fleharty's journal.

I was looking for a spot near the railroad, and Stewart's Creek, since Companies E, K and G of the 102nd had camped somewhere near where these two landmarks converged. The most likely location of the railroad bridge that crossed Stewart's Creek was just West of where Waldron Road passed over the railroad.

Comparing a historic map from 1863 with Google Earth satellite imagery, the railroad route had changed very little between LaVergne and nearby Smyrna. I was fairly confident that I was in the exact vicinity where Henry had camped while at LaVergne. The City Hall center was close by, and another historic placard stood on the property along a stretch of the Nashville highway, where it crossed a branch of Stewart's Creek. The placard read: "MARY KATE PATTERSON DAVIS HILL KYLE (1844-1931) Heroine of the South worked with Coleman's scouts and Sam Davis to spy in the LaVergne-Nolenville-Nashville area. When a teenager she smuggled vital information and supplies through Union lines. Mrs. Kyle was buried in the Confederate Circle in the Mt. Olivet Cemetery, Nashville. The first woman so honored."

The rain hadn't let up since I had touched down in Nashville, and after walking around the City Hall property, exploring a feline-infested, two-story log home perched above the creek, I was soaked to the skin once again. My first journal entry gives an accurate description of how my first night in Tennessee turned out.

*Thursday, July 4, 2013 - Poole Knobs Campground, LaVergne, TN*

How fortunate for me that the Fourth of July fell on a Thursday this year, with a free Friday, a full weekend, and a Monday off to follow, before I'm due back at my POE on Tuesday. I sit in a tent, wrapped in a sleeping bag beneath towering pines, surrounded by hundreds of fireflies. As I reflect on Uncle Henry's many letters written during his long term as a Private throughout the Civil War, I am overcome by an eerie feeling.

Writing by lantern light, not far from his post at Stewart's Creek near LaVergne, Tennessee, I hear thunderous reports from airborne shells being flung in celebration of our nation's 237th birthday! Eyes closed, I imagine cannon fire reaching Henry's ear in similar fashion from the battle of Murfreesboro that took place just a few miles from where I have pitched my tent. As Henry wrote his letters to his mother and brothers back in Illinois, Iowa and New York, he was camped in this vicinity for many months in 1862 and 1863, and I am having trouble making it through just a single night! Since I landed in Nashville this morning, it has rained heavily, non-stop...but I continue to explore, look and learn, non-stop. The monotonous dripping on my tent flap from the tree branches above won't allow for much sleep tonight. Note to self: Next time, remember to pack earplugs.

*A rainy day on the streets of downtown Gallatin, Tennessee*

*Looking into the fog from the summit of Lookout Mountain, Tennessee*

# Lookout Mountain, Georgia

Stephen Fleharty's journal describes Henry's encampment in the Wauhatchie Valley, nested in the shadow of Lookout Mountain. To the North, the ground still smolders from the great battle of Chattanooga, which had occurred only 5 months prior. For many of the troops in the 102nd —Henry included— the war was to have ended long before their reorganization at Wauhatchie. Unbeknownst to the surviving lot of volunteers, Sherman's Atlanta campaign, and his famed march to the sea was about to launch from this very post.

*Marched 14 miles on the 6th (of March), and reached Stevenson, Alabama.*

*Passed through Stevenson on the 7th, marched 11 miles and went into camp near Bridgeport on the Tennessee River.*

*Remained in camp during the 8th. Marched next morning through Bridgeport and across the Tennessee, past Shell Mound, followed up the river and passed from Alabama into Tennessee. Camped 13 miles from Bridgeport.*

*Followed up Falling Water Creek on the 10th. Passed Whiteside Station and Sand Mountain. Marched 12 miles; reached Wauhatchie Valley at 3:00 PM and the tedious march was over. There, the troops were to rest preparatory to a general movement against General Joe Johnston's rebel army.*

*While the regiment was encamped in the valley, the weather was much of the time very cold, and on 22 March an extraordinary fall of snow took place. It commenced about 2 o'clock in the morning; before noon the ground was covered to the depth of a foot. Such an immense fall of snow, in the spring season, so far down in the Sunny South must have been a novelty to the oldest inhabitant.*

*Snowballing became for a brief period, and all exciting pastime in camp.*

*A few days of alternate rain and sunshine sufficed to leave the earth bear again.*

*A grand review took place on the 19th. Major Generals Howard and Hooker were the chief reviewing officers.*

*The men were much occupied during the last weeks of March, in constructing and beautifying their quarters. The month of April was occupied in active military exercises. There were daily drills, company and battalion. Dress parade each day. Regimental inspection every few days. Brigade drill almost every day, and occasionally division drill. Our regiment had an officer's school, and our enterprising chaplain, as if to vary the monotonous routine, commenced a phonographic school.*

*Officers and men improved the opportunity while at Wauhatchie to ascend Lookout Mountain. The scene from the summit is said to be grand beyond description. The eye roams until wearied over vast plains, varied by occasional elevations which seem in their dim and shadowy outlines, to be the boundaries of some fairy land.*

*From the highest elevation on old Lookout, the territory of seven states come within the range of vision.*

*On 14 April there was a grand review of the division by Major General Thomas.*

*An order was received on the 16th announcing that our brigade would until further orders, be known as the 1st Brigade of the 3rd Division, 20th Army Corps, the 11th and 12th corps having been consolidated, forming the 20th – Major General Joseph Hooker commanding, – Major General Daniel Butterfield commanding the division, and Brigadier General W. T . Ward, the brigade.*

*While at Wauhatchie, the mounted companies of the regiment gave up their horses, in accordance with orders from corps headquarters. An order was also received directing the regiment to turn over their Spencer rifles to an ordinance officer, and draw Springfield rifled muskets. Want of time prevented the execution of this order previous to the commencement of the Atlanta campaign. After that time it was inexpedient to make the change.*

*The camp at Wauhatchie Valley will be remembered as the most beautiful and romantic as the regiment ever occupied. The scenery was grand. Old Lookout Mountain loomed up magnificently a short distance eastward, the clouds wreathing themselves around her rugged summit; her sides covered with a dense growth of cedars and pines.*

*As if in a rivalry with nature, the different regiments of the brigade surpassed all previous ideas of taste and elegance in decorating their encampments.*

*The camp of the 102nd was on a small table-land, just large enough for one regiment. It was laid off with great care. The houses were of a uniform size; the streets were graded and macadamized. Elegant arches, made of cedar bows, were put up in the quarters of each company. Interwoven with the arches were various beautiful designs. One bore the names "Grant" – "Sherman" – "Thomas",– arranged in a triangle. Another bore masonic emblems, – the compass, square, etc. A large eagle was represented beneath one of the arches, apparently in the act of flying. Among other beautiful objects, a pulpit was prominent. It was erected in open air, and was a perfect model of taste and ingenuity. The design was very similar to that of an ordinary church pulpit, with columns at each side. Between the columns was a cross. The cross and the columns were wreathed with evergreens. The flag and banner were drooped in elegant folds at each side of the cross. The back part of the pulpit was elegantly wreathed. The floor and steps were carpeted with green boughs. The pulpit was constructed for Reverend Mr. Rider, of the First Universalist Church, Chicago. It was occupied by him on one occasion. Subsequently it was occupied by other ministers.*

*A chapel was also built, and services were held in it each Sabbath, and sometimes during the week. The camp was visited by Major Generals Thomas, Howard, Hooker and*

*Butterfield; all of whom expressed their admiration of the taste and skill exhibited in decorating the quarters.*

*It would hardly be supposed that soldiers, who are usually considered very rough specimens of humanity, could exhibit such a fine appreciation of the beautiful, but that lovely camp, embowered among the arches seemed more like the abode of fairies then of "boys in blue."*

Reflecting on his short career as a cavalryman, as he travelled the 150-mile journey from LaVergne on horseback, Henry stopped to write his brother, Willis while in camp in the Wauhatchie Valley, near Lookout Mountain. He describes the view of Lookout Mountain from his perspective in the low valley, and reflects on the battle that took place there.

*April the 10 1864*

*in Camp in the valley of the lookout mountains*

*Tenn*

*Dear Brother  I thought I woud seat myself this Sabath morning to pen you a few lines for the first time sens I have bin in the servis of this united states army you must exscuse m not writing to you  I did not know where to direct a leture I never coud think where  I wrote to Mother to ask her where to direct  I supose you wer in the same fix to  I got a leture from her & she gave me the directions the other day  they wer then in good health ther & allso one from David  they wer allso well  I have had very good health for the last 10 months  the first of my serving was prety hard on me untill last June every sens then I have had as good a helth as eny man  meande(?) ask for in this world of sin & trials & hardships & above all the gratest sinse Sivell ware (Civil War) whitch brings meny a inesont (innocent) to his endear (to endure) on this poluted urth (earth). well Willes I Supose I am the onely one of the banks family that is in the survis of the united states I have sean a few of the hardships of a soldiers life there is good bad & indiferant  next to getting(?) in this armey & eavel temptations beond dis cription I sometimes think that sutch a cruell & wicked armey as this cant prosper to sucess in the battells our brigugade has not bin in a fite yet our regiment had a small schurmish with a few gorilleys when we wer at gallaton (Gallatin, TN) on the rail road  they undertook to capture the exspress but they wer defetd & flew like wild dears we have bin on the railroad every sens we hav bin out  we wer at Gallaton a bout 8 month  from ther we moved to Lavarng (LaVergne, TN) in June stade there untill last february  our Briguade left thair th 16  we wer 15 days on the martch 6 of our Companys wer Mountaid (mounted) while we wer at Lavurng we acted as scouts threw the woods(?)  we scouted a grate deal while we wer their  Co E  Co G  Co I  Co C  Co B  Co. F wer the mounted infentrey  there  is  on  good  conculation (consolation?)  we got to wride on this long and very hard martch that we had from Lavurng to this plase over 150 mil  it was a very hard martch on the men over the Cumberland Mountains  our scouting on hors back is plaid out now  our horses are taken from us & turned over to the government & they wer taken to Chattanoogy this morning  we  are within  7 mi of Chattanoogy  we are on the front of our lines  there is a large forse in camp hear  we are in the 1 Brigade 1 Division 20 Armey Chore (corps)  when we wer at Gallaton we wer in the 12 reserve Chore  when at Lavurn we wer turnd over to the 11 chore & sens we have bin here we have bin in the 18 from that to the 20  ther has bin a grate taring up in the armey for the last month I ges  Old Grant is gointo __ with us to sid___ his ___ more in the futcher (future) than they have bin in the past  we are campt in in a valley surounded by hills in all side & the high rockey range of the loockout  on our rite east of us  I can se the point of the mountain where our poor boys charged on the rebels & fout them & all matcheral (natural) dis advantidge  the rebels had brest works to defend them they had brest worcks all along on the east side & on the west side  there is a range of high rocks runing strate up for nearley 100 feat  my opinion is furmely seteld if the enemy coudant (couldn't) defend themself & whip our armey they I say might as well throw down there arms & quit  5 states can be sean from this mountain  I have bin out on afew scouts sens we have bin hear  we have not sean eny rebels  have bin in Georgey a few times  we are thre quarters of a mild from the Georgey line  25 from the Atlantey line  we have had very disagreable wether sens we have bin heare  wet chilly wether sens we have bin hear  we have had a very deape snow*

*the 20 day of Martch  it snoad all of one day & night  it snoad
16 intches    there was not no snow th other side of the
Cumberland mountains  well all seames to be quiet on the front
& has bin for te past few months but I exspect th armey will
sone begin to move then ther will come the slautering of
menagain for there countrys writes  a Solgers life is a very hard
life take it as it runs he is exsposed to all kinds of wether &
hardships  I am in good helth at presant & hope these few lines
will find your family the same   write sone & I will try to
answerit  with love to your family as ever your loving brother*

*Henry I Banks*

*Directions  Co. E 102 Rt.*

*Ill. Voll*

*By the way of Nashvill*

*Loockout Vally*

*Tenn*

☆ ☆ ☆

*Friday, July 5, 2013 In Camp, Calhoun, GA*

   More wet stuff! It doesn't seem to want to let up! I
managed to sleep for a sporadic total of about three hours.
That's probably the average for the above-average union
private! I wanted the experience; I guess I asked for it.

   I lit out for the Lookout Mountain area at about 7am. I
drove the distance from LaVergne, TN that Henry got to cover
on horseback, during his brief stint as a Union cavalryman. His
mount being confiscated and returned to Chattanooga, he
would march from here to Resaca, just in time for the epic
battle that took place there in May 1864. While at the Lookout
Mountain area, however, his unit was afforded a brief respite in

the Wauhatchie Valley. The 102nd's camp was described as very beautiful! Based on what I know of its described location, I believe a Walmart now occupies the area. – Nice. *(A map has since surfaced, that was drafted apparently on-site during this period. It shows the 102nd Illinois camped along Lookout Creek, on a plateau further south of Walmart)*

As I explored the Wauhatchie Valley in my sporty Hyundai, Lookout Mountain stood obscured in a distant shroud of clouds, but the summit still beckoned. From Highway 24 I followed Brown's Ferry Road to Highway 11. Cutting left, I ascended the mountain by way of the old Wauhatchie Pike Road. The scenic highway escalated into the low-hanging clouds, past the Incline Railroad – and past beautiful homes with views that stretched far into neighboring states. One home that was under construction looks like a Frank Lloyd Wright testament in stone with a copper roof and two opposing prominent chimneys, both adorned with ornate capstones. Amazing!

I reached the summit, where it seemed that the Parks Department and hilltop souvenir shop we're competing for business. Aside from my normal donation to the park, I paid the ranger my $3.00 entrance fee to the "Point Park". I admit that I was fairly disappointed in the weather, as it obscured anything beyond about 100 feet of visibility. In retrospect, I was happy that I could experience Lookout Mountain in similar conditions that prevailed on the day of the grand battle that took place there on November 24, 1863.

After chatting with the rangers, I studied their maps, compared notes, then set off to find a good vigorous hike…er, march! True to form, I snapped numerous photos of cannons set upon Rocky parapets. The mist and fog created an eerily beautiful aura that I was thankful for upon examination of the photos. A trailhead invited me to descend the steep aluminum staircase built against rugged rocky crags. How could I resist?

The sign at the bottom announced that I would be descending the mountain for 1.5 miles. That obviously meant I would be ascending it according to the same measurement. Since my health club back home was not reachable, I continued, for I was craving a workout. My rain gear came in very handy on the trail leading down the southern face of

Lookout Mountain. I was surrounded by dense forest that wept great drops from millions of leaves in concert with the downpour that pelted the mountain relentlessly, and constant.

I snapped a photo of myself and shared it with friends on Facebook. One coworker exclaimed *"Oh God! I work with Ted Nugent!"* It must've been the hat!

The hike was just what the doctor ordered. I didn't mind the rain, since my early days in the Cascades were spent in similar conditions, hiking and fishing with my dad and friends. I was in my element. Though I would have preferred a sun-drenched, clear day with blue sky, I was loving the moment, and paused a few times, just to drink in the sights, sounds, and smells of a rainy day in a Tennessee forest.

Once the trail came to an end, the green canopy opened up to a lawn-covered plateau that was the "Cravens" home, the residence, built and rebuilt antebellum by Robert Cravens. The Confederate Army used the house as a signaling point, one that actually "tipped off" the blue coats, and started the infamous battle.

I wandered around the property for a while, stalling, in anticipation of the 1.5 mile ascent that was about to commence. The mud and slippery, moss-laden stones had made the first leg a challenge, wrought with close calls, and my mind entertained a lightning-fast montage of alternative modes of transportation that would speed me to the summit. "How far was the incline railroad entrance from here?" "How much would a cab cost?" "Is there a horse nearby that I could steal?" "A helicopter?"

Once again, I entered the hole from whence I had emerged, and the sky opened up right on cue! The trail upward turned into a gravity-fed creek, sending rushing streams of rainwater over my soaking hiking boots. Despite it all, I made it back to the car soaked, but safe!

The closer I got to the Doll Mountain Campground, the more concerned I became. A palpable uneasiness probed at my gut as the pavement turned to gravel, and the gravel -to mud. Had I opted for a jeep, I may have continued onward, but the Hyundai struggled against the mucky terrain. Instinct, and a quick call to a different campground in Calhoun made my decision an easy one. I was within only 50 feet of the remote mountain campground where I had planned to settle, when I pulled over, and drove back down the 22-mile stretch of Highway 136. I arrived in the suburban campground in Calhoun well before dark. I pitched my tent, lit a campfire, cracked open a cold beer, and lit a cigar. A peacock crowed at me with its "May-aww!!" "May-aww!!" repeating through the camp. What? Would this be my morning alarm? Not too early, I hope. I crawled into my bedroll after the rain had doused my blazing piñon logs. I drifted off to sleep for a couple of hours, when suddenly, "Bang!! Kapow!! Ratatatatatatatatatat!! The locals living next door to the camp had decided to blow through their leftover fireworks at midnight! I must say, they had quite the arsenal. Distant thundering booms echoed as well, probably from postponed fireworks shows from the previous night.

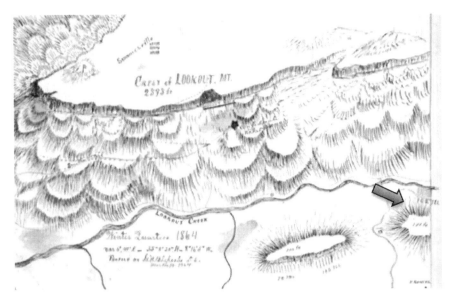

*An 1864 map of the Wauhatchie Valley Federal Camp beneath Lookout Mountain, featuring the position of the 102nd camp near the "table land" lower right*

*My temporary address on the Legacy Road, Calhoun, Georgia*

*Saturday, July 6, 2013. Starbucks, Calhoun, GA*

I slept much better —despite the interruption of fireworks at midnight—than I did on the night of the Fourth. I made sure to select a tent site that wasn't on an incline, which improved my sleeping conditions. Of course, the peacock was eager to rouse me out of my tent at about 7am. I hadn't noticed the petting zoo next to my campsite, until the goats began to scream for their breakfast. I walked over to their pen, and introduced myself. There were three of them, and they didn't seem to mind sharing their space with a very well nourished potbelly pig. He was very friendly, and seemed happy to receive a few pats on his head and muzzle. I grabbed a change of clothes and made a beeline for the showers – I was determined to get my $30 worth of campground services. I poured a generous cup of coffee in the office, and ventured out again – to locate the Resaca battlefield site.

Upon entering my vehicle, I discovered that a large colony of ants had taken residence in my car, most likely to avoid the rains. I sprayed them down with my mosquito repellent, which brought their caravan to an instant, and deadly halt.

Eventually, I arrived at a gigantic field, split by the 75 highway, which ran North-South from Chattanooga to Atlanta. My previous attempts to invite response to my inquiries as to the official location of Van Den Corput's Battery —the cannons that Henry reportedly had charged, and seized with his company E— had been ignored so far. So as I entered the construction site that would become the official Resaca Battlefield Visitors Center, I parked the car closest to the area where my own sources had placed General Hooker and his forces of the XXth Corps, and I began to explore. I did find some trenches and evidence of earthworks, and even some old bones protruding from the earth, but had no luck locating the site of the actual battery. It was a breathtaking scene, however, a wide-open field flanked by two wooded rises that were understandably difficult to navigate through, even by way of the trails that I followed. Henry and Company E must've really struggled when climbing through this terrain before overtaking those Confederate guns.

I do not exaggerate when I state that the hard rains

ceased to fall just as I had begun my exploration, and did not
again continue until the second that I returned to my car. A red-
tailed hawk circled above me as I emerged from the thick
Georgia pines, and his resounding shrieks guided me down the
road to where my Hyundai was waiting. He dropped a peace
offering in my path, and I found a pretty good spot for it, here in
my journal.

This beautiful, brown feather, layered with white down,
a stripe of iridescent copper, and a tip of bright orange
reminded me of a poem that I wrote back in 2011, which was
based on my last visit to the Pacific Coast near our home in
Southern California.

*I caught a feather in midair,*
*a seagull shed at sunset's flare.*
*It brought to mind, a native tale,*
*a Chieftain long-ago regaled.*

*He said,*
*"A plume may fall, where hawks abound.*
*Catch it, lest it touches ground.*
*Your heart will change, your vision too.*
*Hawk Spirit, now inside of you!"*

*I pondered, as I held this gift*
*that came to me, from gulls adrift.*
*So wise, those words from ancient lore,*
*but I felt no different than before…*
*Except this craving for a dish*
*of dumpster trash, and fresh shellfish.*

The rains pummeled my rental car as I twisted through
the winding path of fresh concrete, releasing that "creosote
scent" that filled my nostrils. I yawned repeatedly. It was either
time for a catnap, or coffee. I chose the latter. I spent about 2.5
hours at Starbucks, with two trips to the counter for my
predictable *"grandé drip with room for cream."* Seated,
watchful at a window table, I completed a few pages of journal
jottings, while keeping an eye on the weather.

The torrent did not let up. Patrons came and went, running at full gallop, using unconventional means, to remain dry. Impromptu umbrellas were fashioned from newspapers, napkins, and various articles of clothing were "hiked up" to serve as hoods. The windows were completely steamed over, and weeping heavily from the battle of humidity outside and air conditioning inside. Finally, as it began to grow dark outside, I ran to my silver four-door, and dove into the driver seat to avoid as much rain as possible. My efforts were ineffective. I patted myself dry, and turned over the ignition, only to discover more ants marching across my dashboard in a neat line, carrying eggs, I suppose, to a safer location. After a brief episode of devastation with a cluster of napkins and mosquito spray, I made another grim discovery. The air conditioning in my Hyundai was on the fritz! I tried everything, but finally had to resort to blasting heat through the system in order to keep the windows from fogging over.

By the time I arrived back at my campsite in Calhoun, finding my tent just as I had left it, I was a soaking, sweaty mess! The campsite was flooded, and the others downslope from mine had been transfigured into a veritable trout pond. I pulled a cigar from my backpack, and rushed to the covered porch of a nearby cabin. It had been occupied that morning, but was now vacant, except for a pure white peacock who was not about to abandon his dry, comfortable post, just because I happened to drop in. I plopped down in an oversized Adirondack chair next to my new friend, fired up my cigar, and gazed out at the campground property as it gradually sunk beneath the rising water. The downpour let up after a while, and I ran about 100 feet across the swamp to the campground office. They were about to close for the night, so I got directly down to business.

*"How much to upgrade from my tent site to one of your cozy cabins?"* I inquired. With sopping wet bags in each hand, I kicked open the door to Cabin 2A. It was equipped with a double bed, a pair of bunks, a fridge and freezer, heater, air conditioning and cable TV! I threw my bags up on the top bunk, and collapsed on the double mattress... I was exhausted! I closed my eyes for what was meant to be a brief rest, then bolted up suddenly out of bed at about 9 PM. It sounded like hailstones pelting my roof! What? Seriously? I pushed open the heavy, creaking wooden door, where three ducks were

standing upon my covered porch, next to the bag of piñon logs that I had purchased for my fire pit. To my surprise, the weather had cleared, and as I inspected my roof, I discovered a fourth bright white duck with red flesh around his eyes, his snowy crest split down the middle with a spiky gray mohawk! I laughed out loud at his comical appearance. He was the tap dancing culprit that I had mistaken for hailstones. I scolded him, but he just reared back, flapped his wings and turned his back on me..."little wisequacker!"

Since I was awake, I built a fire, and cracked open a warm beer. The rain had subsided, and my pine knots roared to life with the single strike of a match. The smoke mixed with steam from the rain-soaked ashes filled the air with a heavy gray-white veil. The scent of pine under flame always stirs up something spiritual or aboriginal inside of me at the deepest level. It sets all of my restless parts at ease, and as the embers smolder, I am completely grounded, and internally at peace. Many of my fondest and most detailed memories of experiences and conversations with family and friends often occurred at fireside.

As the blaze spewed forth its final puffs of sweet-scented smoke, I took a final swallow of my lukewarm lager, and bid my feathered friends Bonsoir! Before retiring to my bed, I set up my video camera and recorded some narration from Stephen Fleharty's description of Resaca from his book, Our Regiment. Again, I can't help but repeat what a splendid gift his journal has been. Paired with scans of Henry's letters from the field provided by my cousin, Mary Emma Allen, I am equipped with very helpful and valuable navigational aids that have enabled me to visit sites of enormous significance, and locate them with precise coordinates. Rest assured, this quest would've taken place, with or without them, but it would've been a much more frustrating, and time-consuming process, plagued with errors, and dead ends.

Eventually, I would visit Resaca again during the following year, this time by invitation! I would have yet another chance to attempt to locate the Battery site, where Henry experienced his moment of glory, while facing enemy crossfire. For now, my travels southward would continue toward the site where the once thriving southern town of Cassville stood, that is until its ill-fated destruction.

# Kingston & Cassville, Georgia

The Division had seen some heavy fighting on the road between Resaca and Cassville. An order drafted by General Butterfield describes the movements of the operations of the division, as they occurred on the 18th and 19th of May, 1864:

> *"On the 18th, the Division marched twenty miles — much of it in the heat of the sun; partially making its own roads; moving five miles in line of battle, and driving the enemy before them. On the 19th the Division again moved to the enemy's extreme right. The advance of the First Brigade unsupported, driving the enemy to within one and a half miles of Cassville, by the Adairsville road; the reconnaissance of the 3rd Brigade to the railroad between Kingston and Cassville, unsupported, and in the presence of five times its number of the enemy, the defiant attitude of the Division, alone and unsupported, when threatened by thrice its number; the assault and capture of Cassville, by the 2d Brigade; the daring and boldness of the artillery, especially the section of Battery C, 1st Ohio, Lieut King, commanding; their fine practice at the enemy's retreating columns, and the conduct and bearing of the whole Division throughout the two days, especially while in the presence of the main army of the enemy, are worthy of the highest commendation. Resaca and Cassville are proud names for our banners."*

Fleharty continues:

> *During the 20th, 21st and 22nd of May, the troops were permitted to rest in the vicinity of Cassville.*
> *On the 23rd we moved on to the Etowah River. Crossed the river during the afternoon — slight skirmishing in front and cannonading off to the left. Camped a mile south of the stream. There is some beautiful country in the vicinity of Etowah and many elegant residences.*

☆ ☆ ☆

While resting at Kingston near the railroad with the Third

Brigade, Henry drafted a letter to his older brother, Willis. Most of the contents pertained to his activity during the conflict at Resaca, his letter is therefore reserved until later in this chapter.

*Sunday, July 7, 2013 – cloudy, rain.*

Rising at 0630, I strapped on my Nike half boots that were still soaking wet from my trench exploration at Resaca. I cracked the heavy barn style door to observe the weather. Still, it poured! I gathered all of my various camping items, and stowed them in anticipation of my last day afield, which would be Monday. I was packed except for what I needed for the next leg of my journey. Camera? Check. Video camera? Check. iPhone with extremely valuable GPS, Compass, Internet? Check. Water? Check. Rain gear and hat? Check. Check.

After a shower and a brief visit to the office to arrange for one more night in my cabin, I ventured off toward the direction of Atlanta. Uncle Henry was always kind enough to open his letters home by announcing his whereabouts, e.g. "In camp, near "Kingston, Georgey" – here is a curious pattern that I have noticed when reading Henry's letters, and those from his brother, Egbert. Whenever the name of a town or geographical location ends with the short "A", as in AtlantA, CarolinA, etc. the spelling, – as bad as it already is – is deliberately incorrect, and ends with an "e-y", as in "Atlantey, Caroliney," etc. Since my study of these letters, I have cause for conclusion that much of the misspellings are following literal phonetic speech patterns. It is for this reason that I believe this is how Henry actually spoke.

The path to Kingston brought me far into the green canopy of North Georgey's, eh, Georgia's hidden mountain communities. The popular decor treatment of the region was a plush sofa placed in the middle of the common covered porch, sometimes accompanied by a fridge, or other white appliance. All occupants seemed very content with their place in society. I almost envied the citizens I witnessed, relaxing and conversing together on a lazy Sunday morning under gray skies. As I drove through the winding back roads, I caught glimpses of rail track through gaps in the passing clusters of dark pines, bright crêpe myrtles and Mimosa trees in full bloom. I knew I was close to the camp near Kingston where Henry stopped to write about his close calls and victorious capture of that Confederate battery at the Battle of Resaca. I noticed that Henry's regiment, according to his letters and other sources – were typically chosen to guard bridges, railroads, and river crossings. I had been following Hall Station Road all the way from Adairsville, which ended where Howard Street intersected. Noticing a historic placard placed at the junction, I parked the car in a nearby gravel-covered patch and walked over for a closer look.

It read- *"The Federal Army at Kingston – May 19, 1864. The 4th followed by the 14th A.C. reached Kingston 8 a.m. The 4th turned East to Cassville: a division of the 14th went to Gillem's Bridge, Etowah River, finding no retreating Confederates. Johnston's forces were at Cassville, 5.5 miles East. McPherson's 15th and 16th A.C. moving South from Barnsley's, camped on Wooley's plantation 2 miles West: 4th, 20th and 23rd A.C. at Cassville. Sherman's forces in camp to May 23, when advance across the Etowa River began. Of the three bridges, Millam's, Gillem's and Woolley's, only Millam's was burned by the Confederates."*

Another placard, adjacent to the above stated:

*"Sherman's error in assuming that all of Johnston's army had marched from Adairsville, as William J. Hardee had, to Kingston, caused him to order his forces concentrated here – discovering later that the Confederate Army was 5.5 miles east at Cassville and not at the River south of Kingston."*

So, this spot was very close to where Henry was stationed. And what was one block to the west? A railroad *and* a bridge. Perhaps where a depot for Kingston once stood? Kingston had served as Sherman's headquarters in 1864, and it is said that his approval from U. S. Grant to "make Georgia Howl", and his proposed "march to the sea" had all been orchestrated while he was at Kingston. Cassville, only 5.5 miles to the east was too close, and too significant not to include in my itinerary. As I ventured south toward Atlanta, I took a detour to follow Howard St. west, and crossed over into Cassville. It was a fine period film location, with some beautiful pastureland, cleared between vast groves of green, still slick from the recent rains. It set a beautiful platform, rivaled by innumerable stately homes with covered porticos, and domed rooflines in some cases.

At the exact moment I recalled seeing an old church online while researching this location, I accidentally turned right onto a thoroughfare that was called "Church Street." – I knew I had to be close. I drove down the narrow road, and spied a whitewashed spire with louvered panels enclosing its belfry. I pulled up into the driveway, and parked my silver subcompact on the gravelly part of the lawn that I perceived as being the driveway. I stepped out with my camera in hand. A mossy, roughhewn cross, stood about 100 feet from the church, so I included it in the foreground of a few photos. As I was snapping away, I was approached by a 30-something, well-dressed guy who was clutching a bible. Pastor Gary Eastridge explained to me that during the conflict at Cassville in May 1864, the Cassville United Methodist Church had survived the battle, but her bell took a direct hit from a cannonball, resulting in a large crack, so the story goes. I shared Henry's Bible with Pastor Gary, and he seemed interested in my story. He invited me to their 11am service, but I politely declined, for I had my sights set on Atlanta, and a lot of ground to cover on the way. We shook hands, in parting, and he wished me well with my journey and discoveries. I later sent him an email with a link to my blog.

## New Hope Church, Georgia

Fleharty writes:

*"During the 24th of May, 1864, and the afternoon of the 25th, we advanced in the direction of Dallas (GA). We were in a rough, mountainous region, south of Pumpkin Vine Creek, when about 3 o'clock P.M., May 25th, the 2d Division of our corps found the enemy in force near a place called "Burnt Hickory," —more commonly known as New Hope Church. A battle soon commenced. The roll of musketry was incessant and terrific. The 3d Division immediately moved to take up a position on the right of the 2d, and with it General Butterfield was ordered to make a "vigorous attack" on the enemy's left.*

*Some difficulty was experienced in getting into position. The brigades were not in proper communication with each other, and owing to a multiplicity of orders, the regiments of our Brigade became in a measure separated. Night was coming on apace. The conflict raged fiercely on the left, and the enemy in our front were making the air musical with cannon shot, shells, grapeshot and musket balls.*

*Some who were there will recollect how our line, with one involuntary movement, was swayed for an instant towards the earth—like a field of wheat in a storm—as the screeching shells swept overhead.*

*Finally an irregular advance was made. The 70$^{th}$ Indiana and the 102$^{nd}$ Illinois regiments were at first ordered to remain in reserve. In a short time General Butterfield rode along, evidently somewhat excited, and ordered our Colonel to advance at once with his regiment and make a "vigorous attack." We moved forward, over four lines in our troops, who were prone upon the ground, but were halted to await the 70$^{th}$ Indiana. Again we moved forward. It was growing dark; a drizzling rain set in. The rebel guns flashed fire not more than two-hundred yards ahead, and the grape shot rattled around.*

*At that point we were ordered to halt and lie down. No further advance was attempted. The rebels gave a prolonged cheer of victory, and we felt that we had been slightly worsted.*

*The rain increased as darkness set in, and the night was most dismal. In the thick woods—the darkness rendered more impenetrable by the smoke of battle which hung around the earth—regiments and parts of regiments were moved to and fro in the vain endeavor to reorganize the columns. Pitilessly the rain came down, saturating our clothes through and through. Supperless, at length we went to bed, with our blankets only as our covering.*

*During the night Cos. A and F were detailed to build breastworks on a line which had been established for the purpose.*

*Before daylight the other companies of the regiment moved to this line and commenced building works. A heavy fog enveloped the earth when morning came, but the fog did not prevent the rebels from annoying those at work on the fortifications. They opened a galling fire, and Captain D. M. Sedwick was ordered to deploy Co. E and protect the working parties.*

*The Captain was the man for the occasion, and he did his work well. He had received orders to advance his men 150 yards in front of our line, but had not proceeded more than half that distance when he perceived through the fog that he was but two or three rods from the enemy's works. The enemy succeeded in wounding several of his men before he could withdraw them to a proper distance. Finally they were posted behind trees and logs, and they "let fly" with their Spencers in such an effective manner, that the rebels were compelled to retire, temporarily abandoning two field pieces which they had placed in an advanced position. The artillery horses were killed. Co. E had seven men wounded that morning.*

According to Fleharty's list of casualties at New Hope Church, Henry was one of the seven confirmed wounded that day.

☆ ☆ ☆

The following visit to Georgia was a convenient practice-run for me, before the two additional legs of my journey that would follow. This junket therefore appears here —out of sequence— but in consistent order of Henry's march.

On a stormy September morning I lay in bed, wide-awake at about 3:30am with all the symptoms of an unusual insomnia episode. I carefully rolled out of bed at starboard, as my wife slept peacefully at port, with our cat, Hootie, capitalizing on the warmth from the nest she had made between us. I ascended the stairs to my study, and opened Stephen Fleharty's book, as I had often done during sleepless nights, and lazy Sunday mornings spent on our balcony to observe the sunrise. We had just made flight arrangements from our home in Austin to Atlanta, where we would stay for two nights with Andi's cousin, before embarking on our roadtrip to Seneca, SC to spend Christmas with her father's family. This would be our first Christmas without him, since we had said a sad goodbye, just months before, due to his unfortunate complications with Alzheimer's disease. We thought that spending

Christmas with his closest kin would be a favorable gesture, and a much-deserved salute to a great man who would be missed by many.

The pages in my copy of Fleharty's journal that trapped my bookmark introduced the 102nd's encounter with General Joseph E. Johnston's Confederate Army of the Tennessee at Kennesaw Mountain, just west of Marietta, Georgia. Since this location was only 20 miles from the Vinings suburb of Atlanta, where we would be staying, I began my planning for a side trip to discover yet another location where Henry had spent some time during the war. I remembered Fleharty's reference to Henry's wounded status due to Company E's altercation with the "rebs" at New Hope Church, which was not far from the Kennesaw Mountain location, so I added this spot to my itinerary as well. All of my research up to this early morning had not revealed many details surrounding this particular location, except for a photograph I located online, of a small placard that marked the spot. Its significance, however, as it pertained to Henry's service record, ranked high in my travel priorities as a destination that would not be overlooked. Being one of seven enlisted in his company to receive wounds during a brave assault on a Confederate battery according to Fleharty's record, Henry and his company helped place New Hope Church on the map of historic notoriety, for the encounters there are documented in many popular literary accounts.

*December 21, 2012 - Cold. Breezy. Clear.*

I woke early, next to Andi in a comfortable, but unfamiliar bed that seemed to be nearly 5 feet off the ground. The sun filtered its rays through a thick stand of grand pines wafting in the wind through the east-facing windows in the guest quarters. We had spent the evening at her cousin's home in the Vinings community, just outside of Atlanta. It was a historic plantation-style home atop a thoughtfully landscaped hillock, flanked with pines, and lush shrubbery. After my morning ritual of coffee, and a bit of journaling, I kissed my wife goodbye, as she continued to snooze in the plush poster bed in the guestroom. I was excited to rev up our rental and head west to continue following Henry's path as it meandered through the Georgia woodlands, and along the Chattahoochee River. That landmark was just down the hill from where I was now sitting, waiting for my Ford "something-or-other" to warm up.

I pulled out of the driveway, and checked my GPS for the most direct route to Northbound State Hwy 75, which would lead me to a round-a-bout merge onto the 120. On the screen of my iPhone, I recognized "Paces Ferry Road", which was now leading me from the Vinings suburbs to the main highway. Fleharty described this area near the Chattahoochee River in his journal. I imagine him whispering this description as he beholds it:

*"Still it was a pleasant encampment. The weather was much of the time beautiful. During those calm, delicious autumn days, it was a pleasure to wander along the bank of the dark and rapid Chattahoochee, and into the groves, gorgeous with the many hues of autumn. The forests of the South at that season of the year excel our own in beauty. The variety of colors, and shades of colors is wonderful. There is a general somber hue, but this is varied by deep scarlet, purple, and bright yellow foliage, and intermingled with these, the deep green of the pines."*

As I drew closer to the highway, it occurred to me that I was very near the spot in Buckhead, GA where years ago, as I strolled the banks of the Chattahoochee with my future wife, I was overcome with one of those strange qualms or feelings of uneasy intrusion that I was prone to experience on rare occasion. In my reflection, I made an observation that these "spiritual" sensations only materialized when I was completely unaware of any history or personal connection with the location of the occurrence. It was almost as if the experience itself prompted me to research the area, and in doing so, I would eventually recognize the significance of the spot, in some cases as it would pertain to my personal heritage, as in the case of Henry's presence here, nearly 150 years ago. Often, I might arrive at a familiar historic location, and momentarily attempt to mentally (telepathically?) conjure up that tinge on my own, but to no avail. No answer. Just the same, I still held fast to my deep-seated belief that within its mysterious recesses, the mind demonstrates transmitting functions, complimented by its receiving capacities that tend to spontaneously activate on occasion, unprompted and unbridled.

The sun was bright against a perfect blue expanse, yet the air was sharply cold, and a biting northwesterly blew with consistent force, as I directed my vehicle into the wind, causing a noticeable sway. I gripped the wheel with one hand, and a half-peeled banana with the other. I would rush through my impromptu breakfast as I drove, to avoid any interruption that might rob me of valuable minutes that were ticking away with every mile. Finally, my GPS alerted me to the junction of Highway 120 and East Paulding Drive, where I turned right, and continued on a more northbound course. After a few miles through a series of modest curves along the blacktop, I approached a 3-way intersection, which was flanked by a modern brick-built church on my right, and an antiquated, whitewashed wooden church on my left. Ahead of me, splayed out across the landscape was a giant cemetery, dotted with the familiar gray marble monuments that I recognized immediately as Civil War-era headstones. I idled at the intersection for a few minutes, looking to-and-fro, relishing my arrival, I suppose. I didn't notice the green light until I heard the horn from the impatient commuter behind me.

I pulled into the New Hope Baptist Church parking lot, parked the car, and climbed into my winter parka to defy the elements. The stars and stripes were billowing in the wind, adjacent to the confederate "stars and bars," both of which had been thoughtfully hoisted at "half-mast" due to the recent and unfortunate December 14th slayings of children and teachers at Sandy Hook Elementary School in Newtown, Connecticut. A green and brass placard stood in the middle of a small patch of lawn just beyond the hood of my rental car, which read:

"BATTLE OF NEW HOPE CHURCH" Lt. Gen J. B. Hood's A.C. (ARMY OF THE CONFEDERACY) having marched from the Etowah River, reached New Hope Ch., May 25, 1864, in time to halt Gen. J. W. Geary's (2d) div., 20th A. C. (American Cavalry) which had detoured near Owens' Mill enroute to Dallas by New Hope.

Checked by Hood's outposts near the mill, the Federals advanced & struck Stewart's div. astride the road at this point – the left brigade (Stovall's) in the cemetery, with no entrenchments.

Followed then several hours of bitter conflict –late afternoon & night- in rain & thunderstorm. Battle renewed next day." – GEORGIA NATIONAL COMMISSION

After snapping a few photos, I crossed over to the other side of the road to where the small white church stood. Another placard of a different color and shape stood at the edge of the parking strip, which read:

NATIONAL HISTORIC SITE – ATLANTA CAMPAIGN – NEW HOPE CHURCH – MAY 25 – JUNE 4, 1864.

HERE, AT NEW HOPE CHURCH CONFEDERATE AND FEDERAL ARMIES ENGAGED IN A DESPERATE BATTLE AS THE FORMER BLOCKED THE WAY TO ATLANTA, KEY INDUSTRIAL CENTER OF THE CONFEDERACY. SHERMAN AGAIN OUTFLANKED THE CONFEDERATES AND THE TWO ARMIES MOVED TO RENEW THE STRUGGLE AT KENNESAW MOUNTAIN.

NATIONAL PARK SERVICE – UNITED STATES DEPARTMENT OF THE INTERIOR

With both the Federal office, and Georgia's State "Commission" claiming their armies' victories, I found it fascinating that the two sides still engaged in conflict on this location 150 years later.

Resting at a nearby picnic table behind the small church, I decided to give an actual eyewitness his opportunity to settle the dispute once and for all. I pulled Fleharty's journal from my parka, and read his first-hand account for clarification.

Yet another signpost caught my eye, as I rose from the table, and approached the edge of the parking lot where a grove of pines obscured the property behind the petite church building. It read: "Confederate Dug Trenches - Battle of New Hope Church May 25th, 1864". Of course, I couldn't pass up an opportunity to take a walk through remnants of the Atlanta campaign, even if it was once enemy soil. Judging from the angle of the trenches, they countered a large thicket of woods and a subdivision of newer homes, just a few hundred yards away where I imagined Henry and his company were once entrenched. Referencing an old map I had bookmarked on my iPhone showing the supposed position of each Federal and Confederate column, it became clear that I was now standing where three Confederate batteries had once fired upon Henry and Company E. They would, however press forward, the following morning in fog to commandeer a "field piece" belonging to the rebs. I followed the Confederate trenches deep into the pines, until they tapered off into a carpet of dead stumps and logs that made my navigation through the woods difficult. Still, I emerged from the treeline behind the little white church, with just a few minor bruises and scrapes to tend to. I understood —in the physical sense at least— what Henry meant in his letter to his brother, Willis as he spoke of "ruff countrey."

Since my arrival to New Hope Church, the weather had warmed up significantly, and the wind had subsided, so I shed my heavy cloak, and returned to my vehicle in the empty parking lot. I stood alone at a busy intersection where a multitude of soccer moms and weekend warriors were whizzing by, oblivious to the significance of this sacred spot, where nearly 150 years ago, for just two days in May, the future of this disputed region hung suspended in a deadly exchange of rifle fire and cannon blast.

I crossed over to the northwest side of the Dallas-Acworth Highway, and read a few names of the sons, fathers, brothers and great, great grand uncles who had fallen at New Hope Church. I was amazed at the staggering number of Union headstones scattered among their confederate counterparts, and it was no wonder, for according to the testimony of Confederate Captain Samuel T. Foster, "703 Union soldiers had been killed during the fighting that commenced from May 25-26, 1864." I was grateful that Henry laid low.

With my cemetery exploration complete, I returned to the parking lot, and snapped a few photographs for my blog, to share with my growing network of family and friends who had expressed interest in my discoveries. Glancing at my watch, I noticed it was approaching noon, and I hadn't anticipated the trail's end-payoff that New Hope Church had just presented, so I was running a bit behind schedule. I choked down a sandwich, as I studied my GPS for the shortest route possible to Kennesaw Mountain. I pulled out of the parking lot, and followed the directions at just above the speed limit in order to make up for some lost moments; moments well-spent.

# Kennesaw Mountain, Georgia

Never to disappoint, with a precise measure of detail, Fleharty painted a colorful picture of the aftermath of the Battle at Kolb's Farm, and the deadly conflict at Kennesaw Mountain.

*June 27, 1864: Next morning we marched to the position where Gen. Williams and division repulsed the enemy near the Kulp (Kolb) house. Some of the dead were yet unburied. We camped in line of battle – reserve line – in a hollow where many of them had fallen. A small strip of timber at the bottom of the ravine had been fairly riddled by shot and shell from Williams' division.*

*Pools of blood here and there indicated where the brave but misguided rebels fell. It was one of Hood's slaughter pens. In our position as reserves at that place, we were as much exposed to the enemy's balls as we would have been on the front line. They sometimes passed far beyond us to the rear. At other times dropped uncomfortably near. There we remained until the night of the 26th when we moved up to the front line.*

*During the time we were in reserve the brigade furnished pickets every evening – as was customary when in the front. The men were thus often brought into close contact with the enemy, for the skirmishers were seldom idle, day or night.*

*Our position in the line was about 5 miles southwest of Kennesaw Mountain, and commanded a view of the mountain, and much of the intervening country. Kennesaw Mountain proper is the highest peak of a double mountain, and rises 1828 feet above sea level. The summit is nearly bare. A live tree, which stands on the highest point may be seen as far as the mountain itself is visible.*

*Kennesaw was included within the rebel lines. Upon its summit they had planted heavy artillery.*

*The morning of the 27th the troops were ordered to remain near the breastworks – ready to take arms at a moment's notice. The programme was that there should be a demonstration all along the line, and at 8 o'clock and assault at some point on the left. At an early hour the artillery commenced work, and the firing was constant until 8 AM.*

*At that time the cannonading in a measure ceased. Those who were in eligible positions saw dense columns of blue, far away to the left, advancing across an open field toward the enemy. Soon they disappeared into the woods, and there was a crashing roll of musketry, which increased every moment and held all observers spellbound. From our batteries in the open field referred to, the white smoke leaped; at times from each gun in succession, and then from altogether, and the bursting shells left other white puffs of smoke, away over in the woods near the rebel line. And the rebel guns were not idle. Volumes of smoke arising at different points in the thick woods, indicated their positions. Occasionally their balls would make the dust fly on the hillside near our batteries.*

*Far away beyond the immediate scene of action volumes of white smoke rolled away from the guns on Kennesaw Mountain, as they threw shot and shell into our lines. And above the mountain top, or near its summit, the smoke of bursting shells from Union guns, was occasionally seen.*

*It was a magnificent battle scene, without a realization of all the attending horrors. Alas! Amid that storm of human passion many true hearts ceased to beat forever.*

*The assault was made by parts of the IV and XIV Corps. The enemy's works were impregnable, and the assault was a sad failure. The troops fought with desperate courage. The 27th Illinois Regiment, planted its colors on the rebel works, but could not hold the position.*

*The assaulting column finally threw up breastworks within a stones throw of the enemy.*

## W. T. Sherman reported to Washington:

"*The whole country is one vast fort, and Johnston must have at*

*least 50 miles (80 km) of connected trenches with abatis and
finished batteries. We gain ground daily, fighting all the time. ...
Our lines are now in close contact and the fighting incessant,
with a good deal of artillery. As fast as we gain one position the
enemy has another all ready. ... Kennesaw ... is the key to the
whole country."*

Driving northeast from New Hope Church up Barrett
Parkway, I wondered what was waiting at the enormous
National Battlefield Park that had been established on February
18, 1917 to salute the hundreds who had fought at Kennesaw
Mountain. The park stretched over 11.8 square kilometers, and
I was anticipating the thrill of the climb just as much as the
historic data that I was hopeful to capture. I was cursed with a
dominant wanderlust gene, passed down to me by my father,
and in spending my first 23 years in a habitat between the
Olympic and Cascade mountain ranges, with the great peaks
of Rainier to the south, and Baker to the north, I had always
been surrounded by these salient navigational aids. Living on
the fringes of the "hill country" of Central Texas, I felt lost
without them, and always had to snicker a little when
encountering topographical anomalies like Friday Mountain,
Cat Mountain, Mount Bonnell, etc. in the Austin area. I didn't
qualify any hill whose summit could be reached in under 2-3
hours, a "mountain" by any stretch. For the time being,
however, as long as I lived in the South, I would take what I
could get, Kennesaw included.

After about 15 minutes on the road, a prominent peak
winked at me between a flutter of passing buildings and the
random copse of pines that stood along the highway. The hairs
on the back of my neck tingled, as I caught my first peek at the
hill that I had previously read so much about, both in Fleharty's
journal, and elsewhere. Barrett Parkway presented a direct
portal to the National Battlefield Park Headquarters and
Museum, so I made my turn up the steep three-mile grade, and
did my best to contain my excitement. I pulled into the large
parking lot at the base of the hill, and made note of the official
trailhead that I expected was my anticipated route to the
summit. I packed my small HD video camera, and my Canon

G9 digital still camera to record the details of my visit to this notable landmark. A pair of great bronze cannons stood guard before the museum entrance, and after a carefully choreographed self-portrait staged next to one of them, I entered the main building.

I approached the front desk where two men in their 30's were busy about their retail duties, and fielding telephone calls. One of them approached me eager to assist. I produced Uncle Henry's bible, which he examined as I described its origin, as I understood it. He shared the relic with his colleague, who seemed equally impressed. I expressed my interest as to where the 102nd might have been stationed during the conflict of June 27, 1864. As my eager assistant reached for a large, and well-worn binder on his desktop, I pulled out my video camera, and asked permission to document his description. He obliged. The binder, as I soon learned was a copy of William R. Scaife's "ORDER OF BATTLE" published in 1992 in Atlanta, GA. It covered all forces according to rank, both Union and Confederate. This included Henry's company, a part of the 3rd division, XX Corps led by future President, Colonel Benjamin Harrison, serving under Major General Daniel Butterfield, who's commander was Major General George H. "Pap" Thomas, aka "The Rock of Chickamauga".

It was a mystery at first, where Henry's regiment was actually positioned during the Kennesaw Mountain conflict, since Butterfield's name was missing from the battlefield map we were using as a reference. However, we arrived at the realization that the 1st Brigade's original commander, Brigadier General William T. Ward had been wounded at the battle of Resaca, which had occurred on the 15-18th of the previous month, and Butterfield had been reassigned as Ward's temporary replacement. His brigade's position was clearly marked on the battlefield map, near Kolb's farm at the intersection of Powder Springs Road, and Cheatham Hill Road. The guide gave me accurate directions to the spot where I would be able to walk through the trenches that were still visible in the forest just beyond a well-marked horse trailer parking lot. I was excited to experience the sensation of tracing more of Henry's warpath. First, however, a grand mountain stood between Marietta, and me and it had to be conquered.

After walking through the museum, and purchasing my own copy of Scaife's "Order of Battle", I thanked the gents behind the desk, exited the main building, and wheeled around toward Kennesaw Mountain, where I found a convenient trailhead to follow. It would take me to the peak, which was approximately 551 meters high, and a mile's ascent through a switchback path that twisted through a forest of tall hardwoods, and thick mounds of pine needle carpeting. I was still wrapped in my parka, as the temperature was still in the 40's, but it didn't take long before it became necessary to begin shedding layers. Along the path, I passed an occasional cannon, and thought it might be a good idea to capitalize on these relics as a fitting background for some photography. Pulling Henry's bible from my camera bag, I gently placed it on a split rail fence that surrounded one of the guns, and snapped a photo. A thought occurred to me. Henry's bible had most likely been in his pocket during his time spent in this area. It had come full circle, and I had carried it back. I felt proud, and happy to be here on this day, and glad I wasn't standing here 148 years ago. By the time I reached the summit of Kennesaw Mountain, I was stripped down to my tee shirt, which was now soaked with perspiration. Out of shape, out of breath, and nearly out of daylight, I had just checked a BIG box on my "must-do" list.

After descending the mountain, I returned to the parking lot, and drove to the site of Kolb's farm, where the original house still stood in a recently preserved condition. The busy intersection of Cheatham Hill Road and Powder Springs Road seemed an unlikely spot to find Civil War trenches, yet, behind a parking lot, right where the museum staff had directed me, I found them. I walked their lengths through the heavily-wooded corner, and through the gulleys, still so sharply defined, even after being carpeted with decades of plant matter and needles, shed by the trees towering overhead. Once again, I walked in Henry's footsteps, wondering what he must have been feeling during this, his third year serving his country, rifle and sidearm in hand. One thing is for certain, as he fought and foraged, he was transformed from a Quaker farm boy into a man, unafraid to venture out, establish a 10-acre farm, and then start all over again in Texas with a new wife, new life, new future. It's just a shame that it came to such an abrupt ending.

# Battle of Peachtree Creek, Georgia

Shortly after Confederate President, Jefferson Davis chose to relieve General Joseph Johnston from command for his lack of aggression, his replacement, Lieutenant General John B. Hood launched an attempted counter-offensive at Peachtree Creek, as the Army of the Cumberland tightened the Union grip around Atlanta. Though Uncle Henry did not mention in his letters, his direct involvement in the battle, the 102nd was absolutely in the thick of the engagement. Company E in particular was hailed for their handling of their Spencer carbines. Stephen Fleharty was also there, beholding details he would later record in his journal, near the site of Collier's Mill, where, as reported by Union Major J. D. Cox *"few battlefields of the war had been strewn so thickly with dead and wounded as they lay that evening."*

*At seven o'clock A. M., July 20th, we were again in motion, under orders to occupy a range of hills south of Peach Tree Creek. There had been considerable artillery firing during the two previous days, and it was apparent, by all movements, that the enemy were in strong force a short distance ahead.*

*As we neared the creek, skirmishing became active in front, and we were soon in range of the balls. Crossing the stream we halted for a time in a corn-field at the base of a hill. The day was intolerably warm—scarcely a breath of air stirring. At length we moved a half-mile to the right. While marching by the flank, through a corn-field in the valley, an advance was made by our skirmishers, up the hillside a few hundred yards to the left, or front. The rebels fired briskly and their balls whisked spitefully through the young corn. No one in the regiment was struck. We halted again at the base of the range of hills south of the creek.*

*The rebel sharpshooters were busily at work. Several men were struck while we were in that position. A battery which our artillerymen endeavored to plant on a bare hill a short distance in the rear of our line, was subjected to such a scathing fire that it was taken away as quickly as the horses could remove it under whip and spur. Nevertheless, we did not*

*anticipate any very serious work—nothing more than a slight
skirmish, when we should advance to construct works at the
crest of the hill. The First Brigade had been formed on the
right of the division, and the 102d was on the right of the
brigade—next on the left was the 79th Ohio, and on the left of
that regiment was the 129th Illinois. The 70th Indiana and 105th
Illinois regiments were at first held in reserve, but they moved
forward when the battle was at its height, and engaged the
enemy in a hand-to-hand fight.*

*On the right of our regiment, a battery had been
planted. Near this battery the left of the 2d Division rested,
when the battle commenced.*

*The 102d occupied a knoll, in front of which was a
clump of timber and a small creek. Farther to the left this
stream curved northward, and across it the left of the Brigade
was formed.*

*The rebels advanced in heavy masses down the slope of
a hill in front of the 2d and 3d Brigades, and the left of our
Brigade. The inequalities of the ground prevented them from
advancing in force in our immediate front.*

*On the left of the 20th Corps they struck Newton's
Division of the 4th Corps, and on the right engaged a brigade of
the 14th Corps. Between the 14th Corps and our position on the
line, they hurled a heavy column on the 2d Division of the 20th
Corps.*

*Our position on the knoll commanded a fine view of the
open field through which the enemy advanced on the left.
Sheets of fire blazed along the line of muskets in their front. Yet
without faltering or wavering they pressed forward, their
advance actually piercing the center of our division—the body
of gray intermingling with the line of blue.*

*They were subjected to a terrible enfilading fire from
the 79th Ohio and the 102d Illinois. A perpetual sheet of flame
blazed from their Spencer rifles in the hands of our men. And
the battery on our right with wonderful energy poured shot and
shell into their ranks. Still for a time they persisted firing as*

*they moved forward. Rebel flags waved defiantly in their front line, and were quickly shot down—but quickly taken up and carried forward to the line where waved the stars and stripes. A hand-to-hand contest ensued at that point, the combatants half hidden by fire and smoke and dust.*

*Will the enemy never give back? With intense solicitude we mark the ebb and flow of the battle. At last they waver; numbers drop to the rear, others quickly follow. And finally the entire body is rolled back in utter rout and confusion by our advancing lines. And then the suppressed feeling of the victors find utterance in a shout that rises high above the roar of battle—a wild, thrilling, prolonged shout of victory.*

*Owing to the favorable position our regiment occupied we lost lightly—two men killed and nine wounded. The loss of the brigade was about one hundred and seventy killed and wounded.*

*Although the 102d escaped with so little loss, the regiment inflicted immense damage on the enemy. It was estimated at that time, that five thousand rounds of cartridges were fired from the Spencer rifles alone.*

*Co. E warmed up the Spencer guns as the hearts of the men became warmed with patriotic enthusiasm.*

Henry wrote two letters from his posts near Atlanta that I know of, to his older brother Willis who was living back in New York. Writing only after a week had passed since the battle of Peachtree Creek, he reveals some useful data concerning the losses as a result of the conflict.

*July the 28 1864*

*in Camp Behind*

*Brestworcks, Atlanty*

*Dear Brother I thout I woud write you a few more*

*lines toletyou know how I am geting along to day I am still
well & enjoying good helth as is well to day is very hot there
is considerabell artillery fiting to day the shells come whissing
over our heds ocasionley which loocks very sousey &
dangereous to be hellthey we lose our corps commander to
day Gen Hoocker (Joseph Hooker) he visited the men to day
he sed he regreted to leve us but scurcunstanses compeled him
to he sed he never had men that he coud put so mutch
confedence in as this Corps some ses he is ordered to report to
Washington we regret to part with him for he is a good
commander the report is that our corps lost in the late battle of
the 20 21 & 22 (The Battle of Peachtree Creek) was 27
hundred in kild & wounded well I dont whether the mail will
go out this evening or not well I ges I will now finish this
leture now the mail oes out at 4 ocl. this evening the mail has
come to the company but none for me well canonading is
hevey all along the line the report is that Genral Williams is to
take his plais well Willis you must write when you get this
leture for I am ancious to here fom you & family I hope these
few more scratch lines will find you well my ink is very poor
But good ink is hard to get here & all riting meterrall at
pressent as ever yours with love to you & familey*

*Henry Banks*

*Sunday, July 7, 2013 - cloudy, rain. (continued)*

    Later that morning I had put a good distance between
Cassville, and Acworth, where I was currently positioned with a
gas pump handle my hand. I was surprised at how far I had
traveled on a single tank of gas, and even more shocked when
the tank reached its capacity at just over $20. What? I was so
used to filling up my SUV to the tune of $70 or more, and
traveling half the distance between fill-ups. "Perhaps it was
time," I thought to myself, "to shed the SUV pattern that I had
maintained since I graduated from college over 20 years ago."
Just then, a Jeep Cherokee zoomed past, with a smiling,
panting golden retriever protruding his head through an open
window. I was reminded of a deal struck between Andi and

myself. We had agreed that when our oldest cat passed on into eternity, we would adopt a dog. The SUV saga therefore would continue, and the transition to an economy car would have to wait, for now.

Once on the road again, I began seeing signs for Kennesaw and Marietta. I had explored this area during the previous year, along with New Hope Church, where Henry was reportedly injured during a charge to overtake a Confederate battery. I could've easily stopped to visit those sites again, but only half a day remained, and I had a full agenda meant for exploration of new discoveries. Still, I began to recollect some of the familiar names on highway exit signs, as I drew closer to Atlanta.

My decision to exit Highway 71, and merge onto Paices Ferry Road proved to be wise, for as the steady downpour intensified, the safe, dry shelter beckoned at the Atlanta History Center. My good fortune would follow me inside to the ticket counter, where an easel card announced that all customers belonging to my banking institution could enter the history center admission-free! There was my gas money that would get me back to Nashville on Monday.

Waiting inside the Atlanta History Center was a rich repository full of incredible Civil War relics, some of which were almost too good to be true. Behind a glass-paned display case, for instance was an open ship's log book from the "Shenandoah" featured in one of my favorite books: "*Sea of Gray*". Its captain and crew hunted down Union merchant ships, scuttled or sank them in the name of the Confederacy, and continued to do so, long after Lee had surrendered at Appomattox, that is, until someone produced a newspaper announcing the war's end. Another astonishing relic was an original supply wagon, still emblazoned with hand-painted signage that was faded with age, but applied with the flourish of a masterful hand. One dominant plank was fashioned with heavy blocked letters that identified the wagon as belonging to the XXth Corps. It was therefore a somewhat practical assumption that Uncle Henry could have interacted with this vehicle somehow, even if it simply carried to him, some of the rations that sustained him through the war. Throughout the impressive Civil War exhibit were some of the best-preserved uniforms, weapons, ordinance, flags, and other paraphernalia that I ever laid eyes upon. Once I had my fill of antiques, bullets, bombs, and sepia photos from that bygone era, I got back on the road.

One of Henry's letters had been penned from the railroad bridge at the confluence of Peachtree Creek and the Chattahoochee River, where he and Company E had been standing guard. It was puzzling to pinpoint exactly where the Battle of Peachtree Creek had actually taken place, so when I arrived at a city park that appeared to be dead center within the battlefield site, I parked the car, and stepped out to walk for a while. Referring to an old map of the area, it became obvious to me that the site was too obscured by homes in the sprawling cluster of affluent suburbs to compare details. Being cramped up in my subcompact rental, with faulty AC, I was already soaked with my own sweat, so when the clouds finally parted, and the sun's heat intensified, I hardly noticed the change. I followed a path that led to a narrow greenbelt that straddled both ends of a huge subdivision. The road that intersected it was called Peach Tree Battle Avenue. Surely there would be some sort of monument here. My stroll would prove fruitless, that is, until I arrived at a large plaque on Collier Avenue, on return route to my vehicle. The plaque listed the forces engaged at the great battle. Ward's 3rd Division of the XXth Corps was listed as a part of Sherman's Right Wing. This was evidence enough that I stood where the battle once raged.

## *Atlanta, Georgia*

I love how Stephen Fleharty described in detail the scene that transpired before the great city of Atlanta. He presented a feast for the senses and imagination that satisfied this hungry reader. Painting with his pen, as it were, his description of the scene before him comes alive, like a meticulously crafted rendering, presented in rich living color.

*Some of the most imposing scenes of war are associated with our recollections of the siege of Atlanta. Sherman's grand army formed a line of battle at least fifteen miles in length. Let us look at the picture: First we observe the irregular line of breast-works winding mile-after-mile, over hill and valley. In the rear of these were the small white shelter tents, pitched in regular order, and a little farther to the rear*

*were long lines of red earth, indicating the positions from
which the army had advanced. From several points the city
was plainly visible, and through openings in the forest the rebel
forts and earthworks could be seen; at times thronged with men
in gray. From a high range of hills in the rear of our position
we had a fine view of the situation. Farther to the rear the
immense wagon trains were grouped. Here and there were
clusters of neat hospital tents. All the roads were thronged
with footmen and horsemen, teamsters, orderlies, Generals and
staff officers. In the front the scene was no less active. The
inevitable picket firing, as regular as the "droppings" of a
slow rain, reached the ear from the picket line. Light wreaths
of smoke were visible where our cannons were at work, and
little white "puffs" were occasionally suspended in midair by
exploding rebel shells. The deep dull roar of artillery, far
away, right and left was heard.*

*If a single element was needed to render the
impression intensely vivid, it was supplied by the glorious
music of the field bands, playing those noble campaign pieces,
which will never be heard in these days of peace without
bringing a tear to a soldier's eye.*

*The long delay before Atlanta tested the moral courage
of the army. What would be done next? The enemy's position
seemed impregnable in front. Was Sherman at last brought to
a dead lock? Had his flanking machine entirely played out?*

*Thus we queried, watched and waited.*

On November 8, 1864, President Abraham Lincoln won the
re-election against George McClellan by more than 400,000 popular
votes on the strength of the soldier vote and military successes like the
Atlanta campaign. Henry makes note of Election Day, which would
follow the date on which he wrote this letter to Willis. This example of
his writing is perhaps the most heartfelt of all his letters, where he
longingly wishes to prepare his younger brother Egbert, for the realities
of war that Henry himself has witnessed thus far. Egbert apparently had
opted to enlist voluntarily as a reluctant draftee's replacement.

*Nov the 7 1864*

*In camp on the Chattehootchy*

*Georgia*

*Dear Brother I received your leture to day. I am very glad to hear from you & famaley. but sory to hear that you all are not well I had bin loocking for a leture a long time I am enjoying good helth & I hope thes lines will find you all the same we dont reseave harley eny mail now days there seams to be some grate move goin on in this department the trains are running day & nite to & fro from Atlanty the move seams to be a secret consern no one can find out what is there object unless is the offisers hye in comand we reseaved orders last sabath to be redy to martch but it was countermanderd & we still remain hear lantch on our ores(?) not knowing where we will land before spring comes. I have not had eny leture from home in sometime they wer then all well Mother sed Egbert had vollenteard to take a mans plais in Iowa that was drafffted. Sens then I received a few lines from Egbert the 18 of last month he was then in Nashvill Tennesse he sed he left Davenport Iowa then he sed he liked solgering very well he is in the 17 Corps 11 Iowa Reg Co A Ithink it is Cowelly (Cavalry) but I am not shure I answerd his leture to find out the particlures the 17 Corps is betwean hear & Chatanoogy some plais the report is here that the 16 & 17 are in camp betwene here & Meryeta (Marietta, GA) it is 12 miles from hear I cannot find out for surtin whether it is so or not there is so mutch faults (false) reports one canot hardley beleave what he hears if I knew for surtin I woud try to find him but he coud finde me easeyer for I told him particuler where I am & if he is cavellry he can get around easeyerthan I can I woud like to se him to give him some information about solgering he was speaking a bout liking solgering I think he has not sean the first spark hardly of solgering I think by the time he gose threw a campaign like the past one was he onte (won't) rellishit as good as he dose now for my part I donte want experance the same again if it can posabell be helpt there has bin a grate meny lives destroid in this cruell ware for the love of our countrey & the constitution & the union that our forefathers handed down to us must it be saved or destroid after so meny*

*des perate struggells for its restoration  I apeal before god &
man it must  I have done all in my power  &  I will do more if
nead be  I have laid my life down for its sake for 2 long years
mingeld with hard ships strifes & toil & have sean the strugells
of meny a battel field & the dying grones of  of meny & brave
boy  did these come to waist there lifes for nothing  No God
forbid  we as solgers of the uneion or once auld unieon came to
fite & dy if nead be for the uneion & Constitution as it was
before the ware broke out  not to fe (free?) one negro whitch
has bin medeld a munbeld (mettled with and mumbled about)
at to mutch all redy  let them be  they will fre them selves  we
can saffely say they are all redy fread  as far as the uneion
forses go  well to morow is election day (Lincoln's 2nd term)
whitch will tell the tale for good or bad soone  there is a grate
deal rely in upon that one thing I hope & pray for the President
that can save this now dis tracted contrey & destroy the enemy*

*as ever your brother Henry*

*with love to you all Goodby*

I returned to Atlanta Memorial Park, and reluctantly
folded myself back into the sauna that was posing as my rental
car. I then proceeded to drive into the direction of the
confluence where Peachtree Creek and the Chattahoochee
intertwined. I was certain of this location being where Henry
had camped, based on his description in one of his letters.
Driving back-and-forth across bridges, into dead-end streets,
and fenced parking lots, I was denied access, for the entire
coastline of this key location had been claimed by water
treatment plants, and other industrial eyesores. Frustrated, I
parked at a gas station, walked a half-mile to the center of the
Marietta Boulevard Bridge, which offered a view of the railroad
trestle spanning the Chattahoochee. Satisfied, I snapped a
photo, and returned to my rolling hotbox.

At about this time my iPhone rang. It was Willa, my
wife's cousin. She and her husband Charlie had been
expecting a call and I had lost track of time. Willa reminded me

of her address, and my corresponding GPS displayed their neighborhood location, which was just a stones throw away. I drove down Paices Ferry Road to the Nancy Creek area, and located their home, which was flanked by two opposing magnolia trees in full bloom. I was greeted with a warm hug from Willa, who received a sticky, sweaty embrace from me. This came with a sincere apology and explanation that shamed my rental car company, and their faulty equipment. I joined Willa and Charlie in there beautifully decorated living room, and brought them up to speed with the latest of my escapades through the southern bush, in search of my Great, Great Grand Uncle's campsites. Charlie disappeared briefly, and as I finished my microbrew, he returned with a pair of hiking boots that he began to lace up. "Feel like taking a little hike?" he asked. A loaded question if ever one was asked. "Sure!"

I rose up and beat Charlie to the door. He led me out to the heavily wooded slope behind their home. He recently had his property "staked out," and had more land than he originally thought. We strolled through a narrow path that twisted through ankle-high ivy and lush, mossy carpeting. The rain had subsided mercifully, but the earth was still damp, and I lost my footing intermittently as we negotiated the downward-sloping property. We passed a pit dug out of the ground, which resembled a picket post that I had seen before at other sites. Next to it was a small, rectangular fenced-in an area that looked like a grave of some sort. There were no markers present, so its origin was uncertain. Charlie mentioned that he had some "treasure hunters" pass through a while back. They scanned the area with metal detectors, but reportedly came up empty. The heights above Nancy Creek seemed a likely place where an advancing army might find defilade, or a retreating army, at that. Once Charlie and I had descended down to Nancy Creek's shoreline, some dilapidated shelters, or structures became visible. We entered one building whose roof had caved in, and looked as if it had served as some sort of animal pen, for cattle or livestock. I didn't figure the age of the structures to date back to Henry's time, but they were interesting to stroll through, just the same. The XXth Corps under Hooker had skirmished with the rebels and advanced across Nancy Creek according to some of my resources. Charlie had heard rumors of a Revolutionary War incident that had taken place here, but I have not found record of it, to date. All in all, based on a description of an eastward march that commenced on July 17<sup>th</sup>, 1864, three miles from Paices Ferry, I concluded that Henry and the 102nd quite possibly could have passed through Charlie and Willa's property nearly 150 years ago.

Willa had spaghetti ready for Charlie and I, once we hiked back to the house, and shortly after plates were cleared, I thanked them both for setting aside their afternoon plans to visit with me.

Once I was back on the road, I made a point to stop by the bridge that marked a pontoon span where the XXth Corps had crossed over the Chattahoochee River to the Fulton County side, on their way to seize Atlanta. The spot is known as Paices Ferry, where I found the highest number of historic placards I have ever beheld in a single concentrated area. There was obviously much activity occurring at this spot. After walking across the complete span of the bridge and back to my car, I made a beeline for my cabin back in Calhoun.

The drive north from Vinings to Calhoun was not as congested as the reverse route I had taken earlier in the day. The weather had improved, and Sunday evening traffic was sparse. Still, I took in the passing scenery reflecting sunlit hues of every green shade in the spectrum. Georgia is one of the most beautiful states you will ever visit.

My cabin was just as I had left it, and an almost full bag of firewood was still on the porch, so I splintered off some kindling, and started a nice fire just a few feet from my porch swing. A single can a lager was waiting in my tiny fridge inside the cabin. I fired up a cigar, kicked back in my porch swing, and reflected on the event-filled day while the smoke from my stogie merged in midair with that of my crackling bonfire. The sunset was too good not to share, so I called my wife with a full report of my day. (Cue background sound effects of baying goats and crowing peacocks)

*One of many historic placards in and around the bridge spanning over the*
*Chattahoochee River near Vinings, a suburb of Atlanta, GA*

*Detail of a wagon marked for the 20th Corps on display at the*
*Georgia History Museum in Atlanta*

## *Preparations for the Second Leg*

Shortly after I returned to Texas from my trip to Tennessee and Georgia, a significant life-altering shift in my routine took place. My employer, a high tech data storage company had its third in a series of layoffs in 2013, and this time three of my team members and yours truly were escorted to a conference room, awarded a meager severance packages and a limp handshake. To our surprise, the remaining 200+ employees had been shuffled off into a larger conference room where they would have to wait as we raced the clock to clean out our office, and exit the premises within thirty minutes as the HR Manager stood in the hall tapping his foot and eyeing his watch. Our computers had been seized, and all valued contacts I had established during my year as Marketing Director had been wiped from all devices. I felt particularly horrible, since I had hired my team one-by-one, hand-picked for their various talents, and we had made some great strides together, producing measurable results that gave incremental sales a significant boost. Yet here we sat together, humiliated, and anxious to get through the process and move on.

Eight months later, I reached the tail end of an aggressive job search, I had finally had enough of the routine, and the seemingly endless string of frustrations and disappointments that come with rejection letters, lackluster hiring managers, empty promises, and time wasted answering expired postings. I had obviously reached a point in my career where I was either too experienced, too expensive, or both. Taking stock in my talents, strengths, experience and my writing ambitions, I sat down and wrote myself a letter of recommendation. Passing a series of intimidating interviews with myself, I presented a handsome offer, which I immediately accepted. I formed my own Video Production Company virtually overnight, and fell in with the ranks of the self-employed. Ken, my friend and creative cohort since the 1970's happily accepted my invitation to become my business partner, and it didn't take long before we landed our first paying contract, and another soon followed. I was excited, expectant, nervous, but I was not going to go through another layoff as long as I kept my new venture afloat. That was my motivation.

My writing and research had taken a back seat to that grueling job-hunting schedule, which gave way to the creation of a business plan, a full-blown website, and a handful of capability videos to help market our services. At about that time, an unexpected opportunity presented itself, and reignited my passion to continue my pursuit of Henry Banks that had since come to a grinding halt.

Shortly after my trip through Tennessee and Georgia, I had sent a copy of one of Henry's letters to the Resaca Battlefield Preservation Organization. Through some correspondence, an advertisement arrived in my inbox that announced the 150th anniversary Reenactment that would take place at Resaca over a weekend in May. A few emails later, I had an official invitation to fall in with the 125th Ohio Union Regiment who would be camping out over the weekend of May 16-18 at Resaca, and participating in battle reenactments to take place upon the actual field that Henry had charged across in 1864. When I had originally set forth to capture Henry's story, the notion to actually suit up in the Union blues had never even occurred to me. Looking back across nearly ten years of involvement, and all of the unexpected connections and fortuitous encounters that I had experienced along the way, I had only one response to this unexpected opportunity: "Absolutely!"

I found a download online of a pocket sized field manual derived from Brigadier General W. J. Hardee's Rifle & Infantry Tactics. I sent the file to my printer, and stapled it together to form my own portable study guide to keep with me for quick reference. I had no idea that being a skirmisher required so much preparation. I was both excited and apprehensive to join the ranks of seasoned Reenactors, and to keep up with their drills and maneuvers. One of the officers had written to set my mind at ease, and promised to spend some prep time with me the day before the battle, and to pair me up with an experienced comrade. Still, I kept my handbook within reach, and referred to it whenever the opportunity arose.

The final days of my trip would fall on Memorial Day weekend. I had never visited our nation's capitol, and now that I was approaching my 50th birthday, I figured that it was about time to make that trip, even if it was just for the weekend. Would it be a befitting ending to the entire journey? Or would it produce more open doors into the Banks family saga? Time would tell, but one thing was for certain...I was pumped to get back on the road, and was ready for just about anything. I had a long list of family members, friends, acquaintances, former colleagues, and perfect strangers who were rooting for me, and looking forward to acquiring their copy of my finished book, or at least hearing about the details of the final leg. I wouldn't dare disappoint them. This was going to get interesting.

# The Five Tenders

Thursday, May 15, 2014 Clear. Humid.

I drove off this morning at 0400 hours from Austin and headed northeast towards Resaca, Georgia to fall in with the 125th Ohio Civil War reenactors unit. Yes, though they all live in Georgia, it is a union detachment. My drive was dark and dull as I made my way across East Texas. However, by the time the sun finally broke the horizon, I had nearly made it to the Louisiana border. I passed through Palestine, Texas with my radio blasting and sunroof open, to keep me awake, since I was driving on about three hours of sleep, and I hadn't stopped yet for coffee. I was in need of some rot-gut paint thinner foglifter java, the kind that the convenience stores couldn't provide, so I would have to wait until my favorite haunt, well, chain would open their doors at around 7 AM. Thank God that hour was approaching. I flew through Tyler, Texas at about 6:45 AM, and passed by the entrance to camp Fannin – an Army infantry training camp used in World War II from 1943–1946. I finally crossed into Louisiana, by way of the city of Shreveport.

The rising sun glinted off the high-rise jungle of casinos, with their mirrored windows blinding me with a flash! flash! flash! between garish billboards -their messaging was completely obscured by the bright strobes of sunlight that practically sent me careening off the overpass! I continued motoring East in my new 2014 Jeep Cherokee Trail Hawk. I was averaging about 25 miles per gallon, which was a vast improvement from the poor fuel economy that I had experienced with my Hummer H3 that I had just traded in. Andi had questioned my decision to purchase the trail-rated, four-wheel-drive version, which came with a locking rear differential and "Rock-Crawler Drive" mode. She wanted to settle for the soccer mom version, which I took a very stubborn position against. "When are you ever going to need four-wheel-drive?" she asked. I would need it soon enough. Highway 20 passed beneath my axles as I left town-after-town in my rearview. Baudcau, Red Chute, Fillmore, and a McIntire slipped past in a blur. I wondered if Sibley, Louisiana had anything to do with Sibley tents, a Tipi or Tipi-looking conical tent used periodically by the Union Army during the Civil War.

There had been over 40,000 of these tents produced, and that's the extent of my Sibley tent knowledge, for now. Soon, the turnoff to Gibsland, Louisiana was in view, and following the exit sign was a small billboard directing me to the Bonnie and Clyde Ambush Museum. My memory was instantly populated with a montage of black and white photos that splashed across the spread of some old magazine my father kept in his study. These gory aftermath snapshots were most likely the first crime scene photos that I had ever laid eyes on. I was very young at the time, but they left an indelible impression. I would've liked to stop to pay a visit but it was still early, and the site was a conflict in context. I was, after all, in an 1860's research mode. Soon I crossed over the Ouachita River as I passed through Monroe, Louisiana — the state's eighth largest city. But this passage was significantly trumped by my arrival at Vicksburg, and the long bridge crossing over the great Mississippi. I did decide to stop at this noteworthy city which was a key strategic prize for the Union, where two major assaults were executed against Confederate defenses by U. S. Grant's Army of the Tennessee, resulting in heavy casualties. Enemy forces surrendered Vicksburg on July 4, 1862. This was a major turning point in the Civil War. Uncle Henry was still on picket duty, and drilling at Fort Thomas in Gallatin Tennessee at the time, so I only stopped for a fuel refill, and a large cup of dark roast for the road.

In the parking lot, I encountered a group of teens congregating around a picnic table, smoking cigarettes. One was busily writing with his head buried in a notebook. His green canvas satchel was completely covered with neat cursive writing in black ballpoint ink. Had he at some point, run out of paper? I approached him, and out of curiosity, I asked what he was writing. He reached down, and gave his companion pit bull a welcome pat on the head. "Just journaling." He said. "Are y'all from around here?" I asked. "Nah, we ride trains." I had heard of this subculture of trainhoppers, but I didn't picture them as homeless teens. They all seemed to be enjoying their life of freedom and adventure, and the company of their like-minded peers. I wished the young writer and his sidekick safe travels, and returned to my jeep.

Once I passed through Jackson, Mississippi, Meridian

was not far beyond. Here, my route took a swing from eastbound to a more northerly direction, which offered little more than a leisurely cruise, between opposing stands of towering pine, until I reached Tuscaloosa, Alabama. Merging onto the 59 Highway, I would soon pass through Gadsden. This was a beautiful town with historic façades facing the Coosa River. Second only to the seaport of Mobile, Gadsden had once been the most important commerce and industry port in the state of Alabama.

Gadsden was an attractive and idyllic setting, and my desire to investigate it was overcome by the nagging anticipation that seemed to press my foot harder on my accelerator in route to Resaca.

## *Resaca, Georgia...take two!*

I wound up pulling into the Battlefield Park at about 11 PM. Men were darting about across the parking lot by the light of my high beams, and though I inquired numerous times, no one seemed to know where the Union camp was located, so I kept driving down a dirt road which, by now was only lit by a quarter moon dimly shining through a thin cloud layer above. My eyes were tired, and were beginning to play tricks on me, so I stopped in a designated reenactors parking lot, and leaned back in my driver seat to rest my eyes, but not before reading a passage from Fleharty's journal, to put everything I was about to experience into true perspective:

*Friday morning, May 13, we moved in a direction to the right of Resaca around which place the rebels had entrenched themselves, and were ready to give us battle. The cavalry which had been thrown out in advance, became engaged with the enemy's videttes at an early hour, and we soon learned that General Kilpatrick had been wounded and borne to the rear. The rebels were stubborn. In the afternoon the infantry was pushed forward to "feel" the enemy, and develop his position and strength. We advanced through groves of young pines – the most dense we had yet seen. Among the pines, in line of battle! How indelibly the scene is fixed in memory. What soldier of Sherman's army can view, even at this day, a grove of young pines without having those days of carnage and death recalled to mind?*

*Slowly the enemy's skirmish line was pressed back by our skirmishers, and late in the afternoon the skirmishers in front of the 15th Corps approached, and finally charged and captured a redoubt with two guns.*

*Our division had been separated from the other divisions of the corps, and was formed on the right of the 14th Corps. The advance was continued at intervals until dusk. Halting in an open field at the base of the range of hills, we rested a while, and ate a hastily prepared supper. After dark, moved on by a circuitous route, quietly and carefully, into line of battle, on the opposite side of the hill. The position of the enemy had now been fully developed. Only a narrow valley separated their line from ours. They had been hard pressed during the day, and perceived the necessity of constructing strong defensive works. As we formed in line, the busy click, click, click of their axes could be distinctly heard and they seemed to be working for dear life. We occupied a ravine which ran parallel with the hill about 150 feet above its base. Companies E and G were sent out as skirmishers during the night. Captain McManus had command of the line, and was assisted by Captain Sedwick. Both most excellent men – the former, daring almost to a fault, the latter, perfectly cool and collected in any position of danger. It is related of captain S. that on that occasion it became necessary at one time for him to pass from post-to post in a very exposed position, in plain view of the enemy, and as their balls raised the dust about his feet, the only perceptible change in his manner consisted in the more rapid puffing of the smoke from his pipe.*

*Early in the morning a dash forward to Camp Creek was made. Being then near novices in the art of warfare, many of the men took up positions where they were quite at the mercy of the enemy, and were compelled to remain behind stumps and trees all day – an attempt to escape being equivalent to certain death. It was an exciting day on the skirmish line; firing commenced at daylight, and was kept up until dark. At one time the enemy endeavored to flank the line, and Captain Sedwick discovering the movement from his position in front, recrossed the field to his reserve, and with them advanced on the left and drove the enemy back. Meanwhile there was heavier work on the left. The skirmishing had been lively in that direction all the afternoon, but at 2:00 PM the firing became terrific. There was a perpetual roll of musketry, and the deep base of the artillery reverberated grandly through the woods, and was echoed back by the surrounding hills.*

*At that time we were ordered for work, and the moment we appeared on this little elevation in front of the ravine, the rebel sharpshooters sent their balls whistling around us, killing one man instantly and wounding three. Having proceeded a short distance, we were ordered to halt and lie down.*

*The object doubtless was to make a feint of attacking, in order to divert the attention of the enemy from the left.*

*No further advance was attempted, and we remained in that position until late in the evening, listening occasionally to the whizzing of bullets above our heads, but more deeply interested in the fierce conflicts at our left. The sound at times would run along the line toward us, until it would seem that our corps must soon, also, become engaged, then it would recede, and there would be a lull, like the lulling of the wind in a winter storm. Sometimes it would seem that our men were driving the rebels, and again it appeared that the battle was going against us. O! How terrible the suspense of waiting at such a time for victory, while contemplating the possibility of disaster!*

*The sound of battle at its height could only be compared in my mind to the work of a storm, breaking and crushing to the ground, 10,000 dead trees every instance, amid the roll of heaven's artillery.*

*A battery about 50 yards to the left of our regiment was kept busy throwing shot and shell into the rebel lines, but the guns of the enemy were engaged where the contest raged more fiercely, and they paid no attention to this battery.*

*Towards evening the sounds of battle died away, and finally dwindled down to the irregular firing of the skirmishers. At dusk we retired to our position in the ravine. The regiment had lost during the day three men killed and nineteen wounded.*

*Late at night the camp was hushed in repose, and beneath the lovely foliage of the trees we slept sweetly—but ere we slept, we looked up through our leafy covering to the bright stars that twinkled so peacefully in the calm blue sky, and thought of other and distant skies of peace—of those far away, as dear to us as life—and thought of the morrow.*

*At 2-o'clock next morning we were aroused, and ordered to resume the advance position that had been abandoned the evening before. During the time intervening before day light, slight breast-works were thrown up—the first we ever built.*

*The morning of Sunday, May 15, 1864, dawned luridly upon us. The smoke from innumerable camp fires had enveloped hill and valley in a hazy mantle.*

*At six-o'clock we were ordered to move around to the left of the 14th Army Corps.*

*Quietly we marched back over the hill, and through the shadowy forest, almost feeling the death-like stillness of that memorable Sabbath morning. And how like entering the valley of the shadow of death, seemed our march down through the smoky atmosphere into the deep valley, and around to our new position confronting the enemy.*

*Our Division had been selected for the desperate work of charging a rebel battery, which was supported by a strong force of the enemy behind entrenchments. The ulterior object was to break the enemy's line at that point, and thereby cut the rebel army in twain.*

*The 1st Brigade was ordered to make an assault, while the other brigades of the division were held in easy supporting distance. The brigade was formed in column by regiments,*

right in front, as follows: 70th Indiana, 102nd Illinois, 79th
Ohio, 129th Illinois, 105th Illinois. The men had previously
unslung knapsacks and left them in charge of a guard.

There was evidently some warm work to be done.

At first the real design of the movement was known
only to a few, but when the column was formed, the men were
ordered to fix bayonets, and as the ominous click ran along the
line, the nature of the task before us became apparent. Thought
was busy then, and all faces seemed a shade paler.

The distance from the point where the charging column
was formed to the enemy's line, was about six-hundred yards. A
valley lay between, and their works were upon the crest of a
hill beyond. A heavy growth of young pines covered all the
hills, and completely masked their position.

At length about half-past 11 o'clock the command
"forward" ran along the line, and the column quickly moved
down the hillside. Simultaneously with the beginning of the
movement the rebels opened fire. Then "forward!" was the
word shouted and repeated by almost every tongue. And a wild,
prolonged battle yell that swelled from all lips, arose distinct
and terrific above the roar of battle, as down into the valley
and across the open field – where death rode on every passing
breeze – then up the hillside where the twigs and branches of
the young pines were clipped by the bullets like corn blades in
a hailstorm – the charging columns moved – not in regular
lines, but en masse, disorganized by the inequalities of the
ground and the dense growth of pines – onto the summit,
towards the rebel cannons which belched forth fire, grape-shot
and shell to the last instant –men dropping dead and wounded
on every hand– into the earth works surrounding the guns, and
the guns were ours.

All of the regiments in the brigade were represented
within the earthworks. But the position was occupied only for
an instant. The rebel line had been pierced – not broken. On
the right and on the left of the redoubt, which formed a salient
in their position, their line was intact. They opened a withering
cross fire and our men fell back to a position immediately in

*front of the redoubt, commanding the guns. At that time
someone yelled out that the order was to retreat, and many
retired to the foot of the hill. They were there re-organized and
marched to another part of the field. Most of those who
remained had heard no order to retire, and were sanguine that
the position could be held. Protected in a measure by the rebel
redoubt, and sheltered somewhat by trees and logs, our men
kept up steady fire all afternoon. But the rebel fire was more
active. They were protected by an excellent line of works –
fired low – and their balls cut close around, occasionally
killing or wounding a man.*

*In the squad which held the position, several regiments
were represented. If any fresh column moved up the hill they
did not reach the vicinity of the guns. Toward evening it was
feared the battery would be retaken. One by one the men began
to retire, notwithstanding the expostulations of those who
remained. After dark the enemy opened a sharp fire, as if
menacing a charge to retake the guns. A volley was fired in
return; the boys yelled out a defiant cheer and one shouted to
the Johnnies-"Come over and take your brass field pieces!"*

*Help had been sent for, and at length we heard music
in the valley below. Sweet as the music of heaven, soothing the
soul after the harrowing, discordant day of battle.*

*Interwoven with our very beings, the ecstatic
sensations of that moment, when the soft, plaintive, but
cheering notes of the field band were borne to our ears, will
live in memory forever.*

*We learned afterward, however, that the music did not
herald the approach of a relieving column – but relief soon
came. About 10 o'clock in the evening a strong force marched
into position immediately in front of the earthworks. The guns –
four in number – were held and brought off that night. They
were handsome pieces – brass, 12 pounders. One of them was
named "Minnie, the Belle of Alabama."*

*When the relieving column came, those of the regiment
who had remained on the field marched to the rear.*

*The day's work was over and we were satisfied with the record the 102d had made.*

*None were braver or more worthy of mention than the scores of privates who fought with courage that has never been surpassed. Without injustice to any, I wish it were possible to record the names of all who made a glorious record on that day.*

*Our brigade commander, Brig. Gen. W. T. Ward, was quite severely wounded. It is said that when the ball struck the old General, he evoked a "string of blessings" on the rebels in a style that was more forcible than elegant. He was in the thickest of the fight cheering on the men when struck. Several of our men were doubtless struck by balls from the lines that were directed to support us. At one time the 2d Brigade opened a sharp fire on us, mistaking us for the rebels.*

*During the night of the 15th the rebels evacuated their entire line of works and retreated in the direction of Atlanta.*

*The scene on the battle-ground the following day was sad beyond description. The day was calm − indeed the stillness was oppressive. We were permitted to wander over the field and view the effects of the fierce struggle. The dead of both armies were being buried − some singly where they fell, others in a common grave.*

*In a deep trench surrounded by Evergreen pines, fifty-one of the slain of the 1st Brigade were buried. The scene at the grave was deeply impressive. An immense crowd of soldiers gathered around to hear the remarks of an aged chaplain, ere the forms of their comrades were forever hidden from sight. "Many in one," said the venerable minister, "is the motto borne proudly on our nation's banner. Many in one grave, our fallen brothers rest. And is not the coincidence a fitting one? Will not this common grave be cherished with a sacred pride by all who love our country's flag?"*

*At the conclusion of his remarks the work of burial was accomplished, tenderly and carefully as the circumstances would permit, by the comrades of the slain.*

*But to the living, sad as the surroundings were, the day after the battle seemed like the beginning of a new life. Peace and repose, how sweet, after the weathering tornado of human wrath had swept by!*

This episode at Resaca was probably as close to a "suicide mission" as Henry would ever face throughout the duration of the war. In his letter written to his brother Willis from camp near Kingston, GA, he described his heroic charge in such vivid detail, you can almost hear his voice trembling from the adrenaline still pulsing in his veins.

*Sund May the 22 1864*

*in camp near kingston Georgey*

*Dear Brother I take the opertunity which has bin scares for the fast 20 days we have bin put threw hard thick & thin I supose you know more by the papers what the fiting has bin than eny of the solgers for they can not here eny thing onely what they see  we have bin fiting & twards (?) the enemy prety hard  I have bin in 2day fite it is just one weake a go Saturday Sunday fites are biggest I wer in.  the rebels wer very strongley fortefide we had them nearle surrounded  we were closen on them every day taking those brestworks by the point of the bayonet  we had very hard fiting our regiment lost hevy 7,16 in kild & wounded here  meny in the hole Brigaid  I havent asertaind the enemy lost hevy the enemy found that we were determin to fite them at al haserds and they scadadeld for fear we woud suround them & capture there hole forse  we woud if they staid thair an other day  Sunday nite they left by fireng hevy artillery & fiting to cover there retreat but they did not get away without hevy loss  our men shld them all night well Willess fiting is not what it is cracked up to be as for my part I had rather be excused from goin in to one but now I am in I am bebound (?) to go threw if it dose cill (kill) me the bullets whiseld as close to me as I care to have them to  we captured 4 peases of artillery brass peases they wer cauld the first Georgen ("The First*

Georgian") the bell of Georga ("The Bell of Georgia") the
prisoners say this was the first time they wer repulsed  satur day
our men charged on it & wer driven back every time the 4 armey
corps Old Jose (Old Joe's ref: General Joseph Johnston) corps
tride it Sunday  our Regiment and the 70 indian (ref: 70th
Regiment Indiana joined Henry's Regiment in the 1st Brigade, 3rd
Division, XX Corps, Army of the Cumberland in April, 1864)
charged on the batery at the first charge we cleard them from
there gones (guns) the guners wer all shot ded while in the act of
loding  one canon had a dobell charge of grape (grapeshot) a
canester in it but the poor fllows had not time to put it of  at the
first charge I took my position under the musell of one of the
peases and fired ofer (over) the carig (carriage) of the canon  one
man wasshot threw the head behind me he fell on me & cride for
help

Oh ses he help me I set my gun up against the canon & raised him
up he was allso shot threw the body he cride for a drinck of water
I gave it to him I told him I coud not do eny more for him I then
seased my rifle the bullets fliing as thick as hail but by the kind
hand of providence I was not tutch  Juss then we wer ordered to
fall back we fell back 3 differnt times but the enemy dared not
persue these guns wer nobell ones 20 pounders  our generall was
on the feald with us amonced (amongst) the boys he was wounded
threw the left arm Joseph Hoocker (ref: Major General "Fighting
Joe" Hooker) ses it was the best and most daring & ferosious
charge he ever saw  It is a wonder we wer not all cild (kiled) or
captured we wer under there cros fires the the enemy had a cros
fire on us & threw mestake our one (own) men fired at us taking
us fo the enemy  in our falling back the bushess wer so thick what
was plaid the mifchis(??)  I was never so near exausted in my life
while making the charge threw the thicket & up hill at that  this
was plainest and loudest preatching that I ever atended on sonday
the poind(?) was tested in every plais & none found defended(?)
on the write side the rite is the mite in this ishew the enemy has the
advantige in every sens of the word they left here in sutch a haisty
retreat they did not get time to taer up the railroad  a small town
south from here 2 1/2 mi on the rail road is very strongley fortefid
by the nam wawsackey but they did not stop  it is astonishing to
see what strong fortifide  we have bin resting for the last to days
we wer nearley run down going day & nite hundreds of our men
gave out with heat & fatigue I tel you it is the hardest biseness

*that I ever done caring (carrying) sutch a hevy & bundelling load
I cary over 100 rounds I have my spencer (rifle) & shooter (most
likely a Colt 1851 or 1860 Army model revolver) and I am goin to
stick to it as long as I can  the wether is very warm & dry here
georgey has some very nise farmes tell about starving the south it
dont loock like it hear  grain of all kinds is plenty  catell & hogs
wheat fealds is plenty but as our armey gose it sweapes all of the
catell & evething to fead our armey there is hardley a siezun
(citizen) to be sean here as the rebell retreated they toock every
man and niger  I think this campain is gointo deside the grait
desputing question betwean this aufell conflict that is I hope and
pray that it may for the longer it last the wores it gits  that is in the
slautering of men horibel to think of the site of battell filed will
make the hardest harted man shudder  I saw nofe (enough) of this
a weak agow to day  for me the orders is now that we will lave
here to morow morning to where it is not for a privet to know
there is a long martch on hand that is one thing that I am shure
for we have 4 days rations to cary  wel as for me I am willing to
bare my share of the flames(?) if it will end this ware but it is hard
the men are all in fine spearets (spirits) I stand it beter than I
exspected I could  well I have not had no leture sens I have bin on
this martch but still I feal it my duty to write & let my brothers
know how I am geting along for I know they will be ancious in the
presant surcumstance  write offten you will preserve that (which)
is scares (scarce) down hear  give my love to all inquireng friends
as ever your brother*

*Henry I Banks*

*I send a larell (laurel) ring maid of the root of(f) of loockout
mountain that I maid for your wife   farwell Willis*

*Friday, May 16, 2014. Sunny + fog.*

I must've been more fatigued from the drive than I
thought, for I woke to a rising sun over my left shoulder and a
very stiff and sore neck. I covered my tussled mop of hair with
a baseball hat, and started out on a walking tour of the Resaca

Battlefield property. I had quit my routine of regular shaves and haircuts during the weeks that led up to my trip, and it took a while before she noticed, but days before, my wife called me out on my hygienic negligence.

"Are you growing your beard and hair out for the Civil War thing?" I nodded and smiled as she gave me "that look" and rolled her eyes, as usual. As I continued walking, I emerged onto a gravel road, where a sign hanging on a fencepost directed me to "Federal Camp". The road led me past a large pond on my right, and I realized that I was walking along the dike of a small dam. The road hooked to the left, and was draped on both sides and above with a canopy of trees, until it dipped downward into a fog-laden valley that opened up wide before me. I stopped in my tracks to take in the view in cinemascope. The solitude I was absorbing was disrupted by a distant rumble, soon followed by reverberating wail that echoed through the valley. A long blast, followed by a shorter one, and two more long bursts announced the arrival of a freight train. I was suddenly reminded of the earplugs I had purchased before leaving Texas, and chastised myself for not using them during my attempt at a restful night in my jeep. (No wonder I was having nightmares about freight trains)

Two figures appeared on the gravel road at the base of the hill that I stood upon, so I descended, and approached them. One man was bespectacled and dressed in light blue pants and a navy blue uniform jacket, along with a wide-brim slouch hat. The older gent was dressed in sweats, and a jacket that said "Del Mar, California". I asked them for directions to the Federal Camp, and the older guy pointed to a copse of trees within yards of the railroad tracks. Now I knew for certain that I would need the earplugs. We exchanged notes about San Diego, and compared our histories there, when suddenly our conversation was interrupted with an earth-shattering boom! I don't think I even told the two reenactors thank you, or goodbye, for that matter, but the source of the cannon blast that had just raised the hair on the back of my neck was beckoning. A ridge at my right was crowned with a stand of tall trees that gave way to a rising halo of gray blue smoke. I was briskly ascending the hill toward the battery, and as I cleared the tree line, I recognized an artillery team by their gray uniforms, and butternut-colored hats as a Confederate unit.

They had positioned three cannons behind wooden breastworks atop a crest that offered a birdseye view of the entire battlefield. At that very moment, it struck me. I was on the same battlefield that uncle Henry and his company had charged across 150 years before, almost to the very day, and I would be charging the field myself, in uniform, with rifle in hand, looking down the smoking muzzles of rebel guns. It was almost too much to digest, as I removed my hat, and continued to scan the field in amazement, from the outcrop. I had visited Resaca previously in July, but on a section of the battlefield that was on the other side of the freeway that split the property. This location where I stood seemed different. I had toured the other parcel with some uncertainty as to its authenticity as the 102nd's location of enemy encounter. Standing next to the rebel guns, I had a higher level of confidence that I was in the right spot, and my hunch would soon be proven true.

Just then, I noticed some activity around the perimeter of the Federal camp in the distance, and began to descend the hill toward the neatly arranged canvas tents that were nested within the treeline near the railroad tracks. I walked along the most enormous stack of split cordwood that I had ever seen, and approached a tent that had a canvas "fly" laid out behind it, where a man lay on his back, with one arm across his face, shielding his eyes from the morning sunrise. "Looking for the 125th" I said. The camp seemed deserted, except for the two of us, but an entire village of tents was set up among the pines, so I figured the rest of the unit had to be off drilling somewhere. "Are you Steve?" The man on the canvas fly looked up at me with one eye open. It was almost like he was waiting around for me to show up. "Yes," I answered. "I couldn't find the camp in the dark last night, when I arrived, so I slept in the parking lot." My new acquaintance rose to his feet, dusted off his shirt and said, "Well, your tent was right here, all ready for you." He pointed to a small, canvas true-to-period tent behind a larger, two-man model. It was surrounded by a scattering of hay, placed to keep the wind and moisture out. We shook hands, as he also introduced himself as "Steve".

He explained to me that Greg, Earl and Howard were at breakfast with Earl's wife and mother, and the ladies would be camping with us too. This was unexpected. Steve explained that both ladies participated and dressed in costume, and enjoyed the experience as much as the soldiers did. Suddenly,

I understood whom I was invited to spend the weekend with. These were professional living history actors. My modern LED lantern, high-tech sleeping bag, coffee maker and mess kit would have to remain hidden in my tent for the time being. These folks were after the realism on every level. Steve inquired about my reason for falling in with the 125th Ohio, so I gave him the background, and produced Henry's Bible, which I kept in a leather watch case. I told him that I hadn't even thought about participating in a Civil War reenactment, let alone the 150th anniversary of the Resaca battle, but I looked forward to the experience. Steve assured me that the reenactors were all a great group of guys, and that I would enjoy the camaraderie.

Soon, a small pack of folks wandered into camp, and we commenced with polite introduction. I finally matched faces with the names of my email corresponders from the previous few months of preparation. Earl was the division commander, Howard was company captain, and Greg was first sergeant. He would be my instructor of the art of soldiering. Picture a cross between Robert Duvall and Chuck Connors. That was First Sergeant Krohn. He sized me up, and assured me that after some training, and the actual participation in the battle reenactment, I would have a completely new perspective and appreciation for the Civil War, and of those who actually fought in it. I felt my adrenaline begin to simmer as he described the schedule for the weekend, which would include a "tactical" later in the day, a parade on Saturday morning, followed by a full-scale battle in the afternoon, and another on Sunday. I followed Sergeant Krohn to his tent, where he handed me a military duffel and a long oilcloth sleeve, which was wrapped around a brand-new replica Enfield musket.

"Go ahead and "cooter-up" and we will get you trained for war" he said. I rushed back to my tent, quickly slipped into my uniform, and draped my shoulders and waist with the leathers, which included a belt, cartridge box, percussion cap case, bayonet scabbard and shoulder strap. I previously had purchased some black leather boots that resembled G. I. Brogans, but were more comfortable for a rookie reenactor. They were a little big for my feet, but when I wore them with the heavy wool socks that I pulled from Greg's duffel, they were a perfect fit. I emerged from my tent in light blue wool trousers, dark blue wool jacket with brass buttons, and matching kepi hat, with the rifle in my grip. I walked past Steve who had resumed his reclined position on his canvas fly. "How do I look?" I asked. "Good" he said. "Almost too good, you need to roll around in the mud, for the authentic appearance." Sergeant Krohn approached just then from his tent. "I think I'm about to get dirty" I said.

Steve waved his arm, directing me to Sergeant Krohn's direction. "Private En..., En..yard?? In..hart? How do you....?" As I have so often done throughout my entire life, I interrupted his struggle with the pronunciation of my last name. I held up my musket, "Enfield, just call me private Enfield." Sergeant Krohn smiled. He put me through a series of drills, and taught me how to march, position myself among the rank and file for when Captain Morgan barked out his commands. We moved on to handling the musket, and correct posture and positioning for when the orders were issued to "shoulder arms," "secure arms," "present arms," "parade rest," etc., etc. As I was training, other reenactors began filtering into camp, and setting up their tents. Some just set up bivouacs, and I later learned that they were known as "campaigners" who went after all aspects of authenticity, even when it came to communication, they remained in character during the entire event. I was reminded that busloads of school children would soon be arriving, so tent flaps should be closed to hide anything that was not of the period.

Out came the crude wooden tables and chairs, the wrought iron fire stands, and kerosene lanterns. Hay bales would provide comfortable seating around the fire pits, but not too close! I decided that I would pretend to play the part of the nervous private, whittling a stick beneath the pine tree, as the kids entered our camp. I found a pine branch, and pulled out my "Texas Toothpick" – a small pocketknife that was the closest to "period" that I could muster – and began whittling away at my own piece of "trench art." At about 10:30 AM, the Confederate battery began firing off rounds, and a crowd of school children could be seen on the ridge above the field, with their hands over their ears. It wasn't long before they were being herded through our camp. Some of the seasoned veterans took them through the camp, educating them along the way about the soldier's life, and providing insight into the surrounding accouterments. Once the kids were gone, I carried my wooden folding chair up to the fire pit where others had since gathered.

I sat next to Steve, who introduced me to the crew, explaining the reasons for my presence among them. I was welcomed, and answered a few curious questions regarding Henry's place in the war. Bob, who was our company Corporal, was attending to the fire. He was also responsible for brewing the coffee in the most enormous coffee pot I had ever seen. I sampled a cup, and my heart nearly stopped at first sip – perfect! Steve invited me to tag along on a walk up to the parking area where all the "sutlers" were setting up shop. It was getting close to lunchtime, and I was craving something different than the camp rations that I had stowed in my tent. Corporal Bob, the fire tender, joined us as we made our way out of the Federal camp, through the back way. We crossed a small creek, and passed a clump of trees that was the object of a neighboring Union company's interest. A foursome of boys in blue were studying a small impression in the ground. When I inquired as to what they had found, one of the group spoke up and shared with us that a local historian attached to the "Friends of Resaca" had led him to this spot, which was an original picket post.

We were very near the railroad, so we assumed that it was most likely a Union defensive position. As we continued along our route up the gravel road, I mentioned to Steve and Bob that I was here at Resaca to reenact, but also to make a concerted effort to locate the position of the Confederate battery post where Uncle Henry had seized an enemy cannon. Steve had participated in the Resaca battle reenactment before, and had some insight to share regarding the location of a large Confederate battery that was very near to the sutler area where we were heading. As we continue to walk, he described a high point obscured by a heavy forest where there were still about a half dozen very defined impressions in the earth in a semi circle. I knew by his description that this could only be the location of the famed "Van Den Corput's battery". I felt my pace quicken, and at one point, I had to stop and let Steve and Bob catch up.

I didn't want to be impolite, or worse, accused of desertion! Though I wanted to make a beeline to that hilltop, I remained with my new friends. We arrived at the Sutler Village, which was a neatly arranged collection of large white canvas tents guy-roped to spikes hammered into the earth. (I tripped over one or two, and witnessed others doing the same) Among the four rows of shelters was a photography studio (true to period) and shops that sold everything from books, DVDs, soldier gear, black powder, percussion caps and uniforms, to antique firearms, bayonets, leather accessories, high-quality hats, and costumes for civilians — both men and women. A bakery sold pastries and biscuits along with fresh hot cinnamon rolls – one of my weaknesses – and coffee! Just in case Corporal Bob's Arbuckles blend began to erode my esophagus, I had a more palatable alternative, close to camp. Finally, we arrived at a heavily populated tent affixed with a stovepipe that was spewing gray smoke into the air. I caught a whiff as we approached. Barbecue! A crew of three were busy building fry bread turnovers stuffed with barbecued pulled pork, and I could not resist. We all ordered our lunch, which came with potato salad and a drink. Since sarsaparilla was not an option, I settled for a Diet Coke.

We returned to camp with our meals, and took our seats by the fire, which was still roaring. As we dined, we began to hear chatter through the camp about a "tactical" that would commence at 1400 hrs. "what's the tactical?" I asked. Steve described it as a practice run against the Confederate reenactors. Suddenly, I heard a deep, booming voice call out from the tree line. "Private Enfield!" I shot up from my chair, and reported to Sergeant Krohn's tent. "We have a tactical to prepare for, are you ready?" "Ready as I can be, Sergeant!" I shouted. Sergeant Krohn slipped me a handful of percussion caps, and ran me through the steps of firing the Enfield musket that he had loaned to me. I learned how to present my firearm for inspection; load, prime, shoot, fix bayonet, etc. "let's see how you do out there today, we'll keep an eye on you" said the first sergeant. I was under the strong impression that firing a weapon was not a common privilege for your typical field rookie on his first day out. I filled my cap box on my belt, and told him I wouldn't let him down. "Form company!" he shouted. From the camp streamed out a squad of bluecoats, who all lined up before Captain Morgan's tent. Sergeant Krohn lined us up and called the roll. "Dress your ranks!" We all looked to-and-fro to straighten our lines. I took my place at the right end of the rear rank, next to Steve, and behind Corporal Bob who stood at the end of the front rank, or front row.

The first sergeant would take his place next to Corporal Bob to complete the front rank. "You gonna fire that thing today?" asked Steve. "Just caps." I whispered. "Quiet in the ranks!" roared Sergeant Krohn. He was actually responding to two other soldiers who were loudly discussing politics, which had earlier made Steve's eyes roll. Captain Morgan paced in front of us and announced that we would be engaging the enemy during our tactical, but we would drill, en route across the field. We counted out from right to left establishing our file - "1-2-1-2-1-2!" We each sounded off down the front and rear ranks of our line, to the last man. We marched and drilled, right wheel, left wheel, then we rallied in groups of four, which was a little complicated for a rookie, newbie, greenhorn, cherry, or whatever I was. After a few minutes of drilling with the company, the hot sun and the wool outfit I was wearing began to disagree.

The Georgia humidity had begun to accumulate as well, and I was glad that Sergeant Krohn had loaned a canteen to me along with the other accessories. I stole a long drink while we all faced forward and marched. A detachment of younger reenactors suddenly arrived in a sort of Keystone Cops fashion, to join our ranks. Captain Morgan was quick to assign them the duty of skirmishing. They didn't seem to mind. They ran forward in loose formation as we were ordered to halt. I was impressed that these high school-aged boys were taking part in this recreation, and though they seemed a little scatterbrained at first appearance, the sincerity on their faces made it clear that they were all-business. I remember thinking, as they slinked away from our ranks, that most of the troops that fought in the Civil War weren't much older, in actuality than this lot. As we waited, a Union cavalry team approached us from the right rank. The cavalry Colonel had one empty sleeve, which gave him an authentic appearance. Closer inspection revealed his right arm in a slung cast, but when he gave us a tip of his hat and bellowed, "give 'em hell boys!" I felt an enormous grin populate my face, ear-to-ear. My pulse increased as he put spur to his chestnut steed and galloped ahead of our line. Just ahead, the crest of the hill at midfield was broken by gray puffs of gun smoke.

A chubby little runt in a blue coat and wide-brimmed hat that he held tight to his noggin ran towards us. "Sir!" he panted with cheeks turning shades of red, "we hear drums." He was reporting to Captain Morgan from the skirmisher team. "Drums? your men are firing at drums?" he quipped. The scout gave the captain a puzzled look, and speechless, he saluted and turned about-face to rejoin the skirmishers. I am uncertain, but I think I heard Captain Morgan mention something regarding some skirmisher training that might be necessary. I was, for just a moment, reminded of Henry's letters, and Stephen Fleharty's numerous accounts of Henry's Company E, then under the command of Captain Dan Sedwick, who had often dispatched the company as skirmishers. Company E had been supplied with Spencer repeating rifles when they were assigned cavalry duty at Lavergne, Tennessee. To my knowledge, they kept the Spencers throughout the duration of the war. It is my belief that company E were the Army Rangers of their time. Green Berets? The ragtag skirmisher team that now approached the tree line to the west carried single shot muskets, but still managed to flush out an entire company of rebels, who were now approaching us in a line parallel to our own. Here we go.

Sergeant Krohn took his position next to me, and I noticed that he carried a repeating Henry rifle replica. I made a mental note that I should try to acquire a Spencer at some point, as a keepsake to honor Henry. "How would I explain that purchased to Andi?" I thought. "Company halt!" The order from Captain Morgan was followed by another, which the entire company obeyed in unison. "Ready...Aim..." I brought my musket up and far to the right, a safe distance from Corporal Bob's ear, careful to move my right foot to the right, and not to the rear, as Sergeant Krohn had instructed. "Fire!" Ka-Blam. Blam, Blam-Blam! It was an okay volley with a few stragglers. I savored the unmistakable aroma of gunpowder that had some sulfurous tones, and a kind of earthy pungence that set my mind reeling back to 1864, as I pondered the thought: did black powder have the same flavor and aroma 150 years ago? I was also reminded of a whiskey shot that I shared with a client at a bar in Colorado, which was mixed with real gunpowder. I hadn't tasted it since, until just now.

The rebels returned fire, and with an even more uneven volley than ours. A couple of our guys slumped over as wounded, or dead. Responding sharply to Captain Morgan's order, we wheeled around as a company, and faced the Confederate line in more of a flanking arrangement. "Fire by file!" This was a new one. Steve quickly told me what to do. "Load! Load!" I tossed my spent percussion cap, and quickly replaced it with a live one, pulling the hammer on my Enfield back to first position. "Ready!...Aim..." Again, I raised the musket up next to my right cheek, training the barrel through the site, just above the heads of my approaching adversaries, as I was instructed to do. I then pulled the hammer all the way back until I heard and felt it lock into place. "Fire!!" Corporal Bob and I were the only ones to fire, then Steve and his file partner, then the two troopers next to them, and so on, until the entire line had completed their order. The Confederates who had fallen over wounded or dead opened up a nice even volley in return, which was evidenced by the uniform report of their muskets, but also with the even column of white smoke that wafted across their line.

We returned fire as a company this time, and I beamed with pride as Captain Morgan praised our volley. Our cavalry support came storming up from the tree line at the enemy's right, and they retreated back to their original position. Thus ended our Friday afternoon tactical. We all lined up, primed and fired our weapons into the air to clear any unspent cartridges, and then we turned about-face. From within the ranks, someone spoke up and said, "Captain Morgan, we need to do some drilling." We marched back to our camp as a column this time, along the dirt road that snaked through the battlefield. We stopped in front of our tents, formed a line, and went through a series of drills which Steve and Bob both assisted me with — sometimes vocally, and sometimes with a hard yank on my shoulder, spurring me to fall properly into line. Finally, the order to be dismissed was announced by Sergeant Krohn, and we all dispersed.

Before Steve could finish asking me what I thought of the tactical, I burst out: "That was incredible!" Captain Morgan passed by me, and without eye contact he responded, "Wait till tomorrow." I noticed that a handful of tents had been raised in the Federal camp since we had marched out to meet the Confederates on the field. A few new faces passed by, and a series of greetings, handshakes and backslaps commenced among the men. It became evident to me that many of these reenactors were true-blue veterans of the "hobby" as some called it, and had shared many campfires with each other. I took this reunion as a cue to abandon camp to seek out the site of the original Confederate battery that was only about a half mile up the road from camp. I walked across the wooden bridge over a small creek that split the Federal camp in two. A modest cluster of tents surrounded a crackling campfire that contributed some percussion to a small band of musicians who were belting out familiar tunes. They were seated in a circle, practicing for the entertainment of the crowd, and the morale of the Army.

They handled their classic instruments and sheet music with the same care, reverence, sensitivity and respect that others paid to musket and saber. As I cleared the forest perimeter that opened to the dirt road leading away from camp, I noticed the activity in the sutler village had ramped up somewhat. More soldiers had arrived along with women in their bright gingham dresses, official-looking chaps in garish suits and top hats, and locals in their flip-flops and ball caps. Some Confederate reenactors passed, and I greeted them with a friendly "hello." This was met with silence, and a collective glare, as they passed. "Could there still be some remaining tension or resentment between Union and Confederate ideals-150 years later?" I wondered. An officer in a smart gray uniform with artillery badging approached me. He tipped his hat to me and wished me a good afternoon. His gesture made me feel a little more at ease in this surreal environment, and I had to stop for a moment to take in the cyclorama of activity that surrounded me. I was indeed experiencing living history, and I felt privileged, and fortunate to be a welcomed participant…for the most part.

Over the hill, just a few yards north of the sutler village, I approached the parking lot, and when I spotted the field of vehicles, I was instantly transported back to modern times. I didn't want to linger here for too long, because the 1860's seemed to suit me, at least for the weekend. I stood at the head of a narrow, paved road that led upward into a densely wooded hilltop. A historic marker had been placed next to the road, which identified the original position of Van Den Corput's battery. The sun was warm on my back, as I followed the blacktop upward until the trees that covered the hilltop obscured the sky almost entirely. I felt the temperature drop to a noticeably colder level. The road split off in two directions toward a pair of private residences that appeared to be built in the 1980s. I chose to veer left where I spotted a slight trace of foot traffic wear that led deep into the forest.

I drew closer to the path, as all sounds from camp faded into a faint muffle behind the familiar exchange of calls between two cardinals perched above me. A slight breeze rocked the branches of swaying pines together, creating an eerie creaking chorus. Spotlights of sunshine passed between them to highlight the rims of a half-dozen knee-deep pits in the earth, just beyond the road. I swallowed hard, then followed the path until I stood in the center of a great semi-circular blufftop that overlooked the imposing grade leading down into a valley below. I made a point to stand inside every impression in the earth that had been excavated to accommodate the Confederate cannons that Henry Banks helped seize back in 1864. I knew that I would be standing in one of the pits where he had crouched beneath the cannon's carriage, defending the prize amidst enemy crossfire. I spent about 30 minutes taking photos, and recalling Henry's description of the Federal charge across the field, and up that hillside to overtake the battery.

Though I had read the recorded sketches by Stephen Fleharty and Henry as well, I could now visualize the details in Technicolor, since I stood in the very spot, so well-preserved and protected by the giant pines that stood guard overhead. Satisfied, and energized, I descended the hilltop at a quickened pace, and returned to camp. I passed by the sutler's village, crossed the creek once again, and was approached by a tall uniformed reenactor who introduced himself as "John Smith" from Maine. "No, really, what's your real name?" I asked. I could tell he had heard that one before. His wife had overheard us, and coming out of their tent, dressed in a period costume she said "he gets that a lot." John and I discussed the details of our histories, which had led us both to our participation at Resaca. We eventually came to realize that our ancestors had fought side-by-side as members of the 102nd and 105th Illinois Volunteers. Another reenactor approached us, who had overheard our conversation. John Fritz, from Arizona had found an obituary in his father's effects shortly after he had passed away. It was that of his great-great grandfather who had fought for the 105th Illinois Volunteers also.

John Fritz had recently ordered a headstone for his ancestor's unmarked grave, which he had located through a journey similar to my own. We discovered many more shared parallels that had resulted in our presence at Resaca. The three of us must have stood and exchanged notes and experiences for over an hour. I shared Henry's Bible with them, which I was now carrying in my jacket inside pocket. They both seemed fascinated that the little hunk of red wood had survived for so long, and that it had come full-circle to dwell once again on the hallowed ground of Resaca. As we conversed, Sergeant Krohn emerged from his tent and motioned me over. He spoke in a low tone so only I could hear him. "You know I've been thinking about this a lot, and I think I know what your uncle's Bible is all about...it's his dog tag." "Think about it," he said. What I was thinking is: "Why did I not think of that?" It made sense. Henry had most likely heard about, and seen examples of carnage, rendering victims of a musket ball, or grapeshot completely unrecognizable, resulting in an anonymous burial on foreign soil. Relatives back home would spend the rest of their lives wondering about the fate of their son, or brother, or father who marched off to war – never to return.

In his letters, more than once, Henry mentioned that he had decided to stay the course to the end. Sergeant Krohn was confident that the purposeful inclusion of Henry's name, Company and Regiment, carved onto his Bible was to provide clarity and closure for his loving family, should he join the ever-growing list of casualties. By grace, it would not be necessary.

After some minor housekeeping —well...tentkeeping— I joined the small crowd that was gathered around Corporal Bob's effective campfire. Steve introduced me to some latecomers who were regulars at the reenactments. I passed my cell phone around to share the letter written in Henry's own words as he reflected on his Resaca experience. I was happy to contribute what I could in exchange for the gift of my invitation to participate as a first-timer. I hoped that Henry's words prepared some hearts for the next day's battle, and offered some valuable perspective from an actual survivor of the real thing. As the expansive field before us darkened beneath the descending twilight, a dense layer of fog rolled in, giving the landscape an eerie appearance. A noticeable reduction in temperature followed. Others noticed the same shift, for blankets were produced, and more logs were added to the blaze.

Steve and I both lit up cigars, and he whispered to me

that he had brought some fine, rare cigars..."the origin of which I am not at liberty to divulge." he said. I looked forward to sampling one. It was around midnight, and the diehard firetenders who remained could be counted on one hand. "Kurt!" Steve shouted. A mustachioed reenactor turned his head toward us. "Tell Steve here about your reenactor's rush!" This was apparently what happens when you get lost in the moment, and experience a momentary lapse of discernment, uncertain which century you are living in. It's a sort of transporting, and though it's all a figment of imagination, it's reportedly very real to the transportee. I pulled out my cell phone and fumbled for the voice memo app, and activated the record button, as Kurt proceeded to describe his experience in his own words:

*"We were at the Battle of Atlanta, out in Conyers...and they had candlelight tours...where people got on the carriages, and went from venue to venue to venue. And at each spot they would stop, and the actors there would act out a scene. And I volunteered to act out in a scene where I was a bummer—we were bummers— revisiting a house that had been burned earlier in the day, and the embers were still burning, and outside this were the food slaves that lived there and furniture that people had salvaged. And we were coming up basically to look for something to steal. And Grandpa came running out of the house, and I would club him to the ground, because he had a shotgun. And then we would tell all the slaves they were free, and the whole thing would last about 2 minutes. But before the buggy arrived, we would be in the shadows outside the firelight. Waiting for our cue. Well, every time we would retreat back into the shadows, we would move into this open field, and each time, there would be shots fired, from the tree line...at us. I didn't realize they were shooting at us. But there were three of us. One was a Corporal and one was a Private from a Michigan unit, and the Corporal is the one that realized, "hey these guys are shooting at us." And figured that this was a "hardcore" unit that was just out in the woods...they had a little spot, out in the woods. So he said, "When this is over, we're gonna go investigate those guys, and so when it was done, the three of us began sneaking across the field, and it was completely dark, and they could not see us coming, and we just got completely lost in the moment. And he was saying to us "don't fire...don't fire...don't fire...uh, I've got some coffee, I want to meet with them, I want to barter with them, I want to get some tobacco...I*

*just wanna, but don't shoot...don't shoot." So, we came sneaking up, and we could hear them talking as we came up into their encampment, and the fire was going...and we had to cross a little creek, and so forth, but at some point they heard us. And we were right on the edge of a road that went around past their encampment, and we're right along the margin of the road and there are bushes and trees that are hanging. And they heard us, because all of a sudden things got quiet, and the fire went out. They kicked their fire out. And so we just kinda froze. We had our rifles loaded, ready to go...just froze. They tried to flush us out...after several minutes, tried to flush us out by jumping out into the middle of the road hoping to startle us, and we'd be revealed, and so-on. I was in the lead...they jumped out, and they were right in front of my muzzle, no farther away than he is. (motioning to reenactor sitting next to him) And of course, they didn't have their night vision going, we did. I could see him fine, and I just watched him, as his eyes adjusted, and he thought..."oh shit"...it was just an "oh shit moment" for him. So we went up into the camp with them. I mean we had them...we had 'em. We weren't firing, so we went up into the camp with them. And we just started talking...but everything we were talking about was 1864. We were talking about MacLellan running for President. We were talking about this-that-and-the-other, and the Michigan guy kept talkin about slavery, and "we need to kill all of you guys because you own slaves..." and I kept telling him to "shut up", and we made an exchange, and we talked for about ten or fifteen minutes, and then we said good night, they said good night, and then, we went back into the shadows. But for that whole period of time, we were completely in the moment. That was an amazing experience. Completely spontaneous."*

Kurt's account opened up the forum for other tales to be told at the fire, and we were soon all roaring with laughter. I took this as a good opportunity to fetch some cold beers from my tent. I freely distributed them to the group, and our laughter and conversation continued until the fire was nearly out. Aside from the living history element, it was obvious what kept these guys coming back to the firesides and battlefields. The camaraderie was as intoxicating as the beverages that we shared between us.

*Ready for war, at Resaca for the 150th anniversary reenactment
with borrowed blues and Enfield rifle.*

*Saturday, May 17, 2014 0600 (Still dark...cooold)*

*Braptaraptapbaraptapatapbaraptapatapbrrappptap!!!*

I sat up suddenly in my sleeping bag, inside a strange tent. It took me a moment to remember where I was, but the bugler blowing Reverie at 0600 confirmed for me that I was indeed at Resaca, and not having some surreal dream. I had slept in my wool uniform through the night, and was thankful, for it was about 46° as the camp began to stir. It didn't take long for the realization to set in that the bungling bugler had roused us awake an hour ahead of schedule. The interrupted slumber, and the chill made for some very unhappy campers — what a morning! At least Corporal Bob's fire was already blazing, and the giant coffee pot would soon come steaming to life. After some visiting around the fire, Sergeant Krohn called out "form company!" and all federal troops in first company gathered on the field once again, for roll call.

After a briefing from Captain Morgan, we marched through camp and across the creek, forming a line with other companies upon the dirt road that separated our camp from the parking lot. After inspection of arms, we all marched up the road in a column to report from morning colors. At about 0900, we passed the Settler Village, and judging by the number of camera flashes, and ogling children, a crowd was beginning to gather to observe the battle scheduled for the approaching afternoon. As we marched up the hill adjacent to the sutlers, our adversaries in gray formed their lines across from us. The cavalry came into formation at the top of the hill, and the Union band played as the commanders and their officers and aids emerged to commence inspection of our ranks. We stood at attention in the warm sun, sizing up our Confederate counterparts across the ravine that separated our formations, infantry and cavalry, artillery and musicians all stood still as a lone bugler stood atop the hill and played a tune. Another line had formed along the road at the bottom of the hill where the armies gathered. This was the throng of spectators, which had grown immensely. This was the first time that we were all exposed to the sheer numbers of participants who had turned out for the reenactment at Resaca.

Families, couples dressed in period garb, veterans and their signature black ballcaps, uniformed soldiers in

camouflage utilities, schoolchildren holding giant bottles of
Sutlers' root beer, photographers, and others stood almost as
still as we did, while the music filled the crisp morning air. The
field commanders dismissed us from the morning parade, and
we marched once again in our column formation down
Chitwood Road, came to a halt for a final inspection, and a
briefing with details of the ensuing attack that would occur later
that afternoon. After Sergeant Krohn dismissed the company, I
walked back to camp with Steve, who told me about the ball
that was scheduled that evening, and how I might enjoy
attending. He typically would attend the many reenactments
around Atlanta with his wife, and they would camp together as
many other couples were, here at Resaca. Sergeant Krohn
passed by just then, and Steve called out to him. "Sergeant,
are you gonna let Steve fire his rifle today?" Sergeant Krohn
stopped, looked at me, and in a low tone responded to Steve.
"He has no training, no experience with firearms. I can't risk it."

　　　I didn't argue with him, nor did I blame him. We
returned to camp with about two hours of leisure time to burn. I
decided to try to catch a catnap, so I would be sharp during the
reenactment battle. I deprived myself of sleep on Thursday
night, and Friday night was a sporadic series of brief intervals
between train blasts through the night. I had misplaced my
earplugs, but made a point to locate them during my tent
cleaning session. I crawled into my tent, arranged my gear, and
collapsed on my bedroll. I was out! A coronet solo woke me up
at about 1:15 PM, and the camp began to stir. I emerged from
my tent with bayonet, leathers, uniform, and musket all
assembled. I was ready for the battle. The collective energy in
camp had a different vibe. Everyone seemed to move about
with a heightened level of deliberation compared to their
attitude before the tactical on Friday. This was, after all, the
150th anniversary of the actual battle of Resaca. We would
cross the same field, occupy the same space as the soldiers
who spilled their blood here for their cause, whether it was
based on north or south idealism, and I hoped we would make
them all damn proud. I believe if every volunteer in uniform was
a praying man like myself, they all most likely would ask for the
same thing on this Saturday afternoon – to do right by the ones
whose sacrifice we respected, appreciated and revered, in the
eyes of God, each other, and the gathering throng of
spectators who were blanketing the hillside overlooking the
field.

Our company gathered out on the road once again, and somehow I wound up on the front of the column near Sergeant Krohn, Corporal Bob, and Steve. At Captain Morgan's order, "forward march!" we followed the gravel road south toward the railroad tracks. It was apparent that we were attempting to use the treeline along the tracks to obscure our presence, in order to attack from the enemy's rear flank, on the opposite side of the field from where we were camped. We marched along the trench that laid low between the trees and the elevated tracks. I looked to my rear, and was so astounded by the length of our line, due to our staggering numbers, that I halted, and directed Sergeant Krohn's attention to the sight. "Now that's a regiment" he said. There must've been about 400 men in blue, marching in unison along the railroad tracks. We passed a break in the trees where we could view the field, so we crouched lower as we passed, and observed the Confederate ranks gathering in different pockets throughout the field.

Some of their cavalry passed by, and we were uncertain by their actions whether or not our position was exposed. We found a grown-over service road behind a thicket that provided enough room for our companies to halt and take cover. There, we stayed at ease behind a federal battery position at the southwest corner of the battlefield. We waited for what seemed to be about 10 minutes. Steve thought this might be a good time to produce two cigars "purchased in Dubai" he said with a wink. We lit up our stogies, and of course, after two or three puffs, we were ordered to load muskets. Sergeant Krohn passed by and reminded me that smoldering tobacco and dry gunpowder don't mingle well.

I exhaled with a final puff of smoke and stamped out my cigar in the grass. Steve cringed and moaned. "Sorry." I said. "I enjoyed what little I smoked." Despite the waste of a good cigar, Steve reminded me that he had two more that he thought were better to save for the ball, later in the evening. Finally, we were ordered to form a column, and advance onto the field. As I gazed across the expanse at the multiple detachments of troops, bursting cannons, and galloping cavalry I was overcome by emotion, and I felt a lump form in my throat. Captain Morgan ordered a left wheel motion, and the entire federal line reoriented itself as a Confederate brigade emerged at our right. We halted, and responding to commands, exchanged a spirited series of volleys with our opposers who were only about 60 yards away. A few boys in gray dropped where they had stood, and a few of our federal troops collapsed as well. Me? I kept loading and firing according to Captain Morgan's orders. I must've been doing something right, for amidst the chaos, Sergeant Krohn tapped me on the shoulder and opened my cartridge box – filling it with a large handful of paper cartridges, bulging with black powder.

"Bite off the loose end, pour the contents down your muzzle, and give the stock a light tap on the ground...you're ready to fire." "Fire by company!" shouted captain Morgan. I wasted no time grabbing a paper cylinder from the leather pouch riding on my right hip. I bit into the loose end of the paper cartridge and tasted the metallic powder that coated my lips with the sizzling bitter sting. Emptying the contents into the barrel of my musket, I lightly tapped the stock on the earth to pack the powder, and raised the stock to my shoulder, as Captain Morgan shouted "Ready!" "Aim!" I cocked the hammer back and trained my site just above the head of an official and authentic looking Corporal who seemed to be coaching and encouraging his sidekicks. A thousand thoughts rushed through my mind in a split-second. Did he have children? A wife at home? Who now would those boys look to for leadership? Then... He wouldn't think twice about shooting me. If I don't take him out, he might kill one of our officers... "Fire!" I pulled the trigger with no hesitation, remorse or regret – of course the corporal did not fall, but I somehow convinced myself that he would have, had I loaded a minnie ball with my powder charge.

This time instead of a "pop" of my spent percussion cap, a twin report of cap and charge harmonized with the other rifles in the line... Kaboom! A swift kick against my shoulder from the rifle stock, the fine spray of sparks and sizzling powder against my cheek, and the blossoming plume of gray white smoke, lilting past my face sent me back to 1864 again for just a split second. I looked over at Steve who seemed to be waiting for my response to my first rifle shot. He just smiled like a proud father, as we got back to the business at hand of fending off the rebel attack. Eventually the Confederates fell back, and I quickly spent most of my cartridges as Captain Morgan shouted his order to "fire at will!" Sergeant Krohn was carrying his Henry repeating rifle and stepping out of formation briefly, he popped off a succession of rounds in the direction of some rebel skirmishers who were getting danger close to our right.

His defensive foray was proven effective, leaving two victims lying in the grass. We were ordered to cease fire, as the Confederates retreated. We advanced as a single line, as Sergeant Krohn's order to "dress your ranks" was echoed down the entire Union line by other company first sergeants. I could see down the entire line to my left as we advanced en masse, and straight as an arrow toward the retreating wave of gray. Just beyond them, I could see the hillside canvassed with hundreds of spectators, and attempted to imagine the scene that they were witnessing. I was proud to be playing a small part of an incredible living history experience for this crowd, and hoped to inspire all ages in attendance. After we halted, and emptied our rifles in the air —to clear them of unspent charges, and to salute our adversaries— four buglers emerged, and everyone including infantry, cavalry, artillery, and crowd removed their caps, as the field fell silent to the chorus of "Taps". The mournful chorus echoed across the field from bugler to bugler.

Looking over my shoulder to the position from whence we marched, the dead and wounded lay still, scattered across the grass. Some of the victims had poured stage blood over their faces to add realism to the scene. The buglers' tune resounding against the hillside established a new meaning for me, and rendered the graphic scene before me into an indelible memory. As the buglers held their last note, there was a second or two of deafening silence, broken by the roar of the crowd. The lump formed once again in my throat, and my eyes began to water... I must've got some gunpowder in there somehow. I clutched my pocket where I carried Henry's Bible as we marched back to camp in formation. After some encouraging words from a beaming Captain Morgan, Sergeant Krohn dismissed us. I parked my gear in my tent, and made a beeline to the sutlers village, where I bought my own powder and a freezer bag full of 100 paper cartridges. Back in camp, Steve demonstrated for me how to fill and fold them, and he loaned me his brass powder horn, that premeasured each charge, so that each cartridge held the correct amount of powder.

I spent a couple of hours in my tent, preparing cartridges, and filling my box for the next battle, which would

take place on Sunday. I heard some collective banter and
laughter to the rear of my tent, where Earl, our company
commander and his wife were camped in their tent. Theirs was
a large canvas wall tent, about 12' x 14' with a large 12' fly
which made for a nice covered porch. When the fire wasn't
roaring, this was the social center of the camp. I continued my
fill-fold-and-tuck assembly line, preparing my cartridge box, as I
eavesdropped on the veteran reenactors, reflecting on their
experiences at Kennesaw, Atlanta, Chattanooga, Charleston,
etc. As I finished filling my cartridge box, Steve stopped by my
tent. "I'm going up to the ball later, if you want to come along."
Dancing has never really been my thing, let's be honest, and
watching from the sidelines, well, where was the fun in that?
Steve keyed into my hesitation, and said, "Come on, bring your
camera, I think you'll really enjoy it." "Okay, let's do it." I
said..."but I don't have a thing to wear."

We were the only spectators, as far as I could tell, who
would represent the Federal camp at the ball. We grabbed a
quick bite at the sutlers village, and followed the sound of
fiddle, guitar and voice, arriving at a square grassy patch next
to Chitwood Road, that was staked out by kerosene torches
and hay bales for perimeter seating. A pair of tents arched over
a 4-piece band who were wailing away in classic form, and a
lemonade stand, tended by two ladies in colorful period gowns.
I was blown away by the attendance. There must've been close
to two-hundred participants, all dancing in carefully
choreographed circles and lines. The master of ceremonies, in
an impressive top hat, introduced each dance, over the P.A.
system, and demonstrated the movements slowly for
newcomers, like myself. It began to rain as the sun tucked itself
behind the hills —the torches picking up where it left off. I
captured a few photos of the dancers, all decked out in their
dapper suits, derby hats, bonnets, bows and colorful debutant
gowns. The event was obviously owned by the Confederate
crowd... but it didn't matter. I sat next to Steve, who had found
an unclaimed hay bale. He handed me his last fine cigar "from
Dubai" and said, "try to savor this one." I gladly lit up, and we
indulged in some very fine tobacco while enjoying the
entertainment.

Steve suddenly bolted up and disappeared into the
crowd. Before I knew it, he was twirling around with the ladies –
all smiles. I photographed some couples, the band and

bystanders until Steve returned to his spot at the hay bale next to mine. Before he could catch his breath, a gentleman dressed in his confederate uniform, with long hair and gray beard approached us. He had been drinking something quite flammable, judging by his breath. He began chatting us up, and I got up to offer him my seat. It began as a gag to get him to bend Steve's ear, but the joke was on me, for he turned out to be a very experienced reenactor who wound up telling us a ghost story, which I recorded on my iPhone. His story was fascinating.

*"We was down in Charleston, we go out there every year, camp at the same place, right up against the woods, away from everybody else...you can see as far as a football field that way (motions) and a football field that way...and everyone else is up on the hill, at least a football field away...right behind us is the woods, and there's an apartment complex right there...in the woods.*

*So we set our tents up, facing out this way from the woods. So we got all our stuff out throwed it out there, put the tents up, you know, we got everything out of the van. And I'm standing there sideways, and I can see good out of the corner of my eye. And I look and see this damn person, standing there...you know, I just happened to see him. So I turned around, I stood up, and I said, "Hey man...what's goin' on?" He's walkin' past me, and says "I'm goin' to the dance over here, I'm following those three women." And John Segal, —there's three of us— he says "Three women?...where?" And the guy says "They're all dressed up over there...we're goin to the dance right over here." I says, "Wait a minute, there's no dance over here...not over here...as a matter of fact, it ain't even tonight...it's Saturday night, this is Friday evenin'." It ain't even dark yet, we just got there.*

*He just looked at me...he didn't say, well, hell...somebody told me it was over here...he didn't say that, he's just kept lookin'...he's lookin' right at the dance...he sees it...he's lookin' (gestures) that's the kind of look he's got. He was a rebel. So, my other friend, he come over there, and wanted to talk to him, and he wanted to talk to him about them women. He said, well, what are them women wearin'? He said they're wearin' them big dresses. So we says, there ain't no women up there with* dresses, they're gonna be down that way (pointing in the opposite direction from the woods) ...he looked at us again, and by that time Scott, y'know he's over there he's very intelligent about this Civil War stuff, and he noticed that the guy had this red piping on...red piping...ya see that, ya see that bead around my sleeve right there? (motions) ...he had a little red bead all the way around his uniform.

Scott happened to notice that he had somethin' else on there because Scott told us later that he was a Captain or something...'don't know what he had on, so he come over and said, "I noticed you have the artillery uniform on...what unit are you with? He said "Oh, I'm attached to Battery Wagner." And Scott said, "Oh yeah? well, where do you live at?" and he said, "well I always lived in Charleston all my life." So Scott asked him a few more questions, and the guy went over and sat down. John come up, and started askin' him some more questions, but all he wanted to know about was them women! So, I went, and started puttin' shit in my tent, ya know, and I heard John say, "Well, let me put some of this stuff up, but I want to talk to you some more...I got somethin' else I got to ask you..."

So I'm puttin' some of my stuff up, and as I came out of the damn tent, I seen John goin' into his tent, he's walkin' in, and I'm lookin' and the guy's gone. Well, Scott is over there foolin' around with his stuff, cause he's sleepin' on the ground...he's makin' him a "sasquatch" bed...and this guy's GONE!...I said "Where the hell did he go?! John come out of the tent and says, "Well, he was standin' right there!" And I'm lookin'...(motions)...football field that way, and a football field that way...and the woods back that way...he couldn't have come through our tents...but he did!

He came through our damn tents to go to that dance...you know why? Because everybody out here...all these people...and all these reenactments that we ever go to...the three of us...they stop the whole damn unit...the photographers...and the Captain asks, " What do you want?", and he says "I want that guy, that guy, and that guy..." and we come out there and he takes pictures of us, and then we get back in line and the Captain says, "What else do you want?" and he says, "well, hell...they look original." And that's the reason why he showed us...showed his self to us...was *because we looked original...he thought we was original! ...is the only thing I can figure out why...he showed his self, he thought we was original!... Hey! I tell you it'll mess you up when you think about this shit...I ain't got but half a brain...I shouldn't...I don't...and uh...I told Scott and them, I said "You know what? If he can be here...we can be here at the 200th event! If HE can be here...WE can be here...'you understand what I'm saying?"*

I responded "Absolutely." *"That's good."* he said.

 

There was something otherworldly and spiritual at work here and I wasn't the only one to notice it. I thanked the soldier for his colorful testimony, and I meant it with all my heart, for now I had both a Union and a Confederate Reenactor's perspective of a supernatural experience recorded in digital audio.

When the ball was over, Steve and I walked back to camp beneath a light drizzle. There were two empty spots left at the fireside, so after grabbing a couple of beers from our tents, we joined Sergeant Krohn and others next to another perfect bonfire, courtesy of Corporal Bob. "Steve, tell us what you were most impressed with at the battle today," said the first sergeant. I paused and noticed Captain Morgan watching me intently from the opposite side of the blaze. Sergeant Krohn's question caught me a bit off guard, but I knew the answer. "The turnout...both the reenactors, and the crowd." "I have an enormous amount of respect for anyone who believes in the importance of preserving our history enough, to act on it." "When I looked down the railroad tracks at that long line of blue uniforms, I felt proud to belong to such an elite group, even if it's just for the weekend." We sat around the fire until around midnight, and I listened to reenactor stories — mostly about this film, or that film — and the moviestars that different reenactors had encountered while appearing in Civil War movies...who was polite, and who is an "a-hole," etc. etc.

As embers glowed, the conversation shifted to a deeper reminiscent theme, as stories were shared about reenactments at New Hope Church, Charleston, Fort McAllister, Olustee, and Atlanta. The beer cans crumpled one-by-one as the stories became more fantastic, and the laughter grew louder. The fire continued to roar late into the evening, and I finally rose to my feet, bid the remaining handful of fire tenders goodnight, and wandered off to my tent. I journaled for a while by lamplight, as the symphony of camp conversations, cracking fires, the rattling of gear, and shuffling of feet dissipated into a soothing serenade of crickets and frogs. After dousing the lantern, I drifted off to sleep, but was soon reminded of our close proximity to the Southern Railroad line, formerly known as the Selma, Rome and Dalton railroad. The distant signal from the approaching diesel prompted me to make use of my handy earplugs, and before I knew it, I was out and dreaming.

*Revelry blew promptly at 0700 on the morning of Sunday, May 18, 2014*

—a date that I remembered as the Mount Saint Helens eruption in my home state of Washington, which had also occurred on a Sunday in 1980 when I was 14. My sleeping bag was soaked, and the hay that I had strewn around the daylight gaps at the base of my tent was damp to the touch. Parting my tent flaps, I peered out onto a soaked campground. It had rained consecutively for hours as I slept soundly. I got dressed in my blues, and scurried out into the muddy camp. Sergeant Krohn stood beneath a shelter, holding a snare drum around his waist, and drumsticks in his hands. He began to beat out a rhythm. Next to him, our bugler joined in on a small, high-pitched silver fife. An unattended bass drum stood upright on a stand, so I grabbed the mallet and joined in to complete the trio. We entertained our groggy, soggy audience for a while, performing about a dozen numbers, as the campers shook off the cobwebs, and gathered themselves for roll call. I managed to keep fairly good time, thanks in part to my brief stint as percussionist in ninth grade band class. Soon after we finished, a report came in from command, stating that morning colors would be canceled due to the downpour. I wandered over to the fire, to help myself to a cup of Corporal Bob's java, and found a dry place under the fly cover on the front of Earl and Terry's tent, where others had gathered as usual.

We all sat in repose as the battlefield became soaked with Georgia rains. Just then I remembered that I had loaned my camera to the company commander's wife, and began reviewing the images she captured, which were outstanding! I complimented Terry on her photographic skills. I was impressed by the images of our regiment, as they appeared from the perspective of the crowd. Again, the number of reenactors who showed up for the event was staggering to me, and though the Union uniforms typically were outnumbered by Confederate participants, the current ratio appeared to be well-balanced from my point of view. "That was some fine drumming this morning, Austin!" A deep voice was addressing me from the other side of the shelter, nearly drowned out by the rain that peppered the canvas fly above us.

John Smith from Maine desired to capitalize on our free time to learn more about my book. As we discussed the details, I learned that he owned and operated a small bookstore in his home state of Maine. In the past, he had written and published a book about his ancestor who had taken a bullet at Resaca, while serving in the 105th Illinois volunteers. Obviously, we had covered some common ground. John shared some advice and encouragement with me, regarding publishing options, and I thanked him. He would later send me a copy of the book that he published which provided some valuable background as a reference tool. As morning gave way to the afternoon, I found myself loading more cartridges in my tent, and busying myself with some general housekeeping. My bedroll was still soaking wet, so I spread it out to dry, and hung a makeshift clothesline across the length of my tent to air-dry other articles that also had been soaked. The rain had since subsided, and I sensed the sun beating down through the pines once again, upon our camp. Sergeant Krohn called roll again at about 1300 hours. Once gathered and organized, our unit marched in a line through wet grass to the opposite side of the field.

Fresh earthworks had been created previously for a film project, which we used as our defense, crouching behind it as a group before the crowd of onlookers that gathered on the hill to our left. The hillside was more densely populated with spectators than it had been on Saturday. We were flanked by two Union artillery teams who were preparing their field pieces. Over the ridge before of us, a ragged mass of silhouettes emerged, and drew closer in an impressive line. Captain Morgan ordered us to ready our rifles. I grasped my chest with one hand to make sure that my inside jacket pocket still contained the most important article I had packed for the battle.

It was still there – Uncle Henry's Bible. I raised my Enfield, which now had a full charge of powder, and aimed it just above a young Confederate private in gray jacket, and blue gingham shirt. He and his company halted, and he commenced to train his rifle straight at me. Ignoring my instinct to fire upon him, I waited for my Captain's order. I thought about how frustrating that forced hesitation must have been in 1864 for a soldier who had the enemy in his sites, but was ordered to restrain his instinct to pull the trigger.

Finally, the trench where we stood was instantly enveloped with gray smoke as we fired upon our enemy in a tight volley. A few of their ranks fell to the ground. They returned fire, and I watched two of our men fall to the ground in front of me. For the benefit of the crowd, both of them anointed their heads with stage blood for effect. As I reloaded, I noticed John Fritz had slumped over the earthworks too, and was lying still. Suddenly, I heard it – the wild rebel yell. The entire Confederate company before us charged forward with bayonets fixed. Captain Morgan ordered us to hold the line. We managed to repulse their advance, but only for a few moments. They eventually came charging at us a second time, and though we executed a spirited defense, Captain Morgan ordered us to fall back into the woods behind us. There, we took refuge behind trees and boulders, as the rebels nested themselves in our trenches, and continue to fire upon us at will. Some close contact activity was happening in the trench, and I recognized John Fritz getting swatted and slapped by two reenactors dressed in gray.

Was this some strange, unfamiliar rebel ritual that I had never heard of? Why was John not fighting back? And why was he stripping off his clothes, as the rebels continued to swat and slap at him from shoulders to waist? Apparently, he had collapsed right into a nest of biting fire ants, and the rebs were assisting him in exterminating them. John ran full-gallop up into the woods, stripped down to his skivvies to join us, clutching his musket, hat and laundry. None of us who had experienced our own encounter with those tiny little raiders and their painful poisonous bite were laughing. The over-zealous Confederates had failed to overtake our artillery team, who had trained their barrels on the earthworks that they now occupied. As our cannons fired upon them one by one, their lines ruptured and with our order to "fire at will!" We blew them out of their defenses, and sent them scurrying across the field, back to their original position. The carnage was horrendous! Bodies carpeted the field between our position in the woods, and where the rebels now stood. We were putting on a show for our crowd in Hollywood proportion, and now it was our turn to charge the field. As Captain Morgan beamed proudly, we obeyed his audible, loading our muskets, and joining forces with the other units, we formed an immense single-line that nearly spanned the entire width of the battlefield. "Dress your ranks!" shouted Sergeant Krohn. We advanced, as our collective adrenaline boiled over. This conflict climax was peaking, and we all felt it.

"Charge!" We swept the field in a mighty wave of navy blue, firing at random as we approached our opposers who stood their ground and briskly loaded their muskets, returning fire. Our colors passed impressively through a curtain of gray blue smoke, leading us at full speed toward a brave gang of rebels standing their ground, with barrels trained upon us. I figured this to be my one and only chance to contribute to the drama unfolding, so I charged at my targets, screaming at the top of my lungs, while firing my weapon in their direction. They noticed my advance, and returned fire toward me as a crew, and I tumbled to the ground, as the rest of my company charged forward to engage in hand-to-hand combat with the Confederates. I remained still, with my rifle just out of my reach, and my face in the soil as the sounds of combat eventually subsided to the chorus of Taps, which was blown by a distant bugler. A second bugler echoed the tune, and then the third, who was standing right above me, facing the crowd. Again, I clutched at Henry's Bible, which was still safe in my jacket pocket, and at that very second – the sky parted, spilling rays of sunlight down upon the corpses scattered across the field.

The final note was held at length by the bugler who was nearest to me, followed by a few seconds of silence. The crowd on the hill erupted in spirited applause, and it all became too much to take in without breaking down…which I did. I sat up and gathered myself…attempting to wipe tears, sweat, black powder and dirt from my face, but smeared the mix into a filthy mess instead. I spotted a small cabin, which had been erected on the field. It was currently being put to the torch while the rebs retreated from the field. I suppose it represented

Sherman's penchant for aggravated arson. Our company aligned with the rest of the regiment, and we raised our rifles skyward to salute our adversaries, and to clear charges. The crowd gave a final cheer, as we formed company for one final march back to camp, where we were addressed by each officer, from Captain Morgan to the Union Supreme Commander, who became tearful when we all gave him a collective "hip-hip hoorah" times three, followed by a hearty rendition of "Happy Birthday." He just walked away with his head hidden beneath his hat brim -an imposing figure outside, but a big softy inside. Sergeant Krohn was the last to address us, and offered his congratulations for a successful battle.

He dismissed us, and we all dispersed into our camp. Many went straight to their tents to pack up and prepare for the drive home. I remained behind, and conversed with Captain Morgan for a while. Sergeant Krohn walked by, and I couldn't resist asking him how I did on my first attempt at soldiering. "You were an effective killer." He said. "Something new to put on my resume" I exclaimed. Captain Morgan made a point to invite me to participate anytime at other reenactments that would follow Resaca. I told him that I had planned to only participate in one, but was considering showing up at the Atlanta battle event in September. As much as I hated to, I changed out of my uniform and into a pair of cargo shorts and a teeshirt. As I returned all my gear to you Sergeant Krohn's tent, I was flagged down by John Fritz. He was on his way to his car, and wanted directions to the site of Van Den Corput's Battery. This was an opportunity to visit the sacred spot one last time, so I offered to escort him there.

As we emerged from the Federal camp, we found ourselves surrounded by a chaotic barrage of activities. The Sunday rains had transformed the parking lots into a giant mud swamp. A fleet of tractors was chaining up vehicles one by one, towing them out of the muck, and onto the gravel road that led to the main highway. By the time we reached John's car, it was nearly covered entirely with the thick red goo, which had been splattered, by the passing tractors and vehicles. Once we cleared the windshield, we drove up the hill to the clifftop in the woods, where I pointed out the artillery pits to John. I stood back to allow him to navigate and study the site on his own. John was on his way to Atlanta to visit sites where both of our ancestors had fought, camped and foraged. He was moving

South as I was moving North with a common purpose, so we agreed to text news of our discoveries to each other as we progressed. He thanked me for sharing the battery site, and waved as he drove away. I lingered upon the hill a while longer, walking through the trenches for one last time, enjoying the sounds of the peaceful Georgia forest, and reflecting upon the details in Henry's letter that I had memorized. *"It is a wonder we were not all killed, or captured." "We were under the crossfire of the enemy, and through mistake, our own men fired at us, taking us for the enemy." "I was never so exhausted in my life while making the charge through the thicket and up hill, at that!"* I was presently looking down the East bank of that hill from where I stood, and it was now overgrown heavily with pines, and heavy shrubbery, but I could still see to the bottom, which was a distance of about 300 meters, at about a 50% grade. Imagine charging up this steep incline under enemy rifle fire and grapeshot, just after sprinting across a wide open field, negotiating uneven terrain covered in waist-high underbrush. No thanks!

I hiked down the paved hill, across the Resaca property and across the small bridge that spanned the creek. Many of our tents had been replaced with SUVs and compact cars that were being packed up by their owners, now dressed in their "civvies." Steve had packed up and was saying his goodbyes to the rest of the unit. I stopped in my tracks and ran to my tent. I returned with his powder horn, a full bag of cartridge sleeves, a nearly full tin of percussion caps and a can of black powder. "You're going to need these at Kennesaw" I said. It seemed only fitting to repay him for the ammo that he had been nice enough to loan out to me, not to mention the Cuban cigar that I was ordered to stomp out on the battlefield.

"You should join us again, I think this stuff agrees with you" said Steve. "I couldn't agree more." I said. We shook hands and he wished me good luck with my book. I bid the others farewell, and thanked them as they packed up their gear, and disappeared up the gravel road and out of sight. Soon, only Sergeant Krohn and Earl were left in Camp. I had swapped my canvas tent for my bright orange 2-man nylon dome. I would stay one final evening in the Federal camp and set out early for my drive north, but to my surprise, Earl would remain for one more night as well. His wife, Terry had driven home earlier, and Sergeant Krohn was gathering up his gear, stowing it tightly in his Jeep. Earl and I decided to drive into town to have dinner, since the sutlers had since closed up shop. Sergeant Krohn was anxious to get on the road, so we said our goodbyes, and he extended a kind invitation to fall in with that 125th Ohio anytime. We parted ways with a handshake, but I had the feeling we would meet, or even march together again. Earl and I drove past the parking lot where tractor drivers were still assisting stranded spectators with their vehicles in the rain. Though my wife had questioned the upgrade previously, I had earlier proven the necessity of four-wheel-drive as I relocated my Trailhawk from the muddy parking lot to the Federal camp with ease. Others had looked on with envy as they stood, helpless in ankle-deep mud waiting for tractors to drag their vehicles out to the safety of the gravel road.

The notion of a steak dinner at one of Calhoun, Georgia's fine eating establishments appealed to both Earl and I, so we obliged our appetites at the first spot we could find that seemed appropriate. As we dined together, we discussed the process of becoming a bona fide reenactor, and some of the benefits that accompany the privilege. The satisfaction of preserving our country's rich history, the camaraderie, the outdoors, and the constant pursuit and adherence to authenticity definitely presented some appeal. Earl reminded me, "It gives you an indescribable appreciation for the luxuries they didn't have that we take for granted." I raised my icy cold bottle of beer, and said "I know what you mean." As we drove back to camp, I noticed a giant truckstop on the fringe of downtown Resaca... A sign hung in the window with just a single word in bold print that enticed me, as it was intended to: "SHOWERS". That sounded nearly as good as the steak dinner did. Returning to the battlefield, the monster tractor pull and mud show was over, parking lots were empty, and only our two tents remained in the Federal campsite.

Sergeant Krohn had left for home, but not before building a perfect bonfire setup with kindling and cordwood, all stacked and ready to light. His noble gesture must've taken at least 20 minutes to complete – I emailed him a photo of the blaze that we enjoyed in the late evening hours, and thanked him for everything he did for me. Earl and I had a good fireside conversation until about 11 PM, when we doused the flames and retired to our tents. I journaled by lamplight for a while, then drifted off to sleep, to dream of cannons, rifles, cigars and marching in formation next to Private Henry Banks.

*Placard at the base of the bluff near Van Den Corput's battery*

*Standing in one of the emplacements at the site of Van Den Corput's battery,*
*where Henry seized and defended one of the Confederate artillery pieces*

*Our Union forces advancing at the 150<sup>th</sup> Reenactment at Resaca, GA.*

*Post-battle reactions with Captain Morgan of the 125<sup>th</sup> Ohio Reenactors Unit*

# The Smoke Clears

## Fort MacAllister, Georgia

Monday, May 19, 2014. Sunny and clear.

I woke at about 6 AM and packed all my gear into my Trailhawk, collapsed my tent and said goodbye to Earl, thanking him for the honor of falling in with the 125th Ohio. I asked if he needed help breaking down his tent. He told me that doing it himself was a personal thing and he liked to take his time and reflect while tending to business. I understood completely. We shook hands, and we exchanged waves as I pulled out of the woods and onto the gravel road, past the hill that led to the artillery pits of Van Den Corput's battery, and out onto Highway 41.

It cost the modest sum of nine dollars for a clean towel and a 10 minute shower at the huge truckstop that I had noticed the prior evening en route to dinner with Earl. I felt like a million bucks as I crossed the parking lot to my jeep in a fresh change of civilian clothes, with a full tank of gas, an incredible life-altering living history experience behind me, and a long road of discovery ahead of me. Next stop: Fort McAllister, near Savannah, Georgia. My objective to visit all sites where Henry camped to write his letters still ruled, though I would try to visit other significant Civil War historic sites along my route. Fort McAllister was one of those sites that I could not pass up. Though Henry's regiment did not participate in the Union attack on this enemy stronghold, it seemed like an appropriate launching point for me, being there was a very nicely appointed campground nearby. On my way to the Georgia coast, I passed by Kennesaw Mountain, then sped through Atlanta, since I had already checked those sites off my list the previous July.

I traveled nearly corner-to-corner across the state of Georgia, and I felt the heat and humidity levels rise as I drew closer to the sea. I caught my first glimpse of tropical palms between Savannah and Richmond Hill at about 3:30 PM. I located a campground near the water, along the shore of the Ogeechee River, just a few miles from the fort, so I took advantage of the remaining daylight to select the prime site, and set up for my overnight stay. I had promised my wife to try to select campgrounds carefully, making sure to surround myself with as many watchful eyes as possible, in order to stay safe. The campground near Fort McAllister was heavily populated by the time I completed my staging, and I was thankful that I had arrived early, before the campground sold out. I heard some commotion beyond the trees, and walked past the edge of my campsite to investigate. Peeking out from around the trunk of a tall pine tree I spotted a threesome of young raccoons wrestling in a bed of dry leaves and needles. I took note to pay close attention to my valuables and food while I camped in the little thieves' backyard. Once I had everything in my campsite secured, it was time to explore before dark.

I drove out to Fort McAllister and managed to get a quick tour of the museum, and see a short film before closing time. The ranger collected her fee, and welcomed me to stay and explore the grounds for as long as I liked. I explained to her why I was passing through, and she advised me to return in the morning to speak with the other ranger who was very knowledgeable in Civil War history. I thanked her, and ducked out the back door where the trailhead was located. Maybe it was my strict religious upbringing, or just my disdain for any self-deprecating habit that has always caused me to avoid spouting off profanities, without good reason... The bite of the proliferating deerflies for instance, gave me several good reasons as I hiked out to the earth mounds and barracks to seek shelter from the swarm of pesky bloodsuckers that gorged on my exposed skin. Back at the Federal Camp in Resaca, Steve had mentioned to me that the company had camped in these barracks during a reenactment recently, and suggested... well, dared me to sleep alone in this dark dungeon maze, and I was relieved that my request to do so was refused by the Ranger in the park office.

Besides, my campsite was all set up, waiting for my return. Once I had finished meandering through the barracks, I emerged out into the courtyard lawn surrounded by giant palms and huge cannons aimed out at the sea in every direction. I was impressed by how immaculately the grounds had been cultivated and cared for. The fort itself was in great condition, an obvious result of the respectful team behind its preservation. I learned later that Henry Ford had a hand in restoring the fort and all its facilities back in the day. Fort McAllister had been attacked seven times, according to reports, but it did not fall until Sherman ordered 4000 Union troops to seize it on December 13, 1864. This opened up the strategic position of the Ogeechee River to Union control.

On the 144 Highway that led me across the salt marshes to my campsite on Savage Island, I had spotted a small marina with a tiki bar-styled restaurant complete with outdoor seating, which I could not stop thinking about. I sincerely believe that I was in dire need of my "coastal fix" after being stationed for those few days, land-locked at Resaca.

I sat on a hightop table overlooking the river, watching fishing boats, pleasurecraft and seabirds pass by, as the sun dropped behind the western treeline. I was in a good place, mentally, physically, spiritually. This was obvious, due to the only decision pressing, which was to choose whether I better enjoyed the hot shower after Resaca, or the cold beer presently in my grip. I decided it was a tossup. By twilight, I returned to my campsite, sat at my picnic table and journaled until about midnight by the light of my lantern. After a few hours of undisturbed sleep, I was startled awake by a rustling sound against my tent, and high-pitched chatter that I recognized instantly, from countless camping trips in the Cascade Mountains with my father. Slowly unzipping my tent flap, I was face-to-face with a pair of clever bandits – the raccoons were back. I hadn't left them anything to paw through, so I assumed this rude awakening was their sweet revenge. They scurried away into the pines, and I slid back into my bedroll. My attempt to catch a few z's before daybreak failed, mostly because I was thinking about the road ahead. Today my target would be Seneca, South Carolina.

## Hardeeville, South Carolina

A pivotal point in the XXth Corps' march northward was the crossing of the Savannah River into South Carolina. This territory seen from the open fields and swamps of Georgia must have seemed foreboding to the troops preparing to invade it. This was, after all, where the seed of secession was first planted. In the journal of Stephen Fleharty, it becomes clear that despite the potential threat imposed by the notion of marching into the region, there existed among all troops in the regiment, an eagerness to advance.

> As the Federal picket paced to and fro on the South bank of the Savannah River, his eye often wandered northward, across the wide stream to the dark woods of South Carolina.

> Late in the afternoon the 102d was marched back to Savannah landing. There we boarded the steamer Black Diamond, and went down the river with the intention of flanking the island and effecting a landing on the Carolina shore. As we turned the lower point of the island and began to move up towards the channel north of it, the rebel cavalry pickets could be seen on shore skedaddling in fine style. But we were again thwarted in our purpose. The tide being out, the pilot said he was afraid to attempt the passage of a bar near the point of the island. It was finally arranged that the vessel should steam back to the wharf and make another attempt at high tide the next morning—or rather next year!

> The evening of the 31st of December, 1864, was very cold at Savannah—cold at least for that region. Ice formed during the night a half inch in thickness.

> On the miserable little boat, nearly destitute of rations, shivering with cold, we passed the closing hours of the year 1864, and witnessed the dawn of the new year. The men were stowed away in every nook and corner of the vessel; as many as possible crowded about the boiler works.

> Next morning, the 70th Indiana joined us on the boat, and by noon a landing on the opposite shore was effected without opposition.

> We marched the same evening, five miles out, to Cheves' Farm, crossing the bottom land north of the river. This lowland is also below tide water, and like Hutchinson's Island, is cultivated by the aid of embankments, canals, &c. It extends nearly five miles back from the river.

*The rebels were near by, and had been busy near Cheves' Farm felling trees to obstruct our progress. Their labors subsequently occasioned some heavy fatigue work, but the road was cleared as soon as the army was ready to proceed beyond that point.*

*We camped that evening (Jan. 1ˢᵗ) where the timber was principally pine—which, in its green state, makes for very poor fire-wood. The night was cold; the men had suffered during the previous night, and were therefore more determined to make themselves comfortable. It did not take them long to decide how this would be accomplished—they were in South Carolina!*

*There were several unoccupied houses and barns near by, and we had been in camp but a few moments when the work of demolition commenced. The entire brigade was represented in the work of destruction. The crashing of falling timbers, the ripping loose of the siding, and the general clatter of hammers made such an uproar that some of the men who had lain down to sleep actually thought the enemy was making an attack.*

*Our camp was on the premises of Hon. Langdon Cheves—once a prominent South Carolina secessionist. While we were in the vicinity, his home was used for Division Headquarters. Among his papers were numerous printed copies of a speech made by him at Nashville, in the year 1850.*

*Speaking then of the course the Yankees would pursue, in the case the South seceded, he said: "Will they invade us—where is their army?"*

*It is enough to say that we were then encamped upon his premises; but ah! thought we, where is Mr. Cheves?*

Henry briefly described his experience passing into the state where the trend of secession had begun. In this letter to his brother, Willis, he expresses some guilt as he witnessed the destruction of a church in Hardeeville. Fleharty had witnessed this act as well, and referenced a certain soldier's reaction to the church's toppling, as he cried aloud, *"There goes your damn gospel shop!"* Henry also makes some reference to his opinion of the rebels' fighting spirit, even while facing the futility of prolonging their offense against the prevailing

*Hardeesville January the23 1865*

> *In Camp Northwest of Savannah*

> *20 mi South Carolina*

> *Dear Brother (Willis H. Banks)*

> *I now take the opertunity to write you a few lines once more in the midts of the calametey of ware here in the tretchereous state of South caroliney. I received your very glad welcome leture yesterday dated the 6. I was very glad to receive one for it had bin so long sins I had received any the last one that I received from anyone before yours was from Mother and it was written the 18 of November last. I am well and enjoying good health here in the swamps & mud & mire of south caroliney well time roles on with traters in our front redy to oppose our progress with couradise (cowardice) it loocks so sens ive have enterd south Caroliney I had to laugh one day at them when we wer out foraging we run on to a large squad of Johneys to se them run as same as we or they saw us one day while we wer out we run out to a squad we fired at them they toock to flite like wild deares without fireing a shot with the exception of one riding a creame colored hores he stopt his hores & fired & then put spur the bullet past over our heds whisseling they were on the other side of a river called the Red river & we on this side couredly traters, run from us when we coud not get any nearer to them for they had burned the bridg a crost it I reley beleave they are afraid of Shurmons (Sherman's) armey & men. I want to se every thing in this state burnt level with the urth where they first egg of treson was lade & hatch & this army is the army that can do it & will if they get the chance to this town of Hardeesville that we are now in camp in every hous except a few that the offesers has there hedquarters in have bin toren down or burnt & made in to shanteys for the men to stay in there was a very fine Chirch standing in this town when we came here but now it is no more it was tore down the evening we came in here of the 7 of the month it fell level with the ground what out a solzer doo*

*I thout to my self when I saw it falling it loocks most to bad to
tore a chirch down but I suppose there has bin a grate deal
treson preached in it but it was not bilt nor desined for that   I
don't suppose if the confounded rebells don't give up a come
back in less than 5 or 6 months Shurmons armey will have this
state & north caroliney cleaned out.   The repart is now that
there is to be 40 days armistice   if that is the case we will not
have any more fiting to doo but I am afraid there is nothing of
it  but if the rebells come back to the Union it will be the best
thing they can doo  it will save millions of dollars worth of
property & thousands of lives & millions of money and time
with all.   There is no use of there iting eny longer for they are
over powered & whipt & that badley.   But they are gritey &
determined not it seames untill they get there states all destroid
& they wiped from the fase of the urth no more to be hird of
onely by past history.   You spoke in your leture that Old Jeff
was sick   I never wished eny one to dy but I hope he
sone(soon) may   it has bin reported here that he was ded & all
so that he had run a way I woud sooner believe the latter we
have had the nuse here that Fort Fisher & Williamton were
oures but not offishely.   You say you milk 32 cows it muss keap
you very bissey but I judg you are well pade for it for I suppose
milk is a good prise   I am sory to hear that your wife is not
well   I hope these few lines will find you all well & enjoying
the plesures of this world.   Well I don't think of mutch more
nuse time wares a way sloweley a littell over 6 months more
then gud by to the serviss by me I shall think I hav done justice
in surving my perishing country in the time of nead if I am
spard & we are musterd out of the surviss in the field I shall
probely make you a call   I have a small black finger ring that I
found in a hous here while helping to tare down   I send it in
this leture for your boy (William G. Banks b: 30 Mar 1857, d:
19 Jan 1929) well I don't know whether the mail will gou out
tomorrow or not   I will close & if the mail dose not gou out to
morrow I will write sumore.   Write sone   with love to you all
& all inquireing friends*

*As ever your brother*

*Henry. Ira. Banks*

☆ ☆ ☆

*Tuesday, May 20, 2014 Sunny.*

Rising early, it occurred to me that I hadn't slept in a practical bed in nearly a week, and though I was surprised that my lower back was uncharacteristically pain-free and that my sleep pattern had been fairly consistent, I still looked forward to a night spent sleeping on a comfortable mattress. After a quick bowl of cereal, and a helping of pan-seared Canadian bacon for protein replenishment, I packed up my tent and gear, and pulled away from Savage Island. The 102nd Illinois had reportedly camped on the site of a nearby plantation known as "Cheves' Farm" according to Stephen Fleharty's journal. Henry had penned a letter a few days after being camped at this location, so I would follow Highway 95 Northbound toward Hardeeville, S.C., to attempt to locate the exact spot. I had researched the history of the plantation online, and learned that the Union regiment that passed through the property had not left much of the home intact, partly for want of firewood, but also because the original landowner, Langdon Cheves had been a devout secessionist!

I passed over a bridge that spanned the Savannah River, and left Georgia behind me, at about 9 AM. I had traveled this route a few years back with my wife, her father and stepmother as we joined them for a road trip from Atlanta to Seneca, SC for a family reunion that ultimately became an annual getaway for Andi and I.

The ever-present Palmetto silhouette began to appear on signage, license plates, and all along the freeway, tucked back in the densely packed flora beneath stately pines. The weather was grand, and the sunrays lit up the steam rising from my freshly brewed cup-o'-Joe – gradually warming me up inside, and out. Eventually, I began seeing signs indicating the few miles remaining between my location and Hardeeville. There hadn't been much published on the Internet about Cheves Farm, only that it has been rebuilt in the early 20th century, and was now privately owned and maintained. I found photos of a private wedding that had taken place on the grounds, and learned that it was now known by a different name. Google Earth had revealed a long stretch of road bordered by an even placement of trees that led up from its front gate to the front entrance of the manor. I had attempted to contact the owner of the property, but had no luck, so I was once again at fate's mercy in my attempt to find Henry's campsite. As a town, Hardeeville had a comfortable, welcoming vibe, with banners hoisted on streetlight poles announcing an upcoming festival. At an intersection, I spotted a festive looking Mexican establishment, and talked myself into an early lunch.

My cold Mexican beverage wasn't quite as refreshing as the one that quenched my palate the previous evening at the tiki bar, but it was just the ticket as a complement to my giant chimichanga. I figured the plantation would require a bit of walking, so I succumbed to justification that the calories were affordable.

I didn't catch the name of the security guard that I argued with through a plastic speaker at the front gate of the plantation, but he had that gung-ho attitude that I was all-to-familiar with due to my brief stint as a hotel security officer during my college days. I had worked with some ex-law enforcement personalities that did not consider flexibility and cooperation as job requirements. I gave up trying to convince the voice-in-the-box that I would only be a few minutes, and a quick stroll through the property was an important matter of finding some closure to family history. Never mind the fact that I had driven here all the way from Texas, etc. etc. At the end... I surmised that the long stretch of road to open the gate for me was just too much trouble for the guard to navigate via golf cart at high noon in the summer sun. Frustrated, I circumnavigated the immense property, settled into a spot that offered a prime vantage point, and was satisfied with a good visual of the grounds. I could imagine the sound of hammers and axes echoing through the air as the102nd went to work collecting firewood, building ramshackle huts out of reclaimed lumber from the structures that once graced this riverside acreage.

Once I found the main drag that carried me eastward toward Seneca, my route would lead me through some very lush forests and farmland along the long and lonely two lanes of Highway 3. Once merged onto Highway 68, the small populace of Varnville, Hampton and Fairfax offered welcome relief. The heavy clusters of cypress and oak became even more dense, festooned with their whispy strands of Spanish moss. The canopies they formed above swampy bogs covering the banks of the Salkahatchie River brought to mind tales from Mark Twain. The 641, known as the Confederate Highway, crossed over the width of the Cape Fear River, which was indistinguishable, due to the overgrowth that flourished along its banks, and among the swamps. I felt the humidity rise as I drew closer to my target location, and the screeching symphony of cicadas and birds intensified through my open sunroof. Finally, I arrived at the Rivers Bridge State Historic Site. I parked my Jeep in an abandoned parking lot, walked up to a plaque that outlined details pertaining to one of the Confederate Army's last stands against Sherman that occurred on February 3, 1865. A beautifully constructed split rail fence stretched downward from the parking lot, running parallel with a worn path that disappeared into the trees.

A gentle breeze was blowing, and aside from the chorus of insects, the only sound was that of a Pileated Woodpecker, tapping out his rhythms upon a portion of the fence. I approached the sound carefully, as I walked along the downsloping path, and then I spotted his bright red plume, and black mascara. He had bored several holes in a rail near the ground, and was standing next to an impressive pile of sawdust. I suppose he had discovered a nest of grubs or termites to snack on. Once he spotted me, he hopped up onto the top rail of the fence. *"I see you!"* I said. He stood and cocked his bright red head at me a couple of times, studying my movements, and let me snap a couple of photos before he flew way to latch his talons onto a nearby tree trunk. He stood approximately 20 inches in length, probably 22 inches with his plume at full mast –a majestic and curious trailguide that would appear and reappear, numerous times during my visit.

The well-worn path leading from the parking lot took me in a full circle around the park, which featured some of the best-preserved parapets, trenches, and gun battery impressions I had ever seen. I continued to hike along the interpretive trail, reading placards along the way that outlined the charge of Weaver's Brigade, which was more of an organized wade through the swampy Salkehatchie River. I can describe it as a peaceful uneasiness. That is the feeling that possessed me during my tour through the trails and mounds of this battlefield. The battle had taken place here on February 3, 1865, but I felt like it had only recently occurred – the heavy energy of this place still hanging over it. The last time I felt this sense of unwelcome intrusion was at the Confederate graveyard at Resaca. In wandering through this battlefield, I found the mass grave where rebel casualties had been reburied in 1876. Their marker still stood in its place, and it read: "in memory of our Confederate dead who fell in battle at Rivers Bridges, February 4, 1865." On the back of the stone, an inscription read: "soldiers rest, your warfare over, sleep the sleep that knows no breaking, dream of battlefields no more. Days of anger, nights of waking." Union casualties numbered 124 against Confederate losses of 97. Henry and Company narrowly missed this conflict. They were marching about ten miles or so up river, fresh from a miniature battle that took place near Lawtonville, then as a matter of course, they managed to burn a palatial southern residence to the ground.

Once I had exchanged the rough washboard of country backroads for the consistent hum of Interstate 26 against my tires, I was free to admire the passing scenery. I had driven through these parts of South Carolina twice, while visiting Andi's cousins during the holidays, and was reminded of the adverse affects brought on by the relentless Kudzu. The terrible devastation, as evidenced by dead and dying pines, once standing tall and unopposed, was sickening. "Where did this infestation come from, and why was it so difficult to eradicate?" I wondered. I came to learn that this climbing, corkscrewing vine, also known as the Japanese Arrowroot is native to much of eastern and southeast Asia, and some Pacific islands. It had originally been introduced in the Japanese pavilion at the Philadelphia Continental Exposition of 1876 as an ornamental bush, and low-maintenance shade source. Later, it was used frequently to aid in erosion control and soil enhancement. The invasive vine has been recorded lately to be spreading as much as 150,000 acres annually. Herbicide, prescribed burning, and even grazing goats and llamas have been initiated to combat the creepy crawler, but there is apparently much more effort necessary to slow the Kudzu's proliferation.

## Columbia, South Carolina

As the 102nd approached the capitol of South Carolina, Fleharty recorded the general anxiety of the forthcoming defense that they expected, once they arrived at Columbia.

> *No skirmishing ahead. Surely they will not yield the city without a struggle. At length we approach the summit of a hill not more than two and a half miles from the city. At the summit there is a farmhouse and a fence. From that point something extraordinary is visible. The men far in the rear are sure of this, for those in front are climbing the fence in regular succession to "take a look."*

> *In our turn we do the same, and beyond the Congaree River behold the famed city of Columbia—the cradle of secession.*

> *At the opening of the year 1865, Sherman's grand army carried the Stars and Stripes to the gates of Columbia, with a protest, which in words simply meant "South Carolina cannot secede."*

> *The enemy had crossed to the north bank of the stream and still occupied the city, but not in force. Skirmishers from the right wing of the army were exchanging shots with the rebel pickets, and there was light artillery firing. We camped in line of battle about two miles from the city.*

After driving many miles in my trusty Trailhawk, I arrived on the outskirts of Columbia, the state capitol of South Carolina. I drove off the main drag, and slowly through a neighborhood, stopping at a park that offered a perfect vantage of the state house, which was just across the Congaree River. Despite its structural condition being incomplete, at the time of Sherman's raid, its west walls seemed perfectly suited for target practice. The high ground where I now stood must've been very near where the regiment's artillery had dug in, for as I strolled through the west lawn of the state house, a few moments later, examining the damage that is still evident, I could plainly see the area, far across the river where I had previously parked. At the front steps of the state house stood a bronze statue of George Washington. The lower half of his walking cane was missing, and the adjoining placard blamed Sherman's forces for "brick-batting" poor George when they seized the city. I tucked my pocketknife under George's shoe for safekeeping, to avoid its confiscation by the guards who screened the crowds entering the giant doors at the top of the north steps.

The interior of the state house contrasted its drab exterior, decorated in bright, garish pigments. Its grand dome sparkled above the recently recessed house delegates who now congregated on the floor in their impressive professional garb, carting leather briefcases, and satchels. I found a chair that put me dead center within the chaos, and I felt like an eavesdropping spirit in my cargo shorts, graphic tee, hiking boots and ballcap – I may as well have been invisible. Impressed, I spent about 30 minutes wandering through the halls of the state house. reminding myself that the first state to secede from the union made that fateful decision here. I remembered reading somewhere about a monument that stood near the railroad tracks where the city was formally surrendered to General Sherman. Of course it had to be located. After driving around for a while through more of Columbia's suburbs, I located the stone on the front lawn of a historic church, just north of a railroad tunnel. It read: *"Erected February 17, 1914 by Wade Hampton Chapter, U. D. C. On the spot where Mayor T. J. Goodwyn surrendered the city of Columbia to General W. T. Sherman February 17, 1865."*

"Oh, crap!... My knife!" I've got to hand it to George Washington – he's a good knife-sitter. Unbelievably, my pocketknife was still right where I left it, safe underneath his shoe! Since I had driven all the way back to the state house from the monument, I took a few more minutes to walk around the building. I made a point to locate all the bronze stars that had been attached to the exterior walls, marking the spots where cannonballs had struck their targets, flung from the Union artillery positions across the river. It was late in the day, and Seneca beckoned, so I embarked on my 2.5-hour drive through the South Carolina countryside. I passed through my father-in-law's childhood stomp, Westminster, recognizing the landmarks that he pointed out to us during previous visits. I soon crossed over a bridge that rose above Lake Keowee, where Andi and I had navigated by boat with her cousins during a previous summer. Finally I pulled into the long driveway that led to the Stevensons' beautiful home at the lake. A warm family greeting welcomed me to Seneca, and the sound of a small bell tinkled from down the hallway as Simon the cat came running toward my familiar voice. Missing my own feline threesome, waiting for me back home, I happily stroked his thick gray coat as he squinted at me through his soulful green eyes, expressing his gratitude with a resounding "meooow." All of us went to dinner at a favorite restaurant where I had to sample the local specialty: shrimp and grits! It wasn't the first time, nor would it be the last! After my first sample of this succulent delicacy in a restaurant in Charleston, SC, I hadn't sampled a recipe that rivaled it, but always hopeful, I ordered it nearly every time it appeared on a menu. A creature of habit, I suppose…I exercised the same practice when I spotted "Molé" on the page.

We all stayed up late and shared spirited conversation out on the Stevensons' balcony that overlooks Lake Keowee. I reached a point of fatigue, where I could barely keep my eyes open, said good night and descended the stairs to find my comfortable guest quarters waiting. I think I collapsed in mid air before hitting the pillow, and I slept like the dead until sunrise the next morning. I didn't waste much time getting back on the road, and since the Stevensons were both medical staff at the local hospital, their day started early too.

### *Wednesday, May 21, 2014 Sunny.*

After a strong cup of coffee, I thanked my hosts for their hospitality, and we followed each other in our vehicles down their long drive, crossed the bridge over Lake Keowee, and eventually parted ways. Well-rested, I was now headed back into the eastern direction where I would try my luck at locating the site where Henry wrote his next consecutive letter. I set my GPS to Raleigh, North Carolina. Upon my route, I would pass a notable Revolutionary War site known as "Cowpens." It was here that on January 17, 1781 Brigadier General Daniel Morgan won a decisive battle over British Lieutenant Colonel Banastre Tarleton, a turning point in the reclaiming of South Carolina from the British. – Back to the campaign at hand – my drive toward the coast brought me to an area in South Carolina called Coosawatchie.

Here, I found another well-appointed campground tucked away in the woods behind the Frampton House Plantation, which I toured for about 30 minutes. I was amazed at the sturdy condition of the historic home, which had been put to the torch, then reconstructed in 1868. The grand oaks that stood guard in the front yard were ominous, and draped with veils of Spanish moss, which made for a nice photograph. Robert E. Lee had spent some time at this location and some of the original entrenchments were still visible in the mansion's backyard. The nearby campground was quiet, and it offered campers the rare opportunity to sleep in a real railroad caboose or boxcar. I opted for my own tent, however, and though I had arrived a little earlier in the day, I chose to stay put, help myself to a cold beer from the campground commissary, and journal at my picnic table for a while. I had a lot of catching up to do, and many blank pages to fill. At dusk, I lit a small fire and warmed up some beef stew for dinner. My campsite bordered the edge of a thick grove of palmettos that stood about 8 feet in height. It reminded me of a prehistoric jungle where a T - Rex might come crashing through at any moment – sniffing out my beef stew, which I would gladly forfeit...but not my beer. No sir!

I continued to record details in my journal by lamplight, until I started to drift off. I hoped the contents within my journal would not have the same effect on any future readers, whomever they might be. The few neighbors who had moved in during the evening had all since retired. I doused my lantern, and dove into my tent. The forest creatures did their best to distract me with their serenade, but all they did was speed me off to sleep.

## Averasboro, North Carolina

According to Fleharty's account, in March of 1865, Henry's Company E was once again assigned to scout before the grand army as skirmishers, while they closed in on the rebels entrenched near Averasboro.

*March 16th. The troops moved early and soon found the enemy. When about four miles south of Averysboro heavy firing commenced in the front. The 1st Brigade, except the 70th Indiana, which was "train guard," was formed on the right of* *the road in line of battle, and preparations were made for an advance. Finally we moved by the left flank, crossed the road, and made a detour of about three-fourths of a mile to the left. Then moved to the front, the skirmishers became quickly engaged. As we advanced cautiously through the young pines to the edge of an open field, it was perceived that the Brigade had completely flanked the rebel position. Not more than one-hundred and twenty-five yards in advance, they were visible in great numbers, running forward to their front line of works to reinforce the rebels there engaged. At that instant a number of our men yelled out, "Don't fire—they're our own men!" For a moment our line was undecided. It was thought barely possible that we had become bewildered and were about to charge our own troops. Many months of active campaigning had rendered the uniform of the opposing armies almost indistinguishable. Many of the rebels wore blue, and many of the Federals, having worn out their blue, were dressed in citizen's gray. The enemy in the meantime had kept up a galling skirmish fire, and heavy artillery and infantry firing was going on in the front, where the 3$^{rd}$ Brigade confronted their breastworks. Soon all doubts as to the identity of the rebels in our front was dispelled. The Brigade raised a yell, and, as if by an intuitive perception of the duty required, rushed forward—the 102$^{nd}$ on the right, the 79$^{th}$ on our left; the 129$^{th}$ and 105$^{th}$ in the second line. The rebels, completely outflanked, instantly broke. Yelling like wild men, the Brigade swept magnificently forward, directly in rear of and parallel with the rebel line of works. Three pieces of artillery fell into our hands and many prisoners—recumbent in a trench behind their works—held up their hands and handkerchiefs begging for mercy. But the main body of the charging column rushed by them and continued on after the flying enemy, who abandoned blankets, haversacks, canteens, guns, cartridge boxes—everything that could impede their progress. Reaching heavy timber, the pursuing column halted, reformed the line of battle, and rested for a time, keeping up a sharp skirmish with the enemy.*

*Thursday, May 22, 2014 - sunny.*

The sun peeked through the forest that loomed above my campsite at about 0700, projecting shadows and light that animated across the wall of my tent. Mesmerizing as it was, I was preoccupied by the thought of hot coffee waiting in the campground office. I rose and walked over to the front door, let myself in, and help myself. The manager asked me what I was up to, and when I answered, he lit up and began educating me about the local history. He reminded me that Robert E. Lee's headquarters had been established here early in the war from 1861-1862. The earthworks that I had seen in the backyard of the plantation, represented just a small portion of those built along the nearby Broad River, to defend against Union boats that might wander inland upriver. Though I had my sights set on Raleigh, Fleharty's journal had mentioned a significant battle that occurred nearby in which the 102nd had been involved.

I had come this far, and I had a little time to kill, so I decided to kick northwest. Highway 95 carried me over the great Peedee River and past the famous Camden Battlefield where British General Cornwallis won his great victory over our Colonial ancestors — but enough about him. The border between North Carolina and South Carolina was not far away. This was obvious, due to the Burma-Shave-style outdoor billboard campaign that led to an enormous multi-use compound that seemed to cover nearly a square mile, boasting a gas station, restaurants, bathrooms, gift store, carnival rides... Dear God...I was appalled – a quick glance at my fuel gauge was followed by a deep sigh of relief – I would luckily have every reason to avoid the truck stop from hell! I was tempted however to stop at Lumberton, North Carolina to visit the world's largest cigar store. Instead, I pressed on to Henry's camp at Averasboro. It was about 3:00 p.m. when I finally pulled into the gravel parking lot where a sign read: "Averasboro Battlefield and Museum". I stopped, as I often did, to read Stephen Fleharty's description of the site, and the happenings here that were relevant to the history of the 102nd Illinois Volunteers, and the XX Corps.

Suddenly my iPhone rang with an alert. A text had come over from John Fritz, who I had met at the Resaca event. He was busy exploring the Peachtree Creek Battlefield in

Atlanta. He reminded me that I was near Bentonville, and asked me to share with him what I found there if I was able to visit, for it was on his itinerary as well.

The museum building at Averasboro was smaller than I had expected, but the fields that surrounded it were immense. As I emerged from my jeep, it felt as if someone wrapped me in a heavy wool blanket that had been soaking in boiling water. The humidity was that intense. That familiar, deafening chorus of cicadas greeted me once again from the opposing treeline that bordered the battlefield, as I strolled across the parking lot, and up the steps to the museum's front door. It seemed to be a converted house. What the Averasboro Museum lacked in size, however, it made up for in quality content. A vast collection of firearms in every condition stood behind Lexan panels. Some well-preserved uniforms and sabers shared space with hundreds of unearthed relics. In a separate room, a Union cavalry officer's saddle was on display.

The curator escorted me to a back room not yet open to the public, and proudly showed me a very rare, recently donated Confederate Cavalry saddle in stages of preservation. The curator tendered further assistance, as he pointed out the area on a map where fragments of the XX Corps (the 102nd Illinois included) showed up as the rebels were gaining ground with a counterattack, and helped drive the Confederate forces to withdraw. Further research confirmed that Henry's unit had pushed through the enemy's first of three lines of defense from the left flank near the Cape Fear River. Once satisfied, I exited the museum and lumbered across the parking lot towards a group of log huts. The battlefield stretched far south, where the sun began to flirt with the treetops that stood defiant along the field's western edge. It was easy to imagine the sights, sounds and smells of war, being fresh from the Resaca reenactment. I was reminded of Sergeant Krohn's comment, warning me that I would never again view the Civil War in the same way. He was right.

"You'd better get a move-on if you're going to
Bentonville!" The voice calling out to me belonged to the
museum curator. I saluted to him from across the parking lot
and ran to my jeep. My GPS announced that it was a 40-minute
drive to Bentonville, but I arrived in about 35 minutes, avoiding
the Interstate and barrelling down "Stricklands Crossroads",
and over "Devil's Racetrack" where I sped past "Oak Grove"
the impressive plantation home of John Smith, which was used
as a Confederate hospital during and after the conflict at
Averasboro. I would receive news later from John Fritz, my
new acquaintance from the reenactment at Resaca, that upon
his visit to this building, evidence of blood spilled upon the
floorboards in 1865 was still visible.

## *Bentonville, North Carolina*

A brief glimpse through Fleharty's eyes as he witnesses the
aftermath of Averasboro paints a grim picture of the war. Signs of
deterioration begin to emerge on the part of the Confederate army. The
great war will soon be at an end, yet the 3$^{rd}$ Brigade continues to
advance, despite the difficult terrain of the region, which apparently
makes for slow progress. Fleharty also reveals the reason why there
was such a noticeable gap of time between Henry's letters.

> *Everything indicated that the rebels had been badly cut
> up in the fight. Their dead and wounded were found in almost
> every house in the vicinity of Averasboro — one house contained
> sixteen of their dead. In the town itself we found thirty of their
> wounded. An abandoned ambulance, which we passed,
> contained a dying rebel officer. The poor fellow moaned
> piteously.*

> *We followed the main army on the Goldsboro road, the
> morning of the 18$^{th}$. Crossed a number of swamps; roads very
> bad — in some places almost impassable for teams. All night we
> were on the move or waiting to move, and between sunset and
> sunrise passed over but three miles of the road.*

> *The march was continued on the 19$^{th}$. In the afternoon
> of that day the battle of Bentonville took place. Gen. Joe
> Johnston then hurled all his available force on the left flank of*

*Sherman's army. The cannonading early in the afternoon
became very heavy directly in our front. We were then
guarding a wagon train, but the Division was ordered forward
to assist those engaged, and the teams were left to come up at
leisure. Then there was a rush towards the front—cavalry,
artillery and infantry all crowding along one narrow road. As
we approached the scene of action the roar of the conflict
became perfectly terrific. The advance brigade of Carlin's
Division, 14<sup>th</sup> Corps, had been repulsed, and affairs looked
somewhat critical. Our batteries were being served with
wonderful energy. The crashing roar of musketry reminded us
of Resaca. Our Division was quickly hurried to a position on
the left of the 1<sup>st</sup> Division, and breastworks were quickly
thrown up by the 1<sup>st</sup> Brigade in almost no time. The men
thought they would be needed, but they were not. The extreme
left did not become engaged.*

*On the 20<sup>th</sup>, orders were issued for a general assault
upon the enemy's works—to take place the next morning. This
order was not communicated officially to the troops, but it was
soon noised around, and that evening there was much sober
thought about the work to be accomplished on the morrow. In
such a case the soldiers dislike to be in suspense.*

*But the contemplated assault was abandoned.*

*We remained in the vicinity of the Bentonville battle
ground until the morning of the 22d; in the intermediate time
built a new line of works—marched to them—returned to the
old line—then back again to the new. There was picket firing
and cannonading on the right much of the time. The morning
of the 22d, the enemy having retired to Smithfield, we resumed
the march to Goldsboro. A high wind was blowing; otherwise
the day was beautiful. A star (Venus) was visible at noon-day
in the clear sky. It attracted general attention, and the soldiers
called it "Sherman's Star," and was sure it was a star of
peace. At dusk we reached Falling Creek. The bridge across
the creek was in a miserable condition—indeed it was the
worst bridge we crossed during the campaign. Our brigade
occupied two hours in getting over.*

*On the 23d, we crossed the Neuse River. Previous to*

*crossing we waited for a time in a plowed field. The wind was blowing a hurricane, and we were almost suffocated with dust that was swept up in great clouds from the field. During the day we passed some of Major General Terry's troops—two divisions, one composed of white troops the other of blacks. Some of the men from the white division complained very bitterly of their hardships. They "had been cut off from communication and had been without letters for seven days." Our men answered tem very consolingly saying, "It is too bad—a real shame—but then we have had no letters since January 12th—our latest news from home is only seventy days old. We camped near Beaver's Creek that evening nine miles southwest of Goldsboro. The rebel cavalry skirmished there with the pickets. The 102d being detailed to guard the pack mules into town, we were up at 1 o'clock A. M., March 24th. Moved without breakfast an hour and a half later—reached Goldsboro at daylight. Finally the Brigade went into camp and constructed breast works two miles north of the town.*

*During the raid the 102d lost 44 men—killed, wounded and captured.*

*Excepting for one of two intervals of rest, we had been raiding fifty-two days, and according to Gen. Sherman's own statement, had marched nearly five-hundred miles. The troops were ragged beyond all description. Swarthy, smoked and worn out—many without shoes—no wonder the negro soldiers of Terry's command said, as the raiders marched by, "Sherman's men are a hard lookin' set, suah." If the army could have marched through a northern city, appearing as it did, the people would have held up their hands in amazement and inquired, "What wretched ragamuffins are these?"—and some independent soldier would have replied, "Only Sherman's Greasers."*

I pulled into the parking lot at the Bentonville Battlefield at about 4:30 PM. The gate was still open, but there were only two other vehicles in the parking lot. I raced to the park office, and found the door still open. A young lady stood behind the cash register counting a stack of currency, so I figured my visit here would be brief. I explained my reason for visiting, and she kindly dropped her project, and proceeded to mark for me on a map where the 102nd would've been during the Bentonville battle. She highlighted some key points to visit around the property, and though the office would be closing soon, she invited me to stay as long as I wanted, and to enjoy the property and its historic structures. I made a generous cash donation to the museum collection box as I exited, and wandered out onto the property. The museum had featured an enormous topographical map of the battlefield, complete with fiber optic technology, which would've been a great source to observe and study, but it would have to wait. Strolling through a stand of enormous oaks that offered welcome shade from the afternoon sun, I entered into a spacious clearing, arriving at the "Harper House".

The Harper House had served as a makeshift field hospital in March, 1865. I peeked through the windows to observe the great care that had been administered to achieve impressive levels of realism, from the furnishings to the period-perfect tools and instruments that were neatly arranged on top of a large table. A mass Confederate grave, and the Harper family cemetery was near the two-story home. The Harper House was occupied by Union troops during the conflict, and the Harper family had cared for over 500 wounded soldiers including 45 Confederates. I was excited to find at the end of an interpretive trail leading from that location, a portion of earthworks erected, or at least used by the XX Corps. My corresponding map confirmed this as the general area where Ward's troops had established their flanking position on the left, near where Harper House Road, and the Mill Creek Church Road intersected. As promised, I snapped a series of photographs and emailed them to John Fritz, who was still scouting about the vicinity of Peachtree Creek. He shared some of his discoveries with me as well. The sun had since disappeared behind the forest to the east, and I was a long way from my next destination, which was near Raleigh, North Carolina.

## Raleigh, North Carolina

In chapter XI of Fleharty's book, "Our Regiment", we join the 102nd in a cause for celebration, as they approach Raleigh, N. C., though the collective euphoria would be short-lived.

*The news of severe fighting at Petersburg and Richmond reached us about the 4th of April. On the 6th there was a grand review of the division by Major-Gen. Mower, who had succeeded Gen. Williams in the command of the 20th Corps. As we were coming in from the review, we heard heavy cheering from far away in the direction of Goldsboro. Gradually the wave of enthusiasm approached our part of the line—one regiment following another in such outbursts of deafening cheers as can only be heard from soldiers in the hour of victory.*

*What could it mean? We approached our camp and glad news was then on every tongue—"RICHMOND IS OURS." Then the old "First Brigade" swelled the deep chorus of voices that went up from all the hills and valleys around Goldsboro. Everybody became happy.*

*That afternoon, business was almost suspended in high military circles. The army was wild with joy. Additional news in regard to the great victories, occasioned new outbursts of feeling. With enthusiasm that knew no bounds, the troops received the order of Gen. Grant announcing the result, and saying substantially to Gen. Sherman: "Move immediately against Johnston, and let us finish up the job at once."*

*Camped the night of the 11th a quarter mile east of the town (Smithfield, N. C.) Moved at sunrise next morning—on the road leading westward through Smithfield. As the head of the column approached the ancient little town, cheer after cheer reached us from the camps of other troops. "More good news" the soldiers said and pressed forward to hear it announced. An Aid soon rode along the column, and the electric words thrilled every heart, "LEE HAS SURRENDERED WITH HIS WHOLE ARMY!"*

*Then the cheering surpassed all previous manifestations. Hats flew into the air as thick as the flying leaves of autumn. Oh ! the unspeakable joy of that moment to the war-worn soldiers. The glorious words needed no comment. All felt that the war was virtually over—the Union saved. A few moments later we passed Gen. Sherman, who was walking rapidly to and fro on the sidewalk, his hands crossed behind him. He was evidently absorbed in deep thought, but his thoughts could only have been of a happy nature, for he had just issued an order in which the following noble sentiments were uttered, substantially in these words:*

*"All glory to God! And all glory to our brave comrades towards whom we have been marching! A little more toil ; a few more days of labor, and the great race is won ; and our government stands before the world redeemed and disenthralled."*

*Moved at daylight the 13th, and reached Raleigh without opposition at 2 o'clock P. M. Went into camp southeast of the city. The rear of Johnston's army had retired the previous night.*

*Saturday, the 15th, according to previous orders we were ready to move at six o'clock in the morning. But the order was countermanded. Joe Johnston, as we subsequently learned, had offered to talk with Gen. Sherman about surrendering.*

*While negotiations were pending, the news of the assassination of the President reached us. The army during many days had been intoxicated with joy, but when this terrible news was confirmed, the general joy, was turned into mourning. Had all the bright omens of peace suddenly swept away the reaction could not have been as violent as it was under the effect of this one harrowing thought—Lincoln slain in the hour of victory. O! how the great heart of the army throbbed and swelled; first with the wild thirst for vengeance, and then with a profound sorrow, that would heed no words of consolation.*

*The morning of the 25th the new campaign opened. It was destined to be short.*

*Our regiment, with the corps, marched out about fourteen miles on the Holly Springs Road. Camped six miles from the springs, and remained there during the 26th and 27th. In the mean time Johnston surrendered. We returned to Raleigh the morning of the 28th, and immediately commenced preparations for the homeward march.*

Henry wasted no time responding to brother, Willis' letter that was received the evening of April 20[th,] 1865. As I studied this letter from Henry, in comparison to Fleharty's journal, there were many corresponding notations to contemplate. However, actually moving through these paths in person made it even more exciting for me, and easy to visualize what these two witnesses were experiencing as they described their surroundings, and the events that unfolded near Raleigh, North Carolina.

*April the 21, 1865*

*In camp near Raleigh North carolina*

*Dear Brother I take my pen in hand this morning to answer your very welcome received leture that came to hand last night I was glad to get a leture from you once more but sory to hear that your family is not well I am well and enjoying the pleasure of a solgers life what pleasure there is in it. we received the glorious nuse (news) of the capture of Richmond and leas (Lee's) army the 12 of this month at Smithfield on our martch from Goldsboro to this city of Raleigh. Goldsboro is 60 miles from here we wer fore days coming here as Johnson (Johnston) left our side of this plase. Old Hill (Bill?) came in the other side following him up lose with glorious nuse (news) we have sorefull nuse of the assasenation of President Lincoln cheaf magestrate it has bin douted for a long time to be untrew but this morning Rauleh (Raleigh?) papers confirm it it castes a glome (gloom) of sore over this army as a grate loss but still his being kild will not prolong the ware (war) neither stop the progress of peas (peace) being restored once more to our one bleeding countrey I ges old Johnson (Johnston) has surendured him and Shurman has enterd into an agremand (agreement) of some sort he has ishwed (issued) orders for hostiliteys to seas (cease) & has sent the artecul (article) to Washington conserning the surender to be refroved (resolved?) by the President whitch I dout but what it will be sanctioned if it is peas will be maid from the patomac to the Rio Grand God spead the day & our (hour) of the restoration of peas for there is nothing like peas. 4 years of a bloodey ware (war) is a nufe (enough) of stuch a turebell (terrible) ware of this sort God grant that the peopel of this nation may live in peas hence*

*forth. you spoke of receiving a leture from Egbert the last time
I saw him was at Goldsboro he was then geting better sens we
have bin here I have not sean him I have bin to the corps to
find him sense (since) we have him here to I was on the hunt of
him on Sunday last but did not find him. I went up on the
Northwestern RR (railroad) for 4 or 5 miles as far as the 3rd
Division. They said the 4 division was 5 mil futher out on the
road & I concluded I would not go eny futher I thout it was to
far 10 miles from our camp or this town or rather city You
spoke of my coming to help you harvest I would rejois of the
chance but I am afraid I will not get the chance for they say we
will half to go to our one (own) state to be mustered out if that
is the case the chance is not very good to make you a visit Well
if I don't get the chance then I will come after I get back home
some time if I live that long the reports are that we leave here
for Washington in side…*

(Henrys Letter continues on small piece of dark paper):

*…of ten days some say we are to march three But I cannot rest
for the men are bound to destroy more or less property on
there march there if that should be the case I hope we will not
have to martch for there is no fool? in marching in warm
wether well suppose you would like to hear something about
this capitol it is a butiful place, I have not been over it mutch
just past threw it last Sunday hunting Egbert I saw the state
house it is an elegant building there is a monument erected
close to it with the Statue of Washington on the of it maid of
brass or some other metal part? there is some of the finest ???
I ever saw & ornamented ??? ---yard, with all kind of
shrubbing well this is all of the paper that I have and it is
dark you can see for yourself well I think I shall enjoy the
Blessings of a sitezens life in a month or so god speed the day
for I am tired of wearing (warring) you said was an oner
(honor) to be in Sherman's armey I am proud of this army for it
has accomplished things thought imposiball a year a gow.*

*Goodby*

*as ever your loving brother*

*Henry Banks.*

☆ ☆ ☆

Henry had written his brother from camp near Raleigh on April 21, 1865. Steven Fleharty reported in his book that the regiment had marched 14 miles from that camp down the Holly Springs Road, and wound up 6 miles from the actual springs.

After traveling for about an hour Northwest on Highway 40, I found the old Holly Springs Apex Road, and backtracking about 15 miles from where the road appeared to be 6 miles from the actual springs, I arrived at a spot southeast of the capitol, where at the intersection of Harrington and Cabarrus Streets, the train depot stood, precisely where it appeared on a historic map I had uploaded earlier in the day. This was as close as I would get to Henry's Camp, but I was fairly certain of its location, based on the history of his regiment's habit of taking up residence near railroads, rivers, or creeks, etc. On the 1872 map, here was a great deal of open land surrounding the depot, and numerous fresh water sources nearby. If my calculations were correct, this was the location of the Union Camp where Henry heard the news of both Robert E. Lee's surrender, and Lincoln's assassination.

It was about 6:30 PM, and I found a nearby restaurant that coincidentally shared my wife's first name. I ordered a salad, and called her on my cell from the restaurant patio. I adhered to my promise, to check in at home every day, but out of necessity I went against my promise of avoiding night drives, and followed Highway 85 North, passing through the state line into Clarksville, Virginia. Crossing the bridge over the John H. Kerr Reservoir, I found my campsite at Occoneechee State Park. My drive from Holly Springs had been a long one, and my day had been packed full, with a rush of activity, resulting in another successful scouting session. Once I killed the engine, fatigue got the best of me, and I wound up sleeping through the night, sitting upright in my jeep.

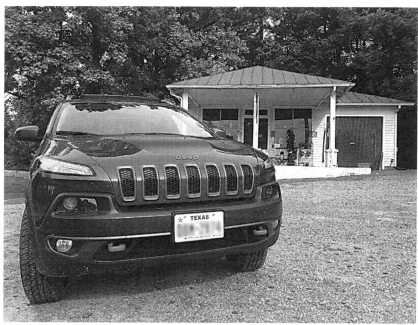

*The Trailhawk taking a much-deserved break near Appomattox, Virginia*

*The Cloverhill Tavern ca: 1819 still stands in the village of Appomattox, Virginia*

## Appomattox, Virginia

*Friday, May 23, 2014. Chilly. Fog.*

Ahhh, my neck! I had closed my eyes to catch a cat nap once I had arrived at Occoneechee, and I actually dreamed that I locked my jeep, set up my tent in the dark, and crawled into my sleeping bag – my brain's way of giving me license to pass out right were I sat – strange. I shook off the cobwebs, and stretched my neck, as I walked from my jeep down to the lake shore, where the sunlight began piercing through the tree trunks, thrusting bright golden shards across the lake's surface. The forest was the most fragrant I had ever sensed, and rivaled any department store perfume counter. Of course, I was craving some Java, but decided to treat myself to a hot shower first, before venturing out to satisfy my fix. While enjoying my breakfast in nearby Clarksville, I studied my choice of routes to my next destination, and decided to wander off the beaten path again. Once on the road, I pointed the Trailhawk north, and commenced traveling upon one of the most scenic drives I have ever experienced. Following Highway 15, which paralleled the Staunton River, I passed by enormous farms, with rolling fields shrouded in fog. Historic structures representing every decade since Colonial times, still stood all along the roadside — a testament to the vision and skills of their builders.

Two notable Virginia plantations were situated along my route: the Roanoke Plantation, and the Prestwood Plantation, which is celebrated as the most intact, and best-documented of its kind in all of Virginia. Along this stretch of blacktop known as the "Kings Highway", I could physically feel the history that passed my left and right as I followed the old trail past crude log homes, whitewashed, abandoned storefronts, and tinroof shacks. I could have easily spent a month alone with my Canon still camera along a few miles of this stretch, with a gallery full of incredible images to show for it, but that was not the purpose of my current mission. Finally, I passed through a more modern intersection, complete with a convenience store, and a colonial brick home, overgrown with ivy. It appeared long-abandoned, but full of exploration potential. I walked into the store with intention to obtain a coffee refill. Inside was an elderly woman who had obviously spent a good part of the morning filling the entire, poorly-ventilated establishment with secondhand smoke from her pack of filter kings. I turned on my heels and returned to my jeep, gasping for fresh Virginia mountain air. Continuing along Highway 15, I stopped at a picture postcard corner, where I spotted an old two-story wood-sided building with a rusty tin roof, that was too perfect to pass up. I gave the jeep a well-deserved rest, and walked around the property to capture some photos, and stretch my stiff, sore legs.

Numerous placards were posted along what I came to know as Patrick Henry Highway. Somewhere near Farmville, I spotted an ancient stone chimney standing alone in a wide, green pasture. A placard nearby read: "March to Appomattox." "Part of Lee's Army passed here, retreating westward, April 8, 1865." I was evidently drawing near to a location that I could not bypass. On this day, I wanted, above all things to enter the McLean house at Appomattox, where Grant received Lee's surrender. After a few more scenic miles, I was turning into the driveway of the Appomattox Battlefield Park, with two packed school buses filled with school children in my rearview mirror. "Oh, nooooo." I said aloud. I had to stop myself, for I was being a little selfish, wishing to explore the grounds on my own without distraction. I was suddenly reminded that one reason I decided to participate as a Civil War reenactor at Resaca was to create a living history experience for the present AND future generations. I would rather see these kids learning about their history first-hand, than to see them with their faces buried in their smart phones, or sitting at home playing video games. Still, I speed-walked past the chattering mob as nonchalant as possible, and arrived at the museum, ready to conduct my own private tour. Appomattox was preserved as a complete village, near to its original condition in 1865. I took a seat to take in the scenery on the elevated porch at "Mr. Hicks's Tavern", also known as the Cloverhill Tavern, which had originally opened in 1819 on the Richmond-Lynchburg Road for travelers.

I learned since that the Tavern is the oldest original structure in the entire park. As I relaxed, a Park Ranger approached the tavern with a small crowd, and a 20-something guy emerged from inside the Tavern dressed in union blues, and a cavalry hat. The ranger addressed the reenactor as "Private Dowler". Remaining in character, Private Dowler rose to his feet, and described the final conflict that occurred on the very ground where we stood, and the history-making event that commenced shortly after, just a few yards away from the Tavern, at the McLean house. His commentary describing the behavior of the soldiers occupying the village was intriguing. Before, during and after the signing of Lee's surrender, the blue and the gray rarely spoke to one another, but with rigid tolerance, held their hostilities in check. Private Dowler fielded a few questions from the crowd, and we eventually dispersed. I thanked him for his service and sacrifice – as I do, most every veteran that I encounter – and made my way down the steps, and onto the gravel path that led to the McLean house.

The two-story home appeared as you would expect; a red brick-built residence with whitewashed embellishments and trimwork. Upon my arrival to the historic house, the sky exploded in a brutal thunderstorm that pounded the property with a tremendous torrent. I stationed myself on the backside of the McLean house, safe and dry beneath the eaves, where I was at least partially sheltered from the rain. Looking down at my feet, I noticed that a stream of water had developed and was tracing along the ground from beneath the foundation of the house. A small piece of rough-hewn weathered wood with two nail holes punched through it floated down the trickling stream, and came to rest near my right foot. I decided that, like Henry's Bible, this was a gift. I wasn't pilfering for relics —which I firmly detested— but I kept this souvenir to add to my small collection of Civil War keepsakes, because to reject it – considering the manner in which it was given – would be disrespectful. I had grown to trust, believe, marvel at and respect unexplainable forces at work —that some would dismiss as coincidence— and decided to surrender to every hint of unsolicited guidance throughout my journey. I believe the timing of this gesture was nothing short of benevolent, judging by the timing, in conjunction with the personal thoughts that I was entertaining at the time while I waited for the weather to improve. The rain finally subsided, and the crowd that occupied the house filed out onto the front yard, as I entered the home through the back door.

The rain had detained the crowd that was vacating the premises, and detoured the next wave of visitors waiting up the gravel walkway, so for a few minutes, it was just me and the ghosts wandering between the walls. The home was beautifully preserved and cared for, as one would expect. The period furnishings, artwork and textiles were spot-on trend for the time, and I was mostly surprised at the diminutive space where the dignitaries had crowded in to formally commence with the conclusion of the Civil War. I had seen many images of this parlor, one of which had featured the presence of George Armstrong Custer in the room. The space only measured about 20' x 30' roughly. I later learned that the original structure had been dismantled in 1893 with intentions to reconstruct it on site at the World's Columbian Exposition in Chicago. Instead, it sat in a pile until its resurrection in the 1940s. Still, it was an honorable moment to relish alone in this room, whether or not it was the room, its history still resonated powerfully.

I strolled through the rest of the McLean home, and walked the entire park afterward, encountering more living history reenactors going about their business, interacting with some of the school kids, and other visitors. I was impressed by the preservation efforts poured into this enormous facility, to create a portal into 1865 for modern-day citizens. I hiked to the parking lot, once satisfied with a data card full of photos, and drove into the direction of Alexandria, Virginia.

## *Alexandria, Virginia*

Fleharty's journal reveals details of the long and arduous march that occurred in May of 1865. The Sergeant was sick at the time, and unable to march with the rest of the army, so he passed along his quill to Corporal E. S. Ricker, of Company I, who offered a ponderous, yet insightful outline of the soldiers' trek from Raleigh to Washington. This movement of an enormous army and their gear covered over 250 miles in twenty days!

> *At seven A.M., on the 30th of April, we left Raleigh en route for Washington, via Richmond. Marched thirteen miles and camped on the west side of the Neuse river, near Faust's paper factory. Ward's Division in the rear. May 1st—Early in the morning crossed the river—marched twenty miles—Ward's Division in the rear. May2nd.—Marched thirteen miles, and went into camp on the north bank of the Tar river. May 3rd.— Marched twenty-five miles and passed from North Carolina into Virginia. Crossed Roanoake river after night, and camped near that stream. Our division (Ward's), which had been*

*previous to that time considerably in the rear, came up with the
corps at Roanoke, and passed over the river in advance. May
4th.—Moved at half-past four A. M., Gen. Ward in advance.
Crossed Meherrin river, at Safford's Bridge. Marched twenty
miles that day. May 5th.—Moved again at half-past four in the
morning. Ward in advance. 102nd in the rear of the division—
acting as train guard. Reached camp at three o'clock P. M. on
the north side of the Nottoway River, having marched 18
miles—weather very warm. May 6th.—Moved out soon after
daylight, marched about fifteen miles—passed through Black's
and White's and Wellville Stations, on the Petersburg and
Lynchburg railroad. At the former place found some of the
Sixth Corps—Army of the Potomac—on duty. Went into camp
at noon; weather excessively warm. A ration of whisky was
issued to the men. Moved May 7th, at 4.30 A. M. Harrison's
Brigade in advance of the corps. Crossed the Appomattox
River before noon and reached camp at Clover Hill, twenty-
one miles from Richmond, at 12.30 P. M., having marched
about eighteen miles. May 8th.—Moved at 4.30 A.M., and went
into camp at noon, seven miles from Richmond; weather very
warm. May 9th.—Moved two and a half miles in the direction
of Manchester. Orders were received from Gen. Halleck,
(Union General Henry Wager Halleck, Commander of the
Military Division of the James, headquartered at Richmond)
directing the army to resume the march towards Washington
on the following morning. The order announced that the
troops would pass in review before Gen. Halleck's
headquarters. That evening Gen. Sherman arrived from
Savannah. May 10th—Orders received on the previous day
were countermanded. May 11th, at 11 A.M., the march was
resumed, but the troops did not march in review through
Richmond. Passed Castle Thunder and Libby Prison. We were
treated with marked attention by the people. They supplied the
thirsty soldiers with water and in some cases with wine. We
camped four miles from Capitol Square, and on the road
leading to Washington, and at the point where Kilpatrick
(Union Cavalry General Hugh Judson Kilpatrick) trained his
artillery in Richmond in one of his dashing exploits when
connected with the Potomac Army. May 12th.—Marched nine
miles. Roads in bad condition. Waited in the morning for the
17th Corps to pass. The 14th Corps was in advance of the 20th—
crossed the Chickahominy and camped one mile south of*

*Ashland. May 13ᵗʰ.—Crossed the South Anna in the forenoon, marched fifteen miles and camped at night on the south side of Little River. May 14ᵗʰ.—Crossed Little River and the North Anna. Ward's Division in the rear. Marched about 17 miles and camped within seven miles of Spottsylvania C. H. (Courthouse) May 15ᵗʰ.—Marched fifteen miles ; passed through Spottsylvania; saw many evidences of the hard fighting that took place there; camped that evening on the old Chancelorsville battle ground. May 16ᵗʰ.—A march of four miles brought us to the Rappahannock, which we crossed at United States Ford. Camped at sunset near White Ridge—a hamlet of half a dozen houses. Distance marched about twenty-one miles.*

*Early that morning, Adjutant J. H. Snyder, with a mounted orderly, W. O. Jones, of Co. I, rode off from the column to view the battle-ground. They never returned, and no clue to their fate has since been obtained.*

*May 17ᵗʰ—Marched fifteen miles and camped at Occoquon Creek. May 18ᵗʰ.—In the forenoon crossed Bull Run Creek, a wide, shallow stream, with gravelly bottom, and clear water. Marched 18 miles, and camped two miles northeast of Fairfax C. H. (Courthouse) Weather excessively warm. May 19ᵗʰ—Moved at an early hour and reached camp two and a half miles from Alexandria, a little after noon.*

In Henry's letter written in camp, just 8 miles from Washington he refers to a reunion in the field with brother, Egbert. He also shares a similar list of landmarks passed over by the 102ⁿᵈ, and his personal disdain for certain officers who forced their army to "double-time it" on this insanely rigorous march from Raleigh to the capitol.

*May the 27ᵗʰ, 1865*

*In Camp at Cloudes Mills (Clouds Mill)*

*3 miles northwest of Alexandarah, Virginia*

*Dear Brother as the male gose out this evening, I thout I woud*
*scratch a few lines to you an inform you how I am getting a*
*long & where I am. I am well and hartey the last time I saw*
*Egbert was the day we left Richmond and he was then well and*
*hartey I have not received eny leture from the north sense we*
*left Raleigh we left Raleigh the 30 of April   Crost the Nuse riv.*
*The tar river & the Roanoke riv & went to camp Southwest of*
*Ritchmond the 8 of (April) past threw Ritchmond the 11. Past*
*by Lidey Prison & thunder casle the too grate holes the rebells*
*keep our prisoners in torment and martch on for this plase.*
*Crost the South anah. North anah river went within 30 miles of*
*the Blew ridg crost the alexandarah & Menases railroad at*
*farfax station. From there in here where we are now in camp 8*
*miles from Washington  the report is we are to be musterd out*
*at Washington and paid off but still kept under control of our*
*Colnel untill we get to Illinois if this is the case I shall try hard*
*to get to go and see you and Daniel & the rest of my relation*
*our martch was a long and hard one  we martch very fast you*
*can se that by the papers  I think if eny set of men go to hel the*
*offesers that martch or caused to be martch so fast the offesers*
*of our armey will go there  it is nearly as bad as fiting rebells*
*to use men in sutch brutell way as we wer used.  I will not give*
*the particulers in the way we wer used  well I must close for the*
*mail gose out son with love to you all as ever your brother*
*Henry.*

As I made my way east on Highway 15, I was thankful
that I was driving this 160-mile stretch during the daytime. I
reflected upon my midnight run to Lake Occoneechee, and
ostracized myself for driving at night, under a spell of
drowsiness. It reminded me of another bad decision I made
when I was 18. I had spent the weekend east of the Cascade
Mountains in Washington State one summer at Lake Chelan
with some friends. Instead of heading home early on Sunday, I
took a chance and extended my stay until after sundown, which
would still allow for a few hours of sleep before I had to report
to work on Monday morning. The drive home from the lake was
about the same distance that was now between me and
Fairfax, VA. At the halfway point, I was descending West from
Snoqualmie Pass, when I began feeling groggy. I pulled my

1978 Fiat Spider over to the median, parked beneath a streetlight and opened the convertible top, since the weather was warm and clear. Nothing beats cruising in an Italian rag top under the stars, and the rush of warm wind through the windows has a way of keeping a driver awake on desolate roads. After pulling out onto the highway once again, out of nowhere, a topless blue Fiat like mine pulled up alongside of me, with an attractive brunette at the wheel. Her contagious smile and expression woke me right up, and we drove in tandem together for over 50 miles! She finally pulled off with a blast of her airhorn, as I continued towards the city lights of Seattle. I arrived safely at home. As I unpacked, I wondered if she was saying goodbye, or signaling me to exit along with her.

I would never know, but I can still remember the details of her face, over 30 years later. Who knows if I would have remained awake at the wheel without her company?

One of Henry's last letters that he wrote home was dated in May of 1865, where he reported his position in camp to be about 3 miles north of Alexandria, Virginia. Corresponding the dates in Fleharty's journal, I found the encampment of the 102nd to be at a location called Cloud's Mill. After Highway 15 had carried me through familiar Virginian towns like Stafford, Dumfries, and Woodbridge, I would reluctantly bypass the turnoff to Manassas, or Bull Run as it is widely known. Despite its historic significance, I was burning daylight and was forced to focus on the objective to locate all of Henry's camps, where he wrote his letters home. Referring to a map provided by a Civil War Campaigner's website, Cloud's Mill was situated along the Cameron River near the Orange & Alexandria Railroad.

A small patch of trees with a tiny creek running through it, stood just beneath a street sign titled: "Clouds Mill Drive". It was surrounded by enormous single-family homes in an affluent suburban neighborhood. The creek was next to a busy highway, and was most likely one of the only patches of undisturbed soil for miles around, so I decided to park my jeep, stretch my legs, and investigate. The sun was hot, but I hiked down into the deep gulley surrounded by tall trees waving in the wind. I was soaking wet with humidity-born sweat within minutes, yet I traversed the entire length of the grove until I was staring at the capitol beltway. A quick glance at

GoogleEarth showed that the small creek that I stood before was a tributary leading just yards away into the great Potomac, which flowed toward the Atlantic Ocean. A spanning matrix of railroad tracks, industrial buildings, and connecting creeks occupied the land just across the beltway from the Clouds Mill neighborhood. I trusted my gut that I was most likely as close as I was going to get to Henry's camp which was apparently long mowed over by bulldozers and zoned off to the surrounding subdivisions. My expectant vision of a historic gristmill, like one that I had once visited at Babcock State Park on Glade Creek in Colorado when I was a resident, was not to be. A few notations have since emerged from other Civil War accounts, showing numerous Union regiments that were mustered out at Clouds Mill. The 102nd Illinois Volunteers, however would not muster out until one final trek across the Arlington Heights to Washington D.C., which was exactly where I was heading next. Hot on Henry's trail, the shadowing continues.

As I emerged from the gulley in the burbs, my phone vibrated in my pocket. It was Fleming, my wife's cousin from South Carolina. She had just recently graduated from Clemson University, and had accepted a position with a company in Washington D.C. She was currently living in Fairfax Virginia, and invited me to use her apartment as my base while I explored the capitol. We coordinated our schedules and I set my GPS for Fairfax, near Chantilly. The name of this neighborhood had a familiar ring to it, but I couldn't place it at the time of our phone conversation. So off upon the beltway I drove, past Springfield, and up the Little River Turnpike through scenic Oldtown Fairfax, finally arriving at Fleming's apartment complex. I opened the front door, and was immediately greeted by Stedman, Fleming's black-and-white cat. He was cordial, vocal, and happy to show me the direct route to his treat stash. I reciprocated his hospitality with a handful of morsels. As Stedman chomped away, Fleming texted that she was on her way home from work in traffic, so I passed some time on her sunny balcony, catching up on my journaling. Once Fleming had arrived and turned her keys over to me, we wound up spending the evening at a local jazz club where I was introduced to her boyfriend, Chris. He was what you might call a Washington insider, when it came to leading an outsider to all the popular tourist hotspots. Chris offered to give me a guided tour of Washington D.C. over Memorial Day weekend. Lucky me! I was extremely disappointed that Andi would not be joining us, as we had originally planned, but I would be the better tour guide for her eventual visit to D.C., after my preview with Fleming and Chris that would commence in the morning.

*Fleming and Chris, my capable D.C. tour guides*

*Looking down Pennsylvania Avenue, where Henry marched in the Grand Review*

## *Washington, D.C.*

For many of the soldiers of the 102$^{nd}$ Illinois Volunteers, this would be their first visit to their nation's capitol. It would also be my initial visit, but definitely not my last. With the grand age of fifty, just over the horizon, I was about due to experience the Capitol City, and I was fortunate to have some wonderful guides to make my Memorial Day weekend in Washington so very memorable and exciting.

The remaining pages in Fleharty's book were thinning out, as were the remaining days of camp life for Henry and the 102$^{nd}$. However, one final march was in order. This would be a peaceful, and celebratory movement for the 65,000 men of Sherman's Army of the Tennessee, and the Army of Georgia, parading proudly down Pennsylvania Avenue before their leaders. Before their country. Before the world. I think about the mixed emotions that must have been experienced by the troops during this six-hour event. The relief existed certainly, now that the war was at its end, finally! And yet, what degree of mettle would it take to abandon these camaraderies formed over four years together in camp, marching, fighting? How could one keep a brave face on parade, after withstanding the great loss of friends, brothers, and those brave officers —many of whom were looked upon as father figures—now gone?

*While camped at Alexandria, preparations were made for the grand review in Washington, and on the 24$^{th}$, at an early hour in the morning, the army was in motion. It was a beautiful morning, and as the columns, following a serpentine course, passed over Arlington Heights, the scene was magnificent. There the soldiers caught their first view of the grand dome of the Capitol building. About 9 o'clock A.M. we crossed the Potomac over Long Bridge, and felt that we were out of the land of Secessia. The head of the column was halted at Capitol Hill, and from that point the review commenced.*

*Marching around the Capitol building, we passed into Pennsylvania Avenue, thenceforward for two miles—to the President's house—dense masses of humanity occupied the pavement on each side of the street, and at some places crowded upon the marching column.*

*Saturday, May 24, 2014... Sunny and clear.*

I woke early, and laced up my running shoes to race the rising sun at a moderate pace, and to get some fresh morning air. Across the road from Fleming's apartment, I spotted a sign for Chantilly Park, and proceeded to step over the white rail fence that surrounded the property, with the expectation to find a nice shady jogging path. Instead I found a large, monolithic stone among a neatly arranged stack of boulders, with a free-standing placard above the site, which read, "Boulders and quartz stone -the spot where General Stevens fell." Also known as "the Battle of Ox Hill," I put two and two together and remembered why "Chantilly" struck such a familiar chord with me. I had long ago written a paper about General Isaac Stevens when I was in ninth grade. Washington State History was a mandatory course that year, and I studied about Stevens' contributions to Washington State as he served as its first territorial governor. He was commissioned as Colonel of the 79th New York Volunteers at the outset of the Civil War, and had led his troops into numerous battles. At Chantilly, he was reported to have recovered his regiment's fallen colors in the thick of the fight, raised them high above his head, and beckoned, *"Highlanders, my Highlanders! -follow your General!"* He then received a rebel bullet in the head, and died instantly. It was a strange sensation that I felt, looking at the white quartz obelisk, placed by the original landowner, at the position where Stevens had fallen. I had written about this place at one time, and now I was standing at the very spot, and later in the evening I would write about how I had once before written about it. I continued my run, saddened at the loss of a great leader, yet enlightened by another unexpected surprise, stumbled upon by accident. The resulting flood of memories from ninth grade brought a smile to my face as I continued onward down the hike-and-bike path.

After a breakfast, Fleming, Chris and I boarded the train to Washington from the Fairfax station. The train ride was smooth, convenient and comfortable, and after a quick 16-mile trip, we were ascending the stairs onto the mall, in the shadow of the Washington Monument. This was my first visit to the capitol, and I was instantly overcome by how close every point of interest was to the next. It was like a great scroll filled with historic monuments had been unfurled before us and we were free to discover each one at our leisure.

One of our first stops was at the newly erected World War II monument with its multiple pillars representing each state in the union. As was the tradition, we each found the pillar that represented our home states and had our photos taken standing against each one. The most personal, and powerful monument on the mall for me was undoubtedly the Vietnam Memorial. Where the atmosphere at the World War II Memorial was festive and engaging for the crowd, in sharp contrast, the collective mood at the Vietnam Memorial was somber and silent. I scanned through the multitude of names etched into the shiny black marble until I found the name of Raymond R. Enyeart Jr. The unique spelling of his last name being identical to mine, Raymond had to be related somehow. Accessing information via iPhone, a private website mentioned that he was from Tracy, California — an army private who was killed in action in 1971. This would require more research. Note: I later found that he was actually killed in a vehicle accident on January 1st, somewhere in the Phuoc Long Province while serving with the 1st 11th ACR (Armored Cavalry Regiment) as a general vehicle repair man. He was 22.

The weather was fair and hot, and our walk was long, across the Capitol Mall and through the Constitution Gardens, but the sweat and struggle was instantly forgotten once the three of us finally reached the Lincoln Memorial. Spellbound, I ascended the grand staircase and wandered around the immense vestibule. Marveling at the enormous likeness of my favorite President, my peripheral vision went ablur, as I slowly read aloud, the words of the Gettysburg Address, followed by those of the Second Inaugural speech, both chiseled into giant slabs of carefully selected Alabama marble.

I studied the details of Jules Guerin's colorful and symbolic murals, which were stunning, and thought-provoking. It was difficult to tear my gaze away from them, while I savored their bold statements, but then there was the man. Seated, regal and contemplative at 19 feet in height, the Piccirilli brothers' masterpiece dazzled in brilliant white Georgia marble. Above Lincoln's head was his epitaph, etched as follows: "In this temple – as in the hearts of the people – for whom he saved the union – the memory of Abraham Lincoln – is enshrined forever."

Once we weaved our way through the crowd at the

memorial, we wound up having lunch at the restaurant on the roof of the W Hotel which afforded a picture-perfect profile of the White House, and its guards dressed in black, pacing the rooftop with their binoculars, and curious large black duffels. We then walked down to a location where Henry had once marched, and of this, I was 100% certain. Pennsylvania Avenue was as busy as ever, and once we walked past Pershing Park, the Avenue doglegged left at 13th St., where I could see the grand dome of the Capitol Building, eight blocks away. We passed the Federal triangle where I would have loved to spend a good solid month in the National Archives building.

It had been 149 years to the day, on May 24th, 1865, when over 60,000 Federal troops, including the remaining soldiers of the 102nd Illinois Volunteers marched a length of two miles down this same thoroughfare from Capitol Hill to the White House. I stood on the far edge of the raised platform of Freedom Plaza, and tried to visualize what the city must have looked like on that sunny afternoon. I attempted to identify some of the surrounding buildings that would have stood during that impressive procession. There weren't many. The old Willard Hotel that I had passed a few blocks behind me was present in the background of a rare photo taken during the Grand Review. It had since been remodeled and converted from its original modest four-stories to a huge building and was now a part of a large hotel chain.

An enormous Memorial Day celebration was being prepared at the capitol building, so it took a while for the three of us to get through the security line, but we finally managed to climb the capitol steps, at least part of the way. The building itself was closed, surrounded by armed security and heavily barricaded. Denied! Again! Here, I was assuming that Washington would be especially welcoming to a new visitor on Memorial Day weekend, but the Capitol Building would have to wait for my next visit toD.C. After the sun set behind the spectacular monuments and structures rising just west of us, we sampled some of D.C.'s vibrant nightlife, then boarded the train bound for Fairfax.

*Sunday, May 25, 2014. Sunny.*

In the morning, we boarded theD.C. commuter rail car again and spent the day museum-hopping. Most of our time was spent at the enormous International Spy Museum, and Ford's Theater, which was not to be missed. I skipped the Smithsonian altogether, for I knew that I would need to allow for at least a week to effectually explore the facility.

Early in the evening, I met a former colleague and his wife downtown for dinner and caught up with their progress since relocating from Colorado in 2005. Afterward, I met up with Fleming and Chris for cocktails, after which we caught a late train back to Fairfax. My recollection of the Spy Museum tour was that it was long, but very engaging, with a good deal of interactive displays and activities. My inner James Bond was thoroughly entertained.

Ford's Theater was captivating, and the line of visitors hadn't been as long as I had expected. The line at the Petersen House across 10th Street, where Lincoln was taken after the assassination was another story. Seated in Ford's Theater near the orchestra pit, a guide walked us and talked us through the events of that fateful night, detail by detail. After his presentation, I climbed up into the balcony, and gazed into the box where the murder occurred. The engraving of George Washington that hung between two flags was thought to be the original that was placed there as part of the decoration. I found it interesting that this balcony box had not been decorated prior to that evening of April 14th, 1865. The museum in the basement of Ford's Theater was top notch! We exited the theater feeling like we had almost been in attendance on the night that John Wilkes Booth murdered our President. I also walked away with an appreciation for my birth in a free society, thanks to Lincoln's vision, among others. Seeing the Derringer pistol that was used to commit the crime, the pillow from the bed where Lincoln had expired, still stained with his blood, and finally the President's death mask brought it all home for me. All the books I had read, programs, films and documentaries about Lincoln that I had watched up until now had a new, clarified perspective for me, thanks to my visit to Ford's Theater.

*The impressive Pennsylvania State Monument at Gettysburg National Battlefield*

*The ominous rock formations of Gettysburg's Devil's Den*

# Gettysburg, Pennsylvania

*Monday, May 26, 2014 - Memorial Day. Sunny.*

Memorial Day in Gettysburg, Pennsylvania. Fulfilling this objective was a deliberate decision. After packing my gear in the Jeep, I treated Chris and Fleming to breakfast at an excellent local diner in Fairfax, and thanked them for an unforgettable tour of D.C. They really did make a charming couple, and I hoped to myself that they would stay together for the long-haul. (We would meet again at Christmas, and I would learn then that my wish was to be granted). After fueling up the Trailhawk, I was on the road again after giving her a much needed and deserved two-day rest. Today would mark a personal achievement. Washington D.C. was the final rendezvous point where Uncle Henry and I would part ways. His duties in the 102nd Illinois Volunteers complete, he was off to Camp Fry in Chicago to collect his compensation for his service. I had completed most of what I had set out to do, and honored my ancestor and my Father to the fullest extent that I could, by following my heart. I wasn't expecting anything in return from the muses, from fate, from God. I could only hope that through my actions, someone might benefit from my experience, find some inspiration, or just learn a little more about our country's rich history. At any rate, upon the completion of the journey, I knew I would be a better, and wiser man for it.

Gettysburg was represented with a red pin on my giant historic map of the United States which hung on a wall in my office back at home in Austin. All of the camps mentioned in Henry's letters were represented with a green pin. The significance of Gettysburg earned it a ranking in my simple planning system all its own, as a site that I would not dare to miss.

I reserved the entire day to spend at Gettysburg in order to remember the fallen who had made the ultimate sacrifice for their cause. I didn't think I could be taken very seriously as one who took pride in telling a Civil War-based story without experiencing this grand battlefield for myself. I would take it one step further, however. I would march...well, hike through the entire park, of course! The weather was glorious, as I followed the Eisenhower Memorial Highway toward Gettysburg with the morning sun at my back. While driving, I was playing a CD compilation of Civil War tunes that were setting the day's context, and providing the appropriate soundtrack to the scenery passing by –much of it unchanged since Henry's day. For instance, the 1587-acre battlefield near Frederick, Maryland called Monocacy, also known as "The battle that saved Washington." Nearby, the "Best Farm" site, made famous by the discovery of Robert E Lee's lost special order 191 which was fortuitously obtained by Union soldiers, stuffed in an envelope, wrapped in a piece of paper with three cigars! Someone had to have lost their job that day, or worse! I always wondered if a fed-up Confederate had left the bundle exposed on the field deliberately, to bring about the war's end sooner than anticipated. The blacktop passing beneath me curved gradually to the right, which pointed me due North along the scenic Catoctin Mountain Highway.

Just west of Thurmont, Maryland I stopped at Cunningham Falls State Park to see the 78-foot cascade —the largest in Maryland. Catoctin Mountain Park looked very inviting for a future hike, and the Catoctin Furnace would provide my "history fix." Here, they produced iron cannonballs for the American Revolution. Rumors tell that actual cannons were constructed here as well. Driving through Emmitsburg, Maryland I spotted the attractive campus of Mount St. Mary's University, and contemplated how one would get such a rich education as a history major while attending this college, with so many significant historic sites nearby. I thought it would be a shameful waste if they didn't offer such a program. Just a stone's throw from campus stood The National Shrine, Grotto of Lourdes, which traces its roots to the beginning of Catholicism's interweaving into the religions of early America. It is a replica of the original shrine in France, where, the Virgin Mary supposedly appeared to St. Bernadette Soubirous, asking for a chapel to be built at the site of a French garbage dump. After two hours on the road, I pulled into the parking lot at the Gettysburg National Battlefield Park. Washington D.C. had proposed much appeal, but I had not felt this exhilarated since my arrival at Resaca.

As you would expect, for such a hallowed site of American historical significance, the Gettysburg Visitors Center was very impressive. It was just opening up for business when I arrived, and the crowd was already gathering, so I didn't linger much before purchasing my ticket. I opted for the self tour. First, I ascended the stairs, which led to the viewing platform of the great cyclorama painting, by Paul Phillipoteaux. The giant canvas work was mounted on an inward facing drum, which measured 377 feet in circumference, by 42 feet in height. At its base were cleverly constructed three-dimensional enhancements, which made the painting seem to come alive, spilling out onto the ground at its base. It depicted the well-known Confederate attack on Union forces that occurred on July 3, 1863. Pickett's Charge. The ranger who presented the painting made note that this impossibly detailed image was one of four that had been created. The original had been completed in 1883, only 20 years after the great conflict. The facility where I now stood had been completed in September 2008, and was purpose-built in a circle around the painting, which opened for viewing in 2005. The presentation helped put the battlefield into a clear perspective for me, though in retrospect, I would suggest to any park visitor to tour the battlefield beforehand, to appreciate the cyclorama program in its entirety.

The sun was obscured slightly by a thin layer of clouds, which cooled things off for me, at least for the time being, as I disappeared into the trees, en route to the Evergreen Cemetery which was just a half a mile or so Northeast. It was important for me to find the exact location where Lincoln delivered his famous address, and in researching this spot, I discovered some controversy. Apparently the location of Lincoln's platform is marked incorrectly, with a sign stating that the platform stood where the Soldier's National Monument is presently located. Reliable sources concur that the exact location is not far North and East of Jennie Wade's grave, in the Evergreen Cemetery. For the record, Jennie Wade was the only civilian killed during the Gettysburg conflict. Apparently, she was baking bread when a stray minnie ball struck her in the heart. An ever-watchful angelic figure stands atop her head stone, with the Stars and Stripes gallantly waving from an adjacent flagpole. From here, the platform spot was easy to locate. I did my best to take in "Lincoln's view" 150 years later, then pressed on to Cemetery Ridge.

Upon arrival, I could instantly make out the famous J-shape that formed the Union's line of defense. It skirted the edge of a shallow plateau that overlooked a vast valley to the west, where Pickett's Charge took place. I smiled as I peered

South, and recognized Roundtop, and Little Round Top standing in its shadow. Devils Den was low in a valley beneath them, but presently obscured. Still, I would not miss it. Along the ridge were numerous artillery pieces, poised and aimed West. The eminent copse of trees still grew inside "The Angle", where a defined zigzag in the Union line followed a stone fence along the ridge. The trees had been the focal point of Pickett's Charge. Here, the rebels did manage to break through the Union line, nearly changing the course of the war in their favor. Though I had seen them many times in photographs and documentaries, the state memorials along Hancock Avenue were much larger in person than I had expected. It appeared to me as a competitive exercise of design and scale between states. Some were more powerful in theme, featuring shining bronze likenesses of officers and troops attached to contrasting bright marble pedestals. Others were more interactive, allowing for internal exploration, with staircases leading into the structures, and to wide observation platforms exposing stunning views of the battlefield.

By far, the most impressive Memorial in my opinion was Pennsylvania's, with its enormous arches and dome, crowned with an enormous bronze angel wielding a sword. I climbed up into one of the pillars, which led to the rooftop deck, and took in the view, while plotting out my route. I thought to myself, "I hope you're ready for a long march." Continuing my hike to the south on Hancock Avenue, a horse trail into the forest led me eastward, then veered South again for a cooler, shady trek. More memorials peeked out from behind the trees were certain activity had transpired in July, 1863. The trail ended where I crossed Wheatfield Road, then led into another patch of woods, where a paved footpath brought me up to the summit of Little Round Top. Studying the placards and the well-defined points of interest, I was given a very detailed sketch of what the 20th Maine experienced under the brave leadership of Major General Joshua Lawrence Chamberlain, as they defended this coveted position. Knee-high walls built of stacked stones were intact, which I supposed represented some hastily fashioned breastworks, and peeking over them, one could see clearly through the trees where the base of Little Round Top began. It was easy to see how important this position was for the 15th Alabama to capture, with its vantage of the Peach Orchard, and the Wheat Field where Union forces were gathered, but it was difficult to imagine the stamina needed to ascend this hill twice under heavy Union rifle fire.

The 20th Maine held their ground through subsequent attacks for over 90 minutes. As I descended the west face of Little Round Top, I caught my first glimpse of Devil's Den. Hiking across Plumb Run, I drew closer, and noticed a crowd of children were crawling all over the Devil's Den site. At first, I admit that I was a little annoyed that more respect wasn't being paid to this mound of boulders, where so many casualties once lay, spilling their sacrificial blood into the crevices in between. I recognized certain areas of the site from Timothy O'Sullivan's haunting photos, where both Union and Confederate soldiers had fallen. As I strolled among the rocks, dodging shrieking rug rats, darting to-and-fro, I recalled a certain nine-year-old running amok through the Whitman Mission Museum in eastern Washington State, pressing the play button over and over again to hear the gory details of the massacre of white missionaries at the hands of Cayuse warriors. I carried that memory with me for years, and understood the history better, by visiting the actual spot where the deed was done. What I initially felt as disappointment in the behavior of the kid crowd converted to hope, that they too would take with them a thorough understanding of this site's significance, and its worthiness of respect.

The boulders at Devil's Den had a sinister, otherworldly appearance, which is why it was understandable that the original residents of the valley awarded it with such a menacing epithet. Facing south, directly across from Devil's Den was another site with an equally disturbing moniker – "The Slaughter Pen". Different from the Slaughter Pen that I visited at Murfreesboro, or Stones River Battlefield —but no less notorious— this rocky gorge dangerously exposed numerous Confederate troops who died here, fighting. From this spot, I followed the worn footpath, which led to the backside of Devil's Den, followed Sickles Avenue on to Cross Avenue, which led into the Wheat Field. This was the site of a battle that claimed more than 4000 dead and wounded on the afternoon of July 2, 1863. A sense of heaviness came upon my soul as I hiked back up Hancock Avenue, across Taneytown Road, through the woods, and back to my waiting vehicle. This trek had given me plenty of time to reflect on all that I had witnessed, and since I had a video camera with me, I documented exactly what I was feeling: *"I'll never look at Memorial Day the same way again. Every American should see this place, and really get a true understanding of what to be thankful for on this holiday. It's crazy what these guys went through...absolutely nuts! – but necessary. Let's hope it never happens like this again."*

The sun was casting long shadows across the battlefield, but there was still enough time to explore the city of Gettysburg before dark. Taneytown Road led me North past Evergreen Cemetery, and Gettysburg National Cemetery, then down Steinwehr Avenue where the tourist traps were ready to pounce. I drove slowly, gathering intel, as the busy avenue gave way to Baltimore Street, where I found a parking spot along a row of restaurants and taverns. After conducting my "sweep", I made note of a few locations that peaked my interest, so I locked up the jeep, and began walking south in the direction from where I had driven. At first blush, I would describe Gettysburg as a wonderfully preserved Victorian borough, just on the brink of ruin, not as a result of age or neglect, but of commercialization.

Ghost tours seemed to be a very competitive racket, as I was propositioned by about half a dozen ladies in period attire within two city blocks to attend their tours. The historic sites were revered and protected, as was the case of the Farnsworth House Inn, an original brick-built structure dating back to 1810. It's south-facing brick exterior was riddled with bullet holes, still visible. It apparently sheltered Confederate sharpshooters during the three-day conflict in 1864. The Inn is one of the few places that I know of where you can step back in time, and enjoy dining with an authentic retrospective menu, decor and waitstaff –followed by, what else?...a ghost tour! After browsing through a few souvenir shops, I began feeling peckish. Who wouldn't, after an exhausting march through the Gettysburg Battlefield. I stumbled upon an establishment known as "The Dobbin House". Originally built in 1776 by Rev. Alexander Dobbin, it was reportedly a classical school for over two decades, and is recorded as the oldest standing structure in Gettysburg. Did I mention that it is now a tavern? This place definitely was begging to be explored. Some might argue that my random, crapshoot approach to exploration and travel itinerary preparation (or lack of) is a little haphazard, but I enjoy the occasional surprise that occurs when I leave the door open for fate to step in.

The Dobbin House made up for the handful of disappointments that I experienced along the legacy road – locked museum doors, plantation access denial, and overcrowding campsites, just to name a few. A beautiful stone built, two-story colonial home, skirted with a whitewashed picket fence, and matching shutters made for an impressive exterior, but the interior opened up a passage that transforms the tourist to time-traveler. Ascending a narrow stairway, ducking beneath giant roughhewn beams, the din of laughter, and spirited conversation filled my ears, as my eyes adjusted to the lamplight. The Dobbin House Tavern was a scene out of any Hollywood Revolutionary War period film. A rosy-cheeked barmaid presided over a youthful staff of waitresses, all dressed according to the era. Each table and booth was bathed in a warm splash of kerosene flame, which gave the entire room and inviting glow. One could scarcely make out the details of the dark wood and stone walls that surrounded the dungeon-like public house, but that was its charm.

I took a seat at the bar on a heavy wooden stool, and ordered the house's best ale. The bar itself had a brass plaque inlaid into its scarred wooden surface, which read: *"Original Colonial Bar – this bar was built before 1818 by George Dick. It has been used by his descendants for six generations, over 160 years, even though it has been sold to antique dealers, it has found its way back to the family."* After enjoying the ambience of the tavern, I wandered through the common areas of The Dobbin House. Ascending the stairs, I noticed a cutaway section in the wall, exposing a large cavity. Behind plexiglass, I could see a thoughtfully constructed display of realistic mannequins crouched beneath the floorboards, representing the widely rumored tale that The Dobbin House had been one of the first stops along the famed Underground Railroad. It was fascinating to me, since I'd recently discovered possible evidence that an ancestor of mine had offered his home as a safe haven for runaway slaves in the eastern States. Exiting through the front door, I found myself transported back to my own century, and I walked up Steinwehr Avenue, holding my breath, for I had overstayed my visit beyond the time limit posted above my parking spot. As fate would have it, I managed to drive away in my jeep without a citation to ruin my good humor, which had been brought about by my visit to the House of Dobbin.

It was just after dusk when I reached my camp, just a stone's throw from the battlefield site. I hoisted my tent from the back of my jeep, and had it pitched in no time. I had plenty of practice at this juncture. I ignited my propane lantern, and journaled at a dilapidated picnic table for a good hour, recalling as many details as I could muster. In the morning, I would begin my long drive home. In my sleep, I strolled for a second time through the museum at Gettysburg, adjacent to the cyclorama, and recalled in detail, some of the surviving relics and well-preserved items on display. I believe it was my mind's method of dealing with the regret of not having a week to tour through the complete collection of other like-facilities in town, like the New Heritage Center, the Lincoln Train Museum, and the intimate but prolific Gettysburg Museum of History.

## Frankfort, Kentucky

### Tuesday, May 27, 2014. Sunny.

I rose to a chilly but clear, beautiful morning, laced up my hikers, and creaked and cracked at every joint, as I zigged and zagged through the open tent flap. I was definitely feeling the effects of my Gettysburg walkabout from the previous day. It was early, and though the sun was streaming full strength through the treetrunks surrounding my camp, I had to blow into my hands to warm them before striking camp. I mixed and warmed some oatmeal at the rickety picnic table for some quick nourishment, and I was soon on the road again, eastbound this time. Along the Lincoln Way, or Highway 30, I passed through Fayetteville, and Chambersburg was soon to follow. Here, I stopped to fuel up the Trailhawk with unleaded, and myself with hot black java. I wandered off the main route for a stretch down Highway 11, also known as the Molly Pitcher Highway. It was an everyday main street —residential on one side, industrial on the other— but its namesake intrigued me enough to select it as a temporary diversion. "Molly Pitcher" was apparently a handle given to a woman who was said to have fought in the Battle of Monmouth, during the Revolutionary War on June 28, 1778. Her true identity was believed to be that of Mary Ludwig Hays McCauley, a New Jersey citizen. Finally, Molly Pitcher may also have been used as a universal term for women who brought water to thirsty soldiers on the field during the Revolution.

Once the highway reached Greencastle, I resumed my route onto Highway 81 traveling South. Soon I was driving on the fringe of Hagerstown, a city rich with Civil War activity, and not far from the sites of the famous Battle of Antietam, or Sharpsburg, an early conflict in the war resulting in over 3500 casualties. Connecting next to Highway 70, I began traveling East, along the banks of the great Potomac. I was tempted to stop at Big Pool, where Fort Frederick State Park is located. This enormous stone fortress, originally built in 1756 during the French Indian war, standing on 585 acres would have been a suitable campsite if my schedule allowed an extra day. I continued my drive, however through beautiful postcard countryside on a perfect Spring morning. Along Highway 68 in the distant West, I could make out an enormous gap, which interrupted a seemingly endless plateau. It loomed over the highway as I drew closer to it, and as the grade steepened, I eventually passed through the giant trough at an elevation of about 2300 feet.

This was the landmark known as Sideling Hill, within the Allegheny Mountains. The large notch, known as the Sideling Hill Bypass had replaced an obsolete two-lane tunnel, once the blasting and paving was completed in 1968. This threshold invited me into one of the most picturesque valleys I've ever witnessed. Passing through the Western Maryland Panhandle, I promised myself to repeat the same route some Autumn in the future, and to allow enough time to capture photos of the numerous country farms, surrounded by an immense spectrum of fall colors. – A definite "must-see" on my bucket list...the perfect "tree-peepin" opportunity, here at the gateway to Appalachia. The breathtaking scenery continued down the remaining stretch of the National Freeway, with these pastoral homesteads, stamped out of a mammoth expanse of heavy native forests, and streams and creeks that I was now crossing by the dozen. I was bit by a tinge of envy while driving past quaint towns like Bellegrove, Frostburg, and the inviting "Friendsville", Maryland, population: 490, or thereabouts. What fortunate townsfolk were these who made this beautiful valley their home.

The appeal of little scenic towns like this one, as well as one of my favorite mountain towns in my home state of

Washington called Leavenworth, seems to dissipate when I am reminded of their hard winters. Still, there is ample cause to be envious of the citizens of Friendsville, and the like, when sitting at an eight-minute stoplight, or passing beneath an overpass splattered with senseless graffiti. Looking off into the west, a storm was gathering, and seemed to be heading slowly into my direction. It was therefore disheartening to see a sign along the highway that said *"Noah's Ark being built here!"* The sign stood next to an ominous skeletal structure in midstream of construction, and appeared to be built to scale!

At 9:37 AM, I passed into West Virginia, but it may as well have been Austria or Switzerland. I was enjoying the majestic scenery, the fresh morning air blowing through my sunroof, the sun beating down upon my sore shoulders, and thoughtful classical guitar streaming through satellite radio. I was "in the zone" and feeling at ease, with all the world's problems tuned out, for the time being.

Fortunately, the approaching storm cell – though it had increased in sinister appearance– had swung South, as I skirted its edge with only a few drops to wipe off my windshield. Shortly before crossing over Cheat Lake, I drove through the Coopers Rock State Forest area, which was named after a legendary fugitive who was in hiding from local law-enforcement, but still managed to make and sell barrels from his mountain hideaway. The entire Cheat River Gorge area featured panoramic overlooks like "Coopers Rock", and "Raven Rock Overlook", just to name a pair. I made a mental note to add this spot to my future trek list, which was getting longer with every passing mile. Highway 79 carried me Southwest through Fairmont, and along Pleasant Valley, which it most certainly was. I passed Stonewall Jackson State Park, surrounded by the enormous lake of the same name. It was quite a distance before I noticed any civilization, until I passed through Sutton and over the Elk River. Soon I was racing the rushing currents of the great Ohio River as I drove through Huntington, and the convergence of three states: Ohio, West Virginia and Kentucky.

It had been a very long haul so far, since I had left Gettysburg. I had driven over 380 miles of the most heavenly scenery I could imagine, and my final point of interest was not far. I was heading for Frankfort, Kentucky where Henry had written home, as a very green Private during his version of boot camp in 1862. The camp at Frankfort was the first mentioned in a collection of letters that were my guideposts for this journey of discovery, and I didn't want to miss it. Even though this location was nonsequential, according to the order of Henry's march, it was an important stop along the path, worthy of a lengthy visit. By this time, I was in sensory overload, and the impressive landscape held no further appeal. Instead, I became extremely anxious to reach Frankfort, and complete my search for Henry's camps. I even forgot to eat lunch. That's not like me! I had hoped to fuel up when I reached my destination, but the fuel gauge needle was danger-close to empty, so I stopped in Winchester to gas up and stretch my legs. Soon, I was entering the metropolis of Lexington, a city one year older than United States itself, and predating the state of Kentucky by 17 years! I drove a few more miles down Highway 64, past world-class horse farms, and finally, a sign directed me to the site of Daniel Boone's grave, at the Frankfort Cemetery, which was incorporated in 1845.

It stood on a high plateau that overlooked the Kentucky River, and the city of Frankfort. I strolled through the ancient property for a while, and peered down into the capitol city. The Kentucky River split the city in two — the older portion on the north bank, where the original state house still stands, and the newer part to the south. Five main bridges crossed the Kentucky River, connecting the city's main arterials. Sergeant Major Stephen Fleharty described the march into town as coming from Shelbyville, which was due west of the capitol. Further, Fleharty revealed the location of the Union camp, exactly 2 miles East of the city. I would eventually trace that march and attempt to locate the campsite, but I was presently famished!

I parked the Trailhawk behind the historic train station on the north end of town. Though the heat was bordering on hell borne, I walked down Broadway, eventually wandering into a nearby luncheonette, I ordered a local delicacy called the "Kentucky Hot Brown". "Stevie Ray?" the waitress called the name I periodically give to get a reaction out of people. Sometimes it would open up a spirited conversation about music, or my present home in Austin, Texas. Other times, it would just launch a smile, as it did in the case of my waitress. One of my favorite burger joints encourages the practice of submitting your alias, or alterego, which would be called when your order is ready. It's entertaining to sit with the lunch crowd and hear the crew announcing the names of Bruce Lee, John Wayne, and Lizzy Borden, as blushing, technogeeks walk up to claim their lunches as their peers giggle and scoff from their table. The tinfoil platter I brought to my table contains a steamy, open-faced sandwich served with slices of turkey and bacon covered in bubbling Mornay sauce and sliced tomatoes. At any rate, while I journal here at the table, my "Hot Brown" is getting cold.

Some Kentucky Hot Brown trivia while I indulge: the Kentucky Hot Brown was apparently invented by a chef at the Brown Hotel in Louisville, Kentucky in the 1920's, as an alternative to their ham and egg sandwiches, ordered by late night diners. I instantly understood why the tradition had survived this long. It was delicious, though the Mornay sauce had been replaced with a more economical white cheese sauce on this particular model. Once I had polished off my platter, I was ready for a march around town. My first stop was the Capitol City Museum behind the train station. The museum was diminutive, compared to the larger State History Museum across the street, which was closed, of course! The Capitol City Museum offered a nice collection of historic artifacts to observe, all arranged in a sort of timeline. This made it easy to target the Civil War items quickly, since I had little time to squander. The curator mentioned the location of Fort Hill, just North of the original state house. A series of trails, an interpretive center inside a house built in 1810, and other items of interest were just a short drive away. A trail which led from the city uphill to the site of two earthen forts was said to be an old military road used to haul equipment and supplies in the 1860s. This was no doubt the uphill heartbreaker hike that Fleharty had described in his journal on the evening of October 8, 1862: *"...up, up, up a hill that seemed as if it would reach the sky..."*

I was more interested in targeting the 102nd Regiment's camp location, which would be established 10 days later, when Henry wrote his detailed letter to his mother, Cynthia on October 18th. He and Stephen Fleharty had both lamented over the futility of "standing at arms" before sunrise every morning, while in camp during those early days in 1862. After being cooped up in the jeep since Gettysburg, a hike around Frankfort on a sunny afternoon was just the ticket! My impression of Kentucky's capitol was that it was a city with a Hollywood studio backlot around every corner. Frankfort's facades were a larger-than-life testimony to its 19th-century heyday. Passing the original state house, I found myself tramping up Broadway once again, and began to follow it toward the Kentucky River. This street stretched East-West, in tandem with the railroad tracks, and appeared to have the wear, and permanence of an original thoroughfare. As my luck would have it, the paved portion of the bridge had been barricaded with chain-link and posted with a "no trespassing" sign! I could go no further from here. In a huff, I ventured South on Sutterlin Lane, which led me to Main Street. At the corner of Main and Wilkinson I found one of Frankfort's most striking backdrops known as the "Hoge House", or the "Garrard/Crittenden House".

This was a stately, two-story clapboard home, painted in bright red, with cream shutters and trim. I was walking through a historic district known as "Corner in Celebrities". As I walked down Main Street, it was difficult to tear my gaze away from the surrounding period architecture, but time was running out, so I decided to tap modern technology for guidance. I located a map from 1871 on the Internet, and took note that only two bridges crossed the Kentucky River at the time of it's printing. They were the Broadway span that I had previously encountered, and another that appeared to be close to my present coordinates. Toggling over to Google maps, I found its location at "Bridge Street". *"Well, that figures,"* I said out loud. I arrived at St. Clair Street, then made my way South to Wapping Street, where traces of the original bridge we're still evident. Upon a base of stacked limestone blocks stood a steel-girdered bridge that stretched across the river. Cottonwoods lined the banks, which solved the mystery behind my sneezing attack, and red, watery eyes. I crossed the bridge on foot, and snapped a few photos, knowing that Henry and company had crossed at this point in October 1862, or, possibly at the railroad bridge on Broadway. Either way, I was satisfied that I had occupied that same space, and was ready to discover the Regiment's camp location.

I wandered East, down 2nd Avenue, which led to Capitol Avenue, where I could clearly see the grand spire of Frankfort's newer capitol building. I crossed the busy bridge leading back to Main Street and found a historic marker that told a grim tale of Frankfort's cryptic past. The marker stood in front of an early whitewashed stone house, once belonging to Colonel Mason H. P. Williams – Franklin County Sheriff. On the eve of March 26, 1879, Williams entertained Judge John Milton Elliott of Kentucky's Court of Appeals. Later that evening, at the Capital Hotel, across the street from the stone house, Elliot was met by another judge, Colonel Thomas Buford. Buford's late sister had just lost her land in order to pay back a debt. Elliot had presided over her case, and ruled in the plaintiff's favor. Buford stepped up to Elliot, and invited him to a *"snipe hunt."* He then emptied both barrels of a shotgun, point blank into Elliott's body. Buford later died in an asylum after being ruled "insane"! *The New York Times* had been quick to condemn the homicide, pronouncing that it *"could scarcely have taken place in any region calling itself civilized except Kentucky or some other Southern State."*

Capitol Avenue led me back to the old train station, where I had parked the Jeep. I sat with the engine idling, while I read a passage from Fleharty's journal that described the Regiment's final camp at Frankfort, which was 2 miles due east of the city. The primary artery leading uphill in that direction was Main Street. It was easy to isolate exact locations when they corresponded with the dates of record in Fleharty's book. According to the description I was reading, the Regiment had camped east of town, on a high point just beyond the ridge where Daniel Boone was buried. Behind the wheel of the Trailhawk, I adjusted my rearview mirror to shield the setting sun that was flashing into my eyes, as I drove up Main Street's steep incline. My odometer measured out an even 2 miles, and I found myself in an area once known as Green Hill, according to a map from a 1924 survey. It was now occupied by an expanse of residential subdivisions. I was satisfied that I was close to, if not dead-center within the location where Henry spent his final week drilling in camp at Frankfort. I parked in an empty lot next to the Green Hill Cemetery, and shielded my eyes to survey the mound where I stood. It seemed large enough to accommodate a thousand men in tight quarters. Making note of the dates etched in stone, my walk among the monuments proved that the property had not served its current purpose until the end of the 19th century. The oldest grave that I could identify was marked in 1904.

Stephen Fleharty had denied me his typical topographical description of the camp, except that the men in the 102nd had been packed together in bell tents, and stacked upon one another like cord wood. A large monument stood beneath an American flag, just a few yards away from where I stood, and I was drawn toward it by curiosity. It was a beautiful and boldly designed monument saluting the 25,000 African-American Kentuckians who served in the US Colored Troops throughout the duration of the Civil War. The African-American Civil War Memorial was established by the Women's Relief Corps, No. 8 in 1924. It was a 14-foot gray marble, four-sided column with the names of 142 men from Central Kentucky etched on each side — a thoughtful testament to some brave sacrifice, the likes of which few will ever fully comprehend. Looking down the hill towards the setting sun, I realized that Frankfort truly was the launching point into the war for Uncle Henry, with the long and harrowing winter experience at Gallatin, Tennessee waiting to ravage his regiment, just around the bend.

In contrast, Frankfort, Kentucky was where my journey would end...or would it? On this final leg of my quest, I had counted 13 days on the road, driven over 2500 miles, and now I would — with relief and a little reluctance — be heading South for Texas...for home. Following Highway 65 out of Elizabethtown after refueling and grabbing a bite for dinner, I drove off into the twilight. Fatigue caught up with me near Nashville, where Highway 65 handed me off to Highway 40. I pulled off at a well-lit rest area, where a veritable armada of semi-trucks were parked. Their running lights were so numerous, that they illuminated the low-lying cloud cover above to such a degree, that it appeared to be high-noon. Rest was difficult, sitting upright next to idling truck engines and the array of bright orange light beaming through every window of the jeep. I was too tired to drive away to scout an alternative shelter, so I improvised instead. I stepped out to open the rear hatch, and located my last pair of earplugs in my sea bag. Returning to the driver seat, I leaned back, fitted my earplugs in place, then slid my sunglasses over my tired eyes, and I was soon sound asleep.

*Wednesday, May 28, 2014. Partly cloudy.*

I had camped…er, parked near Brownsville, which was very near a site called Fort Pillow. This was a notable Civil War Battlefield, and the last one I would notice on my way home to Austin Texas. Fort Pillow was a Confederate defensive stronghold built along the Tennessee River, and named after Gideon Johnson Pillow, a Confederate General, and as I later learned, was a distant cousin of my wife, Andi. The battle of Fort Pillow, which occurred on April 12, 1864, was also known as the Fort Pillow Massacre. According to numerous accounts, the Union garrison was nearly equally divided by white and African-American troops. Northern newspapers reported that Confederate General Nathan Bedford Forrest had his cavalry men slaughter surrendering black troops. *"Remember Fort Pillow!"* Was a common rally cry for black troops throughout the remainder of the Civil War. I tipped my baseball cap toward Graceland, as a salute to "the King" as I passed through Memphis, Tennessee at daybreak. The sun danced along a heavy blanket of fog as the Hernando De Soto Bridge escorted me over the Tennessee River.

## *Camp Fry, Chicago, IL*

Time unfortunately did not allow me to visit Henry's home states of New York, or Illinois, though I would add these two significant locations to my future travel "must-do" list. Fleharty's final pages refer to the last stop for the 102nd, which was the Windy City! Both Fleharty and Henry mentioned how coldly they were treated by the citizens of Chicago. The indifference must have been very anti-climactic, and disappointing for the 102nd, given their recent emergence from their long march, and heavy sacrifice. Finally, as we would expect, the Sergeant Major eloquently closes his journal as follows:

> *We were assigned quarters at Camp Fry. There we received our pay and final discharge on the 14th of June, and the men took the first trains for their respective homes. Each company on reaching the town or neighborhood, were organized, met with magnificent welcome, which went far towards removing the impression produced by the cold comfort extended us by the chief city of our State.*

*With the disbanding of the regiment the thread of our
story ends—yet I am loth to quit the interesting theme. There is
a charm connected with the active military service which no
other pursuit can give. Emotions are awakened, which, as
citizens we can never feel again. We almost long to experience
the sensations produced during the most eventful moments of the
great campaigns; to hear again the grand roll of artillery, to
observe the bursting shells, and to shout once more the shout of
victory.*

*Since the dark cloud of war has passed by, it seems
even more black than when the storm was at its height. But the
sunshine of peace is upon us once more.*

*In the midst of the sunshine there are shadows. Our
minds revert to the Southern battle-fields, and to the many
thousand graves which mark the route followed by the great
army. "Sleeping for the flag," among the pines of northern
Georgia, along the line of march to the sea, and in the far-off
Carolinas, our hero-comrades rest—but not unremembered.
The "Old Flag," consecrated afresh by their blood, floats
unopposed in every State where its defenders are buried.*

Henry wrote one of his most graphic and entertaining letters
while he waited for his final payment from Uncle Sam. The 102nd and
the 105th Illinois Volunteers were stationed in barracks of a former
POW lockup, known as Camp Fry, which was very near the shores of
Lake Michigan. As the regiment waited for their final pay and
discharge, they would not be denied what they so duly deserved on a
hot Sunday in June, 1865.

*STATIONERY: (logo) U. S. Christian Commission*

*IMPRINT:    "This is a faithful saying, and worthy of all
acceptation, that Christ Jesus came into the world to save
sinners; of whom I am chief."*

*Chicago Ills. June the 13 . 1865*

*Camp Fry.*

*Dear Brother with lesure I seate my self to answer your glad
received leture that came to hand yester day glad to heare that
you are all well but regret to heare that Olive is still out of
health I am well I have cot this near home in the hellish hole
Chicago this is the onerestabell name that I can give it we left
Washington the 6 of this month for Chicago past threw
baltimore the same day past threw Haris Burgh the next day
got to Pitsburgh at 100 in the morning of the 8. here we wer
treted with grate respect we wer taken to a large bilding & got
our breakfast donated by the Citazons of Pitsburgh all of the
Solgers that past threw treted with grate respect whitch will
never be forgoten by the Solgers of this state all threw Ohio &
Indianah we wer received with grate reseption by both grate &
small but I regret to say when we got in this city our one (own)
state that out (ought) to be proud of her brave solgers but we
did not get a chear neather apeared to be received welcomly
so it has bin with all of Ills. troops some wer used wores than
our Regiment the 105 when they came in they wer orderd of the
sidewalcks by the poleasman but it was not of no use the Colne
(Colonel) told them to go to hell. this is the reception we
receaved in this grate metrop elas (metropolis) city we wer
received with grater responce in the city of Ritchmond Our
Regiment & the 105 maid a raid on what is cald the Dutch
Gardin last Sunday ad joying (adjoining?) this camp they wer
orderd by the city orthoriteys not to open it but disobaid the
solgers colected around thick they wer seling bear (beer)
whiscy souer wine & wine & drincks of all kinds in this way a
big row was raised the bar ceaper (barkeeper) was hird to say
that Shurman & his men wer Coper heads & soforth then the
boys went for it the Poleas (police) tride to stop it but this onely
made the thing worse the Poleasman wer all nocked down one
was nearley kild I now dout they woud all have bin kild if they
had not got out of the way everything was cleaned out
compleat there was no les than 5-or 600 druncan men sutch a
big row I never saw before in my life we let them know that
Shurman men woud not be run over & used like hogs or worse
there was a settelver shop (?) cleaned out all so (also) &
severall other plases we gave them a slite intereduction of how
we done in the Southern States we are 4 miles north of the city
on the lakeshore the Solgers threten the city we donte get as
mutch to eat as we did when we wer before Atlanty not hafe
ration it is a disgrase to the state the way we are used worse*

*than dogs here they are ceaping (keeping) us here in these nastey steanking baricks & dont seame to be of no hury to pay us of (off) & let us go to our homes I wish chicago coud have one cleaning out I think she woud then apreshieate the horers of ware & the hardships of a Solgers life but they dont seam to have no more respect for a Solger than they do a daug they apear to think because he is a Solger he is a discrase there is one thing if they donte tray in there hornes (?) & use the Solger better the city will get cleaned out I under stand they are doing better some troops came in yesterday there is some more coming in to day there is betwene 10 & 15 regiments here now the report is we mite get our pay before to morow or next day when I am paid of (off) I shall go from here to the city of Fulton this state on the missippi R & cros to Lions from there to Lowmoor well I will close hopeing these lines will find you all well I hope to be at home the next time I write but it seames the devell is to pay now day*

*as ever your brother*

*Henry Banks*

☆ ☆ ☆

The final letter in Henry's collection was unfortunately gnawed apart by rodents, but there was enough information left to give us a good feel for Henry's mood, and palpable relief to be back in the normal swing of farm life. He was living near Clinton, Iowa where his mother, Cynthia and younger brother William had apparently settled shortly after selling the farm in Illinois. He also mentions being only a few miles from David, his older brother, and my great, great grandfather. I would have liked to have been present at this reunion of Banks family members, welcoming home their son and brother. Could it be that this was when Henry's bible was handed off to brother, David —my great, great grandfather— where it began its journey down the line into my possession? I like to think so.

*Lowmoor, IA*

*Lowmoor _____1865*

*Dear Brother (Willis) I happily take pen in hand this morning
to pen again a few lines to let you know how I am getting along
here in Iowa and the wrest of us  I never enjoyed my self better
in my life than I have sens I have bin home in health ad spearit
like a man let out of a prisin and losened from the chanes of
bondage.  I beleave the last leture that I wrote to you  was
when I was in Chicago  I have not ___ eny answer from it  I
write thinking that you write not think & direct to the regiment
if you have it will not get to me for the regiment was
discharged & paid at Camp Fry Chicago the 14 of ___  From
there I went to monmouth Iowa ____there 12 miles___to where
we used to live on_____there used to_____staid 3 days
with____is worcking ___John Lafferty. fr___me
here_____walleses(Wallaces?) found_____he is well
____smart & all of the____lks I was __to se David & William
___rk 27 mi. from here  they have some very nise I like it better
than eny I have sean in the state for raw pererid (period?)  I
think of bying about 80 acors grain of all kinds loock
promesing in these western state as far as I have seane  I like
to have forgoten to tell you that I got a leture from Egbert
yesterday  he is well and he is now in Louis ville ken at presand
he thinks he will get home before his time exspires but I think
not _____I ges the ware is finelly settled but I see it
grines?_____very hard ____gainsed? some of the big___s &
big guns___the south to haff to com____the laws of the United
States they____whiped & subdude____m are leaveing the
united ____for my part I am ___ing they woud all leave
f___there rome? Is more exseptabell than there presant
___write sone direct to Lowmoor Post Clinton Co Iowa*

*As ever thy brother*

*Henry Ira Banks*

*Austin, TX*

My remaining drive was rich with scenery through Arkansas, but not so much as I crawled through Dallas at rush hour. I parked in my driveway at about sunset and wrote in my journal for a while, reflecting on recent details. Before beginning the process of unpacking, I called my wife who was on her commute toward home. She asked how my trip was, and I found myself at a loss for words to accurately describe my experience at first, but finally arrived at a solution to sum it all up in a brief and satisfactory response.

*"I guess you could say that whoever that guy was who drove away from Texas two weeks ago was kicked out and left at the side of the road, somewhere out in West Virginia. There's a different man waiting here for you." "A better man."*

The journey had opened my eyes to so much history, and brought to life the sacrifices made by so many American families like Henry's during the 1860's. The enormity of it all, made my own internal conflicts seem insignificant in comparison. Still, the journey helped me loosen some emotional knots, and was an experience that I was exceedingly grateful for. Andi had allowed me the time to establish some clarity in my own life, by revealing the lost details of another. Henry's trail was thankfully still warm, thanks to the precious collection of letters shared with me by my cousin Mary, and the details within —much like breadcrumbs— left for me to follow, 150 years later. I was grateful for the opportunity and freedom that few people have, to drop everything and set out to visit sites that have relative significance attached to their heritage. Though there were still many questions that remained unanswered, I had returned to Texas, coming full-circle with a new confidence in my identity, feeling fulfilled and satisfied with the results of my mission. I couldn't wait to share my experiences with friends and family. There was, however one final trip to complete, and this time, I would not attempt to approach it alone.

# A Proper Stone

It was a bitter cold and overcast Saturday when two of my friends met me at my home in Austin early in the morning, in preparation for a long, 3.5-hour drive to Baird, Texas. After discovering the location of Uncle Henry's grave back in 2009, I knew this day would eventually come, though I always imagined taking this trip alone, since this journey began as a very personal one. However, Julio, my friend from college who had just recently relocated to Texas from Seattle, and Jeff, my close friend and Austin native insisted on coming along for support, and to participate in the profound event.

The weather outlook was not the best. It was a gray and chilly morning, which was uncharacteristic for early October in Austin. Still, we each dressed for outdoor manual labor, but packed jackets for uncertain weather. This proved to be a wise decision, for the rain did begin to fall, once we arrived at our first stop for refueling along Highway 183 near Brownwood, Texas. It was a kind of cold miserable spit...the kind you feel from the inside out...the kind of wet cold that drove me to leave my Seattle birthplace for the warmer climes of Southern California in 1989. A slight breeze from the Southeast added insult to injury, but we managed our way to Baird with our eminent task at hand.

We drove into town by way of East 4th Street, once a major thoroughfare that used to carry traffic into Baird, resulting in a flow of commerce that has long since subsided with the introduction of Highway 20, built just a few blocks north.

The old courthouse served as a landmark, which stood at the head of Market Street where we turned left into the heart of "The Antique Capitol of Central Texas". The familiar storefronts hadn't changed since my initial visit in 2009, and it was doubtful that they had changed much since Henry's short-lived term as a local. The Whistle Stop Cafe was open for business, and would serve as our rendezvous point where we would meet Tom Ivey, the man in charge of all things Veteran in Callahan County.

Julio, Jeff and I popped out of my SUV at the end of Market Street where the great brick-built train depot stood. Winding around to the backside of the structure, I noticed that the building design was just as impressive as the street-facing side. Cameras in hand, we walked around the depot, and some neighboring historic structures that made for some good "Instagram" material. We piled back into the Hummer, and followed Market Street back to The Whistle Stop, where Tom Ivey was obviously waiting. The pickup truck with the dogs in the cab, and tools and granite headstone lying in the bed was a dead giveaway. No pun intended.

Tom also had a second headstone onboard for me, which was a blunder, courtesy of the United States Veteran's Administration. After gathering, and sharing all the necessary documentation in order to qualify Henry for a proper stone, the VA shipped the first marker with the unfortunate misspelling: H_E_R_N_Y    I_R_A  B_A_N_K_S. Herny? Really? Thankfully, Tom had noticed the mistake upon receipt of the stone, and once the government office was made aware of their error, it didn't take them long to rectify their negligence by quickly shipping a replacement. Had we made the trip to Baird, just to discover a useless stone, there's no telling what kind of ranting, indignant chauffer poor Julio and Jeff would have at the wheel once we were back on the road to Austin. Once Tom had received the correct headstone, the V. A. never asked for the original to be returned, so I asked him to bring it along, though I wasn't certain what I would do with it.

World-class chicken-fried steak was beckoning, and we didn't want to keep Mr. Ivey waiting, so we stepped inside where it was warm, and claimed our seats around the table where Tom was already seated, scouring through the local paper. After proper introductions, we discussed our plans to place Uncle Henry's stone at his plot at Ross Cemetery. There was still some question as to the exact location of Henry's remains, but careful examination of a cemetery map from the early 1900's confirmed the spot that Tom and I had collectively targeted during our initial 2009 survey. (Since this writing, an official dowser has examined the grave, reporting the presence of a male occupant) We continued our discussion about Baird history, and the local Bowlus family that Henry had married into before his hasty relocation from his Kansas farm to Texas in 1888. What a strange transition that must have been for him. I often wonder, instead of his lingering ailments, if the impossibly humid summer climate had actually attributed to his untimely passing, as it nearly did me in, after my own relocation from California.

Mr. Ivey insisted on treating us to our Chicken Fried Steak lunch, which more than lived up to my boasting about it to Jeff and Julio, all the way from Austin. Excited about the task ahead, I nearly forgot about my tripod and camera that I had packed. We paused for a group photo in front of Baird's landmark cafe.

Climbing back into the Hummer, the three of us let out a collective groan as our lunches settled heavily in our stomachs. We followed Tom in his truck up Market Street, and onto Cherry Street, which led us North across Highway 20 to Ross Cemetery. Pulling up next to Henry's plot, we carefully, and respectfully examined the small parcel to determine the most appropriate location for the stone. Once we reached a consensus, we went to work. Jeff pulled an ancient pair of posthole diggers from the bed of Tom's pickup. I grabbed a shovel, and Julio manned the camera. Tom assumed cement-mixing duty as we began to clear a small trench for Henry's headstone.

It is important for me to comment that manhandling a 300+lb. slab of granite, not to mention leveling, and positioning is thirsty work. Jeff and I are both strong, capable guys, yet it took both of us to manipulate the headstone into its final position. I earned a great deal of respect for those who do this for a living. If I'm not mistaken, I think I've seen them use cranes in certain cases. In retrospect, I think that might have been an option to consider. At any rate, we jogged the stone into position, aligned it with neighboring stones, poured our cement and replaced the soil around it.

After a final photo, we packed up our tools and walked around the cemetery for a few minutes, as Tom regaled us with some local Baird stories and Callahan County legends attached to certain graves in the cemetery. It was during this time that I reflected on the journey, and how it had begun, years ago with the discovery of Henry's bible in my father's study. I thought about all the new friends and contacts I had made along the way, and how I couldn't have completed this journey without their help and support. And finally, I shook hands with Mr. Ivey, and returned to the warmth of my SUV with my two loyal sidekicks. On the way, I smiled proudly, for I had completed some unfinished family business that Henry's two brothers, Egbert, and my Great, Great Grandfather, David Banks had intended to, but obviously never did complete. I couldn't wait to update my blog, and my book with this, the final chapter...or was it?

*Julio Rivera, Jeff Robison, Tom Ivey and I in downtown Baird, Texas*

*Finishing some long overdue family business with Jeff Robison*

*Mission accomplished. Ross Cemetery, Baird, Texas*

# The Dust Settles

Still, remnants from the journey manage to wind up on my doorstep. Just the other day, a box arrived in the mail. It was a collection of intimate letters shared between a mother and daughter in the early 1900's. They were cousins on the Enyeart branch of my family tree. The daughter had recently passed away, and a family friend had purchased this box of letters at her estate sale. Thoughtfully, this individual posted the details on the web. When I responded via email that I was related to these ladies, he kindly shipped the box to me. While examining the contents, I found a randomly included booklet inside. The cover featured a flourishy rendering of a clock with wings, lying on top of a scythe, surrounded by the title: MONTHLY TIME BOOK. The pages were preprinted with a template for recording time spent, and income earned. In light, but legible pencil, the owner had recorded his hours spent working at a series of gold mines in California between 1914 and 1917. He entered his name repeatedly in the left column, as "D. D. Enyeart."

Andi was startled as I bolted into the kitchen, waving the small booklet in the air. Enthusiastically, I exclaimed, "Check this out!...this just came in the mail with a box of old letters, it belonged to my great-grandfather, Daniel D. Enyeart...he was a gold miner...in California!" My wife was silent. I glanced over at her, expecting acknowledgement, but... "Hey," I said, "don't give me that look."

The location of another grave was also recently discovered. The grave belongs to an 18-year-old girl named "Minnie Ola" Banks. Her headstone was a crude limestone slab with details inscribed by hand: "Sept. 22-'84—June 7-'02 Dau. Of Emma Crawford". Census records confirmed that "Mineola" was Henry's adopted stepdaughter. Even though he and Emma Bowlus-Gain-Banks-Crawford were married for only a year before he passed on in 1889, Henry was apparently able to briefly experience the role of fatherhood to a 4-year-old girl. I imagine there must have been something special about that relationship, since she assumed Henry's last name, and kept it until her untimely passing at age 18.

Henry's legacy did not end there. It continued through generations, even though its impact would not be fully appreciated but by his great, great grand nephew, more than a century into the future. If there is one thing that Uncle Henry had taught me throughout this journey, it was that in order to perpetuate a legacy, a bloodline isn't necessarily required to influence future generations.

I labored over the decision for quite a while, but finally thought it best to donate Henry's Civil War keepsake to an institution that would look after it in perpetuity. I chose The National Civil War Museum in Harrisburg, PA, which was just north of Gettysburg. I had considered donating it to the excellent collection of Civil War artifacts at the Atlanta History Center, but instinct strongly suggested to respectfully station it north of the Mason's and Dixon's line. Henry's little wooden bible had survived its long journey, being passed down through generations of Banks family members and their heirs, to finally wind up in my possession. The small artifact's journey would not end there, for it accompanied me through every step of my personal pilgrimage that covered well-over 10,000 miles.

By the time my wanderings had reached their conclusion, Andi and I had relocated again to the tropical climes of Florida's Gulf Coast. Both of us knowing since 1993, when our relationship was consummated in San Diego, that we are more "islanders" rather than "inlanders", we agreed that this move would be our last. Looking back over the span of nearly twelve years, to the day when Henry's bible first emerged from my late father's study, it was difficult to fathom all of the changes that had transpired since that warm afternoon in Washington State, June, 2003. Changes in our daily routine, careers, interests and environment were evident. New friends, acquaintances and neighbors had come into our lives, and many had bowed out, while others remained as close as family. Some old friends and family had passed on during that period, some of who were promised a copy of my finished project, and that regret was the most painful consequence for me. Still, despite the many times I was tempted to relinquish the completion of Henry's story, I stayed true to the original objective and finished what I had started, though I never dreamed it would have taken over a decade to complete.

In reflecting upon all those years of research, travel, and introspection, the journey did not distract from that struggle that had surged within my soul since my father had passed on. That barrage of internal Q-and-A had constantly gnawed at me, putting my *faith* and *doubt* at odds with one another, both equally armed, as it would seem. I had given the two adversaries ample time to duke it out on a battlefield that spanned between the opposing corners of Washington State and Florida, over a period of twelve years, with no apparent defeat, surrender or truce in sight. With restored strength, I decided to step in and settle the raucous dispute, once and for all. For guidance, I looked to my ancestors for wisdom, and example.

Was it *doubt*, I wondered, that saw the Banks family though the tragic loss of *their* father, Nathan in 1849? Did they succumb to their *doubts* in the face of the horrible locust attacks, and other disasters that devastated their crops in Kansas? As Henry marched from Tennessee to Georgia, and up though the Carolinas —fighting for his life, and for the Union— was *doubt* the force that enabled him to withstand those long marches, inclement weather, his bouts with poor health, and injuries from enemy engagement? On the contrary.

Henry made the deliberate decision to carve a bible out of a block of wood while he endured a hard winter at Fort Thomas in Gallatin, Tennessee. Of all the subjects a whittler could have selected, he set about rendering a symbol of his *faith*.

I came to understand that his unwavering faith in God was hereditary. Just like Henry's bible, that faith was passed down to me through generations, braided into my spiritual DNA like a dominant genetic trait. This was a trait, however that I could freely choose to abandon, or preserve. Moreover, just like Henry's bible, I recognized that enduring faith as a priceless inheritance, worthy of preservation.

The void that resulted from the loss of my parents manifested a long and intense spiritual struggle, and my choice was not easy, but at the very least, I made up my mind to choose one path. By the same token, anyone whom I might encounter from these days forward, that has soldiered through similar internal conflict, shrugged off the mediocrity of indifference, and committed to a decision —no matter which side they have chosen— will have earned my most profound respect! It's fundamental that doubts and misgivings will tend to creep in on occasion, especially when I am at my weakest. Yet, I rest assured that no matter how hard my journey becomes, for the rest of my days, it will never compare to the hard road that my Great, Great, Grand Uncle, Private Henry Ira Banks marched upon from 1862 to 1865. And now that our travels together are complete, we can celebrate it as *our road*. Henry's. Mine. Yours.   The Legacy Road.

# Guideposts for Your Own Road

Bear in mind that this list of references represents a sampling of what is available at the present time. Advances in technology, the constant flux of trends, and inevitable obsolescence may affect this list as time progresses. I wish you the best of luck with your discoveries!

**Discover and organize your family tree:**

*www.ancestry.com*

*www.geni.com*

**Collaborate with others discovering their heritage:**

*www.rootsweb.com*

*www.werelate.org*

**Locate an ancestor's grave:**

*www.findagrave.com*

**Search for a Civil War Soldier, Sailor or Prisoner by name:**

*www.nps.gov/civilwar/soldiers-and-sailors-database.htm*

**Request a Civil War Soldier's Compiled Service Record:**

*www.archives.gov/researchmilitary/civil-war/resources.html*

**Find millions of books online:**

*www.books.google.com*

**Explore cities and towns:**

*www.EPodunk.com*

**Purchase and study maps from an enormous archive:**

*www.historicmapworks.com*

**Find answers to just about any question:**

*www.answers.com*

# *Acknowledgement*

It wasn't my intention at first, to write a book about the life of Henry Ira Banks, and my experience following his march. It was strongly suggested that I share the story in some way, not just with my immediate family and friends, but with everyone. By nature, I rarely lift the curtain to reveal the complicated process of thoughts, victories, struggles, beliefs, doubts and emotions that constantly churn within. However, at the urging of close friends and family, through the completion of this book, I have stepped far outside of the boundaries that I usually keep at arm's length, and to my surprise, it has been liberating to share it all. Though the journey along the Legacy Road was a very personal, and lonely journey at times, all the while I never felt alone. I had the support and encouragement of relatives, friends and colleagues who helped me stay focused and determined to complete the journey and finally, the project. There are so many who helped make this effort possible, that I would be remiss not to acknowledge their generous contributions.

Andrea Enyeart, James and Mary Emma Allen, Max and Delilah Beougher, Chris Noll, Ron Taylor, Ken Willits, Karen Gilchrist, Jeff and Susan Robison, Julio Rivera, Tom Ivey, Ken Vanden Hoorn, Bob and Sandi Kimball, Hal and Jean Willits, John and Cheryl Teehan, Brennan and Lindsey Teehan, Ande O'Farrell, Heather O'Farrell, Chuck and Marge Woods, CJ Borer, Fleming Stevenson, Keith and Ellen Stevenson, Bill and Cathy Stevenson, Greg and Lindsey Coutu, Charles and Willa McGimsey, Greg Krohn, Howard Morgan, Mike Couch, Steve Babcock, John Fritz, Earl and Teri Zeckman, John Smith, Pastor Gary Eastridge, Marie Prestmo, Karen Holmstrom, Alicia Kibodeaux, Sean and Robin Leenaerts, John Coinman, John and Linda Bernard, Lindy Couch, Carrie Enyeart, Eli and Hazel Rico, Victor and Sonia Rico, Dr. Stu Weber, Junior Ramsey, Carolyn Tucker-Myers, Raul Mireles, Mike and Christina Couvillion, Virgil and Thea Claussen

…and my most sincere gratitude extends to the host of others who I encountered on the road, and along this gratifying path of discovery.